Stripping the Gurus

Stripping the Gurus

Sex, Violence, Abuse and Enlightenment*

GEOFFREY D. FALK

* The inclusion of any particular individual in this book is not meant to suggest or imply that he or she represents him- or herself as a guru, nor is it meant to suggest or imply that he or she has indulged in sex, violence, the abuse of others, or any other illegal or immoral activities.

Million Monkeys Press

Copyright © 2009 by Geoffrey D. Falk. Earlier versions © 2005-2008. No part of this book may be reproduced in any form or by any electronic or mechanical means including information storage and retrieval systems without permission in writing from the publisher, except by a reviewer, who may quote brief passages in a review.

Published by Million Monkeys Press
P.O. Box 68586
360A Bloor St. West
Toronto, Ontario
Canada M5S 3C9
Web: www.strippingthegurus.com

ISBN 978-0-9736203-1-3 (cloth)

Credits and permissions can be found on the Permissions page (p. 509), which constitutes an extension of the copyright page.

Trademarks: "TM" and "Transcendental Meditation" are service marks registered in the U.S. Patent and Trademark Office, licensed to Maharishi Vedic Education Development Corporation. "Coke" is a registered trademark of the Coca-Cola Company. "Spiral Dynamics" is a registered trademark of the National Values Center, Inc.

Library and Archives Canada Cataloguing in Publication

Falk, Geoffrey D., 1966-
Stripping the gurus : sex, violence, abuse and enlightenment / Geoffrey D. Falk.

Includes bibliographical references and index.
Also available in electronic format.
ISBN 978-0-9736203-1-3 (bound).—ISBN 978-0-9736203-2-0 (pbk.)

1. Cults. 2. Religious leaders—Biography. I. Title.

BP603.F36 2009 200 C2009-902813-0

First edition. Printed in the United States of America.
10 9 8 7 6 5 4 3 2 1

CONTENTS

INTRODUCTION

ONE OF MY DEAR, late mother's most memorable expressions, in attempting to get her children to behave, was simply: "Be sure your sins will find you out."

It may take a minute, an hour, a day, a year, ten years or more, but eventually the details of one's behaviors are likely to surface. Whether one's public face is that of a saint or a sinner, ultimately "the truth will out."

This book, then, concerns the alleged sins which have been concealed behind the polished façades of too many of our world's "saintly and sagely" spiritual leaders and their associated communities, with a marked focus on North America over the past century.

Why, though, would anyone write such a book as this? Why not just "focus on the good," and work on one's own self-transformation instead?

First of all, one hopes to save others from the sorrow inherent in throwing their lives away in following these figures. Even the most elementary bodhisattva vow, for the liberation of others from suffering, would leave one with no moral choice but to do one's part in that. Likewise, even the most basic understanding as to the nature of "idiot compassion" would preclude one from ignoring these reported problems just to be "nice" or avoid offending others.

As a former follower of Carlos Castaneda eloquently put it, in relating the depressing and disillusioning story of her experiences with him, amid her own "haunting dreams of suicide":

> [I]f some reader, somewhere, takes a moment's pause and halts before handing over his or her free will to another, it will all have counted for something (Wallace, 2003).

Or, as Margery Wakefield (1991) expressed her own opinion:

> As trite as it may sound, if I can prevent even one other person, especially a young person, from having to live through the nightmare of Scientology—then I will feel satisfied.

Second, I personally spent the worst nine months of my life at one of Paramahansa Yogananda's approved southern California ashrams (i.e., hermitages/monasteries), and have still not recovered fully from that awful experience. I thus consider this as part of my own healing process. That is, it is part of my dealing with the after-effects of the "wisdom" meted out in that environment by its loyal, "God-inspired" participants.

Third, with my own background in Eastern philosophy, we may hope to do all this without misrepresenting the metaphysical ideas involved. With or without that, though, it is not the validity of the theoretical ideas of each path which are, in general, of concern here. Rather, of far greater interest are the ways in which the leaders espousing those ideas have applied them in practice, frequently to the claimed detriment of their followers.

Fourth, the mapping of reported ashram behaviors to psychologist Philip Zimbardo's classic prison study, as presented in the "Gurus and Prisoners" chapter, yields significant insights into the origins and pervasiveness of the alleged problems cataloged herein.

Fifth, to paraphrase Sherlock Holmes, if we eliminate everything which is impossible, then what is left, however improbable it may appear, must be the case. Becoming aware of the reported issues with our world's "sages" and their admirers, then, eliminates many pleasant but "impossible" hopes one may have with regard to the nature of spirituality and religion.

This book will not likely change the mind of any loyal disciple of any of the spiritual figures and paths specifically addressed herein. Indeed, no amount of evidence of alleged abuse or hypocrisy on the part of those leaders could do so, for followers who are convinced that they have found "God in the flesh," in their spiritual hero.

This text may, however, touch some of those devotees who are already halfway to realizing what is going on around them. And more importantly, in quantitative good, it may give a "heads up" to persons who would otherwise be suckered in by the claims of any particular "God-realized being"—as I myself was fooled, once upon a time. And thus, it may prevent them from becoming involved with the relevant organization(s) in the first place.

Ultimately, the "see no evil, hear no evil, speak no evil" approach to life simply allows the relevant problems to continue. No one should ever turn a blind eye to secular crimes of forgery, incest, rape or the like. Much less should those same crimes be so readily excused or forgiven when they are alleged to occur in spiritual contexts. That is so particularly when they are claimed to be perpetrated by leaders and followers insisting that they have "God on their side," and that any resistance to their reported blunders or rumored power-tripping abuses equates to being influenced by *Maya*/Satan.

To say nothing in the face of evil, after all, is to implicitly condone it. Or equally, as the saying goes, "For evil to triumph in this world, it is only necessary for good people to do nothing."

In the words of Albert Einstein:

> The world is a dangerous place to live; not because of the people who are evil, but because of the people who don't do anything about it.

The alert reader will further note that, aside from my own relatively non-scandalous (but still highly traumatic) personal experiences at Hidden Valley, all of the allegations made herein—none of which, to my knowledge, except where explicitly noted, have been proved in any court of law—have already been put into print elsewhere in books and magazine articles. In all of those cases, I am relying in good faith on the validity of the extant, published research of the relevant journalists and ex-disciples. I have made every effort to present that existing reported data without putting any additional "spin" on it, via juxtapositions or otherwise. After all, the in-print (alleged) realities, in every case, are jaw-dropping enough that no innuendo or taking-out-of-context would have ever been required in order to make our world's "god-men" look foolish.

As the Dalai Lama (1999) expressed his own opinion, regarding the value of such investigative journalism:

> I respect and appreciate the media's interference.... It is appropriate ... to have journalists ... snooping around and exposing wrongdoing where they find it. We need to know when this or that renowned individual hides a very different aspect behind a pleasant exterior.

As to the quantity of reported "sins" covered uncomplimentarily herein, please appreciate that I myself am, in general, in no way anti-drug, anti-alcohol, anti-dildo, anti-secret-passageway-to-the-women's-dormitory, anti-whorehouse or anti-orgy, etc. It is simply obvious, by now, that any of those, when put into the hands of "god-men" who have carved islands of absolute power for themselves in the world, only make an already dangerous situation much worse.

Of course, all such protests to the contrary, it is the very nature of the gathering and publicizing of information such as this that one will be regarded as being either puritanical or shadow-projecting for doing so. Why else, after all, would anyone object to guru-disciple sex, etc., in situations where the "non-divine" party too often is a psychological child in the relationship, unable to say "No"?

The guideline that "all's fair among consenting adults so long as no one gets hurt" is reasonable enough. So then simply ask yourself as you read this book: In how many, if any, of the environments covered here has no one "gotten hurt"?

Finally, with regard to the use of humor herein, the late Christopher Reeve put it appropriately: "When things are really bad, you have to laugh."

January, 2009
Toronto, Ontario

Geoffrey D. Falk
www.geoffreyfalk.com

Stripping The Gurus

CHAPTER I

SPEAK NO EVIL

> The wicked are wicked no doubt, and they go astray, and they fall, and they come by their desserts. But who can tell the mischief that the very virtuous do?
>
> —William Makepeace Thackeray

ONE WOULD LIKE TO BELIEVE that our world's recognized saints and sages have the best interests of everyone at heart in their thoughts and actions.

One would also like to believe that the same "divinely loving" and enlightened figures would never distort truth to suit their own purposes, and would never use their power to take advantage (sexually or otherwise) of their followers. They would, that is, be free of the deep psychological quirks, prejudices, hypocrisy and violence which affect mere mortals.

One would further hope that the best of our world's sages would be able to distinguish between valid mystical perceptions and mere hallucinations, and that the miracles and healings which they have claimed to have effected have all actually occurred.

Sadly, none of those hopes stand up to even the most basic rational scrutiny.

Thus, it has come to be that you are holding in your hands an extremely evil book.

It is so, simply because it attempts to expose, to a wider audience, the worst of the alleged abuses which various "god-men" have reportedly visited upon their followers, and on the world at large, over the past century or more.

In tracing that line of degeneracy more or less chronologically, from the introduction of Eastern philosophy into Western thought and action up to the present day, we will meet the following "saints and sages":

- Ramakrishna, whose worship of the Divine Mother did not exclude comparable ritual veneration for his own penis, or an equal interest in fondling the genitals of his male followers
- The brothel-visiting Vivekananda, Ramakrishna's chief disciple, who first brought yoga to America via the 1893 World's Fair, and thus paved the way into the West for all following Eastern teachers
- Jiddu Krishnamurti, the Theosophical Society's eagerly anticipated "World Teacher," who later broke from that organization, fully repudiating it, and then embarked on a quarter-century affair with a woman whom he believed to be the reincarnation of his late mother
- Japanese Zen masters and scholars, whose support of the use of Zen principles in the training of the Japanese military during times of war, and reported physical abuse of disciples in times of peace, will give us serious pause
- Satchidananda, the "Woodstock Swami," who repudiated drugs and rock 'n' roll, but reportedly retained a fondness for sex with his female disciples
- The Maharishi Mahesh Yogi, famed for his involvement with the Beatles, his alleged failed attempt at seducing Mia Farrow, and his efforts at teaching the "real magic" of levitation to the late magician Doug Henning, among others
- Swami Rama, renowned for his purported demonstration of parapsychological abilities under Elmer and Alyce Green in the 1970s, as another "holy celibate" who apparently couldn't keep his robes on

- Bhagwan Shree Rajneesh, who reportedly once admitted, while sniffing laughing gas to get high, that he was "so relieved to not have to pretend to be enlightened any more"
- Satya Sai Baba, whose claimed "miracles" have included raising people from the dead, producing streams of "sacred ash" from his hands—a feat easily replicated by secular magicians—and allegedly molesting hundreds of young boys
- Sri Chinmoy, the "stunt man of the spiritual world," whose disciples to this day periodically canvass campuses across North America with flyers touting the purported benefits of meditation under his guidance
- Buddhist monks in Thailand, who have been known to proudly exhibit expensive collections of antique cars, and to don disguises, sneak out to local karaoke bars, and be caught with pornography, alcohol, sexual paraphernalia, and *more than one woman* at a time
- Scientology founder L. Ron Hubbard, whose FBI files contained the observation, "appears mental"
- Werner Erhard, originator of est group training, who brought us the phrase, "Thank you for sharing"
- Yogi Bhajan, the claimed "only living master of white tantric yoga in the world"
- Chögyam Trungpa, who brought Tibetan Buddhism to America, and proceeded to drink himself into an early grave
- Swami Muktananda, whose ashram living quarters in India reportedly contained a well-used secret passageway to the adjacent young girls' dormitory
- Muktananda's name-changing disciple Adi Da (Da Free John, Da Love-Ananda, etc.), whose "crazy wisdom" exploits propelled him to exile in Fiji in the mid-'80s, following allegations of sexual abuse
- Andrew Cohen, whose own Jewish mother has regarded his closed authoritarian spiritual community as embodying a "fascist mind-set," with its members behaving like "Gestapo agents." (Such closed communities are of homogeneous beliefs, have little exchange of ideas with the outside world,

and possess no option of questioning the leader while still remaining a member in good standing. Further, to leave the community is typically claimed to be to throw away one's only "chance in this lifetime for enlightenment" [van der Braak, 2003].) She has further rejected Cohen's claims of enlightenment, comparing him instead to the "cult" leaders Jim Jones and David Koresh, and even to Adolf Hitler

- Ken Wilber, the "Einstein of consciousness studies," who has at times spoken with unbridled enthusiasm for the effects of discipline under both Adi Da and Cohen
- Yogi Amrit Desai, formerly of the Kripalu yoga center, whose followers there, when news of the claimed sexual activities between the married Desai and his devotees surfaced, displayed unique discrimination in reportedly forcing him to leave the center he himself had founded
- Assorted sexually active Roman Catholic priests—pedophile, ephebophile and otherwise
- The Findhorn community in Scotland, which actually functions without a guru-figure, arguably doing more good than harm for exactly that reason
- Paramahansa Yogananda, author of the spiritual classic *Autobiography of a Yogi,* whose troubled ashrams the present author can speak of from first-hand experience

With only a few exceptions, the above figures have taught authentic Eastern philosophy of one variety or another. They have further been widely recognized and duly advertised as possessing high degrees of spiritual realization. Indeed, one can easily find loyal followers singing the praises of each of these individuals and paths, in books and sanctioned websites. (Both Steven Hassan's www.freedomofmind.com site and the Rick A. Ross Institute at www.rickross.com have many such links to "official" websites.) To find the reported "dirt" on each of them, however, requires a fair bit more effort. Nevertheless, it is those alleged worst aspects, not the often-advertised best, which leave formerly devoted disciples picking up the pieces of their shattered lives, and wondering aloud how they could ever have been so blind as to buy into the "perfect master's" propaganda in the first place.

This is, therefore, a very "dirty" book. For, it presents not only the representative (and, after a while, completely unbelievable) claims to perfection or God-realization of each of the forty or so major and minor "authentic" spiritual figures considered herein, but also the alleged shortcomings of each, as those have affected their followers. Obviously, then, to cover all of that in a single text requires that only the most grandiose of the claims, and the worst of the foibles and alleged abuses, of each "sage" be mentioned herein.

Unless one enjoys seeing other people suffer—or effecting or reliving one's own process of disillusionment—however, this is not going to be pretty. For, in probing this lineage, we will find legions of alleged emotional, physical and sexual abuses perpetrated "in the name of God," by persons neither impotent nor omnipotent, yet claiming to be "one with God."

By the end of all this unpleasantness, then, at least one thing will undoubtedly be clear. That is, that with "gods" like these, we do not need devils. For, every evil which one might otherwise ascribe to Satan or *Maya* has allegedly been perpetrated by one or another "God-realized avatar" or ostensibly "perfected being."

Of course, the forthcoming shocking disclosures will predictably result in a good amount of "wailing and gnashing of teeth" among obedient followers. Indeed, that is to be expected particularly among loyal adherents to each path for whom the "perfection" and infallibility of their own leader is not open to questioning, even if they may allow that none of the *other* "sagely" individuals considered herein are what they claim to be. (Part of the value of grouping all of these pretenses and alleged abuses together in a single book is exactly that one can see that the "unique" claims of one's own path are also being made, equally untenably, by numerous *other* paths.) Nevertheless, if we are really interested in truth, we should still *welcome* having the hypocrisies and (alleged) abusive evils of persons in positions of spiritual authority be laid bare to the world. Exposing them to the public eye, after all, is the only way to get them to stop.

Thus, "onward and evil-ward."

CHAPTER II

A BIT OF A BOOBY

(SRI RAMAKRISHNA)

> [Ramakrishna] is a figure of recent history and his life and teachings have not yet been obscured by loving legends and doubtful myths (in Ramakrishna, 2003).

> Ramakrishna ... gained recognition from his devotees and admirers that he was [an incarnation of] Christ.... When [Mahendra Nath Gupta, a prominent disciple] told his Master that he was the same person as Jesus and Chaitanya, Ramakrishna affirmed enthusiastically: "Same! Same! Certainly the same person" (Sil, 1998).

> I am an avatar. I am God in human form (Ramakrishna, in [Nityatmananda, 1967]).

THE STORY OF YOGA and yogis in the West—and of their corresponding alleged abuses of power, most often reportedly for sexual purposes—really begins with Swami Vivekananda's lectures at the Chicago World's Fair in 1893.

Vivekananda's story, however, begins with his own guru, Sri Ramakrishna, the latter having been born in India in 1836. ("Sri" is an East Indian title of respect, akin to the English "Sir.") Thus, it is to the latter that we shall first turn our attention.

As a child, the boy Ramakrishna—who later claimed to be the incarnation of both Krishna and Rama—"loved to dress up and act like a girl" (Sil, 1997). He was, indeed, aided in that activity by relatives who bought him feminine outfits and gold ornaments, to suit his own relatively feminine body and psyche.

> One can very well see from the extant photograph of Ramakrishna [e.g., online at Ramakrishna (2003)] he possessed quite well-formed and firm breasts—most possibly a case of *gynecomastia*....
>
> Ramakrishna could also be described, in the jargon of modern medical psychology, as a "she male," that is, a male who, despite his male genitalia, possesses a female psyche and breasts resembling those of a woman....
>
> [Saradananda] writes, apparently on the basis of the Master's testimony, that he used to bleed every month from the region of his pubic hair ... and the bleeding continued for three days just like the menstrual period of women (Sil, 1998).

Nor was that the extent of the great sage's appreciation for the microcosmic aspects of the feminine principle:

> Once he sat after a midday siesta with his loin cloth disheveled. He then remarked that he was sitting like a woman about to suckle her baby. In fact, he used to suckle his young beloved [male] disciple Rakhal Ghosh....
>
> He ... exhibited his frankly erotic behavior toward his male devotees and disciples.... He often posed as their girlfriend or mother and always touched or caressed them lovingly (Sil, 1998).

Anyone who is suckling an adult is explicitly viewing/treating that adult as a child. If there is any sexual attraction at all from the "parent" to the "child" in such a context, there is no escaping the obvious psychological pedophilic component, even if the suckled one is of legal age, as was the eighteen-year-old Ghosh. And if one grown man (a "she-male," in Ramakrishna's case) is having another grown man (his junior) pretend to be an infant, so that the first of them can pretend to be the mother to the second, and literally suckle the second, in any other context there would be no doubt at all as to the fetishistic nature of the behavior.

Further, after having met his foremost disciple, Vivekananda, for the first time, in the throes of an "agonizing desire" to see the young man again, Ramakrishna confessed:

> I ran to the northern quarter of the garden, a rather unfrequented place, and there cried at the top of my voice, "O my darling, come back to me! I can't live without seeing you!" After some time, I felt better. This state of things continued for *six months*. There were other boys who also came here; I felt greatly drawn towards some of them but nothing like the way I was attracted toward [Vivekananda] (Disciples, 1979; italics added).

Ramakrishna went on to describe his favorite disciple variously as a "huge red-eyed carp," "a very large pot," "a big bamboo with holes" and a "male pigeon."

In later days, the prematurely impotent, married guru once went into *samadhi* (i.e., mystical ecstasy, generally involving a loss of awareness of the body) after having mounted the young Vivekananda's back.

As to what excuse the great guru might have given for such mounting had it *not* sent him vaulting into ecstatic perception of God, one can only guess.

> [W]e cannot ignore [Ramakrishna's] obsession with the anus and shit in his conversations. Even the experience of his highest realization that there exists within the individual self the *Paramatman,* the repository of all knowledge, was derived from his beholding a grasshopper with a thin stick-like object inserted in its anus!....
>
> His ecstasy [i.e., as trance] was induced by touching his favorite young [male] devotees. He developed a few strategies for touching or petting the body (occasionally the penis, as was the case with Vijaykrishna Goswami, whose cock he calmed by his "touch") of devotees (Sil, 1998).

Of course, none of Ramakrishna's documented homoerotic behaviors in the above regards would equate to him having been a practicing homosexual. They equally, however, cannot be unrelated to his own view of the female body as being nothing more than "such things as blood, flesh, fat, entrails, worms, piss, shit, and the like" (in Nikhilananda, 1984). Indeed, the "incarnation of the Divine Mother" himself divulged:

> I am terribly scared of women.... I see them as a tigress coming to devour me. Besides, I see large pores [cf. vagina symbols] in their limbs. I find all of them as ogres....
>
> If my body is touched by a woman I feel sick.... The touched part aches as if stung by a horned catfish (in Nikhilananda, 1984).

Even the mere sight of a woman could reportedly so negatively excite Ramakrishna as to prompt him to

> either run to the temple or invoke the strategy of escape by getting into *samadhi*. His attraction for young boys that may be considered as muted pedophilia is often associated with aging impotent males....
>
> Ramakrishna's contempt for women was basically a misogynist attitude of an insecure male, who thought of himself as a woman in order to fight his innate fear of the female (Sil, 1998).

On other occasions, the mention of any object which Ramakrishna did not desire (e.g., hemp, wine) would send him fleeing into *samadhi;* as could strong emotion (e.g., anger) on the sage's part. At his cousin's suggestion that those odd behaviors might have been psychologically based, Ramakrishna "responded by almost jumping into the river in order to end it all" (in Sil, 1998).

* * *

With those various factors acting, it should not surprise that Ramakrishna's own spiritual discipline took several odd turns.

> During his ascetic practices, Ramakrishna exhibited remarkable bodily changes. While worshiping Rama as his devotee Hanuman, the monkey chieftain of the Ramayana, his movements resembled those of a monkey.... [Ramakrishna was also an accomplished childhood actor.] In his biography of Ramakrishna, novelist Christopher Isherwood paraphrased the saint's own description of his strange behavior: "I didn't do this of my own accord; it happened of itself. And the most marvelous thing was—the lower end of my spine lengthened, nearly an inch! Later, when I stopped practicing

> this kind of devotion, it gradually went back to its normal size" (Murphy, 1992).

> During the days of my ["holy"] madness [as priest of the Kali temple in Dakshineswar] I used to worship my own penis as the Shiva *linga*.... Worship of a live *linga*. I even decorated it with a pearl (in Nikhilananda, 1984).

Nor was the sage's manner of worship confined to his own genitalia:

> [Ramakrishna] considered swear words [to be] as meaningful as the Vedas and the Puranas and was particularly fond of performing *japa* (ritual counting of rosary) by muttering the word "cunt" (Sil, 1998).

Indeed, as the claimed avatar himself told his devotees:

> The moment I utter the word "cunt" I behold the cosmic vagina ... and I sink into it (in Sil, 1998).

That is actually not quite as odd as it might initially seem, for "cunt" itself derives from *Kunda* or *Cunti*—names for Kali, the Hindu Divine Mother goddess, beloved of Ramakrishna.

It is still plenty odd, though.

In any case, in 1861 the recently wedded Ramakrishna began tantric (sexual) yoga practice with a female teacher, Yogeshwari. (His marriage was actually to a five-year-old child bride, chosen by the twenty-three-year-old yogi himself, and then left with her parents to mature.) Rituals performed by the eager student during that *sadhana* (i.e., spiritual practice/discipline) included eating the culinary leftovers from the meals of dogs and jackals. Also, consuming a "fish and human meat preparation in a human skull" (Sil, 1998). Attempts to have him participate in the ritual sex with a consort which is an essential component of tantra, however, were less successful. Indeed, they ended with the sage himself falling safely into trance, and later simply witnessing *other* practitioners having ritual intercourse.

Comparably, upon his wife's coming of age, Ramakrishna tried but failed to make love to her, instead involuntarily plunging into a "premature superconsciousness." (Their marriage was actually, it appears, never consummated.) That, however, did not discourage the young woman from staking her own spiritual claims:

> [W]hile regarding her husband as God, Sarada came to be convinced that as his wedded wife she must also be divine. Following her husband's claim that she was actually Shiva's wife, Sarada later claimed: "I am Bhagavati, the Divine Mother of the Universe" (Sil, 1998).

Such was evidently the compensation for her being confined to the kitchen for days at a time by her husband, cooking, not even being allowed to relieve herself in the latrine.

* * *

> [Ramakrishna was] one of the truly great saints of nineteenth-century India (Feuerstein, 1992).

In a demonstration of the high regard with which every loyal disciple holds his or her guru, Vivekananda himself declared that Ramakrishna was "the greatest of all avatars" (Sil, 1997). That evaluation, however, was not shared by everyone who knew the great sage:

> Hriday, the Master's nephew and companion, actually regarded him [as] a moron (Sil, 1998).

The venerated guru later formed the same opinion of his own earthly mother.

In any case, as part of his alleged avatarhood, Ramakrishna was christened with the title "Paramahansa," meaning "Supreme Swan." The appellation itself signifies the highest spiritual attainment and discrimination, by analogy with the swan which, it is claimed, is able to extract only the milk from a mixture of milk and water (presumably by curdling it).

In mid-1885, Ramakrishna was diagnosed with throat cancer. He died in 1886, leaving several thousand disciples (Satchidananda, 1977). As expected, Vivekananda took over leadership of those devotees.

After all that, Sil (1998) gave his summary evaluation of "the incarnation [of God or the Divine Mother] for the modern age," concluding that, the swooning Ramakrishna's status as a monumental cultural icon notwithstanding, he was nevertheless "a bit of a baby and a bit of a booby."

CHAPTER III

THE HANDSOME DUCKLING

(SWAMI VIVEKANANDA)

> [Vivekananda] is seen not just as a patriot-prophet of resurgent India but much more—an incarnation of Shiva, Buddha and Jesus (Sil, 1997).

> Perfect from his birth, [Vivekananda] did not need spiritual disciplines for his own liberation. Whatever disciplines he practiced were for the purpose of removing the veil that concealed, for the time being, his true divine nature and mission in the world. Even before his birth, the Lord had chosen him as His instrument to help Him in the spiritual redemption of humanity (Nikhilananda, 1996).

BORN IN 1863 IN CALCUTTA, Vivekananda began meditating at age seven, and claimed to have first experienced *samadhi* when eight years old.

> He regarded himself as a *brahmachari*, a celibate student of the Hindu tradition, who worked hard, prized ascetic disci-

> plines, held holy things in reverence, and enjoyed clean words, thoughts, and acts (Nikhilananda, 1996).

A handsome and muscular, albeit somewhat stout and bull-dog-jawed youth, he first met his guru, Ramakrishna, in 1881 at age eighteen. As the favorite and foremost disciple of that "Supreme Swan," the young "Duckling," Vivekananda,

> was constantly flattered and petted by his frankly enchanted homoerotic mentor [i.e., Ramakrishna], fed adoringly by him, made to sing songs on a fairly regular basis for the Master's mystical merriment, and told by the older man that he was a ... realized individual through his meditations ... [an] eternally realized person ... free from the lure of ... woman and wealth (Sil, 1997).

Vivekanandaji took his monastic vows in 1886, shortly before his guru's death, thereby becoming a swami. (The suffix "ji" is added to East Indian names and titles to show respect.) "Swami" itself—meaning "to be master of one's self"—is simply the name of the monastic order established by Shankara in the thirteenth century. The adoption of that honorific entails taking formal vows of celibacy and poverty.

Interestingly, in later years, Vivekananda actually claimed to be the reincarnation of Shankara (Sil, 1997).

In any case, following a dozen years of increasing devotion to his dearly departed guru, Vivekananda came to America at age thirty. There, he represented Hinduism to American men and women at the 1893 Parliament of Religions, held in Chicago.

> A total stranger to the world of extroverted, educated, and affluent women, he was charmed by their generosity, kindness, and frankly unqualified admiration for and obsession with a handsome, young, witty, and somewhat enchantingly naïve virgin male from a distant land (Sil, 1997).

The earlier-celebrated purity and enjoyment of "clean acts," and "freedom from the lure of women" guaranteed to Vivekananda by Ramakrishna, would nevertheless at first glance appear to have been somewhat incomplete. For, the former once admitted that, following the death of his father in 1884,

> he visited brothels and consumed alcoholic beverages in the company of his friends (Sil, 1997).

Thankfully for his legacy, though, Vivekananda was not actually partaking of the various ladies' delights in those houses. Rather, by his own testimony, he was simply dragged there once by his friends, who hoped to cheer him up after his father's death. He, however, after a few drinks, began lecturing to them about what might become of them in their afterlives for such debauchery. He was subsequently kicked out by his friends for being that "wet blanket," and stumbled home alone, thoroughly drunk (Sil, 2004).

So it was just a few drinks too many. In a whorehouse. Nothing unexpected from a savior "chosen by God as His instrument to help Him" in the salvation of humanity.

Either way, though, "if you keep on playing with fire" you're going to get burned, as Vivekananda himself observed:

> Once in me rose the feeling of lust. I got so disgusted with myself that I sat on a pot of burning tinders, and it took a long time for the wound to heal (in Sil, 1997).

* * *

> [I]t is my ambition to conquer the world by Hindu thought—to see Hindus from the North Pole to the South Pole (Vivekananda, in [Sil, 1997]).

It was not long after that announcement that Vivekananda was proudly claiming to have "helped on the tide of Vedanta which is flooding the world." He was likewise soon predicting that "before ten years elapse a vast majority of the English people will be Vedantic" (in Sil, 1997).

The enthusiastic young monk's hopes of effecting global change, further, were not limited to a spiritual revolution, of "Hindus 'round the world." Rather, among his other vast dreams were those of a socially progressive, economically sovereign and politically stable India (Sil, 1997).

The realization of those goals, however, was to come up against certain concrete realities not anticipated by the swami, including the need to think ahead in manifesting one's ideas. Indeed, Vivekananda was, it seems, explicitly opposed to such an approach:

> Plans! Plans! That is why you Western people can never create a religion! If any of you ever did, it was only a few Catholic saints who had no plans. Religion was never, never preached by planners! (in Nikhilananda, 1996).

Not surprisingly, then, given this antipathy, before the end of 1897 Vivekananda was already down-sizing his goals:

> I have roused a good many of our people, and that was all I wanted (in Nikhilananda, 1996).

Further, as Chelishev (1987) observed with regard to the social improvements advocated by the naïve monk:

> Vivekananda approached the solution of the problem of social inequality from the position of Utopian Socialism, placing hopes on the good will and magnanimity of the propertied classes.

Understandably, within a year the swami had realized the futility of that approach:

> I have given up at present my plan for the education of the masses (in Sil, 1997).

> It will come by degrees. What I now want is a band of fiery missionaries. We must have a College in Madras to teach comparative religions ... we must have a press, and papers printed in English and in the vernaculars (Vivekananda, 1947).

As one frustrated devotee finally put it:

> Swami had good ideas—plenty—but he carried nothing out .... He only talked (in Sil, 1997).

* * *

Vivekananda claimed to have experienced, in 1898, a vision of Shiva Himself. In that ecstasy, he "had been granted the grace of Amarnath, the Lord of Immortality, not to die until he himself willed it" (Nikhilananda, 1996).

The chain-smoking, diabetic sage, apparently "going gentle into that dark night," nevertheless passed away only a few years later, in 1902, after years of declining health. Reaching only an unripe age of thirty-nine, he "thus fulfill[ed] his own prophecy: 'I shall not live to be forty years old'" (Nikhilananda, 1996).

Of course, there are prophecies, and then there are earlier prophecies:

> Vivekananda declared solemnly: "This time I will give hundred years to my body.... This time I have to perform many difficult tasks.... In this life I shall demonstrate my powers much more than I did in my past life" (Sil, 1997).

* * *

In spite of those many reversals, Vivekananda foresaw great and lasting effects on the world for his teachings:

> The spiritual ideals emanating from the Belur Math [one of Vivekananda's monasteries/universities], he once said to Miss MacLeod, would influence the thought-currents of the world for 1100 years....
>
> "All these visions are rising before me"—these were his very words (Nikhilananda, 1996).

The Vedanta Society which preserves Vivekananda's brand of Hinduism has a current membership of only around 22,000 individuals, and a dozen centers worldwide. It would thus not likely qualify as any large part of the "global spiritual renaissance" grandly and grandiosely envisioned by the swami. The better part of Vivekananda's actual legacy, then, beyond mere organizational PR, may consist simply in his having paved the way for the other Eastern teachers who followed him into America in the succeeding century.

CHAPTER IV

MOTHER DEAREST

(AUROBINDO)

> When it was also understood in the East that the Great Chain [or ontological hierarchy of Being, manifesting through causal, astral and physical realms] did indeed unfold or evolve over time, the great Aurobindo expounded the notion with an *unequalled genius* (Wilber, 2000a; italics added).

IN "SIDEBAR A" TO HIS *BOOMERITIS* novel—originally written as a non-fiction work—Ken Wilber (2002), the "Einstein of consciousness research," has one of that book's characters refer to Aurobindo (1872 – 1950) as "the world's greatest philosopher-sage." Even in his much earlier (1980) *Atman Project,* he already had Aurobindo designated as "India's greatest modern sage." And, more recently, in his foreword to A. S. Dalal's (2000) *A Greater Psychology,* he has again averred that "Sri Aurobindo Ghose was India's greatest modern philosopher-sage." Likewise, in his own (2000) *Integral Psychology,* he has Aurobindo appointed as India's "greatest modern philosopher-sage."

So, if there's one thing we can safely conclude....

The yogic scholar Georg Feuerstein, among others, fully shares Wilber's complimentary evaluation of Aurobindo. Agehananda Bharati (1976), however, offered a somewhat different perspective:

> I do not agree with much of what he said; and I believe his *Life Divine* ... could be condensed to about one-fifth of its size without any substantial loss of content and message.... [Q]uite tedious reading for all those who have done mystical and religious reading all their lives, but fascinating and full of proselytizing vigor for those who haven't, who want something of the spirit, and who are impressionable.

Bharati himself was both a scholar and a swami of the Ramakrishna Order.

Aurobindo, in any case, whether a "great philosopher" or not, could well be viewed as having wobbled mightily about the center, if one were to consider his purported contributions to the Allied World War II effort:

> Sri Aurobindo put all his [e.g., astral] Force behind the Allies and especially Churchill. One particular event in which he had a hand was the successful evacuation from Dunkirk. As some history books note, the German forces refrained "for inexplicable reasons" from a quick advance which would have been fatal for the Allies (Huchzermeyer, 1998).

Other admirers of Aurobindo (e.g., GuruNet, 2003) regard that Allied escape as being aided by a fog which the yogi explicitly helped, through his powers of consciousness, to roll in over the water, concealing the retreating forces.

Aurobindo's spiritual partner, "the Mother," is likewise believed to have advanced the wartime labor via metaphysical means:

> Due to her occult faculties the Mother was able to look deep into Hitler's being and she saw that he was in contact with an *asura* [astral demon] who is at the origin of wars and makes every possible effort to prevent the advent of world unity (Huchzermeyer, 1998).

> When Hitler was gaining success after success and Mother was trying in the opposite direction, she said the shining be-

> ing who was guiding Hitler used to come to the ashram from time to time to see what was happening. Things changed from bad to worse. Mother decided on a fresh strategy. She took on the appearance of that shining being, appeared before Hitler and advised him to attack Russia. On her way back to the ashram, she met that being. The being was intrigued by Mother having stolen a march over him. Hitler's attack on Russia ensured his downfall....
>
> Mother saw in her meditation some Chinese people had reached Calcutta and recognized the danger of that warning. Using her occult divine power, she removed the danger from the subtle realms. Much later when the Chinese army was edging closer to India's border, a shocked India did not know which way to turn. The Chinese decided on their own to withdraw, much to the world's surprise. Mother had prevented them from advancing against India by canceling their power in the subtle realms (MSS, 2003).

Nor were those successful attempts at saving the world from the clutches of evil even the most impressive of the Mother's claimed subtle activities:

> She had live contacts with several gods. Durga used to come to Mother's meditations regularly. Particularly during the Durga Puja when Mother gave *darshan,* Durga used to come a day in advance. On one occasion, Mother explained to Durga the significance of surrender to the Supreme. Durga said because she herself was a goddess, it never struck her that she should surrender to a higher power. Mother showed Durga the progress she could make by surrendering to the Supreme. Durga was agreeable and offered her surrender to the Divine (MSS, 2003).

The Mother further believed herself to have been, in past lives, Queen Elizabeth of England—the sixteenth-century daughter of Henry VIII and Anne Boleyn. Also, Catherine of Russia (wife of Peter the Great), an Egyptian Queen, the mother of Moses, and Joan of Arc.

> Her diary entries reveal that even during her illness she continued through her *sadhana* to exert an occult influence on men and events (Nirodbaran, 1990).

> [The Mother] is the Divine Mother [i.e., as an incarnation or avatar] who has consented to put on her the cloak of obscurity and suffering and ignorance so that she can effectively lead us—human beings—to Knowledge and Bliss and Ananda and to the Supreme Lord (in Aurobindo, 1953).

> In the person of [the Mother], Aurobindo thus saw the descent of the Supermind. He believed she was its *avatara* or descent into the Earth plane. As the incarnate Supermind she was changing the consciousness on which the Earth found itself, and as such *her work was infallible*.... She does not merely embody the Divine, he instructed one follower, but is in reality the Divine appearing to be human (Minor, 1999; italics added).

India's independence from British rule followed soon after the end of WWII. Aurobindo himself marked the occasion in public speech:

> August 15th, 1947 is the birthday of free India. It marks for her the end of an old era, the beginning of a new age....
>
> August 15th is my own birthday and it is naturally gratifying to me that it should have assumed this vast significance. I take this coincidence, not as a fortuitous accident, but as the sanction and seal of the Divine Force that guides my steps on the work with which I began life, the beginning of its full fruition (in Nirodbaran, 1990).

This, then, on top of his believed Allied war efforts, was the grandiose state of mind of "the world's greatest philosopher-sage." Note further that this, like the Mother's diary entries, was Aurobindo's own documented claim, not merely a possible exaggeration made on his behalf by his followers. For all of the private hubris and narcissism of our world's guru-figures, it is rare for any of them to so brazenly exhibit the same publicly, as in the above inflations.

And, as always, there are ways of ensuring loyalty to the guru and his Mother, as Aurobindo (1953; italics added) himself noted:

> [A student] had been progressing extremely well because he opened himself to the Mother; but if he allows stupidities like [an unspecified, uncomplimentary remark made by an-

> other devotee about the Mother] to enter his mind, it may influence him, close him to the Mother and stop his progress.
>
> As for [the disciple who made the "imbecilic" remark], if he said and thought a thing like that (about the Mother) *it explains why he has been suffering in health so much lately*. If one makes oneself a mouthpiece of the hostile forces and lends oneself to their falsehoods, it is not surprising that something in him should get out of order.

To a follower who later asked, "What is the best means for the *sadhaks* [disciples] to avoid suffering due to the action of the hostile forces?" Aurobindo (1953; italics added) replied: "Faith in the Mother and *complete surrender*."

> [Physical nearness to the Mother, e.g., via living in the ashram] is indispensable for the fullness of the *sadhana* on the physical plane. Transformation of the physical and external being *is not possible otherwise* [italics added] (Aurobindo, 1953).

Such teachings, of course, provide a compelling reason to stay in the ashram. In all such cases, whatever the original motivations of the leaders in emphasizing such constraints may have been, there is an obvious effect in practice. That is, an effect of making their disciples afraid to leave their communities, or even to question the "infallibility" of the "enlightened" leaders in question.

As with other important spiritual action figures, of course, the exalted philosopher-sage known as Aurobindo did not evolve to that point without having achieved greatness in previous lives:

> Sri Aurobindo was known in his ashram as the rebirth of Napoleon. Napoleon's birthday was also August 15th.... In his previous births, it was believed he was Leonardo da Vinci, Michelangelo, Krishna and many other persons too. Someone asked Sri Aurobindo whether he had been Shakespeare as well, but could not elicit an answer (GuruNet, 2003).

Being an incarnation of Krishna would, of course, have made Aurobindo an avatar, as he himself indeed explicitly claimed (1953) to be regardless. As we will see more of later, however, there is competition among other spiritual paths for many of those same reincarnational honors.

Further, da Vinci lived from 1452 to 1519, while Michelangelo walked this Earth from 1475 to 1564. Given the chronological overlap between those two lives, this reincarnation, if taken as true, could thus only have been "one soul incarnating/emanating in two bodies." That is, it could not have been da Vinci himself reincarnating as Michelangelo. Thus, the latter's skills could not have been based on the "past life" work of the former.

Or perhaps no one ever bothered to simply look up the relevant dates, before making and publicizing those extravagant claims.

At any rate, the purported da Vinci connection does not end there:

> [E]arly in 1940, [a disciple of Aurobindo's] came in and showed the Mother a print of the celebrated "Mona Lisa," and the following brief conversation ensued:
>
> Mother: Sri Aurobindo was the artist.
>
> Champaklal: Leonardo da Vinci?
>
> Mother smiled sweetly and said: yes.
>
> Champaklal: Mother, it seems this [painting] is yours?
>
> Mother: Yes, do you not see the resemblance? (Light, 2003).

Evidently, then, not only was Aurobindo allegedly the reincarnation of Leonardo da Vinci, but his spiritual partner, the Mother, claimed to be the subject of the Mona Lisa portrait.

> "Since the beginning of earthly history," the Mother explained, "Sri Aurobindo has always presided over the great earthly transformations, under one form or another, under one name or another" (Paine, 1998).

For my own part, however, statements such as that remind me of nothing so much as my own growing up with a hyperactive cousin who could not stop arguing about which was the "strongest dinosaur." My own attitude to such conversations is simply: "Please, stop. Please."

In any case, even such "great earthly transformers" as Aurobindo still evidently stand "on the shoulders of other spiritual giants":

> It is a fact that I was hearing constantly the voice of Vivekananda speaking to me for a fortnight in the jail [in 1908]

> in my solitary mediation and felt his presence (Aurobindo, 1953).

Aurobindo and his Mother again claimed to have single-handedly turned the tide of WWII, and asserted that the former sage has "presided over the great earthly transformations" for time immemorial. If one believes that, the impressiveness of the spirit of Vivekananda allegedly visiting him in prison would pale by comparison. The same would be true for the idea of Aurobindo being "the world's greatest philosopher-sage." For, the yogi made *far* more grandiose claims himself, and indeed could therefore have easily taken such contemporary recognition of his greatness as being little more than "damning with faint praise."

At any rate, short of believing that Aurobindo's and the Mother's vital roles in WWII were exactly what they themselves claimed those to be, there are only two possible conclusions. That is, that both he and she were wildly deluded, and unable to distinguish fact from fiction or reality from their own fantasies; or that they were both outright fabricating their own life-myths.

So: Do *you* believe that one "world's greatest philosopher-sage" and his "infallible" spiritual partner—who herself "had live contacts with several gods," *teaching them* in the process—in southern India radically changed the course of human history in unparalleled ways, simply via their use of metaphysical Force and other occult faculties?

I, personally, do not.

There is, of course, competition for the title of "India's greatest modern sage." For example, in his foreword to Inner Directions' recent (2000) reissue of *Talks with Ramana Maharshi,* Wilber himself had given comparably high praise to Ramana:

> *"Talks"* is the living voice of the *greatest sage* [italics added] of the twentieth century.

That feting comes, predictably, in spite of Wilber's having never sat with, or even met, Maharshi, knowing him only through his extant, edited writings.

One may well be impressed by Maharshi's "unadorned, bottom-line" mysticism of simply inquiring, of himself, "Who am I?"—in the attempt to "slip into the witnessing Self." Likewise, his claim that "Love is not different from the Self ... the Self is love" (in

Walsh, 1999) is sure to make one feel warm and fuzzy inside. Nevertheless, the man was not without his eccentricities:

> [T]he Indian sage Ramana Maharshi once told Paul Brunton that he had visions of cities beneath the sacred mountain of Arunachala where he resided all his adult life (Feuerstein, 1998).

Indeed, in Talk 143 from Volume 1 of the infamous *Talks with Sri Ramana Maharshi* (2000)—the very text upon which Wilber has above commented—we find:

> In visions I have seen caves, cities with streets, etc., and a whole world in it.... All the *siddhas* ["perfected beings"] are reputed to be there.

Were such subterranean cities to be taken as existing on the *physical* level, however, they could not so exist now or in the past without previous, historic "Golden Ages" and their respective civilizations, with those civilizations being more advanced than our own. That idea, however, is generally explicitly taken as being the product only of magical/mythical thinking and the like:

> [T]he romantic transcendentalists ... usually confuse average-mode consciousness and growing-tip consciousness, or average lower and truly advanced, [and] use that confusion to claim that the past epochs were some sort of Golden Age which we have subsequently destroyed. They confuse magic and psychic, myth and subtle archetype (Wilber, 1983a).

The question then becomes: Do *you* believe that "all the *siddhas*" are living in (even astral) cities and caves, beneath one particular mountain in India? (Mountains are actually regarded as holy in cultures throughout the world, and as being symbols of the astral spine. To take their holiness and "natural abode of souls" nature *literally,* however, is *highly* unusual.) If not, was the "greatest sage of the century" hallucinating? If so....

Or, even if not:

> All the food [in Maharshi's ashram] was prepared by *brahmins* so that it should remain uncontaminated by contact with lower castes and foreigners....

> "Bhagavan always insisted on caste observances in the ashram here, though he was not rigidly orthodox" [said Miss Merston, a long-time devotee of Maharshi] (Marshall, 1963).

> [Maharshi] allowed himself to be worshiped like a Buddha (Daniélou, 1987).

"Greatest sage"—for whom "the Self is love," but lower castes and foreigners evidently aren't, in spite of his supposed impartial witnessing of all things equally, and in spite of the fact that he was not otherwise "rigidly orthodox" or bent on following religious proscriptions.

Sadly, as we shall see, that sort of brutal inconsistency should be no less than expected from the "great spiritual personages" of our world.

CHAPTER V

THE KRINSH

(JIDDU KRISHNAMURTI)

The messiah, or World Teacher, was made to correspond with the traditional Hindu figure of the Avatar, a deific person sent to the world at certain crucial times to watch over the dawn of a new religious era (Vernon, 2001).

No one used that term [i.e., "World Teacher"] in my childhood. As I could not pronounce his name, Krishnamurti, he was known to me always, as Krinsh (Sloss, 2000).

Madame B
Down in Adyar
Liked the Masters a lot ...
But the Krinsh,
Who lived out in Ojai,
Did NOT!

JIDDU KRISHNAMURTI WAS DISCOVERED as a teenage boy by Charles Leadbeater of the Theosophical Society, on a beach in Madras, India, in 1909.

The Theosophical Society itself had been founded in New York City by the east-European "seer" Madame Helena P. Blavatsky (HPB), in 1875. Its membership soon numbered over 100,000; an Asian headquarters was established in Adyar, India, in 1882.

> The Theosophical Society ... was at first enormously successful and attracted converts of the intellectual stature of the inventor Thomas Edison and Darwin's friend and collaborator Alfred Russel Wallace (Storr, 1996).

> No less an authority than [Zen scholar] D. T. Suzuki was prepared to say that [Blavatsky's] explication of Buddhist teachings in *The Voice of Silence* ... testified to an initiation into "the deeper side of Mahayana doctrine" (Oldmeadow, 2004).

Perhaps. And yet—

> W. E. Coleman has shown that [Blavatsky's *Isis Unveiled*] comprises a sustained and frequent plagiarism of about one hundred contemporary texts, chiefly relating to ancient and exotic religions, demonology, Freemasonry and the case for spiritualism....
>
> [*The Secret Doctrine*] betrayed her plagiarism again but now her sources were mainly contemporary works on Hinduism and modern science (Goodrick-Clarke, 2004).

Interestingly, when Blavatsky and her co-founder, Colonel Henry Olcott, sailed to India in 1879, the man whom they left in charge of the Theosophical Society in America was one Abner Doubleday, the inventor of baseball (Fields, 1992).

Blavatsky herself taught the existence of a hierarchy of "Ascended Masters," included among them one Lord Maitreya, the World Teacher whose incarnations had allegedly included both Krishna and Jesus. Those same Masters, however, were modeled on real figures from public life, e.g., on individuals involved in East Indian political reform (Vernon, 2001). They were fraudulently contacted in other ways as well:

> [Blavatsky's housekeeper, Emma Cutting, demonstrated] how she and HPB had made a doll together, which they ... manipulated on a long bamboo pole in semi-darkness to provide the Master's alleged apparitions. Emma had also

> dropped "precipitated" letters on to Theosophical heads from holes in the ceiling, while her husband had made sliding panels and hidden entrances into the shrine room [adjoining HPB's bedroom] to facilitate Blavatsky's comings and goings and make possible the substitution of all the brooches, dishes and other objects that she used in her demonstrations [i.e., as purported materializations or "apports"]....
>
> The Russian journalist V. S. Solovieff claimed to have caught [Blavatsky] red-handed with the silver bells which produced astral music [in séances].... Blavatsky confessed to Solovieff quite bluntly that the phenomena were fraudulent, adding that one must deceive men in order to rule them (Washington, 1995).

Madame Blavatsky died in 1891. Prior to that passing, however, Leadbeater had already begun claiming to channel messages himself, from Blavatsky's fabricated "Masters."

The famously clairvoyant Leadbeater, further, had before (and after) been accused of indecent behavior toward a series of adolescent males:

> One of Leadbeater's favorite boys [accused him] of secretly teaching boys to masturbate under cover of occult training, and insinuat[ed] that masturbation was only the prelude to the gratifying of homosexual lust (Washington, 1995).

In any case, the young "Krishna on the Beach" was no typical teenager, in need of such mundane lessons, as the clairvoyant well noted. Indeed, upon examining his aura, Leadbeater found Krishnamurti to be a highly refined soul, apparently completely free of selfishness, i.e., ego.

Krishnamurti was soon thereafter declared by Leadbeater to be the current "vehicle" for Lord Maitreya, and schooled accordingly within the Theosophical ranks. (An American boy had earlier been advanced for the same position by Leadbeater, but the latter appears to have "changed his mind" in that regard. Later, Leadbeater was to propose yet another East Indian youth for the title of World Teacher. That boy, Rajagopal, went on to manage Krishnamurti's financial affairs, while his wife handled Jiddu's other affairs, as we shall see.)

> The brothers [i.e., Krishnamurti and his younger sibling] no doubt found Leadbeater's swings of temperament confusing.

> One moment they would be adored, pampered, idolized, and the next scolded for breaching some piece of esoteric etiquette they did not understand (Vernon, 2001).

Throughout this book, we shall see many examples of students and disciples being placed in comparable situations by their teachers and guru-figures. In such psychological binds, persons for whom it is vitally important to earn the approval of their "master" are rather unable to discern how to gain that reward, with often-tragic results. There are, indeed, two possible extreme reactions to such intermittent reward/punishment, where one cannot ascertain the conditions by which the reward will be earned or the punishment given. That is, one can either simply drop all of one's reactions and live in "choiceless awareness" of the moment; or, more often, evolve that impossibility of "guessing right" into neuroses, violence or extreme depression.

Indeed, relevant experiments have been done by students of Pavlov himself (Winn, 2000), wherein dogs were first taught, via reward and punishment, to distinguish between circles and ellipses. Then, the circles were gradually flattened, and the ellipses made rounder, until the experimental subjects could no longer distinguish between them. The dogs were thus unable to give the "correct response" to earn a corresponding prize, instead being rewarded and punished "randomly." The effect on the animals was that initially happy and excitable dogs became violent, biting their experimenters. Other previously "laid back, carefree" animals, by contrast, became lethargic, not caring about anything.

At any rate, even prior to being discovered by Leadbeater, while still in India's public school system, Krishnamurti's own education had been a traumatic experience:

> Never one to endear himself to schoolmasters, Krishna was punished brutally for his inadequacies and branded an imbecile (Vernon, 2001).

> He was caned almost every day for being unable to learn his lessons. Half his time at school was spent in tears on the veranda (Lutyens, 1975).

Not surprisingly, then, in later years Krishnamurti evinced little regard for academic accomplishments:

> [The Nobel-caliber physicist David Bohm] spoke of the humiliation he had experienced at the hands of Krishnamurti who, in his presence, made cutting jokes about "professors" and did not acknowledge the importance of Bohm's work....
>
> He suffered greatly under [Krishnamurti's] disrespect of him, which at times was blatantly obvious (Peat, 1997).

* * *

Krishnamurti's contemporary appearance on Earth offered hope to Theosophists for the "salvation of mankind." After years of being groomed for his role as their World Teacher, however, Krishnamurti's faith in the protection of Theosophy's Masters, and Leadbeater's guiding visions of the same, was shattered in 1925 by the unexpected death of his own younger brother. (Jiddu had previously been assured, in his own believed meetings with the Masters on the astral plane, that his brother would survive the relevant illness.) Thereafter, he viewed those visions, including his own, as being merely personal wish-fulfillments, and considered the occult hierarchy of Masters to be irrelevant (Vernon, 2001).

That, however, did not imply any rejection of mysticism in general, on Krishnamurti's part:

> By the autumn of 1926 [following an alleged kundalini awakening which began in 1922] Krishna made it clear ... that a metamorphosis had taken place. [The kundalini is a subtle energy believed to reside at the base of the spine. When "awakened" and directed up the spine into the brain, it produces ecstatic spiritual realization.] His former personality had been stripped away, leaving him in a state of constant and irreversible union with the godhead (Vernon, 2001).

Or, as Krishnamurti (1969) himself put it, in openly proclaiming his status as World Teacher:

> I have become one with the Beloved. I have been made simple. I have become glorified because of Him.

> [Krishnamurti] maintained that his consciousness was merged with his beloved, by which he meant all of creation (Sloss, 2000).

In August of 1929, reasoning that organizations inherently condition and restrict Truth, the thirty-four-year-old Krishnamurti formally dissolved the Theosophical Society's "Order of the Star" branch, which he had previously headed since 1911.

Even there, however, it was more the organization and its "Ascended Master"-based philosophy, rather than his own role as World Teacher or Messiah, that was being repudiated. Krishnamurti himself explained as much after the dissolution:

> When it becomes necessary for humanity to receive in a new form the ancient wisdom, someone whose duty it is to repeat these truths is incarnated (in Michel, 1992).

Or, as Vernon (2001) confirmed:

> [Krishnamurti] never went as far as to deny being the World Teacher, just that it made no difference who or what he was.

In 1932, Krishnamurti and Rajagopal's wife began an affair which would last for more than twenty-five years. The woman, Rosalind, became pregnant on several occasions, suffering miscarriages and at least two covert/illegal abortions. The oddity of that relationship is not lessened by Jiddu's earlier regard for the same woman. For, both he and his brother believed that Rosalind was the reincarnation of their long-lost mother ... in spite of the fact that the latter had only died two years *after* Rosalind was born (Sloss, 2000).

In the late 1930s, Krishnamurti retired to Ojai, California, becoming close friends with Aldous Huxley. Being thus affectionate, however, did not stop Jiddu from insultingly regarding Huxley, behind his back, as having a mind "like a wastebasket" (Sloss, 2000). Huxley in turn, after hearing Krishnamurti speak in Switzerland in 1961, wrote of that lecture: "It was like listening to a discourse of the Buddha" (in Peat, 1997). Further, when Aldous' house and library were lost in a fire, Krishnamurti's *Commentaries on Living* were the first of the books he replaced.

"Wastebasket," indeed.

With his proximity to northern Los Angeles, Jiddu also visited with composer Igor Stravinsky, writer Thomas Mann and philosopher-mathematician Bertrand Russell, and picnicked with screen legends Greta Garbo and Charlie Chaplin.

The continuing affair with Rosalind was, not surprisingly, less than completely in line with the quasi-Messiah's own teachings:

> Krishnamurti had occasionally told young people that celibacy was significant, indicating that it encouraged the generation of great energy and intensity that could lead to psychological transformation. Krishnamurti seems to have raised the matter with [David] Bohm as well, and the physicist believed that the Indian teacher led a celibate life (Peat, 1997).

Bohm first met Krishnamurti in 1961, and went on to become easily the most famous of his followers (until their distancing from each other in 1984), co-authoring several books of dialogs on spiritual topics with Jiddu. Bohm further sat as a trustee on the board of a Krishnamurti-founded school in England, and was viewed by many as potentially being the Krinsh's "successor."

Consequently, apologetic protests that Krishnamurti's behavior with Rosalind was "not dishonest/hypocritical," simply for him not having spent his entire life preaching the benefits of celibacy or marriage, ring hollow. On the contrary, if we are to believe Peat's report that Krishnamurti "had spoken to Bohm of the importance of celibacy," there absolutely *was* a contradiction between Krishnamurti's teachings and his life. That is so even though the quarter-century affair with Rosalind, hidden for whatever reasons, had ended by the time he met Bohm.

Given that, the only possible verdict regarding Krishnamurti's behavior is that of obvious hypocrisy.

* * *

Considering Krishnamurti's own abusive schooling, it is hardly surprising that he should have perpetuated that same cycle on his students, under the pretense of deliberately creating crises to promote change and growth in them:

> The gopis [early, young female disciples of Krishnamurti, by analogy with the followers of Krishna in the Bhagavad Gita] would seek out private interviews with him, during which he mercilessly tore down their defenses and laid naked their faults, invariably ending with the girls crying their hearts out, but feeling it must be for the best (Vernon, 2001).

Even many years later, employing the same "skillful/cruel means" of awakening others,

> Krishnamurti confronted Bohm in a way that others later described as "brutal" (Peat, 1997).

As we shall see, that is a common problem among the world's spiritual paths for disciples who have endured their own guru-figures' harsh discipline, and have then assumed license to treat others in the same lousy way as they themselves had been treated. The excuse there is, of course, always that such mistreatment is for the "spiritual benefit" of those others, even in contexts where that claim could not possibly be true.

> Quarrels due to what Raja[gopal] remembers as Krishna's frequent lying and undercutting of him, Krishna's agreeing to proposals behind Raja's back, and making promises that could not be kept, became so severe after several months in South America that once Krishna, who could only take so much criticism, slapped Raja. This was not the only time that would happen, but it was the first (Sloss, 2000).

> Krishnamurti lacked ordinary human compassion and kindness; he was intolerant, even contemptuous, of those who could not rise to his own high plane (Vernon, 2001).

"Born with a heart two sizes too small," etc.

At least one of Jiddu's early "gopis," however, saw through his clumsy, "cruel to be kind" attempts at spiritual discipline:

> These supposedly privileged and beneficial sessions consisted of Krishna repeatedly pointing out well-known faults and picking on everything detrimental and sapping one's confidence (Lutyens, 1972).

On at least one occasion, Krishnamurti was likewise inadvertently overheard making unprovoked, uncomplimentary remarks about others ... in his bedroom, with the married Rosalind (Sloss, 2000).

Neither Rajagopal nor Rosalind were ever devotees of Krishnamurti. Nor was David Bohm, whose own response to Krishnamurti's (unsolicited) harsh public discipline—in a context where they were supposed to be in a dialog, not a guru-disciple relationship, by Jiddu's own explicit rejection of the latter—was beyond tragic:

> [T]he physicist was thrown into despair. Unable to sleep, obsessed with thoughts, he constantly paced the room to the point where he thought of suicide. At one point he believed that he could feel the neurotransmitters firing in his brain.... His despair soon reached the point where he was placed on antidepressants....
>
> He once wrote to [Fritz Wilhelm] that he thought that his chest pains were a result of K's [i.e., Krishnamurti's] misbehaving towards him. "This problem with K is literally crushing me" (Peat, 1997).

* * *

Krishnamurti continued to lecture and discipline until his passing in 1986. In those activities, he gradually mutated his teaching style from that of a savior pronouncing cosmic truths to that of a personal counselor, focusing the content of those lectures on the split in consciousness between subject and object:

> When man becomes aware of the movement of his own consciousness he will see the division between the thinker and the thought, the observer and the observed, the experiencer and the experience. He will discover that this division is an illusion. Then only is there pure observation which is insight without any shadow of the past. This timeless insight brings about a deep radical change in the mind (Krishnamurti, in [Lutyens, 1983]).

Through that personal realization, Krishnamurti claimed (completely untenably) to be unconditioned by his own upbringing and, indeed, to have (conveniently) "forgotten" most of his past. Nevertheless, his own teachings have much in common with those of both the Buddha and the Upanishads. Not coincidentally, Jiddu had been intensively schooled in both of those philosophies during his early years at Adyar (Sloss, 2000).

In line with his stultifying ideas on the nature of thought and knowledge, Krishnamurti further gave no instruction in structural/content techniques of meditation. Instead, he taught and practiced the meditative exercise as "a movement without any motive, without words and the activity of thought."

> [R]epeating mantras and following gurus were, he said, particularly stupid ways of wasting time (Peat, 1997).

> And the Krinsh, with his krinsh-feet quite warm in Ojai,
> Said, "Be independent, meditate my way!
> Be free without gurus!
> Be free without mantras!
> Be free without beliefs, intentions or tantras!"

Jiddu himself, however, was a guru in everything but name. The authoritarian pronouncements, intolerance for disagreement, and grandiosity could have come from any of the other "enlightened" individuals with whom we shall soon become too familiar. Though Krishnamurti himself was "allergic" to the guru-disciple relationship, "if it looks like a guru, talks like a guru and acts like a guru...."

> After so many years surrounded by an inner circle, like a monarch attended by his courtiers who adored him and believed he could do no wrong, he had grown unused to being contradicted (Vernon, 2001).

> [E]ven as he was insisting on the vital importance of individual discovery, the transcripts of his conversations with pupils [at his schools] reveal a man who mercilessly bullied his interlocutors into accepting his point of view (Washington, 1995).

> Krishnamurti isolated himself from criticism and feedback, "just like everybody he was criticizing," [Joel] Kramer [coauthor of *The Guru Papers*] said, and had to have "the last word on everything" (Horgan, 1999).

Even as he lay on his deathbed, wasting away from pancreatic cancer, Krishnamurti stated firmly that "while he was alive he was still 'the World Teacher'" (Vernon, 2001). (That terminal illness occurred in spite of his claimed possession of laying-on-of-hands healing abilities, which proved equally ineffectual in his own prior attempts at healing Bohm of his heart ailments.) Indeed, so enamored was the Krinsh of his own teaching position in the world that he recorded the following statement a mere ten days before his passing:

> I don't think people realize what tremendous energy and intelligence went through this body.... You won't find another body like this, or that supreme intelligence operating in a body for many hundred years. You won't see it again (in Lutyens, 1988).

Krishnamurti is supposed to have said that he is even greater than Buddha or the Christ (in Sloss, 2000).

> And what happened then...?
> Well ... in Adyar they say
> That the World Teacher's head
> Grew three sizes that day!

Of course, Krishnamurti's dissolution of the Order of the Star is often naïvely taken as indicating a profound humility on his part. However, as we shall implicitly see with every one of the "sages" to follow, it is only through extensive editing, in the selective presentation of the "enlightened" man's speech and actions, that any of them begin to look so humble and holy.

As to what Jiddu's own legacy may be, beyond his voluminous and arid written and recorded teachings, he essentially answered that question himself:

> Shortly before his death the Indian teacher had declared that no one had ever truly understood his teaching; no one besides himself had experienced transformation (Peat, 1997).

That, too, is a recurring problem with the "great guru-figures" of this world—in generally failing to create even one disciple "as great as" themselves, in spite of their "skillful" discipline. More pointedly, any lesser, non-World teacher who could openly admit that *not even one* of his students had ever "truly understood his teaching" might have begun to question his own abilities in that regard. *This* World Teacher, however, evidently was not "conditioned" by any such need for self-evaluation.

Krishnamurti exhibited a lifelong penchant for fine, tailored clothing. One can further easily see clear vestiges, in his psychology, of the Indian caste system under which he had grown up (Vernon, 2001). Indeed, that background influenced him even to the point of his insisting that used books from others be wiped before his reading of them. In planning for his own death, he had further actually left instructions for the needed crematory oven to be thoroughly cleaned before his own use of it, and for that cleanliness to be verified by one of his followers. Evidently, this was to ensure that no one else's "impure" ashes would commingle with his own holy, *brahmin*-caste remains.

We should all be so "unconditioned" by our own "forgotten" pasts, no?

> [W]hen I interrogated Krishnamurti himself about the whole World Mother affair [i.e., the Theosophical Society's short-lived programme for global spiritual upliftment under a chosen woman after the "World Teacher" plans for Krishnamurti had fallen through], he blurted out, "Oh, that was all cooked u—" before he caught himself in the realization that he was admitting to a recollection of events in his early life which he later came to deny he possessed (Sloss, 2000).

> [Emily Lutyens] said she knew Krishna was a congenital liar but that she would nevertheless always adore him....
>
> My mother asked him once why he lied and he replied with astonishing frankness, "Because of fear" (Sloss, 2000).

> Krinsh was outraged. His voice changed completely from a formal indifference to heated anger. It became almost shrill.
>
> "I have no ego!" he said. "Who do you think you are, to talk to me like this?" (Sloss, 2000).

> One day, history will reveal everything; but the division in Krishnamurti himself will cast a very dark shadow on all he has said or written. Because the first thing the readers will say, is: "If he cannot live it, who can?" (in Sloss, 2000).

> *Then* the Krinsh slowly took off his World Teacher hat
> "If my teaching," he thought, "falls down too often flat....
> Maybe teaching ... perhaps ... is not what I'm good at."

CHAPTER VI

ZEN IN THE ART OF SEX AND VIOLENCE

The Zen tradition has a history of famous drunken poets and masters.... Public encouragement for drinking in several communities where the teacher was alcoholic has led many students to follow suit, and certain Buddhist and Hindu communities have needed to start AA groups to begin to deal with their addiction problems....

Students who enter spiritual communities do not imagine they will encounter these kinds of difficulties (Kornfield, 1993).

[I]t became known that Maezumi [roshi/guru of the Zen Center in Los Angeles] had had a number of affairs with female students and had also entered a dry-out clinic for alcoholics (Rawlinson, 1997).

In 1975 and 1979, as well as later in 1982, the Zen Studies Society had been rocked by rumors of Eido Roshi's alleged sexual liaisons with female students....

Nor were the allegations limited to sexual misconduct. They spread to financial mismanagement and incorrect behavior (Tworkov, 1994).

ZEN BUDDHISM HAS BEEN WIDELY POPULARIZED in the West through the writings of individuals such as Alan Watts and D. T. Suzuki, not to mention Philip Kapleau's *The Three Pillars of Zen* and Eugen Herrigel's *Zen in the Art of Archery*. As means toward enlightenment, it predominantly utilizes *zazen* meditation—sitting and counting/watching one's breath—and koans such as "What is the sound of one hand clapping?" Its Rinzai sect in particular further employs behaviors intended to shock disciples out of their normal state into enlightened awareness, and to aid in the "death of the ego" of the student—for which they also utilize "the stick":

> Zen teachers have an excellent method of dealing with students who start comparing themselves to Buddha or God [after their early enlightenment experiences, says Ken Wilber]. "They take the stick and beat the crap out of you. And after five or ten years of that, you finally get over yourself" (Horgan, 2003a).

That, however, is simply a ludicrously romanticized version of physical abuse meted out in the name of spirituality. In reality, such "crap-beating" behavior only shows the tempers and tendencies toward violence of individuals who are naïvely viewed by their followers as being spiritually enlightened.

> Richard Rumbold, an English Zen enthusiast, who spent about five months at the Shokokuji, a monastery in Kyoto, describes some savage beatings-up administered by the head monk and his assistant for trifling disciplinary offences (Koestler, 1960).

Such brutal discipline could, further, easily get completely out of hand. Indeed, as a true story told to Janwillem van de Wetering (1999) during his long-term stay at a Japanese Zen monastery in Kyoto in the early 1970s goes:

> In Tokyo there are some Zen monasteries as well. In one of these monasteries ... there was a Zen monk who happened to be very conceited. He refused to listen to whatever the master was trying to tell him and used the early morning interviews with the master to air all his pet theories. The masters have a special stick for this type of pupil. Our master has one, too, you will have seen it, a short thick stick. One morn-

> ing the master hit the monk so hard that the monk didn't get up any more. He couldn't, because he was dead....
>
> The head monk reported the incident to the police, but the master was never charged. Even the police know that there is an extraordinary relationship between master and pupil, a relationship outside the law.

Likewise, at a Buddhist repentance ceremony,

> two young monks nodded off. After the ceremony, Dokujiki followed them back to the *sodo,* the monks' hall. Screaming in rage, Dokujiki grabbed the *kyosaku* [stick] and went after the young monks.... Dokujiki repeatedly pounded the two terrified fledglings with the thick winter stick.... Since Dokujiki was in a position of authority, nobody said a word to him about his transgressions....
>
> "Some people would tell you that this is a tough form of Buddhist compassion," said Norman, "but it has nothing to do with Buddhism or compassion. It's a perversity that should be rejected....
>
> "Even the stick should be dropped. The stick and this stupid macho attitude" (Chadwick, 1994).

Indeed, as far as "stupid macho attitudes" go, it would be difficult to top the celebration of Zen masters "beating the crap out of" their disciples. Yet ironically, Wilber himself, quoted earlier in exactly that regard, endorsed Chadwick's above text, enthusiastically blurbing, "I love this book!"

As Robert Buswell (1992) further tells it, such violence is actually not at all foreign to Zen, even outside of the purportedly valid discipline of its followers. For, during the fight between celibates and householders for control of Buddhist monasteries in Korea in the 1950s, after the end of the Korean War, the celibate monks

> sometimes resorted to physical force to remove the married monks from the monasteries; indeed, older *bhiksus* [celibate monks] ... told many stories of celibates ordaining young thugs off the streets to bring muscle to their movement....
>
> According to the main news organ of the celibates ... the married monks submitted false evidence in favor of their claims and illegally invaded temples that *bhiksus* had occupied, trying to retake them.

Such behavior would surely not have surprised Zen priest and scholar D. T. Suzuki, nor was it inconsistent with the attitudes of "enlightened" Zen masters in general:

> With his oft-pictured gentle and sagacious appearance of later years, Suzuki is revered among many in the West as a true man of Zen. Yet he wrote that "religion should, first of all, seek to preserve the existence of the state," followed by the assertion that the Chinese were "unruly heathens" whom Japan should punish "in the name of the religion." Zen master Harada Sogaku, highly praised in the English writings of Philip Kapleau, Maezumi Taizan, and others, was also quoted by Hakugen [a Rinzai Zen priest and scholar teaching at Hanazono University in Kyoto]. In 1939 he wrote: "[If ordered to] march: tramp, tramp, or shoot: bang, bang. This is the manifestation of the highest Wisdom [of Enlightenment]. The unity of Zen and war of which I speak extends to the farthest reaches of the holy war [now under way]" (Victoria, 1997).

Daizen Victoria, quoted immediately above, is himself no unsympathetic outsider, but is rather a practicing Soto Zen Buddhist priest.

As Suzuki's own "fully enlightened Zen master," Soen/Soyen/So-on—who had earlier attended the 1893 Parliament of Religions (Fields, 1992)—put it:

> [A]s a means of bringing into harmony those things which are incompatible, killing and war are necessary (in Victoria, 1997).

The Rinzai Zen master Nantembo (1839 – 1925) would certainly have agreed:

> There is no bodhisattva practice superior to the compassionate taking of life (in Victoria, 2003).

Likewise for the sagely Omori Sogen, "lauded as the 'greatest Zen master of modern times,' whose very life is 'worthy to be considered a masterpiece of Zen art'":

> Instead of a master concerned with the "life-giving sword" ... of Zen, we encounter someone who from the 1920s took an

> active part in the ultra-right's agenda to eliminate parliamentary democracy through political assassination at home and promote Japan's imperialist aims abroad. In short, a man willing to kill all who stood in the way of his political agenda, yet claiming the enlightenment of the Buddha as his own....
>
> Hosokawa Dogen writes: "The life of Omori Roshi is the manifestation of traditional and true Zen" (Victoria, 2003).

Of Philip Kapleau's guru, the Yasutani Haku'un immortalized in *The Three Pillars of Zen* but regarded by some historians since then as being "no less a fanatical militarist" than his own master, Daizen Victoria (2003) opines:

> Hakugen should have written: "Yasutani was an *even more* fanatical militarist, not to mention ethnic chauvinist, sexist, and anti-Semite, than his master!"

Not until 2001 did any of the branches of Rinzai Zen admit or apologize for their zealous support of Japanese militarism (in WWII and otherwise), in equating that militarism with "Buddha Dharma" (Victoria, 2003).

> [D]uring the war leading Zen masters and scholars claimed, among other things, that killing Chinese was an expression of Buddhist compassion designed to rid the latter of their "defilements" (Victoria, 2003).

Zen has further long embraced, even prior to its introduction to Japan in the twelfth century, the idea that enlightened beings transcend good and evil.

> One Zen master told me that the moral precepts were very important for students to follow, but, of course, Zen masters didn't need to bother with them since they were "free." You can imagine what troubles later visited that community (Kornfield, 1993).

And yet, such contemporary attitudes as Kornfield describes are simply "pure Zen," as it has been practiced in the East for over a thousand years. We can and should question such nonsense, but in doing so we are not returning Zen to its original/traditional form. Rather, we are adapting the accepted way of doing things for our modern times. One cannot, after all, assert on the one hand that "enlightened beings are no longer subject to the moral constraints enjoined by the Buddhist precepts on the unenlightened," and then turn around and profess surprise when "troubles" visit not merely their transplants into the West but their own *traditional* communities in the East! Quite obviously, any such "transcendence of moral constraints" would render the particular surrounding social rules irrelevant: If one is not bound by laws, it doesn't matter whether those same laws are strict or lax when applied to others. Put another way: It doesn't matter what the speed limit is, or how fast you were going, if you've got diplomatic immunity from prosecution for breaking laws which apply to others but not to you.

> The scandals, often of a sexual nature, that have rocked a number of American Zen (and other Buddhist) centers in recent years may seem a world apart from Zen-supported Japanese militarism. The difference, however, may not be as great as it first appears, for I suggest the common factor is Zen's long-standing and self-serving lack of interest in, or commitment to, Buddhism's ethical precepts (Victoria, 2003).

Again, that unflattering but unusually insightful observation comes from an ordained Zen *priest*.

Interestingly, albeit for completely different reasons, neither van de Wetering nor Buswell (who spent five years as a Zen monk in Korea) speak positively of the work of either D. T. Suzuki or Kapleau. Rather, those writings on Zen, they respectively indicate, misrepresent how it is actually practiced in contemporary Asia:

> [Modern Zen] monks in Korea train within an extensive web of religious thought and practice.... These monks know that while Zen masters teach sudden enlightenment, they follow in their daily practice a rigidly scheduled regimen of training. They know that while Zen texts claim to eschew doctrinal understanding, monks are expected first to gain a solid grounding in Buddhist texts before starting meditation practice....
>
> The vision of Zen presented in much Western scholarship distorts the quality of Zen religious experience as it is lived by its own adherents (Buswell, 1992).

As to the actual life and mindset of Zen monks in Asia, then, when seeking entrance to a monastery as a trainee the prospective monk will first prostrate himself at the gate for hours or days.

> When asked why he wishes to enter the monastery, the monk should reply, "I know nothing. Please accept my request!" indicating that his mind is like a blank sheet of paper, ready to be inscribed by his superiors as they wish. If a monk fails to give the proper answer, he is struck repeatedly with the *kyosaku* until his shoulders are black and blue and the desired state of mind is achieved (Victoria, 1997).

Having been accepted into the community with that "desired state of mind," even monks who were admitted just hours earlier will exercise authority over the neophyte, preceding him at meals and on other semiformal or formal occasions.

> Those senior monks who have been in training for more than one or two years seem, to the new entrant, to be superior beings (Victoria, 1997).

* * *

What, then, of the widespread enlightenment which one might idealistically wish to attribute to practitioners of Zen?

> I once asked Katagiri Roshi, with whom I had my first breakthrough ... how many truly great Ch'an and Zen masters there have historically been. Without hesitating, he said, "Maybe one thousand altogether." I asked another Zen master how many truly enlightened—deeply enlightened—Japanese Zen masters there were alive today, and he said, "Not more than a dozen" (Wilber, 2000a).

Thus, we have over a millennium of Zen teachers "beating the crap out of" their numerous disciples on a regular basis, to generate a scant thousand (i.e., around one per year, globally) "enlightened" individuals. That, however, would never be a reasonable trade-off, via any "calculus of suffering." That is so particularly since such enlightenment primarily benefits only the specific individual "blessed" by it, not the world at large.

Be that as it may, the "death of the ego" in enlightenment remains a strong motivation for meditators, in Zen and elsewhere.

> [One] of the marks of the meditation monk [as opposed to the monastery administrators, etc.] is to wear old clothes covered with layer upon layer of patches. While such garments are supposed to show his detachment from material possessions, they more often serve as a kind of monastic status symbol. On several occasions I even knew a monk new to the meditation hall to trade a brand-new set of polyester robes for old patchwork clothes. During their free time, the meditation monks can often be found adding still more patches to their raiments (Buswell, 1992).

More accurately, then, the death of *other people's* egos remains a strong motivating factor for meditators everywhere, with the leverage of their respected power both acting to effect that, and aiding in the indulgence of their own desires.

> Mo-san's trap turned out to be his very "noncaring diligence" .... I heard that, some ten years later, he became a substitute master in an American Zen temple on the West Coast. During his tenure he hid his shortness by wearing platform soles under lengthened robes and insisted that his lay disciples buy him a Cadillac to glide about in. He evoked a scandal by trying to trade insights for intimate encounters with tall blondes (van de Wetering, 2001).

> Or, expressed in haiku:
>
> Tall blonde, high heels, wow!
> Is that a lengthened silk robe?
> Happy to see you

We should hardly be surprised that relocating stick-wielding "Eastern truths" into the materialistic and unconstrained West would result in a dilution of their transformative value. But in their native, sacred East?

> Despite the disastrous problems most of his students had encountered trying to study Zen in Japan, [Shunryu] Suzuki [of the San Francisco Zen Center, author of the million-selling *Zen Mind, Beginner's Mind*] continued to explore the possibility.... Suzuki had ordained [a] couple before they went to Japan. The wife did fine at a nunnery, but her husband was forcibly sedated and shipped out of [the Soto headquarters, mountain monastery at] Eiheiji. A woman from Zen Center

had such horrible experiences in Japanese temples that she rejected Buddhism entirely, bought a wig, and moved to L.A. (Chadwick, 1999).

The "Little Suzuki" himself founded the world's first Buddhist monastery outside of Asia, at Tassajara hot springs—located three hours southeast of San Francisco—in 1966. The list of visitors and close associates to the San Francisco Zen Center (SFZC) and Tassajara predictably reads like a "Who's Who" of American Buddhist (real and wanna-be) spirituality: Alan Watts, beat poet Allen Ginsberg and the Pulitzer Prize-winning Gary Snyder. Also, translator Thomas Cleary, social economist E. F. Schumacher, and Stewart Brand (co-founder of the *Whole Earth Catalog*). Plus Robert Thurman, the Harvard-graduated scholarly father of Hollywood-goddess Uma and the self-proclaimed "first hippie in Asia," who was ordained as the first American Tibetan Buddhist monk by the Dalai Lama himself. Additionally, Joan Baez, Mick Jagger, and Earl McGrath, the (former) head of Rolling Stone Records. Also, anthropologist Gregory Bateson, former California governor and 1992 U.S. presidential candidate Jerry Brown, and numerous other recipients of (seriously) autographed fruitcakes later presented by Suzuki's successor, Richard Baker.

For, before passing away in 1971, Suzuki-roshi had named Baker as his sole American "dharma heir," or recipient of the Buddhist "transmission" from guru to disciple. (Baker, for his own part, had earlier organized the first major LSD conference in the United States, in 1966.)

> "[What] does transmission mean?" I asked Suzuki.... "Does it mean that Richard Baker is perfectly enlightened, and that his mind is the same as the mind of Buddha? Is his understanding complete?"
>
> "Oh, no no no," Suzuki said. "Don't make too much of it. It means he has a good understanding. A good understanding and a complete commitment"....
>
> [I]t was the equivalent of getting a teacher's certificate. Suzuki had said in lectures, "Transmission is nothing special," or "Actually, there is nothing to transmit" (Chadwick, 1999).

Baker himself, however, apparently evinced a somewhat more self-flattering understanding as to the significance of his own spiritual inheritance:

> Transmission happens outside the limits of identity and ego. The fact that an acknowledged master *acknowledges you as a Zen master* means "you are no longer a Buddhist; what you do is Buddhism" (Downing, 2001; italics added).

And what, then, "is Buddhism"?

> As abbot of San Francisco Zen Center, between the abbot's budget and use of community-owned residences and resources, [Baker] lived in a style that he estimates could be duplicated by a private citizen with an annual salary of close to half a million dollars a year (Tworkov, 1994).

Discipline under the transmitted "Frisco Zen master" then reportedly (Downing, 2001) included:

- Baker dictating to his followers as to whom they could or couldn't be involved with in sexual relationships
- The master having his followers "stand in rows and bow as he drove away from Tassajara" in a "fantastic to drive" BMW, thereby causing himself to be viewed by at least one of those bowing disciples as the "Richard Nixon of Zen"
- Ostensibly "lifetime" members of the Tassajara Board of Directors involuntarily "going on sabbatical" when not being sufficiently supportive of Baker's wishes

> "What Baker transmitted," said a senior priest, "was power and arrogance and an attitude that 'I have it and you don't'" (Tworkov, 1994).

> At the San Francisco Zen Center, the problems that came to a head in 1983 [involved] a number of master-disciple sexual affairs, as well as a complex pattern of alleged misuses of authority and charisma, both psychologically and financially (Anthony, et al., 1987).

More specifically, the Harvard-educated, married Baker "was forced to resign after his affair with a married student was revealed" (Schwartz, 1996). The frantic husband of the rich, lithe blonde in question—whom Baker reportedly claimed had seduced *him* (we should all have such luck)—was a writer by the name of Paul Hawken. He, in turn, was of upscale Smith & Hawken garden tool (and more) catalog fame, and had previously been seen within the community as being Richard's best friend, even being referred to thusly by Baker himself (Tworkov, 1994).

At least two other women were reportedly cruelly discredited as being mentally unstable by Richard following the termination of his alleged sexual involvement with them (Downing, 2001).

After all that, the author of *The Tassajara Bread Book* expressed his own opinion of Baker:

> A friend of mine said it best: I give thanks to Dick Baker every day for fucking up so incredibly well that it gave me my life back, because I had given it to him (in Downing, 2001).

> Senior priests were testifying at public meetings about physical and psychological abuse Richard had [allegedly] perpetrated....
>
> Richard's close friend and advisor, Esalen's Michael Murphy, told Richard that "the whole alternative movement was crippled by what happened at Zen Center" (Downing, 2001).

And yet, to the present day, Baker reportedly insists:

> The only scandalous thing that happened at Zen Center is how I was treated (in Tworkov, 1994).

This lack of comprehension about what it might mean to "cause no harm" to others, on the part of unapologetic individuals laying claim to enlightenment, profound transmission and grand bodhisattva vows, is something which we shall sadly meet consistently throughout the following chapters. Worse, one regularly sees that persons whose lives have been shattered by their guru-figures, who have then mustered the courage to speak out, are being dismissed and discredited as "crazy," etc. Further, that is done in ways indistinguishable from those in which secular victims of incest or rape are treated, should they dare to come forward.

Baker's own process of recovery from the self-inflicted 1983 "Apocalypse" included a letter from the Nobel Peace Prize nominee,

Vietnamese Buddhist Thich Nhat Hanh, vouching for Baker's sincerity of apology to the community. Also, a spurned offer from the Dalai Lama for him to take refuge in northern India, and a trip to Disneyland with singer Linda Ronstadt.

> Getting ready for an evening out, [Baker] rolls up his sleeves and says plaintively, "I didn't dance enough when I was at Zen Center. I should have danced more" (Tworkov, 1994).

Or, as Nero himself could have put it, millennia ago, upon seeing his own empire burn: "I should have fiddled more."

And how would all of the discontent regarding Baker's alleged behaviors have been handled in the "traditional" Far East?

> The treatment of individual students was the purview of the teacher. This was the *traditional model.* Whatever happened, you could say it was a teaching (Downing, 2001; italics added).

Further, following the 1983 "explosion,"

> people came from Japan and tried to tell us that if we were unhappy with the teacher, we should leave, and the teacher should stay (Yvonne Rand, in [Downing, 2001]).

This pressure to have the unhappy students leave and let the holy teacher stay, too, is very relevant to the unsupportable idea that guru-disciple relationships have "traditionally" worked. (The untenable claim implicit there is that in the agrarian East, such relationships had "checks and balances" in place, which purportedly constrained the behaviors of their guru-figures in ways which are absent in the West.) For, observations such as Rand's, above, clearly show that "traditional" societies have exercised far *less* practical checks and balances on the behaviors of their gurus/kings/emperors than does the modern and postmodern West.

> I was taught in school [that the Japanese emperor] was the [*sic*] god and I believed till I was ten years old and the war [i.e., WWII] over....
>
> We thought Chinese inferior and whites were devils and only god, our god, could win the war (in Chadwick, 1994).

Feudal society, with unquestioning obedience to the guru-like, divine emperor—the "embodiment of Supreme Truth"—actually existed in the "divine land" of Japan until the midpoint of the twentieth century. For the effects of that on the citizens, reflected in past and present society and culture, consult Victoria's (1997) *Zen at War,* Van Wolferen's (1990) *The Enigma of Japanese Power,* and Barry's (1992) *Dave Barry Does Japan.*

Consider, further, the private life of Gyokujun So-on, the Japanese teacher of the late Shunryu Suzuki. Suzuki became a disciple of So-on in 1917, at age thirteen. In those same years, So-on was carrying on an affair with the wife of a local (Japanese) merchant.

> [E]veryone knew about their relationship.... No one did anything to stop their trysts, but there was general disapproval. It was a contributing factor to So-on's loss of students (Chadwick, 1999).

Note that this rule-breaking was met merely with a milquetoast "general disapproval," not with discipline or meaningful censure or career impediments *sufficient to cause it to stop.* That is so regardless of whatever one might propose the local cultural effect of such "general disapproval" to otherwise be in terms of lost honor, etc. In that behavior, further, So-on was merely carrying on a long-standing "tradition" himself:

> In the Edo Era [1600 – 1868], Buddhist priests did not marry, but temples were busy places, and the priests in many cases were somewhat worldly. Women began living in the temples, to work and, at times, to love. They did not show their faces because *they weren't supposed to be there to begin with* (Chadwick, 1999; italics added).

> Otori [1814 – 1904] recognized that a large number of Buddhist priests were already married, *in spite of regulations prohibiting it* (Victoria, 1997; italics added).

> [I]n Zen monasteries in Japan ... sex between men has long been both a common practice and a *prohibited activity* (Downing, 2001; italics added).

> [A]t the same time every evening, there was the faint smell of smoke from the dark graveyard. It wasn't until the third

> or fourth day that I realized that the monks weren't piously lighting joss sticks for the old masters' graves at all; they were sneaking a quick *forbidden* [italics added] cigarette in the shadows of the mossy tombstones....
>
> No one was around when I left the *sodo,* but I thought I heard the sound of female laughter from within the labyrinth of thin-walled rooms, and I couldn't help wondering what other rules might be relaxed when the roshi was out of town.
>
> I walked out through the terracotta courtyard, and as I passed the doghouse I saw that [the dog's] dish contained ordinary mud-colored kibbles. This confirmed my suspicion that the [prohibited in the Buddhist diet] meat on the stove hadn't been for the dog, at all (Boehm, 1996).

In accord with such wholly unpunished, contemporary rule-breaking, Janwillem van de Wetering (1999) relates his own experiences in Kyoto:

> I noticed that the young monks had discovered ways to break the rules of the monastery.... When they put on a suit and a cap nobody would recognize them, and I saw them climb over the wall at night.
>
> "Whatever do you do when you are over the wall?" I asked Han-san, the youngest monk, who had become my friend.
>
> "As long as you don't tell anyone," Han-san said. "We go to the cinema, and sometimes to a pub to have a little *saké,* but it's difficult because at 3:30 in the morning we have to visit the master and we can't be smelling of alcohol. And sometimes we go to the whores."

Zen priests and monks, unlike those in other branches of Buddhism (e.g., Theravada), are not actually sworn to celibacy. Nevertheless, the above clandestine activities, even by non-enlightened individuals who cannot claim to have "transcended rules of good and evil," certainly constituted a breaking of the rules of the Asian community/society. They further again suffered no associated punishment from the monastery leaders—who themselves would surely have violated the same rules in their younger days.

The point here is obviously not that "rules are meant to be obeyed"—as Socrates would evidently have it, in docilely accepting the unfair death-sentence handed to him by the ancient tribunal (Askenasy, 1978), or in "just following the orders" of that authority.

Rather, the relevant point to take from all of these examples is simply that the claim that spiritual aspirants followed the rules in the agrarian East or otherwise in no way matches the documented information. That, in turn, is wholly relevant to the "guru game," simply because the same belief is regularly used to support the false idea that guru-disciple relationships worked in those contexts, even if not functioning properly in our own society and culture.

Nor was it necessary to go out seeking in order to find the enjoyments listed by van de Wetering, above:

> Girls threw rocks into the *sodo's* courtyard with invitations attached with red ribbons.... I once got a rock on my head (van de Wetering, 2001).

Wet night, a rock, ouch!
Her love trails in red ribbons
Falling from the sky

But far, far away from such "enlightenment" ... where noble, revered masters and their humble disciples chop wood, draw water, and have illicit sex ... the quiet, spontaneous grace of a Zen archer, his performance broadcast on Dutch television—

> a Japanese archery-adept in robes, bowing, kneeling, dancing, praying before he pulled his bow's string ... and had his arrow miss the target completely (van de Wetering, 2001).

The young girls throwing rocks over Kyoto monastery walls, however—their sweet offers of love attached by soft red silk ribbons—hit the bull's eye every time.

CHAPTER VII

SEX, BLISS, AND ROCK 'N' ROLL

(SWAMI SATCHIDANANDA)

SWAMI SATCHIDANANDA WAS THE FOUNDER of the Yogaville ashram in Buckingham County, Virginia—begun in 1979—and its satellite Integral Yoga institutes in New York, San Francisco and elsewhere.

He was born in southern India in 1914 and married young but, after his wife's death, left his children and embarked at age twenty-eight on a full-time spiritual quest.

In 1949 he was initiated as a swami by his own spiritual master, the renowned Swami Sivananda, having searched the mountains and forests of India to find that sage in Rishikesh. His monastic name, Satchidananda, means "Existence-Knowledge-Bliss."

He came to New York in 1966 as a guest of the psychedelic artist Peter Max.

Word soon spread that Satchidananda had cured the kidney ailment of a disciple by blessing a glass of water.

He spoke at Woodstock in 1969, having been flown in via helicopter to bless the historic music festival:

> I am very happy to see that we are all gathered to create some "making" sounds, to find that peace and joy through the celestial music. I am honored for having been given the opportunity of opening this great, great music festival (Satchidananda, in [Wiener, 1972]).

Even prior to Woodstock, Satchidananda had sold out Carnegie Hall, being viewed as one of the "class acts" in the spiritual marketplace.

His views on nutrition were solicited by the Pillsbury Corporation.

By the beginning of the 1970s, thousands of Integral Yoga devotees studied at fifteen centers around the United States. By the late '70s, Satchidananda's (1977) followers numbered in the hundreds of thousands. Included in that group have been the health and diet expert Dr. Dean Ornish, model Lauren Hutton, Jeff "The Fly" Goldblum, and Carol "You've Got a Friend" King, who donated Connecticut land to the yogi's organization.

Having acquired other, warmer property for Yogaville in Virginia, Sivananda Hall was built there, complete with a wooden throne for the guru, set atop a large stage at one end of the hall. Life for the poorer "subjects" within that 600-acre spiritual kingdom, however, was apparently less than regal:

> The ritual abnegations of the *sannyasin* [monks] included a pledge to "dedicate my entire life and renounce all the things which I call mine at the feet of Sri Gurudev [i.e., Satchidananda]. This includes my body, mind, emotions, intellect, and all the material goods in my possession." Though they weren't expected to pay for basics like food and lodging, they were relegated to rickety trailers sometimes infested with mice or lice (Katz, 1992).

In the midst of his followers' reported poverty, Satchidananda himself nevertheless acquired an antique Cadillac and a cherry red Rolls-Royce.

Further, and somewhat oddly given Satchidananda's Woodstock background, in the ashram itself

> dozens of onetime children of rock 'n' roll sat down to make lists of "offensive" songs and television shows to be banned within Yogaville's borders. Soon after, dating between ash-

> ram children was banned through the end of high school. Then all children attending the ashram school were asked to sign a document pledging that they would not date, have sexual contact, listen to restricted music, or watch restricted television shows.
>
> Satchidananda never came forth to comment formally on the new restrictions, but residents understood that the rules carried his implied imprimatur (Katz, 1992).

With those restrictions in place, an ashram member was soon reported for listening to a Bruce Springsteen album.

Increasingly oddly, given all that: Rivers Cuomo, the lead singer of the power-pop band Weezer, spent much of his first ten years in Yogaville.

* * *

> Some people take advantage of the language in the tantric scriptures, "I'm going to teach you tantric yoga," they say. "Come sleep with me." With a heavy heart I tell you that some so-called gurus do this, and to them I say, "If you want to have sex, be open about it. Say, 'I love you, child, I love you, my devotee'"....
>
> Yoga monks automatically become celibate when they have a thirst to know the Absolute God, and feel that in order to do so they must rise above the physical body and the senses (Satchidananda, in [Mandelkorn, 1978]).

> [T]he distinguishing mark of a Guru is, as Sri Swamiji [i.e., Satchidananda] says, "complete mastery over his or her body and mind, purity of heart, and total freedom from the bondage of the senses" (in Satchidananda, 1977).

The taking of the monastic vows in which the title of "Swami" is conferred again inherently includes a vow of celibacy. That serious promise, however, may not have stopped the "Woodstock Swami" from, as they say, "rocking out," via Springsteen's *The Rising* or otherwise:

> In 1991 numerous female followers stated that he had used his role as their spiritual mentor to exploit them sexually. After the allegations became public many devotees abandoned Satchidananda and hundreds of students left IYI schools, but the Swami never admitted to any wrongdoing.

As a result, the Integral Yoga organization diminished by more than 1/3. An organization called the Healing Through the Truth Network was formed and at least eight other women came forward with claims of sexual abuse (S. Cohen, 2002a).

[Susan Cohen claims that] Satchidananda took advantage of her when she was a student from 1969 [when she was eighteen] to 1977 (Associated Press, 1991).

Another follower, nineteen-year-old Sylvia Shapiro, accompanied the swami on a worldwide trip.

"In Manila, he turned [his twice-daily massages from me] into oral sex," Ms. Shapiro said (Associated Press, 1991).

Until December [of 1990], Joy Zuckerman was living at Yogaville, where she was known as Swami Krupaananda. She left after a friend confided in her that Satchidananda had made sexual advances toward her last summer, Ms. Zuckerman said (McGehee, 1991).

* * *

A Guru is the one who has steady wisdom ... one who has realized the Self. Having that realization, you become so steady; you are never nervous. You will always be tranquil, nothing can shake you (Satchidananda, 1977).

Satchidananda's own driver, however, recognized characteristics other than such holy ones, in the swami:

After hours of sitting in traffic jams observing his spiritual master in the rearview mirror, Harry had decided that Sri Swami Satchidananda was not only far from serene, he was a bilious and unforgivingly cranky old man. Not once had Harry felt his spiritual bond with Satchidananda enhanced by all the carping, however edifyingly paternal it was meant to be (Katz, 1992).

As they say, "No man is great in the eyes of his own valet."

In describing how a "steady" man would see the world, Satchidananda (1977) further quoted Krishna from the Bhagavad Gita:

> Men of Self-knowledge look with equal vision on a *brahmana* [i.e., a spiritual person] imbued with learning and humility, a cow, an elephant, a dog and an outcaste.

There is, however, always the contrast between theory and practice:

> Lorraine was standing beside one of [Satchidananda's] Cadillacs ... when the beautiful model [Lauren Hutton] and the guru came out and climbed inside. Satchidananda did not acknowledge Lorraine's presence except to glare at her and bark in his irritated father voice, "Don't slam the door" (Katz, 1992).

* * *

Satchidananda passed away in August of 2002. Before he died, he had this to say regarding the allegations of sexual misconduct made against him:

> "They know it is all false," [Satchidananda] had said about eight years ago [i.e., in 1991]. "I don't know why they are saying these things. My life is an open book. There is nothing for me to hide" (S. Chopra, 1999).

Yogaville, meanwhile, is still very much alive, albeit amid a more recently alleged "mind control" scandal involving a university-age woman, Catherine Cheng (Extra, 1999).

CHAPTER VIII

THE SIXTH BEATLE

(MAHARISHI MAHESH YOGI)

> Physicist John S. Hagelin ... has predicted that Maharishi's influence on history "will be far greater than that of Einstein or Gandhi" (Gardner, 1996).

> You could not meet with Maharishi without recognizing instantly his integrity. You look in his eyes and there it is (Buckminster Fuller, in [Forem, 1973]).

> Maharishi's entire movement revolves around ... faith in his supposed omniscience (Scott, 1978).

BORN IN 1918, THE MAHARISHI MAHESH YOGI graduated with a physics degree from the University of Allahabad. Soon thereafter, he received the system of Transcendental Meditation® (TM®) from his "Guru Dev," Swami Brahmanand Saraswati, who occupied the "northern seat" of yoga in India, as one of four yogic "popes" in the country. He practiced yoga for thirteen years under Guru Dev, until the latter's death in 1953. The Maharishi ("Great Sage") then traveled to London in 1959 to set up what was to become a branch of the International Meditation Society there, with the mission of spreading the teachings of TM.

Transcendental Meditation itself is an instance of mantra yoga. The student mentally repeats a series of Sanskrit words for a minimum of twenty minutes every morning and evening. (Such mantras are reportedly selected on the basis of the student's age. And they don't come cheaply.)

> Maharishi was quick to discourage other disciplines. "All these systems have been misinterpreted for the last hundreds of years," he said. "Don't waste time with them. If you are interested in hatha yoga, wait until I have time to reinterpret it. There is no match for Transcendental Meditation either in principles or in practice *in any field of knowledge"* (Ebon, 1968; italics added).

The Maharishi held high hopes, not merely for the spread of TM, but for its effects on the world in general:

> He told the New York audience, as he had told innumerable others before in several around-the-world tours, that adoption of his teachings by 10% or even 1% of the world's population would "be enough to neutralize the power of war for thousands of years" (Ebon, 1968).

> The [TM] movement taught that the enlightened man does not have to use critical thought, he lives in tune with the "unbounded universal consciousness." He makes no mistakes, his life is error free (Patrick L. Ryan, in [Langone, 1995]).

In the autumn of 1967, His Holiness gave a lecture in London, which was attended by the Beatles. Following that talk, the Fab Four—along with Mick Jagger and Marianne Faithfull—accompanied the yogi on a train up to Bangor, North Wales, at his invitation. Reaching the train platform in Bangor, they were mobbed by hundreds of screaming fans, whom the Maharishi charmingly assumed were there to see *him*.

> Like Ravi Shankar before him, [the Maharishi had] been unaware of the group's stature, but, armed with the relevant records, he underwent a crash-course in their music and began to illustrate his talks with quotes from their lyrics. Flat-

> tered though they were, the Beatles were unconvinced by his argument that, if they were sincere about meditation, they ought to tithe a percentage of their income into his Swiss bank account. Because they hadn't actually said no, the Maharishi assured American investors that the four would be co-starring in a TV documentary about him (Clayson, 1996).

> It was reported that Maharishi's fee for initiating the Beatles was one week's salary from each of them—a formidable sum (Klein and Klein, 1979).

In the middle of February, 1968, John, Paul, George and Ringo, with their respective wives and girlfriends, arrived at the Maharishi's Rishikesh meditation retreat in India. They were joined there by Mike Love of the Beach Boys and "Mellow Yellow" Donovan, as well as by the newly Sinatra-less Mia Farrow and her younger sister, Prudence. (The Doors and Bob Weir, guitarist for the Grateful Dead, were also enthusiastic about TM, but did not participate in the Rishikesh trip. More contemporary followers of the Maharishi have included actress Heather Graham and the Nobel Prize-winning physicist Brian Josephson. Plus Deepak Chopra [see TranceNet, 2004], whose best-selling book *Quantum Healing* was dedicated to the Maharishi. Also, at one time, Clint Eastwood and quarterback Joe Namath.)

As Ringo himself put it:

> The four of us have had the most hectic lives. We've got almost everything money can buy, but of course that just means nothing after a time. But we've found something now that really fills the gap, and that is the Lord (in Giuliano, 1986).

The Beatles' 1968 stay in Rishikesh was originally scheduled to last for three months.

Predictably, Ringo and his wife Maureen were the first to leave, after ten days, citing the "holiday camp" atmosphere, the spiciness of the food, the excessive insects and the stifling midday temperatures. Well, it was *India,* after all—what exactly did they expect, if not deathly spicy cuisine, mosquitos, bedbugs and interminable heat? If they wanted bland food and cool weather, they should have stayed in Liverpool, awash in bangers and mash to "fill the gap."

Paul McCartney and Jane Asher bailed out a month later, pleading homesickness.

John and Cynthia and George and Patti, however, persevered, with John and George writing many songs which would later appear on the *White Album*. Indeed, most of the thirty-plus songs on that disc were composed in the Maharishi's ashram. "Dear Prudence," for one, was written for Mia Farrow's sister, who was so intent on spiritual advancement that it was delegated to John and George to get her to "come out to play" after her three weeks of meditative seclusion in her chalet.

The overall calm there, however, was soon shattered by various suspicions:

> [A]ccurately or not, they became convinced that the Maharishi had distinctly worldly designs on one of their illustrious fellow students, actress Mia Farrow. They confronted him, in an oblique way, with this accusation, and when he was unable to answer it, or even figure out precisely what it was, they headed back to London (Giuliano, 1986).

By Farrow's own (1997) recounting, that may have been just a simple misunderstanding based on the Maharishi's unsolicited hugging of her after a private meditation session in his cave/cellar. Less explicable, though, are reports of the same sage's offering of chicken to at least one female student within his otherwise-vegetarian ashram, in alleged attempts to curry her favor (Clayson, 1996).

> The Beatles' disillusionment with the Maharishi during their stay with him in India in 1968 involved allegations that Maharishi had sex with a visiting American student (Anthony, et al., 1987).

"Sexy Sadie" was later composed in honor of those believed foibles on the part of His Holiness.

In any case, within a week Mia Farrow, too, had left the ashram on a tiger hunt, never to return (to Rishikesh).

> [T]he Maharishi burst into the Beatles' lives, offering salvation with a price tag of only fifteen [*sic*] minutes of devotion a day. "It seemed too good to be true," Paul McCartney later quipped. "I guess it was" (Giuliano, 1989).

> The Beatles ... parted with Maharishi in 1969 with the public comment that he was "addicted to cash" (Klein and Klein, 1979).

John and Yoko, interestingly, later came to believe that they were the reincarnations of Robert and Elizabeth Barrett Browning, respectively. (One of Yoko's songs on their joint album *Milk and Honey* is titled, "Let Me Count the Ways.")

No word on who Ringo might have been.

George soon became heavily involved with the Hare Krishnas —as one might have gathered from the chorus to his "My Sweet Lord" single—although ultimately leaving them completely out of his will. Indeed, at one point members of Hare Krishna were signed to Apple Records as the "Radha Krishna Temple." They released at least one chanted single on that label, which made it into the "Top 20" in September of 1969. The Krishnas' Bhaktivedanta Manor headquarters in London, too, was actually a gift from Harrison—which he at one point threatened to transfer to Yogananda's Self-Realization Fellowship instead, when the Krishnas were not maintaining the grounds to his satisfaction (Giuliano, 1989).

The devotional/mantra yoga-based Hare Krishna movement itself is rooted in the extremely patriarchal Vedic culture. It was brought to the United States in the mid-1960s by the now-late Bhaktivedanta Swami Prabhupada—who soon starred in a San Francisco rock concert featuring the Grateful Dead, Jefferson Airplane and Janis Joplin. Prabhupada's own guru was claimed to be an avatar. (George, John and Yoko participated in an extended interview with Prabhupada in 1969, which was kept in print in booklet form by the Krishna organization for many years afterwards. Harrison also wrote the foreword for Prabhupada's book, *Krishna: The Supreme Personality of Godhead.*)

Details along the following lines as to the alleged horrendous goings-on within the Hare Krishna community, including widespread claims of child sexual abuse, drug dealing and weapons stockpiling, have long existed:

> The founder of the institution, the late Prabhupada, was allegedly told about the physical and sexual abuse of minors in 1972, a time when he totally controlled the institution. The victims allege he and others conspired to suppress the alleged crimes, fearful that the public exposure would threaten the viability of the movement (S. Das, 2003).

> [After Prabhupada's death] the Hare Krishna movement degenerated into a number of competing [so-called] cults that have known murder, the abuse of women and children, drug dealing, and swindles that would impress a Mafia don (Hubner and Gruson, 1990).

> The movement's [post-Prabhupada] leadership was first forced to confront the victims of abuse at a meeting in May 1996, when a panel of ten former Krishna pupils testified that they had been regularly beaten and caned at school, denied medical care and sexually molested and raped homosexually at knife point (Goodstein, 1998).

Or, as Hubner and Gruson (1990) alleged:

> [B]oys were ordered to come to the front of the class and sit on [their teacher] Sri Galima's lap. Sri Galima then anally raped them, right in front of the class. Other boys were ordered to stay after class. Sri Galima tied their hands to their desks with duct tape and then assaulted them in the same way.
>
> At night, Fredrick DeFrancisco, Sri Galima's assistant, crept into the boys' sleeping bags and performed oral sex on them.

George Harrison was of course stabbed in his London home at the end of 1999 by a man who believed that the Beatles were "witches." Interestingly, one of the reasons given by his attacker for continuing that attempt at murder was that Harrison kept chanting the protective mantra, "Hare Krishna, Hare Krishna"—interpreted by his disturbed assailant as a curse from Satan.

In any case, returning to Maharishi Mahesh Yogi's mission: The number of people practicing TM grew nearly exponentially from 1967 through 1974. By 1975 there were more than half a million people in America who had learned the technique, over a million worldwide, and the Maharishi had been featured on the cover of *Time* magazine. Were that exponential growth to have continued, the entire United States would have been doing TM by 1979. As it stands, with the law of diminishing returns and otherwise, there are currently four million practitioners of Transcendental Meditation worldwide.

In 1973, Maharishi International University (MIU) was established in Santa Barbara, California, moving a year later to its permanent location in Fairfield, Iowa. Interestingly, when the Maharishi first touched down in the latter location in his pink airplane, perhaps influenced by his contact with the Beatles ("How do you find American taste?/We don't know, we haven't bitten any yet," etc.), he quaintly announced: "We are in Fairfield, and what we find is a fair field."

Approximately one thousand students currently practice TM and study Vedic theory in that "fair field," particularly as the latter theory relates to accepted academic disciplines, including the hard sciences. MIU has since been re-christened as the Maharishi University of Management (MUM). Presently, one-quarter of the town's 10,000 residents are meditators.

* * *

In 1976, the Maharishi discovered the principles which were to lead to the TM Sidhi [*sic*] Program—based on the *siddhis* or powers outlined in Patanjali's *Yoga Sutras.* Those include the technique of Yogic Flying, or levitation ... or "hopping down the yogi trail":

> During the first stage of Yogic Flying, the body—motivated only by the effortless mental impulse of the Sidhi technique —rises up in the air in a series of blissful hops (Maharishi, 1995).

> "It's a form of levitation, you're actually lifted one or two feet by the exhilaration" that some describe as "bubbling bliss," explained Transcendental Meditation spokesman Joseph Boxerman (Associated Press, 2003).

> [*Taxi's* Andy Kaufman had a] consuming devotion to Transcendental Meditation ... he believed it had taught him to levitate (Blanco, 2000).

> [T]he guru himself announced in 1978 on TV ("The Merv Griffin Show") that he had enrolled some forty thousand students in this [Sidhi] course! Griffin then asked the obvious question: How many had learned to levitate? Declared the Great Guru: "Thousands!" (Randi, 1982).

Repeated attempts by the skeptical Mr. Randi to secure documented and believable evidence of that levitation were unsuccessful. He did, however, report (1982) receiving the following admission, from one Mr. Orme-Johnson, director of TM's International Center for Scientific Research:

> "We do not claim," he said, "that anyone is hovering in the air."

Nevertheless, hovering or not, the possible effects of one's missed practice on the world were apparently not to be taken lightly:

> At MIU and throughout the [TM] movement, guilt was used to manipulate students into never missing a flying session. When the Iranians seized the American Embassy, a MIU student friend who had missed a flying session was called into the dean's office and blamed for the hostage-taking in Iran (Patrick L. Ryan, in [Langone, 1995]).

All of that notwithstanding, by 1994 the technique of "Yogic Flying" had been taught to more than 100,000 people worldwide.

> The Maharishi has also claimed that advanced practitioners can develop powers of invisibility, mind-reading, perfect health and immortality (Epstein, 1995).

His Holiness further asserted a "Maharishi Effect," whereby relatively small numbers of meditators are claimed to be able to positively and measurably influence world events. That phenomenon has even been alleged to measurably lower crime rates in regions such as Washington, DC, and Kosovo (in August of 1999), via the "accumulated good energy" of the practitioners.

> As a press release on the website states, "When the group reached about 350 Yogic Flyers, the [Kosovo] destruction ended" (Kraus, 2000).
>
> In the early '90s, four thousand of the Maharishi's followers spent eight weeks in Washington holding large-scale group meditations. They claimed they helped reduce crime during that time. But the District's police department was unconvinced (Perez-Rivas, 2000).

In a more detailed analysis of relevant data, Randi (1982) has presented many additional, quantitative reasons to deeply question the reality of the so-called Maharishi Effect.

Such critical analyses aside, however, there seems to be little doubt within the ranks as to the beneficial effects of TM on the course of world history:

> [A]ll the social good—the move away from potential worldwide disaster toward global enlightenment—that has developed in the last few years I naturally consider to be the result of more people practicing Transcendental Meditation. After all, Maharishi did say that this would happen way back then [i.e., in the late 1950s], and it has (Olson, 1979).

More recently, "the Maharishi said he intends to bring about world peace by establishing huge Transcendental Meditation centers with thousands of full-time practitioners all over the world" (Falsani, 2002).

> Maharishi explains that every government, just by creating and maintaining a group of Yogic Flyers, will actualize the ideal of Administration [of the Natural Law "Constitution of the Universe"], the supreme quality of Administration of government in every generation (in Maharishi, 1995).

"Natural Law" is "the orderly principles—the laws of nature—that govern the functioning of nature everywhere, from atoms to ecosystems to galaxies" (Maharishi, in [Kraus, 2000]).

Governmental "administration," further,

> is a matter of expert intelligence. It shouldn't be exposed to voters on the street [i.e., to democracy] (Maharishi, in [Wettig, 2002]).

> Soon every government will maintain its own group of Yogic Flyers as the essential requirement of national administration, and every nation will enjoy the support of Natural Law. All troubles on Earth will fade into distant memories, and life will be lived in perfection and fulfillment by every citizen of every nation, now and for countless generations to come (Maharishi, 1995).

Such anticipated "fading of all troubles into distant memory" will undoubtedly have been aided by the formation, in 1992, of the politically "green" Natural Law Party, on the campus of MIU/MUM. The party has since fielded U.S. presidential candidates, and legislative hopefuls in California. The late magician and disciple Doug Henning, a long-time sincere TM practitioner and attempted "Yogic Flyer," actually ran for office under the NLP banner in both Britain and Toronto.

In keeping with the hoped-for freedom from our secular troubles, in the wake of September 11, 2001,

> the Maharishi announced that if some government gave him a billion dollars, he would end terrorism and create peace by hiring 40,000 Yogic Fliers to start hopping full time. No government took him up on the offer, which clearly irks him (Carlson, 2002).

And yet, the freedom from war and other troubles anticipated by the Great Sage appears to have its cost:

> I have heard Maharishi say on occasion that in the society he envisions, if someone is not smiling or happy he would be picked up by a meditation paddy wagon and taken to a checking facility for the proper TM treatment and then released (Scott, 1978).

* * *

One of the primary selling points of TM has always been its purported "scientific" nature, and the studies which have been done claiming to corroborate its beneficial effects. However:

> One three-year study done by the National Research Council on improving human performance concluded that "TM is ineffectual in improving human performance" and that pro-TM researchers were "deeply flawed in their methodology" (Ross, 2003a).

Consult Holmes (1988) for additional information regarding the reported effects, or lack of same, of TM and other forms of meditation.

* * *

With or without the young Ms. Farrow's bodacious presence around the Maharishi's ashrams, controversy continues to haunt the $3.5 billion worldwide enterprise of the yogic "Sixth Beatle." (The late ex-guitarist Stuart Sutcliffe was known as the "fifth.")

> His compound in India was the focus of allegations [in *The Illustrated Weekly of India,* July 17, 1988] regarding "child molestation, death from abuse and neglect" (Ross, 2003a).

> The [previous media] reports charged that at least five boys had died under mysterious circumstances and that about 8000 of the 10,000 children admitted to the vidya peeth in the past five years had run away from the ashram, allegedly because of the "torture" they had been subjected to inside....
>
> To make matters more difficult for the ashram administration, [local MLA Mahendra Singh] Bhati and an ayurvedic physician, Dr. Govind Sharma, formerly employed at the ashram, charged that some of the boys were also subjected to sexual abuse by the teachers (Dutt, 1988).

The ashram itself has denied all of those allegations, in the same article.

And how have other, past problems within the sphere of influence of the Late Great Sage been handled? It depends on whom you ask; Skolnick (1991), for one, reported:

> "I was taught to lie and to get around the petty rules of the 'unenlightened' in order to get favorable reports into the media," says [one former, high-ranking follower]. "We were taught how to exploit the reporters' gullibility and fascination with the exotic, especially what comes from the East. We thought we weren't doing anything wrong, because we were told it was often necessary to deceive the unenlightened to advance our guru's plan to save the world."

CHAPTER IX

BEEN HERE, DONE THAT, WHAT NOW?

(RAM DASS, ETC.)

> It is useful here to remember that your guru, even though you may not have met him in his manifest [i.e., physical] form ... KNOWS EVERYTHING ABOUT YOU ... EVERYTHING (Dass, 1971).

RAM DASS, AUTHOR of *Be Here Now*—one of the seminal books stirring widespread interest in Eastern philosophy and gurus in the West—is one of the good-at-heart guys through all this. He has, indeed, endeared himself to many by his sincerity. His ability to admit when he is wrong has also come in handy, in terms of his experiences with the contemporary female spiritual leader Ma Jaya Sati Bhagavati.

Born Richard Alpert in 1931, Dass graduated from Stanford University with a Ph.D. in Psychology. He went on to participate, with Timothy Leary, in a research program into altered states of consciousness at Harvard, utilizing large amounts of LSD under relatively uncontrolled circumstances. Those same activities got him fired from that faculty in 1963.

Four years later, Alpert journeyed to India, meeting two relevant people there: Bhagavan Das, and the man who soon became his guru—Neem Karoli Baba or "Maharajji" ("Great King").

Bhagavan Das had grown up in Laguna Beach, California, coming to India on his own in 1964 at age eighteen, and later becoming one of Ram Dass' teachers. As Ram himself described their first encounter:

> I met this guy and there was no doubt in my mind [that he "knew"]. It was just like meeting a rock. It was just solid, all the way through. Everywhere I pressed, there he was! (Dass, 1971).

Of course, Dass also considered the Grateful Dead's Jerry Garcia to be a "bodhisattva" (Meier, 1992), so "consider the source" in that regard. And indeed, as if to warn us of the gulf which more often than not exists between the real state of any guru or teacher, compared with the pedestal upon which he has been put by his followers, Das himself, years later (1997), gave his own honest evaluation of his earlier spiritual state:

> Ram Dass would describe me [in *Be Here Now*] as if I were some kind of enlightened, mythical being. But I was just a lost child, trying to find my way home to Mother....
>
> Unfortunately, because of my work with Ram Dass and because I was Maharajji's *sadhu* [i.e., ascetic], many of the [East] Indians were starting to overestimate my powers.

At other times, the boons of such "powers" included Das' waking up to a seventeen-year-old blond girl (Swedish) on one side of his Nepalese cowshed bed, and a silent, young Frenchwoman with long, black hair on the other side.

In any case, Bhagavan Das soon left that sylvan paradise behind to drop acid with Alpert in Kathmandu, and then reluctantly road-tripped with him back to India. He soon introduced that new uptight, bisexual (and "too interested in him") friend to Karoli Baba—partly in the hope of getting rid of him (Das, 1997). To Karoli, Das gave Alpert's friend's Land Rover vehicle, while Alpert himself claims to have once fed the guru twelve hundred micrograms of LSD—many times the "safe" dosage—with no apparent effect.

> Some said they'd seen [Neem Karoli Baba's] body grow really huge, and others claimed they'd seen him shrink down very small. And then there were those who swore they'd seen him [as an incarnation of the monkey god Hanuman] with a tail (Das, 1997).

> [Neem Karoli Baba] is God; he knows everything (in Mukerjee, 1996).

Of course, such high reviews of Maharajji naturally came from very hero-worshiping angles. By contrast, Andrew Cohen's former guru, H. W. L. Poonja, offered a perspective on the same sagely individual which is either more balanced, or more unbalanced, as may be left for the reader to judge:

> When I had asked [Poonja] what his opinion was of the now famous deceased guru Neem Karoli Baba, he went on to describe in detail about how he had met him and that he knew that he was completely insane and "mad," but that many people mistook his insanity for Enlightenment.... Several years later [following Cohen's and Poonja's bitter separation] when devotees of Neem Karoli would go to [Poonja] he would praise him as the highest (Cohen, 1992).

The following story, from a female disciple of Baba, does nothing to settle the question as to insanity versus enlightenment:

> The first time he took me in the room alone I sat up on the tucket [a low wooden bed] with him, and he was like a seventeen-year-old jock who was a little fast! I felt as if I were fifteen and innocent. He started making out with me, and it was so cute, so pure. I was swept into it for a few moments—then grew alarmed: "Wait! This is my guru. One doesn't do this with one's guru!" So I pulled away from him. Then Maharajji tilted his head sideways and wrinkled up his eyebrows in a tender, endearing, quizzical look. He didn't say anything, but his whole being was saying to me, "Don't you like me?"
>
> But as soon as I walked out of that particular *darshan* [the blessing which is said to flow from even the mere sight of a saint], I started getting so sick that by the end of the day

I felt I had vomited and shit out everything that was ever inside me. I had to be carried out of the ashram. On the way, we stopped by Maharajji's room so I could *pranam* [i.e., offer a reverential greeting] to him. I kneeled by the tucket and put my head down by his feet—and he kicked me in the head, saying, "Get her out of here!"....

That was the first time, and I was to be there for two years. During my last month there, I was alone with him every day in the room.... Sometimes he would just touch me on the breasts and between my legs, saying, "This is mine, this is mine, this is mine. All is mine. You are mine." You can interpret it as you want, but near the end in these *darshans,* it was as though he were my child. Sometimes I felt as though I were suckling a tiny baby (in Dass, 1979).

Of course, devoted disciples of the homoerotic pedophile Ramakrishna viewed his "divine" motherly/suckling tendencies just as positively.

At any rate, after a mere few months at the feet of Neem Karoli Baba, Ram Dass returned to the U.S. at Karoli's behest, to teach.

Hilda [Charlton] referred to [Ram Dass] as the "doorway of enlightenment for America," incarnated for the age, having once been one of the Seven Sages on the order of Vishwamitra: a full master (Brooke, 1999).

Beginning in 1974, at the height of his fame, Ram spent a good amount of time with a female spiritual leader in New York City: Joya Santana (now Ma Jaya Sati Bhagavati), a claimed stigmatist and fellow follower of Karoli Baba. As Dass himself tells the story:

Joya kept reiterating that she had come to Earth only to be an instrument for my preparation as a world spiritual leader and that ultimately she would sit at my feet....

Joya further professed to be the Divine Mother herself (Dass and Levine, 1977).

That Mother image evidently did not, however, couple sufficiently with Dass' psychological training in Oedipal complexes and the like, to prevent the predictable from allegedly occurring between Joya and him:

> He even found a convoluted way to justify a sexual relationship with Joya [which she insists did not occur], despite the fact that she required all of her students to take a strict vow of celibacy and publicly took one herself. Joya professed no physical desires, and Ram Dass willingly accepted her explanation that by having sex together, she was actually teaching *him* to become just as unattached to physical desire as she claimed she was (Schwartz, 1996).

That reported "thrill of learning," unfortunately, was not to last:

> There were just too many "signals," like the moment Joya and I were hanging out and the telephone rang. She picked up the receiver and in a pained whisper said, "I can't talk now, I'm too stiff" [i.e., in *samadhi*], and let the receiver drop. Then without hesitation she continued our conversation as if nothing had happened. I realized how many times I had been at the other end of the phone....
>
> I began to see the similarity between what I was experiencing and the stories I had heard about other movements, such as Reverend Moon's group, the so-called Jesus Freaks, and the Krishna-consciousness scene. Each seemed a total reality that made involvement a commitment which disallowed change....
>
> It seemed that [Joya's] incredible energies came not solely from spiritual sources but were [allegedly] enhanced by energizing pills. Her closest confidants now confessed many times they were ordered to call me to report terrible cries [*sic*] they knew to be untrue. They complied because Joya had convinced them that it was for my own good.
>
> Such stories of deception came thick and fast. I had been had (Dass and Levine, 1977).

In happier days, the married Bhagavan Das too had, for a time, been part of the same energetic "scene" with Joya:

> We were having a huge meeting and Joya said, "Bhagavan Das, stand up!" I stood up and she said, "Shivaya stand up! Shivaya, take Bhagavan Das to a whorehouse right now!" The next thing I knew I was in a whorehouse in Manhattan on Christmas Day (Das, 1997).

"It's a Wonderful Life."

* * *

So where are they now?

Well, Neem Karoli Baba passed away in the autumn of 1973.

Ram Dass himself sadly suffered a serious stroke in 1997, providing him with the personal background to complete a touching and (thankfully) relatively non-mystical book on aging—*Still Here.*

The sixty-something Joya, in no danger of "sitting at Ram Dass' feet" at any point in the near future, continues her teaching activities at her own Kashi Ashram in Florida. That environment itself, along with its "Ma," has been uncomplimentarily profiled numerous times in various local, regional and national newspapers and magazines since the mid-'70s, as documented at www.kashi ashram.com. Also see Tobias and Lalich's (1994) *Captive Hearts, Captive Minds.*

And what of the "mythical being," Bhagavan Das, in America?

> I ... found myself onstage before thousands of people, I named babies and blessed people, and people fell at my feet. I felt like a king with my patrons and movie stars, but I was still a kid, a guru at twenty-five, sitting on a tiger skin in a Manhattan town house....
>
> After three years of "spiritual life" that was really a party [drugs, groupies, etc.], I got sick of it and wanted to be home with my children. I rejoined the world and [ironically, given the Land Rover incident] sold used cars in Santa Cruz, I became a businessman, and I gradually lost my sense of [the] divine completely (in Kornfield, 2000).

At one point during that Faustian descent into the business world, after having experienced a profoundly moving vision of the crucified Jesus, Das actually became a born-again Christian, thereby returning to his family's Episcopalian roots.

> I was now officially in Bible college, and I was going to be a pastor....
>
> I got rid of everything but my Bible, which I worshiped. I'd go to bed with my Bible, I'd sleep with it, and I'd hug it. And God woke me up at all different times of the night....

> I would go into Denny's restaurant with my Bible, constantly looking for souls to save. I did nothing but read the Bible and pray (Das, 1997).

Thence followed Bhagavan's "speaking in tongues" with his local, polyester-wearing congregation. Also followed an affair with a blond, teenage choir girl "in tight blue jeans," which got Das—in his forties at the time—branded and counseled as a "fornicator" by the church.

None of that latter disrepute, however, could shake the ex-yogi's inner peace:

> I felt completely saved and totally free. The freedom I had felt in that tantric sexual experience with the choir girl was like being with Mary and Jesus (Das, 1997).

Praise! "Gimme that ol' time religion," "ménage a Trinity," etc.

Further, by Das' own (1997) admission: Alcoholism, AA, a nearly six-figure income selling insurance, another "wild 'n' nekkid" Scandinavian teenager, and back into smoking pot and doing magic mushrooms. Finally turned on, tuned in and dropped out of the business world, rediscovered himself as "Bhagavan Das" the mystic, hooked up with another eighteen-year-old girl whom he took as both a lover and disciple, etc.

All of which, one must admit, is still markedly less eye-popping—by California standards, at least—than was Das' earlier cooking of (energy-transferring) placenta soup for his wife (which she, and he, ate) after the births of two of their children, during his yogic days.

"Been here, done that ... what now?"

Indeed, "What now?"

CHAPTER X

SCORPION-MAN

(SATYA SAI BABA)

The words of an aristocratic Indian girl I knew in Delhi rang in my ears, "You foreigners will accept anyone as a guru—people like Maharishi are export items as common as tea, but we Indians will have nothing to do with them. [The Maharishi, however, is also a non-*brahmin* (Mangalwadi, 1992), perhaps accounting for a large part of the indigenous reluctance to accept him and his teachings.] There is only one I have heard of who the Indians trust, he is Sai Baba" (Brooke, 1999).

Swami Amritananda, companion of Bhagavan Ramana Maharshi [1879 – 1950], was convinced that Sri Satya Sai Baba knew yogic science better than anyone else in his experience (Kasturi, 1971).

Although Sai Baba only attended school to the age of thirteen, he has complete mastery of the scriptures, of all the sciences, arts, languages—of all fields of study. As a matter of fact, he knows everything—including the past, present and future of all of our lives (Warner, 1990).

> [Sai Baba] says he is an avatar, or the divine prophet of God for our time (Giuliano, 1989).

> The Avatar is one only, and this one body is taken by the Avatar (Sai Baba, in [Hislop, 1978]).

> By 1963 Baba had begun to claim that he was the incarnation of Shiva and Shakti.... Since the Westerners have begun to follow him, he has also declared that he is Jesus Christ who has come again (Mangalwadi, 1992).

> [W]hen it became obvious that I was not going to leave this issue [of alleged sexual abuses on the part of Sai Baba] alone, a couple of [national coordinators] telephoned me to say that yes I was correct and they had known of this for years. "But he is God, and God can do anything he likes" (Bailey and Bailey, 2003).

FOR THE PAST HALF CENTURY, Satya Sai Baba has been India's "most famous and most powerful holy man" (Brown, 2000), renowned for his production of *vibhuti* or "sacred ash," and for numerous other claimed materializations of objects "out of thin air."

Sai Baba was born, allegedly of immaculate conception, in southern India in 1926.

At the tender age of thirteen, he was stung by a scorpion. Following that, he announced that he was the new incarnation of Shirdi Sai Baba, a saint who had died eight years before Satya was born.

Some accounts have the previous inhabitant of his body "dying" from that sting, and Sai Baba's spirit taking it over at that vacated point, as opposed to his having been in the body from its conception or birth. (Adi Da, whom we shall meet later, claims to have been guided by the same spirit during his *sadhana.)*

In any case, from those humble, Spider-Man-like beginnings, Sai Baba has gone on to attract an estimated ten to fifty million followers worldwide, with an organizational worth of around $6 billion. Included among those disciples is Isaac Tigrett, co-founder of the Hard Rock Cafe; the "Love All – Serve All" motto of that chain is a direct quote from Baba. Also, jazz trumpeter Maynard Ferguson—who has reportedly pleaded with Sai Baba to heal his progressive hearing failure, to no avail—and Sarah Ferguson, the former wife of Prince Andrew.

> It is believed that the guru once granted [George] Harrison a rare personal audience at his Anantapur ashram in India sometime in the mid-'70s. John and Yoko also met with Sai Baba around that time. It was from this experience that Lennon later made the quizzical comment, "Guru is the pop star of India. Pop stars are the gurus of the West" (Giuliano, 1989).

Interestingly, the late, great jazzman John Coltrane's second wife, Alice (now Swami Turiyasangitananda), on the basis of her own visions, claims that "Sai Baba is described by the Lord as 'one of my sacred embodiments'" (Rawlinson, 1997). Coltrane himself had earlier been introduced to the teachings of Krishnamurti by his pianist, Bill Evans.

* * *

No "divine prophet of our time" would so descend, of course, without manifesting numerous "signs and wonders."

> Like Christ, [Sai Baba] is said to have created food to feed multitudes; to have "appeared" to disciples in times of crisis or need. There are countless accounts of healings, and at least two of his having raised people from the dead (Brown, 2000).

The first widespread indications that Sai Baba's manifestations might be less than miraculous, however, occurred in the context of a visit to his ashram by an East Indian prime minister, in which Sai Baba appeared to materialize a gold watch as a gift.

> [W]hen Indian state television workers played back film of the incident in slow motion, they saw that the miracle was a sleight-of-hand hoax. The clip was never broadcast in India but has been widely circulated on videotape there (Kennedy, 2001).

That, of course, would have come as no surprise to any of the skeptical magicians who have, in the past, questioned and consequently dismissed Sai Baba's "miraculous" production of sacred ash and other manifestations:

> Examination of films and videotapes of Sai Baba's actual performances show them to be simple sleight of hand, exactly the same as the sort used by the other Indian *jaduwallahs,* or "street conjurors." Sai Baba has never submitted to an examination of his abilities under controls, so his claims are totally unproven (Randi, 1995).

A formerly devoted, inner circle disciple of Sai Baba has independently confirmed all of that. That is, Faye Bailey claims to have personally seen "rings, watches and other trinkets being palmed, or pulled out from the side of chair cushions" and *"vibhuti* tablets held between [Sai Baba's] fingers before being crushed and 'manifest.'"

> [Sai Baba's] major and most advertised "miracle" is the production from his apparently empty hand of a substance known as *"vibhuti"* ("holy ash") which turns out on analysis to be powdered ashes of cow dung mixed with incense. Street conjurors in India *(jaduwallahs)* perform this trick by preparing small pellets of ashes and concealing them at the base of their fingers, then working their fists to powder the pellets and produce the flow of fine ash. Their trick is indistinguishable from Sai Baba's miracle (Randi, 2000).

> There are fantastic stories going round about Sai Baba's supposed powers, but in five years searching I have not found one to be genuine (Bailey and Bailey, 2003).

Beyerstein (1994) has given a further detailed, critical analysis of Sai Baba's paranormal claims.

* * *

The concerns surrounding Sai Baba are not restricted to questions about the authenticity of his "miracles." Indeed, as early as 1976, Tal Brooke (1999) had told the story of his own experiences during two years as a close disciple of Baba in the late '60s, before converting to Christianity:

> Baba's nudging pelvis stopped. Suddenly a hand unzipped my fly, then, like an adder returning home at dusk, the hand burrowed inside.

With less of a purple (but perhaps more of a tie-dyed) hue, a friend of Brooke's further related the following tale, claimed to have occurred around a year later:

> When all the others left and Baba got [Patrick] alone ... the next thing that happened was that in one smooth motion, Baba reached down and unzipped Patrick's fly, and pulled his tool out....
>
> [H]e worked up a bone all right, and the next thing that happened is really gonna blow your mind. Baba lifted his robe and inserted the thing. That's right. Maybe he's got a woman's organ and a man's organ down there. Yeah, a hermaphrodite. But he honestly inserted it. Patrick said it felt just like a woman.

More serious are the guru's alleged interests in young boys:

> Conny Larsson, a well-known Swedish film actor, says that not only did Sai Baba make homosexual advances towards him, but he was also told by young male disciples of advances the guru had made on them (Brown, 2000).

Larsson himself claims that the guru regularly practiced oral sex on him—and asked for it in return—over a five-year period. "By 1986, Mr. Larsson had talked to many young male devotees, most of them attractive blond Westerners, who told him they too had had sex with Sai Baba" (B. Harvey, 2000a). He says he now receives twenty to thirty emails a day from victims "crying out for help" (Brown, 2000).

> Hans de Kraker ... who first visited Sai Baba's ashram in 1992, said the guru would regularly rub oil on his genitals, claiming it was a religious cleansing, and eventually tried to force him to perform oral sex (P. Murphy, 2000).

Another sixteen-year-old boy whose parents were both Sai devotees told his story to them:

> Sai Baba, he said, had kissed him, fondled him and attempted to force him to perform oral sex, explaining that it was for "purification." On almost every occasion Sai Baba had given him gifts of watches, rings, trinkets and cash, in

> total around $10,000. He had told him to say nothing to his parents....
>
> In 1998 [i.e., at age eighteen], according to [the boy], Sai Baba attempted to rape him (Brown, 2000).

None of the above allegations, however, have unduly swayed the faith of those close to Sai Baba:

> [British Columbia Sai Baba president Nami] Thiyagaratnam ... says he's not surprised that people are trying to ruin the reputation of such a wondrous man. After all, he says, people also persecuted Jesus Christ and Buddha (Todd, 2001).
>
> Dr. Michael Goldstein, the influential U.S. president of the Sai Baba organization, this year dismissed all the accusations. He says they're unbelievable and that Sai Baba remains divinely pure, filled only with "selfless love." The answer for those who doubt, says Goldstein, is to show more faith (Todd, 2001).
>
> Or, as Baba himself put it (in Dass, 1971):
>
> The influence of the Guru is obstructed by mental activity, by reliance on one's own exertions and by every kind of self-consciousness and self-exertion.
>
> Sai Baba is reported to have said recently to his devotees: "Never try to understand me" (Harpur, 2001).

The head of at least one overseas arm of the Sai organization correspondingly refuses to warn families taking children to Baba's ashram in Puttaparthi, about the reports of pedophilia.

> Sai Baba, who hardly ever grants media interviews, alluded to the allegations himself at an address last year, saying, "Some devotees seem to be disturbed over these false statements. They are not true devotees at all" (Goldberg, 2001).
>
> Being "God," after all, means never having to say you're sorry.

CHAPTER XI

EVEN IF IT HAPPENED....

(SWAMI RAMA)

SWAMI RAMA WAS SUPPOSEDLY BORN in 1925, and allegedly grew up as an orphan in northern India. He was soon reportedly adopted there by "one of the greatest masters of the Himalayas," Bengali Baba.

At the age of twenty-four, the story goes that he was given the position of Shankaracharya of Karvirpitham—one of four "popes" in the Hindu religious hierarchy. A mere two years later, however, he apparently simply abandoned that position, leaving without notice to meditate in the mountains instead.

Rama also claimed to have later studied in Hamburg, Utrecht and at Oxford University. It turns out (Webster, 1990), however, that significant elements in the official biography of the swami may well have been merely "pulled out of thin air."

In any case, Rama definitely came to the United States in 1969, and was soon participating in biofeedback demonstrations under Elmer and Alyce Green, at the Menninger Foundation in Topeka, Kansas. There, he showed the ability to consciously control various aspects of his autonomic (involuntary) nervous system.

In 1971, the swami founded the Himalayan International Institute—"HI," publisher of *Yoga International* magazine—in Illinois, with the goal of translating ancient spiritual wisdom into contemporary terms. By 1977, that organization had moved to an ashram in the Pocono Mountains of northeastern Pennsylvania, capable of housing more than one hundred residents and guests, along with their Institute headquarters.

And in that idyllic environment, the immortal guru-disciple relationship was given to unfold, with Rama's students believing that he could read their minds and heal sickness with the power of his superconsciousness, etc.

That, though, is exactly par for the course: for the disciples to think any less of the guru would make them "disloyal," riddled with *mayic* doubt.

* * *

In December of 1990, *Yoga Journal* published an exposé detailing allegations of misbehavior, including sexual abuse, against Rama.

One of the women involved further described a public, nonsexual encounter with the sage. There, the swami allegedly put a dog collar and leash around a woman's neck, walking her around for the amusement of the other loyal followers present. He was also accused of kicking other women in the buttocks when they were weeding, already down on their hands and knees (Webster, 1990).

Pandit Rajmani Tigunait, at the time the resident spiritual director of the Honesdale ashram and a member of the Institute's teaching staff, reportedly responded (in Webster, 1990) to the allegations of sexual abuse in this way:

> Even if it happened, what's the big deal? People say that Mahatma Gandhi slept with women. God knows whether it was true or not, and even if it was true, this is a normal phenomenon....
>
> Even if I found out—how can I find out? Because I do not want to find out. There's no need for finding out, if I know it is completely wrong.

The reported reaction of Swami Rama's community to the women asserting improprieties on his part was further exactly as one would expect. That is, they were allegedly discounted as being "emotionally disturbed," or otherwise reportedly regarded as "liars" (Webster, 1990).

* * *

As Tigunait noted above, Mahatma Gandhi was indeed sleeping with teenage girls (including his cousin's granddaughter) toward the end of his life. As odd as it may sound, however, all reports are that the two parties *were* literally just sleeping beside each other, for him to test his resistance to sexual desire.

> In explaining his position, Gandhiji said that it was indeed true that he permitted women workers to use his bed, this being undertaken as a spiritual experiment at times. Even if there were no trace of passion in him of which he was conscious, it was not unlikely that a residue might be left over, and that would make trouble for the girls who took part in his experiment [cf. "In the presence of one perfected in non-violence, enmity (in any creature) does not arise"—Patanjali, *Yoga Sutras*] (Bose, 1974).

The possible psychological effects of that on the girls themselves, even without any breach of his *brahmacharya* celibacy vow, does not seem to have concerned the Mahatma.

Of course, Gandhi's very human displays of (non-righteous) temper alone would have been enough to demonstrate to him or anyone else that he was not yet perfected in *ahimsa*. Those eruptions were indeed reported by his one-time secretary, N. K. Bose, a distinguished anthropologist who resigned the former secretarial position in part because of his objections to the Mahatma's above "experiments." Gandhi's own admitted "detestation of sensual connection," too, is a type of psychological violence upon himself. For, when it comes to metaphysical questions regarding attachment, repulsion is no better than is attraction.

Both Chapter XVIII of Bose's (1974) *My Days with Gandhi* and Chapter 4 in Koestler's (1960) *The Lotus and the Robot* give reasonable analyses of the all-too-human psychological reasons behind Gandhi's emphasis on celibacy. Included in those is the Mahatma's abandoning of his father on the latter's deathbed to be with his young wife sexually, thus being absent from the old man's death, for which he never forgave himself.

Koestler also covers Gandhi's disappointing treatment of his children, in the same book. That handling included the Mahatma's denying of a professional education to his older sons, in the attempt to mold them in his image. The eldest was later disowned by the "Great Soul" for having gotten married against his father's prohibitions; and died an alcoholic wreck, after having been publicly attacked by Gandhi for his involvement in a business scandal.

Why then are the stories of the Mahatma's "experiments with teenage girls" not more widely known?

> The Gandhians were so thorough in effacing every trace of the scandal that Bose's book is unobtainable not only in India, but also at the British Museum (Koestler, 1960).

* * *

Swami Rama passed away in 1996, being survived by, it has been suggested, at least one child (Webster, 1990).

In the autumn of 1997, Pennsylvania jurors awarded $1.875 million in damages to a former female resident of the Himalayan Institute in Honesdale, PA. The woman in question claimed to have been sexually assaulted by Rama a full thirty times over a Yogic Summer of Love in the early '90s. At the time, she was a nineteen-year-old virgin, just out of high school. Yet, as reported by Phelps (1997), the Institute allegedly "did nothing to stop" that claimed abuse, even though having reportedly been informed not only of those alleged assaults but of similar complaints registered by other female disciples.

Pandit Tigunait, who accepted Rama as his guru when just a child in India, is now the "spiritual head of the Himalayan Institute," and the acknowledged "spiritual successor" to Swami Rama there.

"Even if it happened...."

CHAPTER XII

MO' CHIN-UPS

(SRI CHINMOY)

> Sri Chinmoy is a fully realized spiritual Master dedicated to inspiring and serving those seeking a deeper meaning in life (Chinmoy, 1985).

> Sect members believe that Chinmoy is an "avatar" (Eisenstadt, 1993).

A NATIVE OF BANGLADESH, Chinmoy Kumar Ghose arrived in the United States in 1964, having previously lived for two decades at the Sri Aurobindo Ashram in India. Three years later, he started his own Aum meditation center in Queens, New York.

Once described by the *Wall Street Journal* as "the stunt man of the spiritual world," Chinmoy has earned that appellation many times over, via numerous demonstrated "feats of strength."

> The Supreme doesn't want you to be satisfied with fifty meters. He wants you to run fifty-one meters, fifty-two meters, fifty-four meters.... Otherwise, if you always aim at the same goal, it becomes monotonous (Chinmoy, in [Jackson, 1996]).

> Weight-lifting is "the perfect analogy to the spiritual life," explains one devotee. "As the dead weight is lifted up, so also a person's lower, unilluminated being can be lifted to a level of increased peace, light, and delight" (Rae, 1991).

Chinmoy's publicized weight-lifting stunts (aided by a Nautilus-like machine which does most of the work) have included:

- Lifting one thousand sheep (four at a time) in Australia
- Raising a Piper Arrow aircraft while balanced on one leg
- Hoisting the prime minister of Iceland, two San Francisco 49ers, four Nobel laureates, comedian Eddie Murphy (speaking of "dead weight"), the Reverend Jesse Jackson, a Ford pickup, an elephant and a small schoolhouse (separately) into the air. Also, Nelson Mandela, Desmond Tutu, Muhammad Ali, Susan Sarandon, Jeff Goldblum, Yoko Ono, Sting and Richard Gere (separately)

Nor are the man's quantitative accomplishments limited to weight-lifting. Rather, if Chinmoy's followers are to be believed, the man has written at least 1200 books, 62,000 poems and 14,000 songs.

> In 1974 he wrote 360 poems in twenty-four hours, then the next year batted out 843 verses in a single day. In one hundred days from November 1974 to February 1975 he completed 10,000 "works of art"—pen-and-inks, abstract acrylics, watercolors (Jackson, 1996).

Indeed, by the "avatar's" own count, he has produced over four million drawings of birds, and a total of more than 150,000 paintings.

Chinmoy is in his seventies, so four million drawings would work out to over 150 per day, every day—or one every ten minutes, if he had done nothing during a sleepless life except "draw birds."

Impressive. Indeed, to do all that and still find time for meditation or working out would almost require more than twenty-four hours in a day.

Such record-setting "for God" seems to have rubbed off on at least one disciple of Chinmoy's, a Mr. Ashrita Furman, whose activities have included

> simultaneous jogging and juggling (six hours, seven minutes: three balls); long-distance somersaulting (12.3 miles) along the same route Paul Revere took through Boston; and underwater pogo-sticking (three hours, forty minutes) in the Amazon River (Areddy, 1989).

For the latter stunt, "a lookout was posted to keep watch for piranhas."

As to the spiritual advancement and years of meditation underlying his own evinced productivity and demonstrated strength, Chinmoy (1978) explains:

> After one has realized the Highest and become consciously one with the Absolute Supreme, one has no need to pray or meditate. But I have a number of disciples, so I meditate for them as I used to meditate for myself many years ago.

Chinmoy further leaves no doubt as to his own importance in effecting his disciples' evolution:

> The Guru has the power to nullify the law of karma for his disciple (Chinmoy, 1985).

> Without a guru, your progress will be very slow and uncertain....
>
> The best type of meditation comes when you enter into my consciousness by looking at a picture taken of me when I am in a high meditative consciousness (Chinmoy, 1978).

* * *

Chinmoy himself is a prolific musical entertainer. Indeed, if his press kit is to be believed, the man has performed close to three hundred concerts, for nearly half a million people in thirty countries over the past twenty years.

> This is noteworthy because Chinmoy and his supporters concede that he is not a gifted musician; he sometimes makes mistakes and starts over, and generally improvises the melodies on the spot (Galloway, 1991).

Concert venues have included the Royal Albert Hall of London, Carnegie Hall, Tokyo's Nippon Budokan—made famous in the West by Cheap Trick in the 1970s—and the Sydney Opera House.

According to Chinmoy's website, his own personal record for "most instruments in a single concert," playing music to soothe the savage chakras—purported subtle energy centers in the human body—is now up to 150.

> There is some music that is really destructive to our inner being. This music comes from the gross physical or the lower vital. Undivine music tries to awaken our lower vital consciousness and throw us into a world of excitement (Chinmoy, 1978).

Given that, it is interesting to note that Chinmoy's devotees have included Grammy-winning musician and "guitar god" Carlos Santana who, with his wife, devotedly followed Chinmoy for nine years, from 1972 to 1981. Also, Clarence "Born to Blow" Clemons (Bruce Springsteen's sax man), Roberta Flack and Sheena Easton.

"My guru takes the morning train...."

* * *

Chinmoy claims up to seven thousand disciples worldwide, formerly including the late Zen Master Rama, or Frederick Lenz. (Lenz's first book was dedicated to Chinmoy, prior to their split.) His reported teachings on the relation of sex to spirituality for those students are unequivocal:

> In order to have Self-realization, celibacy is absolutely necessary....
>
> God-realization and the sex life are like the combination of sugar and salt. If we try to put them together we cannot taste either....
>
> Those who are really advanced find that lower vital necessity does not enter into them. For them the life of pleasure is replaced by the life of real joy. And naturally, once realization takes place *temptation can never assail them* (in Ross, 2003d; italics added).

Such a position, however, stands in contrast to the numerous allegations of sexual misconduct made against the guru himself, raised via the Testimonials section on the www.chinmoycult.com website. It likewise does not square with the following allegations:

> Some of his followers left ... amid accusations that Chinmoy was making sexual advances toward the wives of his disciples (Occhiogrosso, 1996).

> Anne Carlton, a former member for twenty years, told *The* [*New York*] *Post* Ghose [i.e., Chinmoy] summoned her for sexual encounters over two extended periods—one in 1991 and another in 1996.
>
> Then, in 2000, Ghose [allegedly] called her at work and told her to have sex with another female disciple while he watched (Ginsberg, 2004).

Chinmoy, through his lawyer, has denied those sexual allegations.

Of course, with the man's penchant for quantity over quality—i.e., "mo' is better"—one almost expects to hear Paul Bunyan-esque tales/allegations of sexual conquest, too. For example, of having slept with 1200 women in a twenty-four hour period while continuously playing the kazoo and sketching thousands of images of assorted waterfowl, etc.

And what did Chinmoy himself have to say about behaviors such as he has been accused of?

> [S]o-called human weaknesses are one thing; but if the Master indulges in lower vital life, sex life, then that Master is very bad and you have to leave him (Chinmoy, 1985).

> The Guru has to be a perfect example of what he teaches. His outer being has to be the perfect example of what he is saying. Otherwise he is not a Guru.... The responsibility of a Guru is tremendous. If the Guru is not a perfect example of his teachings, then he is not a true Guru. He is what in the medical world they call a "quack" (in Ross, 2003d).

Well, if it looks like a duck, meditates like a duck, and lifts weights like a duck....

* * *

Carlos Santana, for one, no longer has any connection with Chinmoy or his community.

> After leaving the group it seems Sri Chinmoy "was pretty vindictive," recalls Santana. "He told all my friends not to

call me ever again, because I was to drown in the dark sea of ignorance for leaving him" (Heath, 2000).

Or, as Santana—Mr. Supernatural himself, whose strong sympathies for Eastern philosophy persist to this day—put it in the same *Rolling Stone* interview, when speaking of Chinmoy's path: "This shit is not for me."

Now that's mo' like it!

CHAPTER XIII

THAI SURPRISE

Confucius say, "Man who go through airport turnstile sideways going to Bangkok."

APPROXIMATELY 95% OF THE SIXTY-FIVE MILLION CITIZENS of Thailand (capital, Bangkok) are Buddhists.

More than 350,000 monks and novices live in Thailand's 35,000 temples—ten monks for every temple, on average. Tenets enjoindered on those devout monks include strict injunctions never to touch intoxicants or women.

Clearly, such restrictions would not constitute an easy or exciting life.

As if to break such monotony, then, we have the renunciant monk who proudly exhibited over sixty vintage cars—many of them Mercedes-Benzes. Some of those were donated, others were purchased with money from his temple treasury, with the claimed investment intention (though questionable business acumen) of opening a museum to benefit that church.

There was also the monk "caught on camera wearing a wig and enjoying a nightlife of loud karaoke singing, boozing and other taboo acts" (Ehrlich, 2000).

There was, further, the highly respected former Buddhist monk, accused of possible embezzlement of funds, who stepped down as spiritual adviser to the prime minister. That, after having also been accused of having sex with some of his female followers and living a lavish lifestyle. "His monastery came complete with the latest sound equipment, elaborate furnishings and luxury cars" (PlanetSave, 2001).

There was the deputy abbot who was recorded, in fine voice, engaging in phone sex with women (Thompson, 2000).

There were the monks accused of selling amphetamines and of hiring some of the country's 700,000 prostitutes (Economist, 2000). "Two girls for every monk."

There was the Chivas Regal-drinking, Mercedes-driving abbot who was disrobed for allegedly ... er, disrobing. With two women at the same time. Two nights in a row. While impersonating an army special forces colonel—a serious crime.

A subsequent search of the holy man's private residence turned up pornographic materials, lingerie and condoms. As well it should, for a monk who was renowned among local law-enforcement officials for going out on the town nearly every night.

There was also, by abstinent contrast, the forty-year-old Buddhist monk who, as a protest against the sufferings of those in his country, planned to immolate himself on the steps of the Burmese embassy in Bangkok.

> As he spoke, I discovered an astonishing thing: although he planned to take his life to protest the great injustices he had fought against for many years, this was not the real reason for his decision. The true reason was that he had fallen in love with this young girl. He had been in monk's robes since age fourteen and for twenty-nine years he had given his life to the order. He had no other skills and couldn't imagine himself married, with a family, yet he loved her. He did not know what to do, so burning himself for political reasons seemed the best way out (Kornfield, 1993).

There was—speaking of burning—the Thai monk who gruesomely roasted babies—already dead babies, thankfully—hoping to utilize the oil collected from them in magical ceremonies. That was done with the intention of creating a "babyish ghost," to be employed in the black magic manipulation of others (Ehrlich, 2000).

There was, even more horribly, the monk accused of raping an eleven-year-old girl.

There was the Buddhist abbot arrested for the alleged murder of a woman whose remains were discovered floating in the septic tank at the house of a neighbor (Ehrlich, 2000).

There was, finally, the monk caught committing necrophilia in a coffin beneath his temple's crematorium.

Thai surprise.

CHAPTER XIV

BATTLEFIELD TEEGEEACK

(SCIENTOLOGY)

Scientology is the one and only road to total freedom and total power (L. Ron Hubbard, in [Burroughs, 1995]).

Werner Erhard, of est fame, called L. Ron Hubbard the "greatest philosopher of the twentieth century" (Corydon and Hubbard, 1998).

Among the many affirmations that Hubbard was known to have used was the following:

> All men shall be my slaves! All women shall succumb to my charms! All mankind shall grovel at my feet and not know why! (Wakefield, 1991).

As religious zealots, Scientologists exceed any that have gone before. They have not simply a deep faith that theirs is The Way. They can present a comprehensible whole; an all-embracing answer to many of the problems that beset humanity (Vosper, 1997).

> [Scientology is] the sole agency in existence today that can forestall the erasure of all civilization or bring a new better one (L. Ron Hubbard, in [Wallis, 1976]).

SCIENTOLOGY (LIKE ITS PRECURSOR, DIANETICS) was founded in the 1950s by pulp/science fiction writer Lafayette Ron Hubbard, who (dubiously) traced the religion's origins to the sacred Hindu Vedas, and further claimed to be the reincarnation of the Buddha.

> Hubbard has been presented, in publications for advanced students, as the Maitreya Buddha supposedly prophesied to appear by Gautama Buddha (Wallis, 1976).

> Most of Hubbard's thousands of followers regarded him as more brilliant than Einstein, more enlightened than Buddha, and quite as capable of miracles as Christ (Atack, 1990).

L. Ron was correspondingly viewed by his devoted disciples as being the only one who could "save the world" (Miller, 1987).

But save the world ... from what?

Evidently, from the high-level Scientology teaching that seventy million years ago, our Earth—called Teegeeack, then—was featured in a galaxy-wide federation oppressed by one Xenu (or Xemu), an evil titan (played by the strictly heterosexual John Travolta). Faced with the problem of overpopulation, Xenu had gathered up the ne'er-do-wells from his empire—among them Jenna Elfman, Narconon spokesperson Kirstie Alley (see Ross [2004b]; Penny [1993]), and the late Sonny Bono. He next confined those individuals in terrestrial volcanoes, and utilized nuclear bombs to explode the latter (and the former). The spirits ("thetans") of those formerly intact beings were then collected, imprisoned in frozen alcohol, and implanted into human beings.

And that, as even Tom Cruise could plainly see and understand, is the cause of all human suffering. Such deeply rooted pain, however, can thankfully be alleviated through Scientology's "auditing" procedures—those being aided by a simplified lie detector called an E-meter. Indeed, through that expensive practice, Scientology "promises to heal the psychic scars caused by traumas in present or past lives" (Richardson, 1993).

The claimed seven million worldwide followers of Scientology have reportedly included jazz pianist Chick Corea, jazz singer Al

Jarreau, pop star Beck, Priscilla Presley, and the voice of Bart Simpson, Nancy Cartwright. (Ironically, Bart's sister is Lisa Marie, named after Priscilla's daughter; and the real Lisa Marie is herself, along with Priscilla, active in Scientology.) Also, Travolta's wife Kelly Preston, Cruise's ex-wife Mimi Rogers, the late Aldous Huxley—who received auditing from Hubbard himself—and Richard de Mille (son of director Cecil). Jerry Seinfeld, Patrick Swayze and Brad Pitt have also "drifted through" Scientology (Richardson, 1993); as have Mikhail Baryshnikov, Van Morrison, Emilio Estevez, Rock Hudson, Demi Moore, Candice Bergen, Isaac Hayes, Mensa member Sharon Stone and O. J. Simpson prosecutor Marcia Clark. Plus, as of 1970, it was claimed that Tennessee Williams, Leonard Cohen, Mama Cass Elliot, Jim Morrison "and possibly the Beatles" were Scientologists (Cooper, 1971). The great jazz pianist Dave Brubeck, too, believed that Scientology's processing had aided his musical career (Evans, 1973).

Charles Manson likewise apparently undertook around 150 hours of auditing while in prison (Atack, 1990). There, he reportedly reached the celebrated level of "Clear," *prior* to his mass-murdering phase (Krassner, 1993).

The imprisoned Manson was actually later doused with gasoline and set on fire by a fellow inmate, an ex-Hare Krishna—who himself had been convicted of killing his own abortion-performing father—following Manson's endless taunting of him for his in-jail chanting and prayers (Muster, 1997).

In more recent years, Dustin Hoffman and Goldie Hawn both signed an open letter to the chancellor of Germany, protesting discrimination against Scientologists there and hyperbolically comparing their treatment to that of Jews during World War II (Bart, 1998).

Be that as it may, the cravat-wearing Hubbard himself suffered no such imagined Holocaust, instead maintaining his own set of privileged, teenaged female "messengers." Those cheerleader-beautiful blond girls, vying for the geriatric Hubbard's attention, had designed their own uniform, consisting of hot pants, halter tops, bobbysox and platform sandals. Their envied duties reportedly included washing Hubbard's hair, giving him massages, and helping him dress and undress (Miller, 1987).

"A man could get religion."

Yet, the life of a messenger was not all fun and estrogen-fuelled games:

> [Hubbard] got mad at a messenger once ... because she overspent some money on an errand, so they took away everyone's supply of toilet paper for ten days (in Corydon and Hubbard, 1998).

Nor was LRH's interest in the financial and anal activities of others limited to pulse-quickening teenage girls:

> Homosexuality is outlawed; Hubbard insisted that the Emotional Tone Level of a homosexual is "covert hostility": they are backstabbers, each and every one (Atack, 1990).

"Ron's" tolerance for equality in other areas seems to have been no higher:

> I don't see that popular measures ... and democracy have done anything for Man but push him further into the mud ... democracy has given us inflation and income tax (in Corydon and Hubbard, 1998).

In spite of such demeaning from above, the reported attitude of devoted members toward their source of salvation is exactly as one would expect:

> Scientologists believe that their survival as spiritual beings is totally dependent upon remaining in good graces with the Church (Corydon and Hubbard, 1998).

> [I]t was well rumored in Scientology that to leave with an incomplete level of auditing could result in death within twelve days (Wakefield, 1996).

In earlier times, Hubbard's dabbling in black magick with renowned chemist Jack Parsons had caused no less than Aleister Crowley—the self-proclaimed "Beast 666"—to remark:

> Apparently Parsons and Hubbard or somebody is producing a moonchild. I get fairly frantic when I contemplate the idiocy of these louts (in Corydon and Hubbard, 1998).

Bringing a welcomed level head to all of that, however, "Superman" Christopher Reeve described (2002) his own experiences within Scientology, including his common-sense method of evaluating their auditing procedures:

> [M]y growing skepticism about Scientology and my training as an actor took over. With my eyes closed, I gradually began to remember details from a devastating past life experience that had happened in ancient Greece....
>
> I could tell that my auditor was deeply moved by my story and trying hard to maintain her professional demeanor. I sensed that she was making a profound connection between guilt over the death of my father when I was a Greek warrior in a past life and my relationship with my father in the present.
>
> And that was the end of my training as a Scientologist. My story was actually a slightly modified account of an ancient Greek myth.... I didn't expect my auditor to be familiar with Greek mythology; I was simply relying on her ability, assisted by the E-meter, to discern the truth. The fact that I got away with a blatant fabrication completely devalued my belief in the process.

Others have come to even less complimentary evaluations of Scientology. Indeed, years earlier, in 1965, the Australian Board of Inquiry into Scientology had produced a report opining that "Scientology is evil; its techniques evil; its practice a serious threat to the community, medically, morally and socially; and its adherents sadly deluded and often mentally ill" (in Miller, 1987). The same report criticized the Hubbard Association of Scientologists International, created by Ron in London in 1952, as being allegedly "the world's largest organization of unqualified persons engaged in the practice of dangerous techniques which masquerade as mental therapy" (in Miller, 1987). (Fellow science fiction writer Isaac Asimov had earlier dismissed Hubbard's Dianetics as being "gibberish" [in Miller, 1987]. The "science of the mind" received no better reviews from Martin Gardner, in his [1957] *Fads and Fallacies in the Name of Science*.)

In a May, 1991, cover story (Behar, 1991), *Time* magazine further described Scientology as allegedly being "a hugely profitable global racket that survives by intimidating members and critics in a Mafia-like manner."

The following books have given much additional disturbing detail as to the alleged nature of life within and around Scientology:

- Jon Atack (1990), *A Piece of Blue Sky*

- Paulette Cooper (1971), *The Scandal of Scientology*. Also see her (1997) diaries. After having been sued eighteen times by the Church, to get a settlement Cooper reportedly "promised she would not republish the [former, *Scandal*] book and signed a statement saying fifty-two passages in it were 'misleading'" (Rudin and Rudin, 1980)
- Russell Miller (1987), *Bare-Faced Messiah*
- Robert Kaufman (1995), *Inside Scientology/Dianetics*
- Cyril Vosper (1997), *The Mind-Benders*
- George Malko (1970), *Scientology: The Now Religion*. Malko's book was reportedly later "withdrawn by its publishers who also paid a legal settlement" (Wallis, 1976)
- Monica Pignotti (1989), *My Nine Lives in Scientology*
- Bent Corydon and L. Ron Hubbard, Jr. (1998), *L. Ron Hubbard: Messiah or Madman?*
- Margery Wakefield (1991), *Understanding Scientology;* (1993), *The Road to Xenu;* and her (1996) autobiography, *Testimony*
- Bob Penny (1993), *Social Control in Scientology*
- For more, see the www.factnet.org website

The aforementioned Behar (1991) further alleged:

One of Hubbard's policies was that all perceived enemies are "fair game" and subject to being "tricked, sued or lied to or destroyed." Those who criticize the church—journalists, doctors, lawyers and even judges—often find themselves engulfed in litigation, stalked by private eyes, framed for fictional crimes, beaten up or threatened with death.

Others have made similar claims:

The Church of Scientology is not known for its willingness to take what it construes as criticism without recourse. Indeed its record of litigation must surely be without parallel in the modern world (Wallis, 1976).

Hubbard has stated, as if invoking a Voodoo curse, that anyone rash enough to take action against Scientology is guar-

> anteeing unto himself an incurable insanity followed by a painful death (Vosper, 1997).
>
> After her first article on Scientology, in 1968, [Paulette] Cooper received a flood of death threats and smear letters; her phone was bugged; lawsuits were filed against her; attempts were made to break into her apartment; and she was framed for a bomb threat (Atack, 1990).

Los Angeles Superior Court Judge Paul G. Breckenridge disclosed his own disturbing impressions of the group in the mid-1980s:

> The [Scientology] organization clearly is schizophrenic and paranoid, and this bizarre combination seems to be a reflection of its founder. The evidence portrays a man [i.e., Hubbard] who has been virtually a pathological liar when it comes to his history, background and achievements. The writings and documents in evidence additionally reflect his egoism, greed, avarice, lust for power, and vindictiveness and aggressiveness against persons perceived by him to be disloyal or hostile (in Miller, 1987).

Justice Latey's opinion of the organization, as expressed in his 1984 London High Court ruling, was no higher:

> Scientology is both immoral and socially obnoxious ... it is corrupt, sinister and dangerous (in Atack, 1990).

Likewise for Conway and Siegelman's (1982) published view:

> According to those who responded to our survey ... Scientology's may be the most debilitating set of rituals of any [alleged] cult in America.
>
> After a survey of forty-eight groups, Conway and Siegelman reported that former Scientologists had the highest rate of violent outbursts, hallucinations, sexual dysfunction and suicidal tendencies. They estimated that full recovery from Scientology averaged at [nearly] 12.5 years (Atack, 1992).

More recently, a wrongful-death lawsuit was brought (and settled out of court in 2004) by the estate of former member Lisa McPherson against the Church of Scientology. For details, see Ross

(2004b) and www.lisamcpherson.org. For the alleged negative effects of participation in Scientology's activities on other devoted followers, see Chapter 21 of Paulette Cooper's (1971) *The Scandal of Scientology,* and Chapter 14 of Corydon and Hubbard (1998) for Cooper's own story. Also, Chapter 22 of the same latter book for Scientology's alleged treatment of lawyer Michael Flynn—who has since frequently represented Paramahansa Yogananda's Self-Realization Fellowship in their own legal concerns (Russell, 2001).

Hubbard himself died in the mid-'80s. By the end, he had become a rather unhappy man, living in a rather unhappy, Howard Hughes-like fashion—reportedly believing, at various times, that his cooks were trying to poison him; and demanding that his dirty clothes be washed thirteen times, in thirteen different buckets of clean spring water, before he would wear them.

> Psychiatrist Frank Gerbode, who practiced Scientology for many years, feels that Hubbard was not schizophrenic, but rather "manic with paranoid tendencies".... However, Gerbode suggests that the best description is the lay diagnosis "loony" (Atack, 1990).

> [T]he FBI did not take Hubbard seriously, at one point making the notation "appears mental" in his file (Wakefield, 1991).

And yet, Bent Corydon and L. Ron Hubbard, Jr. (1998) have equally claimed:

> To be a critic of the Church or its Founder is to be insane. Simple as that....
>
> Labeling any dissident "psychotic" is commonplace in Scientology. This is mandated by Hubbard's written policies.

Good advice, however, comes from—of all places—multiply rehabbed actor and pornography aficionado Charlie Sheen, a former boyfriend of Kelly Preston. (Also, an aspiring poet. "Luckily most of it was written on smack, or it would all be religious fluffy stuff.") For, when asked about reported attempts by Scientologists to recruit him for their cause, Sheen—who would surely have fully appreciated the hot pants and halter tops of Hubbard's blossoming "messengers"—is said to have replied:

"I have no involvement in that form of silliness."

CHAPTER XV

WERNER'S UNCERTAINTY PRINCIPLE

(est/FORUM/LANDMARK TRAINING)

WERNER ERHARD WAS BORN John Paul Rosenberg. He took his new moniker on a cross-country plane trip, as a combination of two names he read in an in-flight magazine: quantum physicist Werner Heisenberg—developer of Heisenberg's Uncertainty Principle—and then-economics minister of West Germany, Ludwig Erhard.

As to the man's character, the late Buckminster Fuller effused in the *New York Times* (in February of 1979):

> I have quite a few million people who listen to me. And I say Werner Erhard is honest. He may prove untrustworthy, and if he does then I'll say so.

That endorsement came, of course, from the same futurist who, only a few years earlier, had whole-heartedly endorsed the Maharishi Mahesh Yogi. At the time, Fuller and Erhard were splitting the proceeds from a series of public "conversations" between the two of them.

Erhard's est training had its roots in many other well-known therapies and disciplines. Indeed, Mark Brewer (1975), in an article for *Psychology Today,* found traces of Zen, Scientology—which Erhard once followed—Dale Carnegie and gestalt therapy in the core teachings of est ("Erhard Seminars Training"):

> What the training is more than anything else [is an] application of classic techniques in indoctrination and mental conditioning worthy of Pavlov himself.

Yet, the relatively low concentration of things "Eastern" reportedly did not stop the former used car salesman, Erhard, from pondering his own high position in the cosmos:

> "How do I know I'm not the reincarnation of Jesus Christ?" Erhard once wondered of a friend (Pressman, 1993).

In other times, Jim Jones asked himself the same question, coming to the conclusion that he was exactly that reincarnation (Layton, 1998)—as well as having more recently been Vladimir Ilyich Lenin. Wanna-be rock star and alleged pedophile David Koresh, too—of Waco, Texas, i.e., Branch Davidian infamy—believed himself to be Jesus Christ (England and McCormick, 1993); as did Marshall Applewhite of Heaven's Gate (Lalich, 2004).

One can, however, always aim higher. Thus, in the autumn of 1977, as reported by Steven Pressman in his (1993) *Outrageous Betrayal,* during a beachside meeting of est seminar leaders in Monterey, one participant got to his feet.

> "The question in the room that nobody is asking," the man told Erhard solemnly, "is 'Are you the [M]essiah?'"
>
> The room grew silent as Erhard looked out to the curious faces of some of his most devoted disciples. After a few moments he replied, "No, I am who sent him [i.e., God]."

Marshall Applewhite's spiritual partner, Bonnie Lu Nettles, likewise believed herself to be an incarnation of God the Father (Lalich, 2004).

Given reported feelings such as the above among the formerly encyclopedia-selling "God"—Erhard—and his seminar trainers, it is hardly surprising that alleged trainee horror stories such as the following should surface:

> "Most of the people I've seen at our clinic—and they come in after the training in fairly substantial numbers—have suffered reactions that range from moderately bad to dreadful," the executive director of New York City's Lincoln Institute for Psychotherapy reported in 1978. "They are confused and jarred, and the same pattern—elation, depression, feelings of omnipotence followed by feelings of helplessness—are repeated over and over again"....
>
> In March 1977 the [*American Journal of Psychiatry*] published the first of two articles ... that described five patients who had [allegedly] developed psychotic symptoms, including paranoia, uncontrollable mood swings, and delusions in the wake of taking the est training (Pressman, 1993).

David Shy (2004) lists additional relevant published concerns.

Erhard himself has reportedly "hotly denied any damaging effects from the est training" (Pressman, 1993).

Early graduates of Erhard's four-day est seminars included John "Windy Kansas Wheat Field" Denver—who wanted to give up his singing career to become an est trainer. Also, Diana Ross, astronaut Buzz Aldrin, and Yoko Ono. More recently, Ted Danson, Valerie Harper, Roy "Jaws" Scheider and numerous other Hollywood stars have taken Erhard's courses.

At any rate, as if to argue that the harsh discipline of any "holy man" directed toward his followers simply begins a cycle of abuse with future generations of disciples, we have the following allegation:

> Those who worked closest to Erhard often witnessed his own tirades and yelling bouts, and sometimes felt free to mirror his own behavior when they were in charge (Pressman, 1993).

Erhard's home life may have taken tragic turns as well. For, Werner's daughter Deborah once alleged that he had

> coerced one of his older daughters ... into having sexual intercourse with him in a hotel room they were sharing during one of his frequent out-of-town trips (Pressman, 1993).*

"Thank you for sharing."

* Erhard has denied all allegations of abuse. Jane Self's (1992) ***60*** *Minutes and the Assassination of Werner Erhard* has further offered a staunch defense of Erhard against the uncomplimentary picture of him painted by the media. There, she alleges that the orchestration of his downfall can be found within the Church of Scientology. In that same book, Erhard's daughters are quoted as retracting their previous allegations of improprieties on his part, having supposedly made them under duress.

Dr. Self does not address the alleged negative effects of Erhard's seminars on their most vulnerable participants nor, in my opinion, convincingly refute Erhard's reportedly messianic view of himself. (Curiously, though, both she and Werner's friend Mark Kamin refer to Erhard's public downfall as his being "crucified.") Nor, unlike Pressman (1993), does she delve into the serious, alleged behind-the-scenes issues with the Hunger Project. (That project was Erhard's failed attempt to wipe out starvation by the year 2000.) Instead, she simply repeats the "public relations" line on that topic.

CHAPTER XVI

COCKROACH YOGA

(YOGI BHAJAN)

YOGI BHAJAN WAS THE SIKH FOUNDER of 3HO, the nonprofit "Healthy, Happy, Holy Organization," headquartered in Los Angeles.

Born in the Punjab, he worked as a customs agent in New Delhi before emigrating with his wife to North America in 1968, at age thirty-nine, to teach kundalini and white tantric yoga there.

White tantra is used "to purify and uplift the being," as opposed to black, which is "for mental control of other people," or red, which is "for sexual energy and senses" or for demonstrating miracles (S. Khalsa, 1996).

> Yogi Bhajan has said that kundalini yoga will be the yoga of the Aquarian Age and will be practiced for the next five thousand years (in Singh, 1998a).

> Guru Terath Singh Khalsa, who is [Bhajan's] lawyer and spokesman, says that Bhajan is "the equivalent of the pope" (Time, 1977).

> Yogi Bhajan is unique among spiritual teachers because he is also the Mahan Tantric of this era. This means that he is the only living master of white tantric yoga in the world,

> since there can only be one on the planet at any given time. He is a world teacher, a very special instrument whom God has appointed and anointed to awaken the millions of sleeping souls on this planet (S. Khalsa, 1996).

The idea that Bhajan is actually the "Mahan Tantric of this era" via any recognized lineage, however, has been questioned by some of his detractors.

In any case, Madonna, Rosanna Arquette, Melissa Etheridge, Cindy Crawford, Courtney Love and David Duchovny have all reportedly been influenced by Gurmukh Kaur Khalsa, one of Yogi Bhajan's devoted followers (Ross, 2002). As of 1980, Bhajan claimed a quarter of a million devotees worldwide, including around 2500 in his ashrams. The yogi himself was reported to live in a mansion in Los Angeles.

The late (d. October, 2004) Bhajan's brand of Sikhism has actually been rejected by the orthodox Sikh community, but that seems to derive more from him including elements of (Hindu) kundalini yoga in it than for any concern about the teachings or practices themselves.

* * *

> As a Master, as a yogi, Yogi Bhajan always sees women—and men—from a cosmic viewpoint. He never forgets that we are primarily souls, paying our karma and learning our lessons in these two different forms....
>
> "I believe that so long as those born of woman do not respect woman, there shall be no peace on Earth" [Bhajan has said] (S. Khalsa, 1996).

The particular brand of "respect" offered to women within Bhajan's community, however, may have stopped somewhat short of any enlightened ideal, as one of his female devotees explained:

> When I moved into the Philadelphia ashram back in the '70s, I was handed a little pink book called *Fascinating Womanhood*.... [I]t is a practical how-to manual on marriage from the woman's point of view, written by a Mormon. It is the philosophical opposite of feminism, completely committed to the belief that the spiritual fulfillment of women is achieved through unquestioning service and obedience to men....

> In most ways 3HOers no longer play such extreme sex roles. It has been a very long time since I have seen a male head of an ashram lounging around while sweet young things ply him with foot massages (K. Khalsa, 1990).

Of course, that implies that there was a time when desirable young women in the ashrams *would* give foot massages to the highly placed men there.

> In a series of lectures entitled "Man to Man," Yogi Bhajan explains women's nature to the males: "One day she is very bright and charming and after a couple days she is totally dumb and non-communicative. This is called the 'normal woman mood.'" And because women fluctuate so much, "a female needs constant social security and constant leadership ... when you are not the leader, she is not satisfied" (Naman, 1980).

Such "fifteenth century" (i.e., when the Sikh religion was founded by Guru Nanak) attitudes toward "the fairer sex," though, would invariably have an alleged flip side:

> Bhajan has repeatedly been accused of being a womanizer. Colleen Hoskins, who worked seven months at his New Mexico residence, reports that men are scarcely seen there. He is served, she says, by a coterie of as many as fourteen women, some of whom attend his baths, give him group massages, and take turns spending the night in his room while his wife sleeps elsewhere (Time, 1977).

When the same Ms. Hoskins became disillusioned and decided to leave the 3HO group, she was allegedly told by Bhajan that "she would be responsible for a nuclear holocaust" (Naman, 1980).

Perhaps in anticipation of such calamities, Bhajan is reported to have suggested (in Singh, 1998):

> We should have a place, which should sustain five thousand children, five thousand women, and one thousand men.

Of course, if we have learned one thing from *Dr. Strangelove,* it is that such women would have to be chosen for their "breeding potential"....

* * *

The proper attitude toward the guru, within 3HO as elsewhere, was explained by Bhajan himself:

> Advice should be righteous, your mind should be righteous, and your advice and activity to that advice should be righteous. If a guru says, "Get up in the morning and praise God," will you do it?
>
> Answer: Yes.
>
> Question: If the guru says "Get up in the morning and steal," will you do it?
>
> Answer: Yes.
>
> Question: Is everything the guru says righteous?
>
> Answer: Otherwise he is not a guru.
>
> Question: Is it righteous to steal?
>
> Answer: Perhaps he is testing, who knows. What is a guru? A guru is an unknown infinity of you, otherwise another human being cannot be a guru to you (Bhajan, 1977).

Note that this quotation is *not* taken out of context: it is a full entry in the "Relationship" chapter of the indicated book by Yogi Bhajan.

The alleged result of such attitudes is not altogether surprising:

> The yogi makes money from businesses run by his yoga disciples, but was sued for "assault, battery, fraud and deceit." He decided to settle out of court.
>
> One of Bhajan's top leaders and yoga enthusiasts was busted for smuggling guns and marijuana and then sentenced to prison (Ross, 2003c).

And what was Bhajan's reported response to such downturns of fortune?

> The critics didn't spare Jesus Christ, they didn't spare Buddha, and they don't spare me (in Naman, 1980).

* * *

At the 1974 3HO Teachers Meeting in Santa Cruz, New Mexico, Yogi Bhajan had allegedly predicted:

In another ten years hospitals will have iron windows and people will try to jump out. There will be tremendous sickness. There will be unhappiness and tragedy on Earth.

Your dead bodies will lie on these roads, your children will be orphans, and nobody will kick them, rather, people will eat them alive! There will be tremendous insanity. That is the time we are going to face (in Singh, 1998).

And from the same sage in 1977 (reported in Singh, 2000):

Now you say there is no life on Mars? Mars is populated ... it is over-populated. The rate of production and sensuality is so heavy, and the beings—they grow so fast that they have to go and make war on all the other planets.

There are beings on Jupiter. There is a hierarchy. Their energy and our energy interexchange [*sic*] in the astral body and it is highly effective.

* * *

For a long time I didn't worry much about the few odd people who left 3HO. I hadn't liked them much when they were in 3HO so it seemed reasonable to me that, after forsaking the truth, they had all become pimps, prostitutes and drug dealers, like the rumors implied (K. Khalsa, 1990).

But again, Bhajan himself saw it all coming:

[Yogi Bhajan] warned all of us who were to become teachers that, "You will be tested in three areas: money, sex, or power —possibly in all of them." It is a great responsibility and privilege to teach kundalini yoga. It is said that if a teacher betrays the sacred trust placed in him, he will be reborn as a cockroach! (S. Khalsa, 1996).

Kundalini yoga. Tantric sex yoga. Pimp yoga. Prostitute yoga ("3-HOs"). Drug-dealer yoga. Gun yoga. Nuclear holocaust yoga.

Cockroach yoga.

CHAPTER XVII

A WILD AND CRAZY WISDOM GUY

(CHÖGYAM TRUNGPA)

CHÖGYAM TRUNGPA, BORN IN 1939, is the first of the "crazy wisdom" masters whose effect on North American spirituality we will be considering.

> The night of my conception my mother had a very significant dream that a being had entered her body with a flash of light; that year flowers bloomed in the neighborhood although it was still winter, to the surprise of the inhabitants....
>
> I was born in the cattle byre [shed]; the birth came easily. On that day a rainbow was seen in the village, a pail supposed to contain water was unaccountably found full of milk, while several of my mother's relations dreamt that a lama was visiting their tents (Trungpa, 1977).

As the eleventh incarnation of the Trungpa Tulku, the milk-fed sage was raised from his childhood to be the supreme abbot of the Surmang monasteries in eastern Tibet.

In Trungpa's tradition, a *tulku* is "someone who reincarnates with the memories and values of previous lives intact" (Butterfield, 1994). Of an earlier, fourth incarnation of that same Trungpa Tulku (Trungpa Künga-gyaltzen) in the late fourteenth century, it has been asserted:

> [H]e was looked upon as an incarnation of Maitreya Bodhisattva, destined to be the Buddha of the next World Cycle, also of Dombhipa a great Buddhist *siddha* (adept) and of Milarepa (Trungpa, 1977).

Having been enthroned in Tibet as heir to the lineages of Milarepa and Padmasambhava, Trungpa left the country for India in 1959, fleeing the Chinese Communist takeover. There, by appointment of the Dalai Lama, he served as the spiritual advisor for the Young Lamas Home School in Dalhousie, until 1963 (Shambhala, 2003).

From India Chögyam went to England, studying comparative religion and psychology at Oxford University. (A later student of Trungpa's, Al Santoli, "suggests that the CIA may have had a hand in getting the eleventh Trungpa into Oxford" [Clark, 1980].) He further caused quite a stir in clashing with another *tulku* adversary (Akong) of his who, like Trungpa himself, had designs on leading their lineage in the West.

> To the amazement of a small circle of local helpers and to the gross embarrassment of the powers that sent them to England, the two honorable *tulkus* entered into heated arguments and publicly exchanged hateful invectives. In an early edition of his book, *Born in Tibet,* Trungpa called Akong paranoid and scheming (Lehnert, 1998).

In any case, Trungpa and Akong went on to found the first Western-hemisphere Tibetan Buddhist meditation center, in Scotland, which community was visited by the American poet Robert Bly in 1971.

> It was, Trungpa remembers, "a forward step. Nevertheless, it was not entirely satisfying, for the scale of activity was small, and the people who did come to participate seemed to be slightly missing the point" (Fields, 1992).

That same center later became of interest to the police as they investigated allegations of drug abuse there. Trungpa, not himself prone to "missing the point," avoided that bust by hiding in a stable.

The Buddhist nun Tenzin Palmo (in Mackenzie, 1999) related her own experiences with the young Chögyam in England, upon their first meeting in 1962. There, in finding his attentive hands working their way up her skirt in the middle of afternoon tea and cucumber sandwiches, Trungpa received a stiletto heel to his sandaled holy feet. His later "smooth line" to her, in repeated attempts at seduction beyond that initial meeting/groping, included the claim that Palmo had "swept him off his monastic feet." That, in spite of the fact that he "had women since [he] was thirteen," and already had a son.

In 1969 Chögyam experienced a tragic automobile accident which left him paralyzed on the left side of his body. The car had careened into a joke shop (seriously); Trungpa had been driving drunk at the time (Das, 1997), to the point of blacking out at the wheel (Trungpa, 1977).

Note, now, that Trungpa did not depart from Tibet for India until age twenty, and did not leave India for his schooling in England until four years later. Thus, eleven years of his having "had women" were enacted within surrounding traditional Tibetan and northern Indian attitudes toward acceptable behavior (on the part of monks, etc.). Indeed, according to the son referenced above, both his mother and Trungpa were under vows of celibacy, in Tibet, at the time of their union (Dykema, 2003). Of the three hundred monks entrusted to him when he was enthroned as supreme abbot of the Surmang monasteries, Trungpa himself (1977) remarked that

> one hundred and seventy were *bhikshus* (fully ordained monks), the remainder being *shramaneras* (novices) and young *upsaka* students who had already taken the vow of celibacy.

Obviously, then, Trungpa's (Sarvastivadin) tradition was not a "monastic" one *without* celibacy vows, as is the case with Zen.

Further, Trungpa himself did not formally give up his monastic vows to work as a "lay teacher" until sometime *after* his car accident in England. This, then, is another clear instance of demonstration that traditional agrarian society places no more iron-clad constraints on the behavior of any "divine sage" than does its postmodern, Western counterpart.

Trungpa may have "partied harder" in Europe and the States, but he was already breaking plenty of rules, without censure, back in Tibet and India. Indeed, one could probably reasonably argue that, proportionately, he broke as many social and cultural rules, with as little censure, in Tibet and India as he later did in America. (For blatant examples of what insignificant discipline is visited upon even violent rule-breakers in Tibetan Buddhist society even today, consult Lehnert's [1998] *Rogues in Robes.*) Further, Trungpa (1977) did not begin to act as anyone's guru until age fourteen, but had women since he was thirteen. He was thus obviously breaking that vow of celibacy with impunity both before and after assuming "God-like" guru status, again in agrarian 1950s Tibet.

In 1970, the recently married Trungpa and his sixteen-year-old, dressage-fancying English wife, Diana, established their permanent residence in the United States. He was soon teaching at the University of Colorado, and in time accumulated around 1500 disciples. Included among those was folksinger Joni Mitchell, who visited the *tulku* three times, and whose song "Refuge of the Roads" (from the 1976 album *Hejira*) contains an opening verse about the guru. Contemporary transpersonal psychologist and author John Welwood, member of the Board of Editors of *The Journal of Transpersonal Psychology,* is also a long-time follower of Trungpa.

In 1974, Chögyam founded the accredited Naropa Institute in Boulder, Colorado—the first tantric university in America. Instructors and guests at Naropa have included psychiatrist R. D. Laing, Gregory Bateson, Ram Dass and Allen Ginsberg—after whom the university library was later named. (Ginsberg had earlier spent time with Swami Muktananda [Miles, 1989].) Also, Marianne Faithfull, avant-garde composer John Cage, and William "Naked Lunch" Burroughs, who had earlier become enchanted (1974, 1995) and then disenchanted with L. Ron Hubbard's Scientology. Plus, the infinitely tedious Tibetan scholar and translator Herbert V. Guenther, whose writings, even by dry academic standards, could function well as a natural sedative.

Bhagavan Das (1997) related his own, more lively experiences, while teaching Indian music for three months at Naropa in the '70s:

> The party energy around [Trungpa] was compelling. In fact, that's basically what Naropa was: a huge blowout party, twenty-four hours a day....
>
> I was in a very crazed space and very lost. One day, after having sex with three different women, I couldn't get out of bed. I was traumatized. It was all too much.

Jack Kornfield offered a less "traumatic" recounting of his own days lecturing there, being invited to teach after he and Trungpa had met at a (where else) cocktail party in 1973:

> We all had this romantic, idealistic feeling that we were at the beginning of a consciousness movement that was really going to transform the world (in Schwartz, 1996).

Befitting the leader of such a world-changing effort, in 1974 Trungpa was confirmed as a Vajracarya, or a "spiritual master of the highest level," by His Holiness the Karmapa Lama, during the latter's first visit to the West (Trungpa, 1977).

* * *

The practice of "crazy wisdom" itself rests upon the following theory:

> [I]f a bodhisattva is completely selfless, a completely open person, then he will act according to openness, will not have to follow rules; he will simply fall into patterns. It is impossible for the bodhisattva to destroy or harm other people, because he embodies transcendental generosity. He has opened himself completely and so does not discriminate between *this* and *that*. He just acts in accordance with what *is*.... [H]is mind is so precise, so accurate that *he never makes mistakes* [italics added]. He never runs into unexpected problems, never creates chaos in a destructive way (Trungpa, 1973).

> [O]nce you receive transmission and form the [guru-disciple] bond of *samaya*, you have committed yourself to the teacher as guru, and from then on, the guru can do no wrong, no matter what. It follows that if you obey the guru in all things, you can do no wrong either. This is the basis of Osel Tendzin's [Trungpa's eventual successor] teaching that "if you keep your *samaya*, you cannot make a mistake." He was not deviating into his own megalomania when he said this,

> but repeating the most essential idea of mainstream Vajrayana [i.e., Tantric Buddhism] (Butterfield, 1994).

> Q [student]: What if you feel the necessity for a violent act in order ultimately to do good for a person?
> A [Trungpa]: You just do it (Trungpa, 1973).

> A perfect example of going with energy, of the positive wild yogi quality, was the actual transmission of enlightenment from Tilopa to [his disciple] Naropa. Tilopa removed his sandal and slapped Naropa in the face (Trungpa, 1973).

We could, of course, have learned as much from the Three Stooges.

> Q [student]: Must we have a spiritual friend [e.g., a guru] before we can expose ourselves, or can we just open ourselves to the situations of life?
> A [Trungpa]: I think you need someone to watch you do it, because then it will seem more real to you. It is easy to undress in a room with no one else around, but we find it difficult to undress ourselves in a room full of people (Trungpa, 1973).

Yes, there was plenty of undressing. At the Halloween costume party during an annual seminar in the autumn of 1975, for example:

> A woman is stripped naked, apparently at Trungpa's joking command, and hoisted into the air by [his] guards, and passed around—presumably in fun, although the woman does not think so (Marin, 1995).

The pacifist poet William Merwin and his wife, Dana, were attending the same three-month retreat, but made the mistake of keeping to themselves within a crowd mentality where that was viewed as offensive "egotism" on their part. Consequently, their perceived aloofness had been resented all summer by the other community members ... and later categorized as "resistance" by Trungpa himself.

Thus, Merwin and his companion showed up briefly for the aforementioned Halloween party, danced only with each other, and then went back to their room.

Trungpa, however, insisted through a messenger that they return and rejoin the party. In response, William and his wife locked themselves in their room, turned off the lights ... and soon found themselves on the receiving end of a group of angry, drunken spiritual seekers, who proceeded to cut their telephone line, kick in the door (at Trungpa's command) and break a window (Miles, 1989).

Panicked, but discerning that broken glass is mightier than the pen, the poet defended himself by smashing bottles over several of the attacking disciples, injuring a friend of his. Then, mortified and giving up the struggle, he and his wife were dragged from the room.

> [Dana] implored that someone call the police, but to no avail. She was insulted by one of the women in the hallway and a man threw wine in her face (Schumacher, 1992).

And then, at the feet of the wise guru, after Trungpa had "told Merwin that he had heard the poet was making a lot of trouble":

> [Merwin:] I reminded him that we never promised to obey him. He said, "Ah, but you asked to come" (Miles, 1989).

> An argument ensued, during which Trungpa insulted Merwin's Oriental wife with racist remarks [in return for which she called him a "Nazi"] and threw a glass of *saké* in the poet's face (Feuerstein, 1992).

Following that noble display of high realization, Trungpa had the couple forcibly stripped by his henchmen—against the protests of both Dana and one of the few courageous onlookers, who was punched in the face and called a "son of a bitch" by Trungpa himself for his efforts.

> "Guards dragged me off and pinned me to the floor," [Dana] wrote in her account of the incident.... "I fought and called to friends, men and women whose faces I saw in the crowd, to call the police. No one did.... [One devotee] was stripping me while others held me down. Trungpa was punching [him] in the head, urging him to do it faster. The rest of my clothes were torn off."
>
> "See?" said Trungpa. "It's not so bad, is it?" Merwin and Dana stood naked, holding each other, Dana sobbing (Miles, 1989).

Finally, others stripped voluntarily and Trungpa, apparently satisfied, said "Let's dance" (Marin, 1995). "And so they did."

And that, kiddies, is what they call "authentic Tibetan Buddhism."

Don't let your parents find out: Soon they won't even let you say your prayers before bedtime, for fear that it might be a "gateway" to the hard-core stuff.

The scandal ensuing from the above humiliation became known as, in all seriousness, "the great Naropa poetry wars." It was, indeed, commemorated in the identical title of a must-read (though sadly out of print) book by Tom Clark (1980). If you need to be cured of the idea that Trungpa was anything but a "power-hungry ex-monarch" alcoholic fool, that is the book to read. (Interestingly, a poll taken by the Naropa student newspaper in the late '70s disclosed that nine of twenty-six students at their poetry school regarded Trungpa as being either a "total fraud" or very near to the same.)

For his journalistic efforts, Clark was rewarded with "lots of hang-up phone calls," presumably as an intimidation tactic on the part of Trungpa's loyal followers.

And incredibly, even after enduring the above reported abuse, Merwin and Dana chose to remain at the seminary for Trungpa's subsequent Vajrayana lectures.

At any rate, Chögyam's own (1977) presentation of the goings-on at his "seminars," even well *after* the Merwin incident, predictably paled in comparison to their realities:

> I initiated the annual Vajradhatu Seminary, a three-month intensive practice and study retreat for mature students. The first of these seminaries, involving eighty students, took place ... in the autumn of 1973. Periods of all-day sitting meditation alternated with a study programme methodically progressing through the three *yanas* of Buddhist teaching, Hinayana, Mahayana and Vajrayana.

"Mature, methodical progression," however, does not quite capture the mood earlier expressed by the traumatized Das or the involuntarily stripped Merwin and his wife.

How then is one to understand Chögyam's "extra-curricular" activities within the context of such Vajrayana teachings?

> The notorious case involving Trungpa ... was given all sorts of high explanations by his followers, none of whom got the correct one: Trungpa made an outrageous, inexcusable, and completely stupid mistake, period (Wilber, 1983).

Trungpa's own insistence, however, was again always that he and his enlightened ilk "never make mistakes." (The explicit quote to that effect, above, is from 1973—a *full decade* prior to Wilber's attempted, and wholly failed, explanation.) Rather, the day following the Merwin "incident," Trungpa simply posted an open letter to everyone at the retreat, effectively explaining his previous night's behavior as part of his "teaching." No apology was offered by him, and he *certainly* did not regard himself as having made any "mistake" whatsoever (Marin, 1995). Even in the late '70s, when Allen Ginsberg asked Trungpa, "was it a *mistake?* He said, 'Nope'" (in Clark, 1980). Ginsberg himself, too, "said Trungpa may have been guilty of indiscretion, but he had not been wrong in the way he had behaved" (Schumacher, 1992). And indeed, any disciple who might ever question the stated infallibility of such a guru would again only be demonstrating his own disloyalty. The only "option" for any obedient follower is then, quite obviously, to find a "high explanation" for the activities.

> "I was wrong," Trungpa might have said. Or, "he was wrong," his disciples might have said. But they cannot say such things. It would interfere too much with the myth [of Trungpa's supernatural enlightenment] they have chosen to believe....
>
> I think back to a conversation I recently had with the director of Naropa's summer academic program.... [W]hen, in the course of the conversation, I asked him whether Trungpa can make a mistake, he answered: "You know, a student has to believe his master can make no mistake. Sometimes Trungpa may do something I don't understand. But I must believe what he does is always for the best" (Marin, 1995).

In 1978, the emotionally involved Allen Ginsberg was confronted with the suggestion that the obedience of Trungpa's followers in the "Merwin incident" might be compared to that of participants in the Jonestown mass suicides. He then gave his own heated, and utterly irrational, analysis:

> In the middle of that scene, [for Dana] to yell "call the police" —do you realize how *vulgar* that was? The wisdom of the East being unveiled, and she's going "call the police!" I mean, shit! Fuck that shit! Strip 'em naked, break down the door! Anything—symbolically (in Clark, 1980).

Yes. "Symbolically."

Further, regarding Wilber's intimation that the guru's actions were an isolated "mistake": When a former resident of Trungpa's community was asked, in 1979, whether the "Merwin incident" was a characteristic happening, or a singular occurrence, she responded (in Clark, 1980):

> It is a typical incident, it is not an isolated example. At every seminary, as far as I know, there was a confrontation involving violence.

In any case, the regarding of such actions as Chögyam's versus Merwin, as being simple "mistakes," certainly could not explain away the reported premeditated means by which disciples were kept in line within Trungpa's community:

> We were admonished ... not to talk about our practice. "May I shrivel up instantly and rot," we vowed, "if I ever discuss these teachings with anyone who has not been initiated into them by a qualified master." As if this were not enough, Trungpa told us that if we ever tried to leave the Vajrayana, we would suffer unbearable, subtle, continuous anguish, and disasters would pursue us like furies....
>
> To be part of Trungpa's inner circle, you had to take a vow never to reveal or even discuss some of the things he did. This personal secrecy is common with gurus, especially in Vajrayana Buddhism. It is also common in the dysfunctional family systems of alcoholics and sexual abusers. This inner circle secrecy puts up an almost insurmountable barrier to a healthy skeptical mind....
>
> [T]he vow of silence means that you cannot get near him until you have already given up your own perception of enlightenment and committed yourself to his (Butterfield, 1994).

The traditional Vajrayana teachings on the importance of loyalty to the guru are no less categorical:

> Breaking tantric *samaya* [i.e., leaving one's guru] is more harmful than breaking other vows. It is like falling from an airplane compared to falling from a horse (Tulku Thondup, in [Panchen and Wangyi, 1996]).

> In many texts, the consequences of breaking with one's guru are told in graphic terms, for it is believed that, once having left a guru, a disciple's spiritual progress "comes to an absolute end" because "he never again meets with a spiritual master," and he is subject to "endless wandering in the lower realms." In the case of disrespect for the guru, it is said in the texts that if the disciple "comes to despise his Guru, he encounters many problems in the same life and then experiences a violent death" (Campbell, 1996, quoting from [Dhargyey, 1974]).

Such constraints on the disciple place great power into the hands of the guru-figure—power which Trungpa, like countless others before and after him, was not shy about exercising and preserving.

> [Trungpa] was protected by bodyguards known as the Vajra Guard, who wore blue blazers and received specialized training that included haiku composition and flower arranging. On one occasion, to test a student guard's alertness, Trungpa hurled himself from a staircase, expecting to be caught. The guard was inattentive, and Trungpa landed on his head, requiring a brief visit to the hospital (Miles, 1989).

We could, of course, have learned as much from Inspector Clouseau.

Or, expressed in haiku (if not in flower arranging):

> Hopped up on *saké*
> I throw myself down the stairs
> No one to catch me

> I was scolded by one of his disciples for laughing at Trungpa. He was a nut. But they were very offended....
>
> He had women bodyguards in black dresses and high heels packing automatics standing in a circle around him while they served *saké* and invited me over for a chat. It was bizarre (Gary Snyder, in [Downing, 2001]).

Interestingly, Trungpa considered the SFZC's Shunryu Suzuki to be his "spiritual father," while Suzuki considered the former to be "like my son" (in Chadwick, 1999).

* * *

There is a actually a very easy way to tell whether or not any "sage's" "crazy wisdom" treatment of others is really a "skillful means," employed to enlighten the people toward whom it is directed.

Consider that we would not attempt to evaluate whether a person is a hypochondriac, for example, when he is in the hospital, diagnosed with pneumonia or worse, and complaining about that. Rather, hypochondria shows when a person is certified to be perfectly healthy, but still worries neurotically that every little pain may be an indication of a serious illness.

We would likewise not attempt to evaluate any author's polemics in situations where the "righteous anger" may have been provoked, and may be justifiable as an attempt to "awaken" the people at whom it is directed, or even just to give them a "taste of their own medicine." If we can find the same polemic being thrown around in contexts where it was clearly unprovoked, however, we may be certain that there is more to the author's motivations than such claimed high-minded ideals. That is, we may be confident that he is doing it for his own benefit, in blowing off steam, or simply enjoying dissing others whose ideas he finds threatening. In short, such unprovoked polemics would give us strong reason to believe that the author is not being honest with himself regarding the supposedly noble basis of his own anger.

We would not attempt to evaluate the "skillful means" by which any claimed "sage" puts his followers into psychological binds, etc., in their native guru-disciple contexts, where such actions *may* be justified. Rather, we would instead look at how the guru-figure interacts with others in situations where his hypocritical or allegedly abusive actions cannot be excused as attempts to awaken them. If we find the same reported abusive behaviors in his interactions with non-disciples as we find in his interactions with his close followers, the most generous position is to "subtract" the "baseline" of the non-disciple interactions from the guru-disciple ones. If the alleged "skillful means" (of anger and reported "Rude Boy" abuse) are present equally in both sets, they cancel out, and were thus never "skillful" to begin with. Rather, they were simply the transplanting of pre-existing despicable behaviors into a context in which they may appear to be acceptable.

In the present context, then, since Akong was never one of Trungpa's disciples, Chögyam's poor behavior toward the former cannot be excused as any attempted "skillful means" of awakening him. Merwin and his wife were likewise not disciples of Trungpa. Thus, his disciplining of them for not joining the Halloween party arguably provides another example of the guru humiliating others only for *his own* twisted enjoyment, not for their spiritual good.

We will find good use for this "contextual comparison" method when evaluating the behaviors of many other "crazy wisdom" or "Rude Boy" gurus and their supporters, in the coming chapters.

* * *

> Allen [Ginsberg] asked Trungpa why he drank so much. Trungpa explained he hoped to determine the illumination of American drunkenness. In the United States, he said, alcohol was the main drug, and he wanted to use his acquired knowledge of drunkenness as a source of wisdom (Schumacher, 1992).

> [Trungpa's] health had begun to fail. He spent nearly a year and a half in a semicoma, nearly dying on a couple of occasions, before finally succumbing to a heart attack (Schumacher, 1992).

> Before he died of acute alcoholism in 1987, Trungpa appointed an American acolyte named Thomas Rich, also known as Osel Tendzin, as his successor. Rich, a married father of four, died of AIDS in 1990 amid published reports that he had had unprotected sex with [over a hundred] male and female students without telling them of his illness (Horgan, 2003a).

> Tendzin offered to explain his behavior at a meeting which I attended. Like all of his talks, this was considered a teaching of dharma, and donations were solicited and expected (Butterfield, 1994).

Having forked over the requisite $35 "offering," Butterfield was treated to Tendzin's dubious explanation:

> In response to close questioning by students, he first swore us to secrecy (family secrets again), and then said that Trungpa had requested him to be tested for HIV in the early 1980s and told him to keep quiet about the positive result. Tendzin had asked Trungpa what he should do if students wanted to have sex with him, and Trungpa's reply was that as long as he did his Vajrayana purification practices, it did not matter, because they would not get the disease. Tendzin's answer, in short, was that he had obeyed the instructions of his guru. He said we must not get trapped in the dualism of good and evil, there has never been any stain, our anger is the compassion of the guru, and we must purify all obstacles that prevent us from seeing the world as a sacred mandala of buddhas and bodhisattvas.

Yet, in spite of that, and *well after* all of those serious problems in behavior had become widely known, we still have this untenable belief being voiced, by none other than Ken Wilber (1996):

> "Crazy wisdom" occurs in a very strict ethical atmosphere.

If all of the above was occurring within a "very strict ethical atmosphere," however, one shudders to think of what horrors an *un*ethical atmosphere might unleash. Indeed, speaking of one of the unduly admired individuals whom we shall meet later, an anonymous poster with much more sense rightly made the following self-evident point:

> One problem with the whole idea of the "crazy-wise" teacher is that [Adi] Da can claim to embody anyone or anything, engage in any sort of ethical gyration at all, and, regardless of disciples' reactions, Da can simply claim his action was motivated as "another teaching." He thus places himself in a position where he is *utterly immune from any ethical judgment* (in Bob, 2000; italics added).

More plainly, there can *obviously* be no such thing as a "strict ethical atmosphere" in any "crazy wisdom" environment.

But perhaps Trungpa and Tendzin—a former close disciple of Satchidananda, who was actually in charge of the latter's Integral Yoga Institute in the early '70s (Fields, 1992)—had simply corrupted that traditional "atmosphere" for their own uses? Sadly, no:

> Certain journalists, quoting teachers from other Buddhist sects, have implied that Trungpa did not teach real Buddhism but a watered-down version for American consumption, or that his teaching was corrupted by his libertine outlook. After doing Vajrayana practices, reading texts on them by Tibetan authorities, and visiting Buddhist centers in the United States and Europe, I was satisfied that this allegation is untrue. The practices taught in Vajradhatu are as genuinely Buddhist as anything in the Buddhist world....
>
> Dilgo Khyentse Rinpoche, *after the Tendzin scandal,* insisted to Vajradhatu students that Trungpa had given them authentic dharma, and they should continue in it exactly as he had prescribed (Butterfield, 1994; italics added).

Dilgo Khyentse Rinpoche—"Rinpoche" being a title meaning "Precious One"—was head of the oldest Nyingma or "Ancient Ones" School of Tibetan Buddhism from 1987 until his death in 1991.

Even with all that, Peter Marin (1995)—a non-Buddhist writer who taught for several months at Naropa in 1977—still validly observed that the activities at Naropa were relatively tame, compared to the oppression which could be found in other sects.

In the end, though, Andrew Harvey (2000) put it well:

> In general, I think that nearly all of what passes for "crazy wisdom" and is justified as "crazy wisdom" by both master and enraptured disciple is really cruelty and exploitation, not enlightened wisdom at all. In the name of "crazy wisdom" appalling crimes have been rationalized by master and disciple alike, and many lives have been partly or completely devastated.

One is of course still free, even after all that, to respect Trungpa for being up-front about his "drinking and wenching" (in Downing, 2001), rather than hypocritically hiding those indulgences, as many other guru-figures have allegedly done. That meager remainder, however, obviously pales drastically in comparison with what one might have reasonably expected the legacy of any self-proclaimed "incarnation of Maitreya Bodhisattva" to be. Indeed, by that very criterion of non-hypocrisy, one could admire the average pornographer just as much. Sadly, by the end of this book, that point will only have been reinforced, not in the least diminished, by the many individuals whose questionable influence on other people's lives has merited their inclusion herein. That is so, whatever their individual psychological motivations for the alleged mistreatment of themselves and of others may have been.

To this day, Trungpa is still widely regarded as being "one of the four foremost popularizers of Eastern spirituality" in the West in the twentieth century—the other three being Ram Dass, D. T. Suzuki and Alan Watts (Oldmeadow, 2004). Others such as the Buddhist scholar Kenneth Rexroth (in Miles, 1989), though, have offered a less complimentary perspective:

"Many believe Chögyam Trungpa has unquestionably done more harm to Buddhism in the United States than any man living."

* * *

> Sometimes the entire Institute seems like a great joke played by Trungpa on the world: the attempt of an overgrown child to reconstruct for himself a kingdom according to whim (Marin, 1995).

Through all of that celebrated nonsense "for king/guru and country," the Naropa Institute/University continues to exist to the present day, replete with its "Jack Kerouac School of Disembodied Poetics." Previous offerings there have included courses in "Investigative Poetry"—though, sadly, no corresponding instruction in "Beat Journalism." Also, at their annual springtime homecoming/reunion, participation in "contemplative ballroom dancing." (One assumes that this would involve something like practicing *vipassana* "mindfulness" meditation while dancing. Or perhaps not. Whatever.)

Indeed, a glance at the Naropa website (www.naropa.edu) and alumni reveals that the '60s are alive and well, and living in Boulder—albeit with psych/environmental majors, for college credit.

CHAPTER XVIII

SIXTY MINUTES

(SWAMI MUKTANANDA)

> Why do false Gurus exist? It is our own fault. We choose our Gurus just as we choose our politicians. The false Guru market is growing because the false disciple market is growing. Because of his blind selfishness, a false Guru drowns people, and because of his blind selfishness and wrong understanding, a false disciple gets trapped. *A true disciple would never be trapped by a false Guru* (Muktananda, 1981; italics added).

> I had a private *darshan* ... with Swami Muktananda in India three days before he died, and I thought he was a magnificent man, an incredibly loving man (Anthony Robbins, in [Hamilton, 1999]).

BORN IN 1908 IN MANGALORE, India, Swami Muktananda, like Neem Karoli Baba, was a disciple of the respected guru Bhagawan Nityananda, whom he met in 1947.

Not coincidentally, in 1970 Ram Dass introduced Muktananda to America.

To aid his world mission in furthering the practice of kundalini yoga, Muktananda in 1974 established the SYDA (Siddha Yoga) Foundation, with headquarters in South Fallsburg, NY.

SYDA admirers have included Jerry Brown, Carly Simon, James Taylor, Diana Ross and Isabella Rossellini. Also, Rosanna Arquette, Meg Ryan, *The Cosby Show's* Phylicia Rashad, *Miami Vice's* Don Johnson and his wife Melanie Griffith, and Marsha Mason (Neil Simon's ex-wife). Plus, singer Mandy Patinkin, celebrated songwriter Jimmy Webb—composer of both "MacArthur Park" and "Up, Up and Away (With My Beautiful, My Beautiful Guru....)"—and astronaut Edgar Mitchell.

* * *

> Whoever has attained spiritual perfection has done so through his Guru. The Guru grants a life full of grace, complete freedom, and liberation of the Self. The Guru's favor is absolutely necessary for lasting attainment. Without a Guru man is unhappy; with a Guru he is full of joy. So *surrender yourself completely to the Guru* (Muktananda, 1978; italics added).

> The Guru should possess every virtue.... He cannot be a true Guru if he ... indulges in sense pleasures....
>
> Without the Guru, it is not possible for a person to understand the Truth (Muktananda, 1999).

Muktananda's specific view toward conjugal relations, further, reportedly took the following form:

> Muktananda advised his devotees to refrain from sex.... "For mediation," he told a South Fallsburg audience in 1972, "what you need is ... seminal vigor. Therefore I insist on total celibacy as long as you are staying in the ashram" (Harris, 1994).

But then, those rules are obviously there only for the benefit of the disciples, not for the guru who no longer needs them.

> At his Ganeshpuri, India, ashram, "he had a secret passageway from his house to the young girls' dormitory," one [ex-follower] reported. "Whoever he was carrying on with, he had switched to that dorm. [He] had girls marching in and out of his bedroom all night long" (Rae, 1991).

One of the girls thus allegedly marching—"Jennifer"—claimed to have been raped by the great guru in early 1978.

> Muktananda had intercourse with Jennifer for an hour, she said, and was quite proud of the fact. "He kept saying, 'Sixty minutes,'" she said (Rodarmor, 1983).

"An incredibly loving man."

The "celibate" guru's reported tolerance for sex, however, apparently did not extend to sexual tolerance:

> "A Guru would never be flirting with mistresses or hobnobbing with homosexuals," a 1976 Muktananda missive reads. "Homosexuals are considered to be eunuchs—disgusting, impure, and inauspicious" (Chew, 1998).

* * *

> If Shiva is angry, the Guru can protect you, but if the Guru becomes angry, no one can save you (in Muktananda, 1999).

Unfortunately for his disciples, then:

> "Muktananda had a ferocious temper," said [Richard] Grimes, "and would scream or yell at someone for no seeming reason." He [claims that he] saw the guru beating people on many occasions (Rodarmor, 1983).

Indeed, Noni Patel, the guru's valet, reportedly once sought treatment for an odd wound in his side.

> "At first, he wouldn't say how he had gotten it," Grimes' wife Lotte recalled. "Later it came out that [Muktananda] had stabbed him with a fork" (Rodarmor, 1983).

A clear breach of etiquette, that.

* * *

Former journalist Sally Kempton, a.k.a. Swami Durgananda, began following Muktananda in 1974. After decades in the ashrams of the "fully enlightened" Muktananda and his successor, she returned to the secular world in 2002, to teach. She has since found work as a columnist for *Yoga Journal,* and been interviewed on Ken Wilber's Integral Naked forum (www.integralnaked.org).

Lis Harris' (1994) article on SYDA, however, contains numerous segments involving Durgananda and her denials of Muktananda's alleged behaviors, all of them very much worth reading.

* * *

Of Muktananda's own sagely guru, Nityananda (who died in 1960), the following information is extant:

> He was a born *siddha* ["perfected being"], living his entire life in the highest state of consciousness (Muktananda, 1999).

> He was an omniscient being; still he appeared as if he didn't know much....
>
> Only occasionally would he speak; however, you could not understand him (Muktananda, 1996).

"He was the best of gurus; he was the worst of gurus," etc.

> [W]hen in his twenties, he would hide behind trees, patiently waiting for a cow to come his way. The moment the animal stood to drop a cowpat, he would rush forward, scoop up the dropping in midair, and then swallow it (Feuerstein, 1992).

Yum. Nor did such feasting exhaust the yogi's interest in cows and their rectal output:

> He would at times be seen in the middle of the road (there was hardly any motor traffic in those days), catching the dropping from a cow before it fell to the ground, putting it on his head, and then whistling just like a railway engine and chugging away, as children often do (Hatengdi, 1984).

"Woo-woo! Next stop, Looney Station."

> [Nityananda] would speak quite frequently about devotees who had the mentality of a crow. A crow, even in heaven, said Baba, insists on eating shit, because that is what he has been accustomed to. And this is exactly how these faultfinding devotees behave (Muktananda, 1996).

Cows, crows, choo-choos ... and more:

> On another occasion, he besmeared himself from head to toe [i.e., including his lips] with [human] excrement. He sat near the lavatories, with large heaps of excrement piled in front of him. Each time a devotee passed him, he would call out, "Bombay halwa [sweets]—very tasty—want to eat? Can weigh and give you some" (Feuerstein, 1992).
>
> South Park Yoga.

* * *

By the time of Muktananda's death in 1982, his SYDA Foundation operated eleven ashrams and hundreds of meditation centers worldwide. He was initially co-succeeded by his disciple Gurumayi (1955 – present) and her younger brother. Following an alleged power struggle in the mid-1980s in which that latter sibling left the organization under disputed circumstances, however, Gurumayi rules alone (Harris, 1994).

Allegations of abuses and harassment by SYDA can be found at www.leavingsiddhayoga.net, as well as in Harris (1994).

CHAPTER XIX

THE MANGO KID

(BHAGWAN SHREE RAJNEESH)

> [Rajneesh] stated that he himself had attained [Enlightenment] at the age of twenty-one.... [H]e went on to declare that ... there was only one Enlightened Master at any particular time, and that he was the one (Milne, 1986).

> *The Rajneesh Bible* ... was really "the first and last religion" (Gordon, 1987).

BHAGWAN SHREE RAJNEESH, BORN in 1931, achieved his first *satori/samadhi* at age fourteen. Prior to embarking on a world mission which was to secure his place as one of the world's most *infamous* guru-figures, he served as a philosophy professor at central India's Jabalpur University in the late '50s and early '60s.

In 1974, he founded his first ashram in Poona (Pune), southeast of Bombay.

Rajneesh's followers have reportedly included the Japanese composer Kitaro, and the former Françoise Ruddy. She earlier, along with her then-husband Albert, had produced *The Godfather* (Fitzgerald, 1986). They and Bhagwan Rajneesh's other disciples followed teachings which were a combination of "rascal"/"crazy wisdom" behavior, tantric sexual practices, and often-violent (i.e., to the point of reported broken bones) Western human potential movement (cf. Fritz Perls, etc.) encounter groups.

Being renowned as the "Guru of the Vagina," Rajneesh was, of course, said to be sleeping with a selection of his female disciples, particularly via "special *darshans*" granted to them in the movement's foundling/fondling years. Vivek, one of the earliest and closest of those, was claimed to be the reincarnation of Mary Magdalene (Milne, 1986).

> Sometimes [Bhagwan] would ask attractive women to strip off in front of him and lie naked while he peered at them intently. Then, after satisfying himself, he would ask them to get dressed again. He also had couples make love in front of him, a definite case of voyeurism....
>
> In the later years, in Poona, many sexual experiments were tried. Bhagwan told one woman how to overcome her phobia of rats: she should indulge in oral sex.... In another tantric session at Poona, the male participants had to eat a ripe mango from between their female partners' legs. The mangoes were very popular with everyone (Milne, 1986).

In the midst of that revelry, vasectomies were "suggested" for the ashram men—a quarter of whom complied.

In 1976, the homophobic (as per Andrew Harvey [2000] and Storr [1996]) Rajneesh made it known that he was going to be selecting twelve female "mediums" from the ashram for nightly, restricted-group "energy *darshans.*" The purpose of those was to be the transferring of his energy through them to the community, and to the world at large.

As to the characteristics which Bhagwan was looking for in his mediums, he soon explained:

> [O]nly women with large breasts could hope for the honor. "I have been tortured by small-breasted women for many lives together," he announced to a startled audience, "and I will not do it in this life!" (Milne, 1986).

At least one of those twelve Buddhalicious Babes was reportedly instructed not to wear panties to the nightly "energy transferring" sessions.

> Rajneesh has said at some time that underwear interferes with the passage of energy (Gordon, 1987).

> Former mediums claimed to have had sexual contact with Bhagwan for the purpose of "stimulating our lower chakras" ... and for "orchestrating our energies" (Palmer and Sharma, 1993).

> He would manipulate my genitals, masturbate me, but it was also as if he was rewiring my circuits (in Gordon, 1987).

* * *

> There were few legal ways in which a Westerner could earn money [to stay at the Poona ashram], and before long many of the girls turned to prostitution....
>
> The other main way of making money in those days was to mount a drug run (Milne, 1986).

For the same financial reasons,

> a large number of strippers working from London's SoHo to San Francisco's North Beach were *sannyasins* (Strelley, 1987).

In Rajneesh's parlance, *sannyasis/sannyasins* were simply initiated disciples, not seasoned monks as the term would be taken to refer to in other traditions.

By the late 1970s and early '80s, this particular "inner city path to spiritual enlightenment" was beginning to have some predictable reported side-effects:

> Three British *sannyasins* ... were arrested on smuggling charges in Paris in 1979. The most ambitious known smuggling attempt was made in 1979 when fifty kilograms of marijuana were packed into the frame and furnishings of a hippie-style bus traveling from [Poona] to Europe. About twenty disciples had invested in the deal and another twenty had worked on the bus. The contraband, however, was discovered in Yugoslavia, and three *sannyasins* were put in jail for a year (Mangalwadi, 1992).

> One *sannyasi* murdered another in one of the hut villages about a mile from the ashram, and another was found dead

with multiple stab wounds beneath the nearby Mulla-Matha bridge (Milne, 1986).

In the midst of those difficulties, seeking to expand his work and desiring to escape a reported $4 million in unpaid income taxes, Rajneesh quietly left India for the United States in 1981, arriving via a 747 jet in New Jersey.

Pausing at the top of the departure stairs as he exited the plane, the sage expansively proclaimed:

> I am the Messiah America has been waiting for (in Milne, 1986).

And this was when the *real* problems began.

Rajneesh first settled in at the Montclair castle in New Jersey, and then founded an ashram ("Rajneeshpuram") in eastern Oregon, purchasing the 120-square-mile Big Muddy ranch in Wasco County there. (That ranch had formerly been the barren filming location of several John Wayne westerns.) His eventual goal was to establish a million-population city in that region.

So as to not unnecessarily alarm their conservative neighbors, the proselytizing materials available from the ashram were screened and re-evaluated. Consequently, "The Fuck Tape"—consisting of Rajneesh "extolling and describing at length the forty different possible uses of the word 'fuck'" (Milne, 1986)—was recast as "a discourse in which Bhagwan makes jokes about human relationships."

Rajneesh went on to assemble the world's largest private collection of Rolls-Royces—ninety-three in total. The combination of Bhagwan's public silence, increasing isolation from his surrounding ashram community, and large Rolls-Royce collection, soon manifested as the new phenomenon of "car-shan," or drive-by blessings. There, the faithful would line up to catch a glimpse of His Holiness during his daily trips into the nearest town—Antelope, population thirty-nine—forty-five minutes away.

Meanwhile, privileged residents and visitors to Oregon and the Rajneesh ashrams/communes elsewhere enjoyed horseback and aircraft rides, boating, swimming and river rafting.

> To complete the Club Med appeal, discos, bar lounges and gaming tables were made available in late 1983 (Palmer and Sharma, 1993).

And thereby was the table set for the fortunate few to "eat, drink and be merry," for

> shortly before [Rajneesh] came out of his three and a half year silence, he prophesied with great drama and precision that two-thirds of humanity would die of the disease AIDS by the year 2000 (Palmer and Sharma, 1993).

That off-base prediction was based on Bhagwan's understanding of a Nostradamus verse. (For a debunking of the latter purported seer, see Randi's [1993] *The Mask of Nostradamus*.)

Fears that insiders at the Oregon ashram may have been plotting to murder Rajneesh soon took root, however. Thus, in late 1984, Bhagwan and his "right-hand woman," Sheela, allegedly commenced with spending $100,000 per month on the installation of wiretapping and bugging equipment throughout Rajneeshpuram (Milne, 1986).

Directing their attention as well to concerns outside of the ashram, followers in the same year

> spiked salad bars at ten restaurants in [nearby The Dalles, Oregon] with salmonella and sickened about 750 people (Flaccus, 2001).

The goal there was apparently to incapacitate large numbers of voters, allowing the Rajneesh-sponsored candidates to prevail in county elections. A contamination of the local water supply was reportedly planned for after the "test" restaurant poisoning.

Investigations into that salmonella outbreak ultimately revealed an alleged plot to kill the former U.S. Attorney for Oregon, Charles Turner. Though the attack was never actually carried out, in the hope of derailing the investigation into their other activities some of Rajneesh's loyal followers nevertheless reportedly

> assembled a hit team in 1985. They bought guns, watched Turner's home, office and car, and discussed ways to assassinate him (Larabee, 2000).

Following all that, and with the continuing failure of his apocalyptic predictions for the near-end of the world to materialize —as they had previously dissipated in 1978 and 1980—Rajneesh was deported from the U.S. for immigration violations in 1985. He was refused entry by at least twenty countries before finally returning to his old ashram in Poona, thereby leaving Americans either waiting longer for their Messiah ... or being glad that he had left.

The Oregon ashram closed down soon after Bhagwan's departure. (Various followers were later convicted on assault, attempted murder, wiretapping and food poisoning charges [Larabee, 2000].) Today, it serves as a summer Bible camp for teenagers safely devoted to following their own, more conservatively acceptable (but still long-haired, robe-wearing, "only one Enlightened Master") Messiah.

* * *

The use of consciousness-altering drugs was never officially approved-of in either the Poona or the Oregon ashrams. In spite of that, by 1982 Rajneesh was allegedly sniffing nitrous oxide (i.e., laughing gas) to get high on a daily basis. On one occasion, six months into that, reportedly reclining in his own $12,000 dentist chair and babbling,

> Bhagwan went on: "I am so relieved that I do not have to pretend to be enlightened any more. Poor Krishnamurti ... he still has to pretend" (Milne, 1986).

Krishnamurti—who actually considered Rajneesh to be a "criminal" for his abuse of the guru-disciple relationship—was the only "sage" whom Rajneesh had ever acknowledged as an equal. (Bhagwan himself denied being a guru, but those denials are no more convincing than were Krishnamurti's own.) Indeed, by contrast to their man-made, imported white-sand Krishnamurti Lake in Oregon, in an open show of contempt for another of his "main competitors" in the enlightenment industry, Rajneesh named a sewage lagoon there after Swami Muktananda. The latter's own guru, the shit-eating Nityananda, would surely have approved ... and perhaps even gone for a dip.

At any rate, having returned to India, Bhagwan's "enlightenment" soon improved to the extent where he could announce that

> Gautama the Buddha had entered his body, and that this had been verified by the seeress of one of the most ancient Shinto shrines in Japan (Hamilton, 1998).

> Rajneesh, as the reincarnation of Gautama Buddha, fits the model of the Second Coming ushering in the Thousand Years of Peace (Palmer and Sharma, 1993).

The Buddha himself, however, made do with a simple Tree in his own spiritual practice or *sadhana,* never having had access to a "Bodhi *Chair"* of Enlightenment.

Of course, Rajneesh was by no means the first "spiritual seeker" to reportedly make use of nitrous oxide in his quest:

> William James thought he had recorded the ultimate mystery under the influence of nitrous oxide. On returning to his normal state, he eagerly consulted the paper on which he had scrawled the great message (DeRopp, 1968).
>
> That message?
>
> Hogamous, Higamous,
> Man is polygamous.
> Higamous, Hogamous,
> Woman is monogamous.

* * *

Rajneesh died of a heart attack in 1990 at age fifty-eight, but not before changing his name to "Osho" ("Beloved Master"), under which authorship his books are currently being marketed. His Poona ashram continues to host devotees from around the world—up to 10,000 at a time—in an increasingly resort-like, "Club MEDitation" atmosphere. Indeed, the environment currently features waterfalls, a giant swimming pool, a sauna and cybercafe, and tennis courts where "zennis" (non-competitive Zen tennis) is played.

> "Osho has become a cocktail party name," said Sanjay Bharthi, thirty-four, a freelance graphic designer who described the Osho lifestyle as "so aesthetic, so juicy, so modern, and at the same time so peaceful" (Waldman, 2002).
>
> In India the once-persecuted Rajneesh is currently the country's best-selling author. His books are on display in the federal parliament library—an honor accorded to only one other, Mahatma Gandhi (Hamilton, 1998).

Indeed, worldwide Osho book (two thousand titles in forty-four languages) and audio-book sales now surpass $1 million annually (McCafferty, 1999). There is, of course, scant mention in those honored books of

- Rolls-Royces
- Homophobia
- Prostitution
- Drug-running
- Tax evasion
- Wiretapping
- Salmonella
- Assassination plots
- Nitrous oxide sniffing, or
- Mangoes ... in syrup

CHAPTER XX

DA AVATAR, DA BOMB, DA BUM

(ADI DA, A.K.A. DA AVATAR, DA LOVE-ANANDA, DA AVABHASA, DA AVADHOOTA, DAU LOLOMA, MASTER DA, DA FREE JOHN, BUBBA FREE JOHN, FRANKLIN JONES)

The works of Bubba Free John are unsurpassed (Wilber, 2001a).

It looks like we have an Avatar here. I can't believe it, he is really here. I've been waiting for such a one all my life (Alan Watts, in [Da, 1974]).

Adi Da ... is the Divine World-Teacher, the Giver of Divine Enlightenment, Who has made all myths unnecessary and all seeking obsolete....

The Divine Avatar, in the guise of "Franklin Jones," had not come to Liberate just a few others, individuals who might be thought qualified for such a hair-raising "adventure." Not at all. He had come to *all* beings (in Da, 1995).

> [Da] has repeatedly said, in recent months, that the year 2000 is the year he will be recognized by the world. He has even gone so far as to claim that Christians will recognize him as the Second Coming of Christ (Elias, 2000).

> Da Love-Ananda tells [his disciples] that he can do no wrong, and they, in all seriousness, see in him God incarnate (Feuerstein, 1992).

BORN ON LONG ISLAND, NY, in 1939, "the guise of Franklin Jones" lived until age two in an internal state which he later called "the Bright."

> [A]s a baby, I remember only crawling around inquisitively with a boundless feeling of Joy, Light, and Freedom in the middle of my head.... I was a radiant Form, the Source of Energy, Love-Bliss, and Light in the midst of a world that is entirely Energy, Love-Bliss, and Light. I was the power of Reality (Da, 1995; all capitalization is in the original).

Following the gradual fading of that perspective as he grew up, the future guru earned a bachelor's degree in philosophy from Columbia University in New York, in 1961. At one point, when asked by his uncle Richard what he wanted to do with his life, Da (1995) expressed the serious wish to "save the world."

And yet, as Wilber (1983) himself has noted:

> [A]ny group "out to save the world" is potentially problematic, because it rests on an archaically narcissistic base that looks "altruistic" or "idealistic" but in fact is very egocentric, very primitive, and very capable of coming to primitive ends by primitive means.

In late 1964, Jones began studying kundalini yoga in New York City under "Rudi" (Swami Rudrananda), a disciple of Muktananda.

> In a sentimental mood, Da Free John once mused, "Rudi loved men and I love women. Together we could have fucked the world" (Lowe, 1996).

Jones visited Muktananda's ashram in India in 1968. By May of 1970, he had made two additional similar trips. Experiences produced in Jones by the intense meditations overseas included a vision of the Hindu goddess Shakti.

Following that, while meditating in the (Ramakrishna-Vivekananda) Vedanta Temple in Hollywood in the autumn of 1970, Jones had a spiritual "experience where there was no experience whatsoever." Through that, he was "spontaneously and permanently reawakened in the Enlightened Condition he had enjoyed at birth." Describing that non-experience, Jones has said:

> I felt the Divine Shakti appear in Person, Pressed against my own natural body, and, altogether, against my Infinitely Expanded, and even formless, Form. She Embraced me, Openly and Utterly, and we Combined with One Another in Divine (and Motionless, and spontaneously Yogic) "Sexual Union" (Da, 1995; all capitalization is in the original).

Or, more colorfully, in referring to the same awakening:

> The Goddess used to say, "Yield to me," and I fucked her brains loose (Free John, 1974).

In 1972, Jones and a friend opened the Ashram Bookstore on Melrose Avenue in Los Angeles, attracting his first devotees, "many of them street people" (Lattin, 1985a).

After another visit to Muktananda in India in 1973, Jones enacted the first of his many name-changes, becoming Bubba Free John. (In the late '70s, Free John took the "Da" epithet—an ancient name of God meaning "the Giver"—and, in 1994, added the "Adi," thus becoming not merely Realized but Palindromic.) He also founded his first ashram on a former resort in Lake County, on Cobb Mountain, California. That location is still referred to by his followers as the Mountain of Attention.

The following year, Free John declared himself to be "the Divine Lord in human Form" (Gourley and Edmiston, 1997).

> [Those who] follow Jones believe he is an "adept," a person who came into this world already enlightened with eternal truth. The sect's publications also call Jesus an "adept," but make it clear that Jones is considered more important (Leydecker, 1985).

Also in 1974, during his "Garbage and the Goddess" period, Bubba apparently

> started his "sexual theater," involving the switching of partners, sexual orgies, the making of pornographic movies and intensified sexual practices (Feuerstein, 1996).

The *Mill Valley Record* (Colin, et al., 1985) further reported:

> [James] Steinberg [head of the Hermitage Service Order] says the destruction [of the pornographic films] took place a few months after they were made. Steinberg also says that the church's dildo collection was either sold or destroyed, he isn't sure which.

"The church's dildo collection." Sold or destroyed. Amen.

"If you'll now open your hymnals to the centerfold, let us all sing together, 'God, Oh God, I'm Coming.'"

Interestingly, one of Da's lingerie-modeling daughters, Shawnee Free Jones, has more recently appeared as an actress in *L.A. Confidential* and *Baywatch.*

At any rate, by 1985 the sect had around one thousand active members—a third of them living in Marin County, California—with another 20,000 on its mailing lists. (To this day, active membership remains at around a thousand.) Members there were reportedly expected to tithe from 10 to 15% of their income to the new church; in the higher levels of the spiritual order, they were asked to donate as much as they could.

In that same year, however, the alleged concerns of former disciples began to surface in public, as exposed in a series of articles published in the *San Francisco Chronicle* and *Examiner:*

> [Da, they claim] would have them watch pornographic movies and engage in anal sex—sometimes in front of him, and sometimes tell them to go to their bedrooms (in Lattin, 1985a).

> As a child, [a devotee of Da] had been sexually abused by a neighbor. To help her through her sexual fears [she] said, Da Free John told her to have oral sex with three group members, and then the guru had sex with her himself.
>
> "I was hysterical," she said. "After it was over, I went out into the parking lot and found an open car, and had a

> good cry and went to sleep. I was traumatized. It's years later that I came to terms with it" (Butler, 1985a).

In later years, a married couple of Da Party Animal's followers were apparently invited over to his house, only to find the guru in bed, drinking beer and surrounded by cigarette smoke.

In short order, the wife was allegedly prepared by other followers, to be taken sexually by the guru. "And so she was."

Suppressing his "irrational feelings" into numbness, however, the husband soon found a suitable rationalization for that, convincing himself that the guru was simply teaching him to not be emotionally attached to his wife.

And yet, doubts linger, both about whether the same lessons could possibly have been learned in some easier way, and otherwise:

> There is one thing that has *persistently* bothered me about the incident, and that was the pressure on me to drink alcohol in an attempt to get me drunk. I still feel I was being manipulated on this count. I also never quite understood why we were asked to keep the whole incident quiet (in Feuerstein, 1992).

Yes, interesting questions, all.

* * *

As of the mid-'80s, the Daists (followers of Da Guru) operated a "Garden of Lions" school in upstate New York. Of the pupils there, it was reported that one thirteen-year-old child and his classmates adorned and venerated a bowling ball. As the student himself put it:

> I always felt a love-connection towards the ball and served it remembering that the Master would touch it someday and give it his attention (in Lake County, 1985).

For my own part, that reminds me of nothing so much as growing up with the '70s sitcom, *What's Happening!!* Specifically, the episode where Rerun got "brainwashed" by a "cult," and ended up worshiping a head of lettuce named Ralph.

It seemed funnier then, than it does now. (No word on whether Da's bowling ball had a name.)

* * *

In any closed society run by a "Divine Lord in human form," of course, it would be rare for any of the peer-pressured members to openly question "the thread-count of the emperor's clothes," as it were. Indeed, as former residents of Da's community have alleged:

> Anybody who dares to stand up to [Adi Da's] bullying is quickly sent packing (Elias, 2000a).

Elias himself taught at Naropa in the late 1970s (Bob, 2000), and later worked as a typesetter in the Dawn Horse Press in the early '80s.

On another occasion, Da Guru was asked about the source of his apparent arrogance. A former community member reported his response:

> I only do this as an act.... It could be much worse (in Lake County, 1985).

Indeed, Jones himself has apparently claimed elsewhere that, regardless of what his behaviors might superficially appear to be, he is nevertheless "always Teaching."

And yet, the contexts in which the same reported behaviors appear, but where they cannot reasonably be excused as a mere "act," betray the real motivations. For example, consider Da's alleged response in a dispute over noise coming from an ashram adjacent to his Hawaiian one, run by a rival guru. After an unsuccessful attempt by Jones' followers to make so much racket at a big New Year's party that their opponent would be sure to support a noise ordinance,

> Jones [allegedly] went completely livid, swearing and criticizing them for coming up with the idea for this, when he himself had endorsed it.
>
> "He always preached that people shouldn't come up with a strategy or plan to life. Here he was, demanding 'Give me a strategy' to get this guy" (Neary, 1985).

Or contemplate Jones' alleged reaction (reported in the *Mill Valley Record*) to the devotee laborers on a construction project having worked many sixteen-hour days in building a home for him:

> The work schedule and the meager fare took a toll on the work force. On Christmas Day, [Mark] Miller says he told Jones, "The people are tired. They need a break." Miller says Jones replied, "They will work for me until they drop and then they'll get up and work some more" (Colin, et al., 1985).

Of course, such evident dearth of compassion has been demonstrated many times before—by Da Scrooge if not Da Avatar.

* * *

In 1980, Ken Wilber penned a fawning foreword for Adi Da's *Scientific Proof of the Existence of God Will Soon Be Announced by the White House!* (I have dealt in depth with the problems with Wilber's character, ideas, and community, in the companion book to this one, *"Norman Einstein": The Dis-Integration of Ken Wilber.*) Most of it was spent in arguing that Da was not creating a harmful "cult" around himself, but Wilber also found space to include the following praise:

> [M]y opinion is that we have, in the person of Da Free John, a Spiritual Master and religious genius of the ultimate degree. I assure you I do not mean that lightly. I am not tossing out high-powered phrases to "hype" the works of Da Free John. I am simply offering to you my own considered opinion: Da Free John's teaching is, I believe, unsurpassed by that of any other spiritual Hero, of any period, of any place, of any time, of any persuasion.

Not finished with hyperbole—or "syrupy devotionalism," as one critic (Kazlev, 2003) reasonably put it—in 1985 Wilber contributed effusive text for the front matter of Adi Da's *The Dawn Horse Testament:*

> This is not merely my personal opinion; this is a perfectly obvious fact, available to anyone of intelligence, sensitivity, and integrity: *The Dawn Horse Testament* is the most ecstatic, most profound, most complete, most radical, and most comprehensive single spiritual text ever to be penned and confessed by the Human Transcendental Spirit.

Obviously, any sincere seeker reading such ecstatic praise from the most highly respected "genius" in consciousness studies (as Wilber has been regarded for the past quarter of a century) might be inclined to experience for himself the teachings of such a unique, "greatest living" Adept. Indeed, had I come across those endorsements in my own (teenage years, at the time) search, and been aware of and unduly awed by Wilber's status in the consciousness studies community, I myself might well have foolishly taken such exaggerations seriously enough to experience Adi Da's community discipline first-hand.

How unsettling, then, to discover a 1987 interview with *Yoga Journal,* only a few short years after the *Dawn Horse* ejaculations, where Wilber stated his opinion that Adi Da's "entire situation has become very problematic." Nearly a *decade* later (1996a), he explained: "'Problematic' was the euphemism that sociologists at that time were using for Jonestown."

For my own part, not being a sociologist, I would never have caught on to the meaning of that "unsafe word" without having it explained to me ... albeit years after the fact, here. I suspect that I am not alone in that regard.

No matter: Three years later, in 1990, Wilber was back to contributing endorsements for Da's teachings, this time to the humbly titled *The Divine Emergence of the World-Teacher:*

> The event of Heart-Master Da is an occasion for rejoicing, for, *without any doubt whatsoever,* he is the first Western Avatar to appear in the history of the world.... His Teaching contains the most concentrated wealth of transcendent wisdom found anywhere, I believe, in the spiritual literature of the world, modern or ancient, Eastern or Western (in Bonder, 1990; italics added).

Note that, in the above quote, Wilber is evidently considering himself fit not merely to pronounce on the degree of enlightenment of others, but even to confirm their avatar status, "without any doubt whatsoever."

Of the above author Bonder (2003) himself—who has since independently adopted the status of teacher, without Adi Da's blessing—Wilber has more recently declared:

> Saniel Bonder is one in whom the Conscious Principle is awakened.

Again, note the oracular nature of the statement, as no mere expression of opinion, but rather as a without-doubt, categorical evaluation of another person's spiritual enlightenment—as if Wilber himself were able to see into others' minds, or clairvoyantly discern their degree of conscious evolution.

Others, however, have reasonably questioned the possibility, even in principle, of anyone executing such over-the-top insight:

> [B]oth mystics and sympathetic writers about mysticism are just wrong if they think that there is a way of telling whether the other person has had a genuine experience or just pretends to have had one....
>
> A man may write excellent love poetry without ever having been a comparable lover; it is the writer's skill as a writer that makes his words convincing, not his skill as a lover. The mystic's talk about his experience may be skillful or clumsy, but that does not improve or weaken his actual experience (Bharati, 1976).

A mere seven years before the aforementioned "problematic" *Yoga Journal* piece, Wilber (in Da, 1980) had again ironically been "protesting too much," in print, that Adi Da was not creating a harmful environment around himself:

> [N]owhere is [Da] more critical of the "cultic" attitude than he is towards those who surround him.... I have never heard Da Free John criticize anyone as forcefully as he does those who would approach him chronically from the childish stance of trying to win the favor of the "cultic hero."

Other fans of Da—even those who have comparably considered him to be "the ultimate expression of the Truth residing in all religions"—however, have claimed to find in his followers exactly what Wilber would evidently rather not see:

> The problem was they were much too friendly, much too happy, and far too nice. More plainly put, they were all busy breathlessly following their own bliss. Not only this, but unless my eyes were deceiving me, *they all looked like maybe they came from the same neighborhood or the same college.* It was uncanny really. And very disquieting, as well. I mean, they all looked and sounded almost exactly alike.
>
> My God, they're pod people, I thought (Thomas Alhburn, in [Austin, 1999]; italics added).

Hassan (1990) gives a completely plausible explanation for such phenomena:

> One reason why a group of [alleged] cultists may strike even a naïve outsider as spooky or weird is that everyone has similar odd mannerisms, clothing styles, and modes of speech. What the outsider is seeing is the personality of the leader passed down through several layers of modeling.

Prior to actually meeting Adi Da and his followers, Alhburn had not only blurbed for Da's books but had actually written a foreword for one of them. Also blurbing have been "stages of dying" expert Elizabeth Kübler-Ross, and Barbara Marx-Hubbard. The former was credited by *Time* magazine as being one of the "100 Most Important Thinkers" of the twentieth century. The latter, Marx-Hubbard, is the president and a founding member of The Foundation for Conscious Evolution; she was once called "the best informed human on the concept of futurism," by Buckminster Fuller.

Sad. Very sad.

Wilber closed his aforementioned (1996a) admonitions regarding Da Seclusive Avatar—sequestered in Fiji, by that point—with the relative caution that, until the day when the "World Teacher consents to enter the World," one might just keep a "safe distance" as a student of Da's writings, rather than as a resident of his community. As to how Adi Da "re-entering the world" from his island seclusion would alleviate the "problematic" aspects of his teachings, however, that was not made clear.

By comparison, would Jim Jones re-entering the world from his isolated agricultural commune in Guyana have made *his* teachings safe? If not, why would a comparable re-entry have been the solution to the "problematic" (Wilber's word) aspects of Adi Da? Isn't it better for the world at large—if not for their unfortunate, already duped followers—if these misfits *do* isolate themselves?

At any rate, none of the above milquetoast caveats from Wilber have ever been included in any of his books, where they might have reached "a hundred thousand" people (Wilber, 2000a). Rather, in terms of kw's own attempts at promoting that version of reality, the (1996a) letter exists, at the time of this writing, only on his publisher/author website ... buried in the Archives section, not sharing the home page with his many accolades.

Wilber later (1998a) offered an explanatory open letter to the Adi Da community. That was posted *anonymously* (i.e., evidently not by Ken himself) on the Shambhala KW Forum for date 8/1/01 in the Open Discussion area, a full three years after the fact. (That forum itself has existed since early 2000.) There, he clarified his position on Da Realizer, back-tracking significantly from any insight which one might have been tempted to credit him from 1996, and explicitly stating that he had not renounced his view of (or love for, or devotion toward) Da as Realizer. Rather, he argued simply that Da's "World Teacher" status enjoindered upon him the maintaining of a presence in the world, and the initiation of an "even more aggressive outreach program" by the community, as opposed to his ongoing seclusion.

An *"even more aggressive outreach program."* To put a positive spin on a "problematic" situation, and "spread the word" to more people, thereby doing *more* harm? Or perhaps simply to warn potential devotees as to what they're getting themselves into, as if that would then clear up all of the reported problems with the community? (Would "Jim Jones with a warning label" have been the solution to *his* "problematic" craziness?)

Again, as posters in Bob (2000)—themselves making no claim to genius, but clearly adept in common sense—have insightfully (and independently) pointed out:

> I find it absurd that Wilber seems to attach more importance to criticizing Da's failure to appear in public forums than he does to examining the very serious [alleged] abuses of trust and misuse of power that have [reportedly] been perpetrated by Da under the guise of spiritual teaching. In light of the well-documented [reported] problems that Da has created in his own life and his follower's [*sic*] lives, it is completely irrelevant to any evaluation of Da whether or not he accepts Ken's challenge to go out into the world at large. Who cares! Why would anyone want to see Da broaden his influence by speaking to a larger audience?

Precisely.

The full text of Wilber's aforementioned (1998a) open letter to the Daist Community is eminently worth reading, toward one's own disillusion regarding the caliber of advice given by even the "brightest lights" in the spiritual marketplace. To summarize its contents: Wilber states that he neither regrets nor retracts his past endorsements of Adi Da; that it is only for cultural and legal considerations (i.e., for evident protection when "Da Shit hits Da Fan") that he can no longer publicly give a blanket recommendation for people to follow Da; that he is pleased that his own writings have brought people to Da Avatar and hopes that they will continue to have that effect in the future; and that he still recommends that "students who are ready" become disciples/devotees of Da.

A month and a half after distributing the above nuggets of wisdom to the Adi Da community, Wilber (1998b) reconfirmed his position in another open letter, posted as of this writing on his website. There, he states—with rarely encountered opacity—that the "real difficulty of 'the strange case of Adi Da' is that the guru principle *is neither understood nor accepted by our culture"* (italics added). He further opines (italics again added) that

> for those individuals who realize full well the extremely risky nature of the *adventure,* but who feel a strong pull toward *complete and total surrender* of their lives to a spiritual Master, I can certainly recommend Adi Da.... [H]e is one of the greatest spiritual Realizers of all time, in my opinion.

Note further that the related title, "The Strange Case of Franklin Jones," was used in 1996 by David Lane and Scott Lowe, in their exposés of Da/Jones and his ashram environment. Unless that was a common phrase going around in the mid-'90s, then, it would seem that Wilber was likely aware of their earlier, insightful critique of the dynamics reportedly going on within Adi Da's community. Rather than properly absorbing the information in that, however, he has evidently simply seen fit to give his own, purportedly more valuable version of the same—even though looking on merely from a safe distance, not as a first-hand, residential participant. That is sad, since Lowe and Lane have offered real insight into the situation, while Wilber has consistently failed miserably to do the same.

One further assumes that in praising Da's spiritual state, Wilber was referring more to the man's later realizations than to early insights such as the following:

> I remember once for a period of days I was aware of a world that appeared to survive in our moon. It was a superphysical or astral world where beings were sent off to birth on the Earth or other worlds, and then their bodies were enjoyed

> cannibalistically by the older generation on the moon, or they were forced to work as physical and mental slaves (Da, 1995).

Then again, the later realizations have their problems, too:

> In 1993, Adi Da Revealed that Ramakrishna and his principal disciple, Swami Vivekananda, are the deeper-personality vehicle of His bodily human Incarnation (in Da, 1995).

"Ramakrishna, Part II: Return of the Booby."

Of course, unless one is inclined to take the visions of "astral moon cannibal slaves" on the part of "Da greatest living Realizer" seriously, one arrives at serious concerns as to Adi Da's mental stability. After all, skeptics have long rightly held that even a single instance of any given medium (e.g., Blavatsky) or ostensibly *siddhi*-possessing sage being caught "cheating" in "manifesting" objects, casts doubt on every "miracle" that had previously been attributed to the individual. Likewise, if even one aspect of an individual's enlightenment has been hallucinated but taken as real, the potential exists for it to *all* have been the product of delusion in a psychiatric, not a metaphysical, sense.

So you have to ask yourself: Do *you* believe that there are B-movie-like "cannibal masters/slaves" on the astral counterpart to our moon?

Wilber, at least, seems (in Da, 1985) to have no doubt, overall:

> I am as certain of this Man as I am of anything I have written.

Well put. I, too, am as certain of Adi Da's unparalleled enlightenment, "astral moon cannibal slaves" and noble character as I am of anything Wilber has ever written.

* * *

Over the years, Adi Da has taken credit for numerous "miracles," such as a "brilliant corona that stood around the sun for a full day" (in Free John, 1974). No scientist or skeptic, though, would ever accept such anecdotal claims as evidence of a miraculous control over nature. And with good reason, particularly given Lowe's (1996) eye-witness testimony of the same "miraculous event":

> I had been outdoors all that afternoon. Not only had I seen nothing out of the ordinary, but no one within my earshot had mentioned anything at all about the miracle at the very time it was supposedly happening! I was not trying to be difficult or obtuse, but this proved too much for me. If a great miracle had occurred, why was it not mentioned at the time? I asked a number of devotees what they had seen and why they had not called everyone's attention to it, but received no satisfactory answers. It slowly emerged that I was not alone in missing this miracle; my skeptical cohorts on the community's fringe were similarly in the dark.

There might even have been *some* (natural) coronal effect visible to *some* members of the community. And they, being "desperate for confirmation of their Master's divinity, [may have] exaggerated the significance of minor synchronisms, atmospheric irregularities, and the like." That, however, would still hardly qualify as a miracle. It would further do nothing to ease one's concern about the members of the community, like Lowe, who didn't see that "authenticated miracle," reportedly being quickly demoted to positions of lower status for not going along with the group version of that reality.

One is strongly reminded, in all that, of the research on conformity done in the 1950s by psychologist Solomon Asch. For there, experimental subjects in the midst of other, unknown (to them) confederates, were required to match the lengths of two lines. After the planted confederates had deliberately given wrong answers, the subjects were asked for their responses.

> [They frequently] chose the same wrong answer, even though they did not agree with it (Lalich, 2004).

Another classic experiment in social psychology involves a participant standing on a busy city sidewalk, and staring up into the sky at nothing in particular. When performed by just that single person, few of the people passing by will glance up, and probably no one will actually stop to stare up with the individual.

Should you, as that participant, bring along several friends to the same spot to look upward with you, however, the result will be quite different:

> Within sixty seconds, a crowd of passersby will have stopped to crane their necks skyward with the group. For those pe-

> destrians who do not join you, the pressure to look up at least briefly will be nearly irresistible (Cialdini, 2001).

Indeed, in one experiment performed by Stanley Milgram and his colleagues, 80% of the passersby were drawn to look at the empty area.

In that light, one may better appreciate the importance of, for example, Adi Da's first "street people" disciples. For, when beginning any movement, it is less important that the first converts be of any high caliber than that they simply be "warm bodies." As soon as a small group is thus formed, others will "look up at least briefly," or "stop and stare" altogether, simply for having seen the social proof of the validity of your new path in the very existence of that group.

* * *

Da's "sun corona" manifestation was again included as a documented "miracle" in his (1974) self-published, and thus Implicitly-Approved-By-Him, *Garbage and the Goddess.* (Nearly all of the "enlightened" figures mentioned herein have gotten their writings into print only via self-publication.) And if, as Lowe hints, the "miracle" itself never happened, Da of all people would have known that from the beginning. Why then would he have proceeded with allowing it into print? To publish something like that in the hope of *decreasing* "cult-like" following would have been an interesting approach indeed, since it could only have had exactly the opposite effect.

Further, since Wilber had read that book prior to writing the above 1980 and 1985 forewords—it is listed in the bibliography for his (1977) *Spectrum of Consciousness*—one must ask: Does this mean that he was accepting that apparently non-existent "miracle" as being valid? One cannot help but assume so, since the alternative would be to say that Wilber regarded Da as not accurately presenting his spiritual accomplishments, but still chose to pen his gushing forewords.

Da's "corona miracle" seems to have come into being not via any trickery, but simply via an "emperor's new clothes" conformist mentality on the part of the witnesses in his community. Still, if *one* such "verified miracle" of Adi Da, "witnessed" by all of the members in good standing of his society, should thus turn out to be invalid, and yet be touted as real by the guru himself, how much confidence should one have, not merely in the community consensus as to Da's "great Realization," but even in the remainder of the claims made by Da Guru himself?

* * *

Having heard Wilber's skewed interpretations of Adi Da's work and environment, now read, if you wish, the 1985 exposé series, preserved in the *Daism Research Index* at www.lightmind.com. Then decide for yourself whether Wilber's point of view on all this has any validity at all.

Or, more pointedly, ask yourself how, in the face of all that easily accessible information, anyone of sound mind and body could still recommend that others "surrender completely" to someone like Adi Da. *What kind of a "genius" would compare an environment to Jonestown, for being (in his own words) "problematic," and yet still encourage others to "surrender completely" to its god-man leader?!*

> By the standards of traditional society, [Adi Da] is like the man in the madhouse claiming to be Napoleon who has convinced a few of the other patients that he is the Boss. But the people walking around outside the walls of his Loka [i.e., his world] with-bars-on-the-windows say "Yes, you think you are Napoleon, but we don't think so. You claim to be the Most Enlightened Being Ever Was and Ever Will Be, but we don't think so. It just doesn't add up. By traditional religious standards, you are quite insane, totally nuts, absolutely bonkers, a real freakazoid nutcase...."
>
> One man against the world ... and about a thousand people have bought his one-way rap (Bob, 2000).

Or, as another disillusioned ex-follower put it:

> One can imagine Da in a previous lifetime as a minor European nobleman, exploiting his impoverished serfs, sleeping with their wives and daughters, and living a splendidly dissipated life of luxury, all in the name of the divine right of kings. As a model for proper behavior in the twilight of the twentieth century, Da seems neither better nor worse than, say, Marlon Brando or Keith Richards (Lowe, 1996).

"Sympathy for the Da-vil."

* * *

Sal Luciana was formerly a close friend of Jones from their Scientology days in 1968 until their falling-out in 1976. He was credited by Da with having achieved a "nearly 'instant enlightenment'" (in Free John, 1974). He further expressed (in Lattin, 1985a) his own evaluation of Jones' perspective on the world, as follows:

> At this point, I think he really thinks he is God.... If you had every whim indulged [since 1972], how would you think of yourself?

And still, "they call him by many names, who is but One God."

Franklin Jones. Franklin, Benjamin. Franklin Mint.
Bubba Free John. Bubba Louie. Da Quicksdraw.
Da Free John. Da Free Paul. Da Free George. Da Ringo.
Da Love-Ananda. Da Love-Bliss. Da Loves-You, Yeah-Yeah-Yeah.
Dau Loloma. Dau La'Samba. Ba-Da-Da-Da-Da La Bamba.
Da Do Run Rerun, Da Do Run Run.
De Do Do Do, De Da Da Da.
Master Da. Master John. Master Bates. Da Dildo.
Adi Da. Da Avatar. Da Bomb.
Da Bum.
D'uh.
Zippity Do Da.

The late Da Hoogivesahoot (d. November, 2008) spent much of the 1980s and '90s living in Fiji, on an estate formerly owned by Raymond Burr. He was reportedly kept company there by thirty long-time devotees, and by his nine (9) "wives." Included among those "insignificant others" was September 1976 Playboy centerfold Whitney Kaine (Julie Anderson), a former cheerleader whom Da Avatar had reportedly stolen away from her tennis-playing, high-school-sweetheart boyfriend, also a devotee of his, back in the 1970s.

Well, "La Dee *Da*."

CHAPTER XXI

SOMETIMES I FEEL LIKE A GOD

(ANDREW COHEN)

> Andrew Cohen is not just a spiritual teacher—he is an inspiring phenomenon. Since his awakening in 1986 he has only lived, breathed and spoken of one thing: the potential for total liberation from the bondage of ignorance, superstition and selfishness. Powerless to limit his unceasing investigation, he has looked at the "jewel of enlightenment" from every angle, and given birth to a teaching that is vast and subtle, yet incomparably direct and revolutionary in its impact (from the "About the Author" section in [Cohen, 1999]; self-published).

ANDREW COHEN WAS BORN in New York City in 1955.

He spent his formative years—either from ages five to fifteen (Cohen, 1992), or from age three into his twenties (Tarlo, 1997), depending on whom you choose to believe—undergoing psychoanalysis.

When Cohen was sixteen years old, he experienced a spontaneous expansion of consciousness "in all directions simultaneously" into infinite space, along with a "revelation" concerning the interconnectedness and inseparability of all life.

A few years later, he was initiated into kriya yoga (a variant of kundalini yoga in general) by a "direct disciple" of Paramahansa Yogananda (i.e., by one who knew the yogi when he was alive). Having practiced that technique for six months, Cohen was blessed with a temporary kundalini surge and a vision of blazing white light.

After giving up his musical aspirations in despair of not finding perfect, lasting spiritual happiness through them (in his version)—or of not having the right stuff to get to the top as a drummer (in his mother's version)—he traveled to India, meeting his future wife (Alka) there. In 1986 in that country, after having experienced several "betrayals" at the hands of earlier teachers, he met his guru, Hari Wench Lal (H. W. L.) Poonja. The latter was presenting himself as an enlightened disciple of the widely celebrated sage Ramana Maharshi. Maharshi himself, however, not only never confirmed anyone else's enlightenment but had no official disciples and no recognized lineage.

With or without that spiritual connection, however,

> Poonjaji told me several stories of people who had faith in him and had experienced miraculous and sudden cures from illnesses (Cohen, 1989).

During Cohen's first meeting with Poonja he fell into a profound enlightenment experience of "emptiness." That was confirmed as real by Poonja, and seems to have duly impressed both Andrew and his guru:

> Poonjaji told me that I had the same look in my eyes as his Guru Ramana Maharshi did. He said that he had seen these eyes only three times in his life: in his Guru's, in his own and in mine (Cohen, 1992).

As Poonja himself put it:

> I knew this would happen—you're the one I've been waiting for my whole life and now that I've met you I can die (Cohen, 2002).

Of course, Poonja did eventually die, but not before using the same "you're the one I've been waiting for all my life" line several years later on a female disciple, whom he reportedly sent to America to effectively "clean up Andrew's mess."

That, however, would be getting ahead of our story.

For the time being, both guru and disciple were very much in love with each other and with the idea of enlightenment. Indeed, as Poonja (in Cohen, 1992) intimated to Andrew's mother Luna Tarlo, who had by then joined them in India:

> You don't know how rare this is. Something like him ... only happens once in several hundred years.
>
> [Poonja] read a list of the names of all the Buddhas that had come into this world. When he got to the end of the list he read out my name and then looked at me and smiled (Cohen, 1992).

Following his enlightenment, and with only a scant two and a half *weeks* of training, Poonja sent Cohen out into the world as a teacher, with great expectations. Andrew himself then reportedly confirmed his own feelings, of now having a special purpose in life—and a fairly messianic one at that—to his mother:

> "Believe it or not Poonja and I might be the only two people in the whole world doing the [enlightenment] work we're doing," Andrew said (Tarlo, 1997).

As another early disciple of Cohen tells it:

> Poonjaji has told him he will create a revolution amongst the young in the West! "I pass my mantle on to you," Poonjaji had said (van der Braak, 2003).

If that "mantle-passing" from guru to disciple sounds disturbingly familiar, that is because the same phrase comes up between the biblical Elijah and Elisha, just before Elijah was taken up to heaven in a fiery chariot, having given a "double portion" of his own blessings to Elisha:

> He [Elisha] took up also the Mantle of Elijah that fell from him, and went back, and stood by the bank of Jordan (2 Kings 2:13).

In the contemporary acting-out of that incident, then, Poonja has placed himself in the position of Elijah—who, in some reincarnation-based interpretations (e.g., Yogananda, 1946), was also John the Baptist. Cohen, on the other hand, plays the part of Elisha, or Jesus Christ.

Such a comparison might well have displeased Poonja, however, given his positively unbridled attitude toward his own spiritual attainment:

> "I'm only jealous of one man," [Poonja] said. "Who was that?" I asked. "The Buddha," he replied, "he's the only one who surpassed me" (Cohen, 1992).

Of course, being the foremost disciple of such an exalted figure is bound to do wonders for one's self-image. Thus, in Andrew's own reported, enlightened words (in Tarlo, 1997):

> [V]ery few people like me exist in the world. I can destroy a person's karma.... If you trust me, I have the power to completely destroy your past.
>
> Anyone who loves me ... is guaranteed enlightenment.
>
> You know, Luna, sometimes I feel like a god.

Regarding "Luna": Cohen always referred to his mother by her first name, even before his "enlightenment."

At any rate, the god-like Andy C. quickly took his wife as a disciple, and reportedly pressured his mother (Tarlo, 1997) into the same—thus exhibiting *atrociously poor* judgment in both of those relationships. Nevertheless, the latter mother, in particular, was soon to benefit from Cohen's spiritual largesse, apparently being informed over afternoon tea—to her own surprise—that she was now enlightened.

Another disciple, Dvora, evidently profited comparably, reportedly being notified one morning by Andrew that "her enlightenment was complete" (Tarlo, 1997). Being thus ostensibly fully enlightened, however, apparently did not absolve loyal disciples such as Dvora of discipline at the hands of the guru. Indeed, she seems to have discovered that the hard way when bleakly informing Andrew of her parents' pressures on her to come home, i.e., to leave India and Cohen:

> "You're a hypocrite, a liar, and a prostitute," Andrew said [to Dvora] in cool measured cadence and he got up, and went to his bed and lay back, and turned on the TV (Tarlo, 1997).

Such, allegedly, were Cohen's applications of "skillful means" toward the enlightenment of his followers.

It would be getting ahead of our story to disclose that Cohen's mother no longer considers herself to be enlightened. Nor does she anymore regard herself as an "unvirgin" holy mother to the erstwhile Messiah, Andrew.

The "messiah" epithet is actually not at all out of place here, for the possibility was apparently actually floated, among Cohen's followers, that he may have been the reincarnation of the Buddha. As Poonja himself declared: "The twentieth century is lucky to have seen the Perfect Buddha reborn to live with them to Free [*sic*] them from the miserable *samsara*" (Cohen, 1992). Not to be outdone, disciples of Cohen reportedly also suggested that Andrew may have been the reincarnation of Jesus Christ (Tarlo, 1997).

Ironically, the messiah-figure in Monty Python's *Life of Brian* also had the surname Cohen. The contemporary namesake wins in quantity, however, counting around a thousand disciples—although only about a hundred live in his *sangha*—to the fictional Brian's mere dozens.

Of course, as with guru-figures in general, we should hardly be surprised to find it claimed that "respect was Andrew's obsession." As he himself reportedly put it:

> I am no longer an ordinary man leading an ordinary life. And from now on, no one will spend time with me unless they treat me with respect (in Tarlo, 1997).

As to the loyalty which the Antidangerfield guru evidently expected from his followers, then, Andre van der Braak (2003) gives the unsettling example of a committed student reportedly needing to be willing "rather to be burned alive than betray Andrew."

Interestingly, Poonja once stated his view of the guru-disciple relationship to Andrew as, "Do not be attached to the teacher" (in Cohen, 1989). Cohen's own perspective in recent years, however, has apparently grown to encompass exactly the polar opposite of that position:

> [O]ne cannot be too dependent upon a truly enlightened person, Cohen said, exasperated. "The more attached you get to a person like that, the more free, literally, you become." Cohen derided the importance that people in general, and Westerners in particular, give to independence....
>
> Cohen's belief in his own specialness kept coming to the fore. Those who are enlightened, he said, by definition can do no wrong. They "are no longer acting out of ignorance, in ways that are causing suffering to other people" (Horgan, 2003).

That, of course, is the most dangerous belief which any human being could hold. Yet, it is the normal attitude of any loyal disciple toward his or her "perfect" guru, invariably demanded by the latter, as we have already explicitly seen with Trungpa, Da, and many sad others:

> Maharishi [Mahesh Yogi] can do no wrong (Scott, 1978).

> [Rajneesh] can't be wrong (Belfrage, 1981).

* * *

It is easy to show, via the same contextual comparison method which we have utilized for previous "crazy wisdom" practitioners, that Cohen's reported rude behavior, like Adi Da's and Trungpa's, apparently lacks any wise or noble basis.

For example, consider that in 1997 an Amsterdam newspaper printed a generally complimentary review of a lecture there by Cohen. The piece ended with the ironic but nevertheless fairly innocent observation that, although the guru had his students shave their heads, Cohen's own hair was well coiffed.

When that article was read to Andrew in English, Cohen reportedly "shows no response until those last lines. Then he pulls a face":

> "What a bastard, that interviewer. He seemed like such a nice guy. Call him up Harry! Tell him he's a jerk."

When Harry sensibly resists burning that PR bridge, Cohen apparently shoots back:

> He's an incompetent journalist. Then just tell him he's no good at his profession (in van der Braak, 2003).

If the journalist in question had been a formal disciple of Andrew's, everyone involved would have had no difficulty at all in rationalizing Cohen's reported temper as being a "skillful means." That is, his rumored outburst would have been meant only to awaken the scribe from his egoic sleep. That hypothetical situation, however, is not at all the case. We should therefore not credit Cohen's reported response, at such absolutely minimal provocation, as being anything more than infantile. Further, we must take alleged eruptions such as that as forming the "baseline" for the man's behavior, against which all other potentially "skillful means" are to be judged.

My own considered opinion is that when the baseline of such "noise" is subtracted from Cohen's reported behaviors in the guru-disciple context, there is nothing at all left to be regarded as a "skillful means" of awakening others in that.

* * *

Cohen has founded numerous spiritual communities or *sanghas* in North America. Initially, he had his disciples rent shared houses in Amherst, Massachusetts, in 1988. They soon moved the community to Boston, and later to Marin County, California, in the summer of 1989. Then back to a $2 million "Foxhollow" ashram in the Berkshires of Massachusetts in 1997. For the latter privilege, each moving disciple reportedly paid one thousand dollars for each year that he had been a disciple of Cohen, to a maximum of five grand.

Andre van der Braak began following Cohen in 1987, living in the latter's *sangha* for eleven years. During that period, he acted at various times as the head of the community editorial department, specifically as an editor for both *What Is Enlightenment?* magazine and for Cohen's first book, *Enlightenment is a Secret.*

He further (2003) expressed his own early, inflated enthusiasm for Cohen's enlightenment work within that shifting community, as follows:

> This is an evolutionary experiment; we are the forerunners in an evolutionary wave that will transform the western spiritual world!

Life within that "evolutionary" community, however, appears to have unfolded in a less than heavenly manner. Indeed, the overall inculcated attitude reportedly involved a banishing of personal or independent life in favor of enforcing Andrew's rules, and of "living for the sake of the whole" (van der Braak, 2003).

It is, however, only by making our own mistakes as individuals that we can learn. If one goes through life simply "making other people's mistakes," obediently following their instructions and rules regardless of how obviously wrong those may be, the best that one can hope to learn from that is to appreciate the importance of thinking for oneself. And that latter realization, as long as it may take for one to properly appreciate, is just the *start* of the unfolding of one's full human potential, never the *end* of it.

Toward the close of van der Braak's own decade-long involvement with Cohen, the enforced *sangha* discipline reportedly took the form of six hundred prostrations each morning, done while repeating a mantra created by the enlightened master: "To know nothing, to have nothing, to be no one."

> This is the message he wants engraved in our brain (van der Braak, 2003).

Tarlo (in van der Braak, 2003) further describes Cohen as exhibiting an "ever growing paranoia and ferocious will to control." Under that alleged mindset, disciplined life in his community is said to have entailed, at one time or another:

- Followers doing up to a thousand prostrations in a ten-hour period each day, on the orders of Cohen
- The guru instructing his devotees to shave their heads and maintain celibate relations to prove their dedication to his path. At one point, approximately one-fifth of the community were shaven celibates
- Disciples willfully destroying $20,000+ cars, at Cohen's instruction and indeed with him present, to demonstrate their non-attachment and sincerity
- Successful painters renouncing their art, at Andrew's misled counsel, for it allegedly being simply "an extension of ego," and thus ostensibly an impediment to enlightenment

- Followers throwing their secular books into the Ganges, and obediently incinerating their life's writings (with no known backups), on Cohen's demand
- Disciples surviving for extended periods on five hours or less of sleep per night, not by choice but by necessity for meeting the community schedule of mandatory activities
- Students on meditation retreats not being allowed to have personal conversations, only being permitted to discuss Cohen's summary of his teachings in his "five fundamentals"
- Injuctions by Cohen against his disciples entertaining intellectual pursuits. As Tarlo (1997) put it: "I mentioned to [Andrew] that I'd glanced at [Wilber's] *Up from Eden* and he told me not to read further in the book because it was intellectually stimulating [*sic*]"
- Cycles of expulsion and readmission to the community, for devotees who had fallen out of favor with Cohen. Those were then given second or third chances to work their way back up into Andrew's good graces
- And, as is the case with every spiritual community, anyone who leaves "is viewed with scorn and contempt. He hadn't the courage to face himself" (van der Braak, 2003)

After all that, Luna Tarlo (1997) summarized her own opinions regarding Cohen's guruship:

> It just seems to me that [Andrew] is as duped by his own propaganda as were all those other brother-gurus in the marketplace who promised deliverance from suffering—from Hitler to David Koresh.

Note that that wholly negative, Hitler-comparing evaluation comes from Cohen's own *Jewish mother* and former disciple. Tarlo still loves him "as her son," but will rightly have nothing further to do with the activities which stem from him feeling "like a god."

* * *

As we have hinted at above, Ken Wilber's writings have traditionally generated a uniquely high level of interest within the inner circle of Cohen's community. Andre van der Braak had actually done his psychology thesis on Wilber, piquing Cohen's curiosity with his associated bookshelves full of kw's ponderous works, and resulting in their reported collective brainstorming as to how to get Wilber in as a student of Cohen's.

> We speculate about why he hasn't been willing to meet with Andrew. *Is he afraid of ego death?* (van der Braak, 2003; italics added).

Their persistent courting evidently paid off, however, for in Wilber's foreword to Cohen's (2002) *Living Enlightenment* we read:

> [Rude Boys] live as Compassion—real compassion, not idiot compassion—and real compassion uses a sword more often than a sweet. They deeply offend the ego (and the greater the offense, the bigger the ego)....
>
> Andrew Cohen is a Rude Boy. He is not here to offer comfort; he is here to tear you into approximately a thousand pieces ... so that Infinity can reassemble you....
>
> Every deeply enlightened teacher I have known has been a Rude Boy or Nasty Girl. The original Rude Boys were, of course, the great Zen masters, who, when faced with yet another ego claiming to want Enlightenment, would get a huge stick and whack the aspirant right between the eyes.... Rude Boys are on your case in the worst way, they breathe fire, eat hot coals, will roast your ass in a screaming second and fry your ego before you knew what hit it....
>
> I have often heard it said that Andrew is difficult, offending, edgy, and I think, "Thank God." In fact, virtually every criticism I have ever heard of Andrew is a variation on, "He's very rude, don't you think?"

Of course, Tarlo's (1997) exposé of Cohen had been published nearly *half a decade before* Wilber's penning of that odd mixture of images. Had kw properly informed himself of that, he would most certainly have heard criticisms of Cohen which could *in no way* be dismissed as arising merely from overly sensitive egos complaining about not being sufficiently coddled. (Needless to say, Cohen disputes the accuracy of the depiction of life in his communities given by his own mother, and presumably does not agree with van der Braak's sketching of it, either. The WHAT enlightenment??! website, though, offers many additional, generally equally uncomplimentary stories from other former disciples.)

If being a "Rude Boy" simply means speaking unpleasant truths, then yes, "every deeply enlightened teacher" has probably done that. Such beneficial behavior, however, is *vastly* different from what Trungpa, Adi Da and Cohen (unlike, say, Aurobindo and Ramana Maharshi) have allegedly indulged in.

Further, just because a "master" is a "Rude Boy" toward others *obviously does not mean* that his own "breakthrough" into claimed radical enlightenment was the product of having previously been treated in that way himself! Indeed, neither Adi Da nor Cohen nor Trungpa have recorded their own enlightenments as arising from being on the receiving end of such behavior. That fact is radically significant, as is the fact that neither Da nor Cohen, explicitly, have managed to produce *even one* disciple as "enlightened" as they themselves claim to be, in spite of their "rude" behaviors.

> It does have to be considered at this point that there are no practitioners in the advanced and ultimate stages (Da, in [Elias, 2000a]).

> None of Cohen's students have become liberated (Horgan, 2003).

Beyond that, the whole disturbingly violent "whack between the eyes" thing is, as we have seen, a rather absurdly romanticized view of Zen. Indeed, one cannot help but wonder: Has Wilber himself ever received such a beneficial, hard blow between the eyes with a huge stick, or literally had the crap beaten out of him? Was that what brought on any of his early, "verified" *satoris,* or his nondual One Taste realization? If not, he has no business recommending such treatment to others.

Notwithstanding all of those concerns, other revered spiritual figures have been equally impressed by Cohen, on the mere basis of his *writings,* as has the easily excitable Wilber. Indeed, as Penor Rinpoche, head of the Nyingma School of Tibetan Buddhism since 1991, put it (in Cohen, 2000):

> I have an appreciation for Andrew Cohen's works on the quest of the spiritual path, which explore the essence of religious faith. His work is very beneficial for anyone curious about Enlightenment as the ultimate goal. I have confidence

that *Embracing Heaven & Earth* will bring great benefit to readers and seekers in their spiritual practice.

Rinpoche's endorsement there, too, came well after the 1997 publication of Tarlo's exposé of Cohen. He and Wilber are hardly alone in that regard, however, in having failed to do the relevant research before offering a confident opinion. Indeed, others in the same embarrassing situation include the head of the Sivananda ashram, who averred that Cohen "shines like a light in darkness." Also, the president of Kripalu, the science fiction writer Amit Goswami, Lama Surya Das, and Swami Chetanananda of the Nityananda Institute. (For the latter, see LNI [2003] and Read [2001].) All of those individuals enthusiastically endorsed Cohen (2000), as did the "God-realized" John W. White (cf. 1997), who there commended Cohen as being a "RAMBO-dhisattva," or spiritual peace-warrior.

Presumably, the titles "Rocky of Ages"—with his trusty, admiring sidekick, the "Bullwinkle of consciousness studies"—and "Cohen the Barbarian" were already taken.

Body Shop founder Anita Roddick, too, has in recent years fallen for Andrew's brand of salvation—inconsistent as that discount brand may be:

> "I don't like unconditional love," [Andrew] says. "Love always has to be earned" (van der Braak, 2003).

Of course, such radically conditioned love would be the complete opposite of what Dr. Elizabeth Debold (in Cohen, 2000) credits Andrew with expressing. For there, she lauds exactly "his demand that we realize and live a love that has no bounds."

A love with "no bounds" would obviously be *unconditional* and not needing to be "earned," after all, would it not?

The "real compassion" of which Wilber speaks with such certainty then allegedly manifests through Cohen in this manner:

> I don't give a damn about your personal evolution anymore. I just want to be able to use you for my community (in van der Braak, 2003).

Of course, not everyone reacts positively to such "compassionate, Rude Boy" discipline. Indeed, the reported experiences of one particularly unfortunate disciple of Cohen, who lived in a "state of chronic panic" and allegedly ultimately ended up "under a psychiatrist's care, thoroughly sedated" (Tarlo, 1997), would reveal as much.

As Pavlov himself again discovered in having animals try to distinguish between flattened circles and fairly round ellipses, initially excitable dogs could easily feel constant panic, in not knowing how to please their "master," when *pleasing the master, however little he may have merited that respect, is all that matters.* Obviously then, when spiritual disciples are driven to such literal panic and madness, that breakdown has nothing whatsoever to do with their own alleged "psychological immaturity." Nor does it have anything to do with the phenomenological nonsense of supposedly being "unable to face up to the fact that naked Reality, which reveals itself when our conceptual grids are removed, is an unimaginable richness of actualities and possibilities" (Feuerstein, 1992).

And what was Cohen's reported "non-idiot compassion"-based response to all of that?

> "Enlightenment and madness are very close." Then he laughed, and added, spookily, "It could happen to any one of you" (Tarlo, 1997).

* * *

Aside from attempting to spread his teachings through his books and personal counsel within his spiritual community, in 1992 Cohen founded *What Is Enlightenment?* magazine. That bi-annual (now quarterly) periodical has been praised by Wilber (in Cohen, 2002) as follows:

> Andrew's magazine ... is the only [one] I know that is ... asking the hard questions, slaughtering [needlessly violent macho imagery, again] the sacred cows, and dealing with the Truth no matter what the consequences.

The avant-garde biologist Rupert Sheldrake likewise opines (in Cohen, 2005):

> *What Is Enlightenment?* magazine is a unique forum for inquiry that goes deeper and reaches further than any other spiritual magazine I know.

Other former residents of Cohen's spiritual community, however, have voiced far less complimentary opinions of that same publication, calling it "a hodge-podge of opinions that go nowhere. A foray into mental masturbation."

At a back-issue price of $9 U.S. per glossy, full-color copy, however, there are cheaper ways of mentally ... um....

Anyway, Cohen's own books are themselves no examples of fine literature, metaphysical or otherwise, being abundantly padded with blank pages and unnecessarily large—generally nearly double spaced—leading between lines of text. For example, of the seventy-two total pages, including front and back matter, in his self-serving (1999) tract, *In Defense of the Guru Principle*, twenty-six are blank, and four others contain only section/chapter headings. Eight more are taken up with the foreword and preface, giving the book an unbelievable "Don't Need To Read This" rating of 38/72 = 53%, even independent of its nearly double-spaced content.

Cohen's equally widely spaced *Living Enlightenment*—endorsed by Barbara Marx-Hubbard—fares marginally better, with a DNTRT of around 30%. A rating of 5% would be more typical for an average book. Beyond both of those unimpressive texts, however, the gargantuan amount of white space in Cohen's *Enlightenment is a Secret* must be seen to be believed. Was there an ink shortage? Or a paper surplus?

When you read and research a lot, you notice things like that. When you pay full price for such vacuous creative artistry and environmental unconsciousness, you notice it even more.

Centering a teaching around "emptiness" is one thing. But blatantly padding books with thick, unruled, empty sheets of paper—useful neither for note-taking nor for toiletry—is taking it to an extreme. Nor would a *real* publisher take that route to such a painfully obvious, tree-wasting degree—which Roddick, of all people, should have noted and objected to at first glance.

Of course, Wilber (2000a; italics added), as usual, sees things differently:

> [U]ntil the ecologists understand that the ozone hole, pollution, and toxic wastes are all completely part of the Original Self, they will never gain enlightened awareness, *which alone knows how to proceed* with these pressing problems.

Anyone with the least comprehension of those issues, however, can easily see that the first step in "knowing how to proceed" is simply to "stop the bleeding." If Cohen's "enlightened awareness" only makes the bleeding *worse*, that is to be expected. For, it has never been the Self-realized "meditation masters" of this world who have stood at the front line of any battles, environmental or otherwise. Rather, it has always been the looked-down-upon and "less spiritually advanced" activists who have taken the risks and effected those changes. (Rare exception: Zen roshi Robert Aitken, whose efforts have at times "depart[ed] radically from the Japanese Zen tradition in which opposition to political authority has been negligible and civil disobedience unknown" [Tworkov, 1994]. In his demonstrations against nuclear testing and sexual inequality, however, he has surely stood side-by-side with many others for whom Zen and the like were little more than distant curiosities. Yet, they were every bit as able to see "how to proceed" as he was. Still, both Aitken and Cohen are arguably doing better than the enlightened Wilber himself, if one considers his black leather furniture [Horgan, 2003a] and Thanksgiving turkey dinners [Wilber, 2000a] from an animal rights perspective. One need not even agree with that often-judgmental alternative view in order to see that Wilber is in absolutely no position to lecture ecologists or the like on how to create a better world by becoming "more like him.")

Cohen's books themselves are all published by Moksha Press, which is again simply the *self-publishing* vehicle for his own teachings. In any such situation, one would confidently expect not merely the text but the promotional materials for any publication to be at least vetted, if not actually written, by the author-publisher himself. Thus, the inflated "About the Author" description of Cohen's greatness which opened this chapter could not reasonably have been put into print without his own full approval.

* * *

Cohen eventually split from his own guru, Poonja, upon learning of various indiscretions in the master's conduct, including his having reportedly fathered a child via a blond, Belgian disciple. He explained that communication breakdown simply in terms of himself having "surpassed [his] own Teacher" (Cohen, 1992).

Of course, all humility aside, Poonja obviously considered himself to have accomplished the same "surpassing the Teacher" feat. For he regarded only the Buddha as being above him, in spite of claiming Ramana Maharshi as his own guru and teaching lineage. That is, Poonja could not have been "second" to the Buddha if he had not, in his own mind, surpassed his teacher, Maharshi.

If Andrew has now surpassed Poonja, that presumably places him too above Maharshi, and second in line to the Buddha himself.

Freely casting aside any remaining sense of perspective, then, in experiencing unexpected resistance to his humble "revolution," Cohen (1992) wrote that it was only the "hypocrisy and self-deception" of others in the face of his "truth" that caused them to be afraid of him.

More recently, following the publication of Tarlo's exposé of her claimed experiences in Cohen's spiritual community, significant concerns were publicly raised about the health of that environment. In response, Andrew (1999) gave his explanation as to the origin of the controversies then swirling around him, as being the product only of his own uncompromising integrity.

Unfortunately, integrity enforced from within the context of an allegedly "fiercely controlling" perspective, coupled with absolute authority in that same position, is still a chilling concept, bound to result in disaster. "Being true to their ideals" in such a context is, indeed, probably something which the leaders of any totalitarian regime could claim just as validly.

> Sociologist Hannah Arendt, who covered [Nazi] Adolf Eichmann's trial, made the telling statement: "The sad and very uncomfortable truth of the matter was that it was not his fanaticism but his very *conscience* that prompted [him] to adopt his uncompromising attitude." Eichmann had said himself that he would have sent his own father to the gas chamber if ordered to (Winn, 2000; italics added).

* * *

It was not so long ago that Cohen was reportedly teaching that "there are no accidents" (in Tarlo, 1997). Conversely, he was (2000) emphasizing the need for all individuals to "take responsibility for their entire karmic predicament":

> The reason that *The Law of Volitionality* [the second of the "five tenets" of Cohen's formalized path] is such a challenging teaching is that we live in a world where most of us are convinced that we couldn't possibly be responsible for everything that we do. And the reason that we believe we couldn't

> possibly be responsible for everything that we do is simply because we are convinced that we are victims....
>
> [T]hose who ... want to be free more than anything else ... are willing to whole-heartedly *take responsibility for absolutely everything that they do* [italics added].

Only slightly more recently, however:

> Cohen derided the notion—promulgated by New Agers and traditional believers alike—that everything that happens to us has been divinely ordained or at the very least happens for a reason. "The narcissism in that kind of thinking is so blatant, I mean, it's almost laughable."
>
> Pain and suffering often occur in a random fashion, Cohen assured me. He and his Indian-born wife, Alka, were crossing a street in New York City a few years earlier [i.e., in 1994] when they were hit by a car and almost killed. "I was going, 'Why did this happen?' And I realized that it didn't happen for any particular reason. It just happened" (Horgan, 2003).

As far as being "almost killed," however, Cohen merely suffered a broken right arm and injuries to his right calf in that accident; his wife sustained a concussion and a fractured jaw. All in all, those are fairly minor wounds, considering the context, i.e., one could just as well feel lucky for having incurred no spinal or internal organ damage. Indeed, a different person might actually manage to turn the same incident into a proof that "God was watching over them." For, considering that they "could easily have been killed," isn't it "a miracle" that they survived with such minor injuries?

Independent of that, the responsibilities shirked by Cohen in his accident—i.e., in him not "taking responsibility for absolutely everything he has done"—boil down to him simply *not watching where he was going*. The taxi, after all, did not ride up onto the sidewalk; rather, Andrew and his wife stepped straight into its path, albeit at a red light. But did we not all learn, well before age ten, to look both ways, even just in peripheral vision, before crossing the street?

Contrast the abdication of responsibility in his own implicit victim-hood, further, with Cohen's reported attitude toward the supposed responsibilities of others under much harsher circumstances:

> For a *self-professed bodhisattva,* [Cohen] was awfully contemptuous of human frailty. He bragged to me about how he had scolded a schizophrenic student for blaming his problems on his mental illness instead of taking responsibility for himself (Horgan, 2003; italics added).

That same contempt is, of course, part of the same "Rude Boy" attitude which Wilber so inexcusably celebrates in Cohen.

This, then, is Cohen's apparent worldview: His own stepping into the path of an oncoming vehicle has no cause, and therefore no responsibility, truly making him a "victim." But severe mental illness afflicting others is to be overcome by an acceptance of responsibility from which he himself explicitly shrinks.

Further, since Cohen gives no examples of *good* things happening equally "without a reason," one might assume that only *bad* things are thus spiritually acausal. Indeed, finding one's "soul mate" or having a book on the *New York Times* best-seller list—Cohen is in no danger of either—would both presumably still occur "for a reason." That is, they would happen perhaps for one's own spiritual evolution, or for the sake of the dreamed-of "revolution" in one's grandiose life-mission.

And to such gibbering "Buddhas" as this, one should then "surrender completely," for one's own highest benefit?

> Cohen describes enlightenment as a form of not-knowing. And yet his guruhood, his entire life, revolves around his belief in—his knowledge of—his own *unsurpassed perfection.* To borrow a phrase, Cohen is a super-egomanic. His casual contempt for us ordinary, egotistical humans is frightening, as is his belief that, as an enlightened being who has transcended good and evil, *he can do no harm.* Cohen may not be a monster, as his mother claims, but he has the capacity to become one (Horgan, 2003; italics added).

All potential monstrosities aside, however, even Cohen would surely agree, after his own "accidents" and many "persecutions"—not to mention having his own *Jewish mother* compare him to Hitler—that "sometimes you feel like a god ... sometimes you don't."

CHAPTER XXII

HELLO, DALAI!

(THE DALAI LAMA)

THE DALAI LAMA IS THE HEAD of the Gelug School of Tibetan Buddhism.

The title "Dalai Lama" itself is Mongolian, meaning "Ocean of Wisdom" or "Oceanic Wisdom Master."

Each successive Dalai Lama, beginning with the first such leader born in 1391, is regarded as being an incarnation of the previous one. They are also seen as incarnations of Chenrezig, the Bodhisattva/Buddha of Compassion.

> Upon the passing of the Dalai Lama, his monks institute a search for the Lama's reincarnation, who is usually a small child. Familiarity with the possessions of the previous Dalai Lama is considered the main sign of the reincarnation. The search for the reincarnation typically requires a few years which results in a gap in the list of the Dalai Lamas (Wikipedia, 2003).

The current Dalai Lama—the fourteenth in that spiritual line—Tenzin Gyatso, was born in 1935. He has lived in Dharamsala, India, since fleeing the Chinese invasion of Tibet in 1959.

Previous incarnations in that same lineage have left their own marks on history:

> [T]he Sixth Dalai Lama ... was said to have been unsuited for his office, said to have loved many women, as well as having a fondness for gambling and drink (Carnahan, 1995).

> He did not observe even the rules of a fully ordained priest. He drank wine habitually....
>
> *"Ignoring the sacred customs* of Lamas and monks in Tibet he began by bestowing care on his hair, then he took to drinking intoxicating liquors, to gambling, and at length no girl or married woman or good-looking person of either sex was safe from his unbridled licentiousness" (French, 2003; italics added).

> One of the early Dalai Lamas was particularly known for his love of women. It was common practice for households in which a daughter had received the honor of the Dalai Lama's transmission through sexual union to raise a flag over their home. It is said that a sea of flags floated in the wind over the town (Caplan, 2002).

That Sixth, Tsangyang Gyatso, lived only a few hundred years ago, from 1683 to 1706, in traditional, agrarian Tibet.

Given this reincarnational lineage, then, we need hardly be surprised that the current Dalai Lama has himself voiced a thought or two concerning sexual matters. For, when questioned as to which common experiences he had most missed out on, the retirement-aged monk "pointed at his groin and laughed: 'I obviously missed this'" (Ellis, 2003).

The non-violent winner of the Nobel Peace Prize also admitted that he "would not have made a good father as he had a bad temper":

> I used to be somewhat hot-tempered and prone to fits of impatience and sometimes anger. Even today, there are, of course, times when I lose my composure. When this happens, the least annoyance can take on undue proportions and upset me considerably. I may, for example, wake up in the morning and feel agitated for no particular reason. In this state, I find that even what ordinarily pleases me may irri-

> tate me. Just looking at my watch can give rise to feelings of annoyance (Lama, 1999).

At any rate, other lamas from the Dalai's own country of birth have evidently not "missed out" on sex to the same degree, as one Western female teacher and devotee of Tibetan Buddhism noted, in attempting to sort through her own feelings on the subject:

> How could this old lama, a realized master of the supreme Vajrayana practices of Maha Mudra, choose a thirteen- or fourteen-year-old nun from the monastery to become his sexual consort every year? What did the lama's wife think?....
>
> I talked to a number of Western women who had slept with their lamas. Some liked it—they felt special. Some felt used and it turned them away from practice. Some said they mothered the lama. But no one described it as a teaching; there was nothing tantric about it. The sex was for the lama, not them (in Kornfield, 2000).

Of course, there are two sides to every issue. Thus, Tenzin Palmo, who herself spent years in Tibet as the only (celibate) woman among hundreds of male monastics, after having earlier laughed off Chögyam Trungpa's "wandering hands" in England, noted:

> Some women are very flattered at being "the consort," in which case they should take the consequences. And some women only know how to relate to men in this way. I sometimes feel we women have to get away from this victim mentality....
>
> A true guru, even if he felt that having a tantric relationship might be beneficial for that disciple, would make the request with the understanding that it would not damage their relationship if she refused. No woman should ever have to agree on the grounds of his authority or a sense of her obedience. The understanding should be "if she wished to, good; if not, also good," offering her a choice and a sense of respect. Then that is not exploitation (in Mackenzie, 1999).

Still, much as one might agree with the need to "get away from this victim mentality," when a "great spiritual being" or an "infallible god" asks you to do something, you are entitled to feel flattered, to even enjoy it ... and still, to not be able to say, "No." After all, it is not possible to separate one's "sense of obedience" and need for salvation out of all that, perhaps even moreso when God "asks nicely." Webster (1990), quite honestly, covered all of those points over a decade ago. Only because all indications are that they have not yet properly sunk in is it worth repeating them here.

We will return to that issue in a later chapter.

In any case, Janwillem van de Wetering (2001) related further experiences with an eighteenth high-lama (i.e., one who had ostensibly been recognized as a lama in seventeen lifetimes before):

> Rimpoche [*sic*] had been given [a] car by his support group of London-based backers and often took girl disciples on outings to the seashore. A month later, when I was in Amsterdam, an accident interfered with the temple's routines. Rimpoche, driving home after visiting a pub in a nearby town, accompanied by his favorite mistress, hit a tree. "Alcohol-related"....
>
> Rimpoche drank constantly and became irritable at times. My wife was about to whap a fly that was bothering her during dinner and Beth [the favorite, mini-skirted mistress] screamed, "Don't kill a sentient being!" and got whacked over the head by Rimpoche, who told her to keep her voice down.

The amorous lama in question, after years of hard living, died in his early forties. A Mohawk Indian shaman, to whom that story of debauchery was told, offered her scattered analysis:

> "Yes," she said, "I've heard of that happening before. It probably was the only way Rimpoche could have stayed here" (van de Wetering, 2001).

The ridiculous idea there is, of course, that the more elevated the soul is, the more he must ground himself into the earth to keep from simply leaving his body and returning to the bardo realms or astral worlds, etc.

By contrast, though in line with the teachings of his own more conservative lineage, the current Dalai Lama obeys and enforces well-defined limits on the "pleasures of the flesh":

> His adamant stand on sexual morality is close to that of Pope John Paul II, a fact which his Western followers tend to find embarrassing, and prefer to ignore. The Dalai Lama's U.S.

publisher even asked him to remove the injunctions against homosexuality from his [1999] book *Ethics for the New Millennium,* for fear that they would offend American readers, and the Dalai Lama acquiesced (French, 2003).

Expounding further on such restrictions, the Lama (in P. Harvey, 2000) has said:

> Sexual misconduct for men and women consists of oral and anal sex.... Even with your wife, using one's mouth or other hole is sexual misconduct.
>
> As for when sexual intercourse takes place, if it is during the day it is also held to be a form of misconduct (Lama, 1996).

Thankfully, some "fun" is still allowed, albeit not during daylight hours:

> To have sexual relations with a prostitute paid by you and not by a third person does not, on the other hand, constitute improper behavior (Lama, 1996).

Interesting. Yet still, speaking of "the other hand":

> Using one's hand, that is sexual misconduct (the Dalai Lama, in [P. Harvey, 2000]).
>
> Masturbation ... includes emitting semen on another person, a monk getting a novice to masturbate him, or himself masturbating a sleeping novice, which could be seen to include homosexual acts. It is a lesser offence, of expiation [i.e., atonement], for nuns "tormented with dissatisfaction" to slap each other's genitals with their palms or any object, with the slapper "enjoying the contact" (P. Harvey, 2000).

"Nuns just wanna have fun."

The present Dalai Lama's views on reincarnation, too, stray somewhat from the spiritual norm:

> There is a possibility that a scientist who is very much involved his whole life [with computers], then the next life ... [he would be reborn in a computer], same process! Then this machine which is half-human and half-machine has been reincarnated (Hayward and Varela, 1992).

Both of those authors, Jeremy Hayward and Francisco Varela, have been followers of Chögyam Trungpa. Hayward helped to found, and has taught at, the Naropa Institute/University; he is currently the "Acharya-in-residence" at the Dechen Chöling meditation center in France. He also sits on the Board of Editors of the refereed *Journal of Consciousness Studies*. Varela sat on the same board until his passing in 2001, and was a founding member of Wilber's Integral Institute. No word on his reincarnations yet, but if your new Xbox or iPod is acting up....

For my own part, though, I do not consider that proposed reincarnational scenario to be at all likely. In the interest of full disclosure, however: I myself used to program computers for a living. Yet, in spite of those sixty-hour weeks, the "non-human" half of me is still more Vulcan than semiconductor.

Interestingly, Ken Wilber (2001a) offered his own opinion on a very closely related subject to the above reincarnational suggestions:

> [T]his whole notion that consciousness can be downloaded into microchips comes mostly from geeky adolescent males who can't get laid and stay up all hours of the night staring into a computer screen, dissociating, abstracting, dissolved in disembodied thinking.

Well, "geeky adolescent males" ... and certain respected lamas. Also, sort of, Allen Ginsberg's semi-coherent, unapologetically misogynistic friend and fellow admirer of Chögyam Trungpa, William S. Burroughs. (Burroughs was also a huge fan of the work of the orgone-fancying and orgasm-celebrating psychologist, Wilhelm Reich.) For, when not busy playing "William Tell"—and missing the target, if not the devoted head supporting it—with his thence-late wife, Burroughs (1974) mused the following:

> They are now able to replace the parts [of the human body], like on an old car when it runs down. The next thing, of course, will be transplanting of brains. We presume that the ego, what we call the ego, the I, or the You, is located somewhere in the midbrain, so it's not very long before we can transfer an ego from one body to another. Rich men will be able to buy up young bodies.

* * *

Interestingly, the hardly pacifistic actor Steven Seagal has been declared, by Penor Rinpoche, to be a reincarnated lama, i.e., a sacred vessel or *tulku* of Tibetan Buddhism. Perhaps for that "trailing cloud of glory," Seagal was once seated respectfully ahead of—i.e., closer to the stage than—Richard Gere, at a Los Angeles lecture given by the Dalai Lama. Of course, if Penor is wrong about Seagal, the former is nowhere near as wise or intuitive as his followers believe. On the other hand, if he is right and Seagal *is* a *tulku,* that only shows how little such titles (including Penor's own, as Rinpoche) mean.

> [I]n 1994 Seagal [reportedly] split with Kusum Lingpa, the exiled Tibetan lama also then favored by Oliver Stone and a number of other Hollywood stars, when Lingpa refused to declare him a *tulku.* Then in 1995, Seagal went to India and chartered a plane to tour Tibetan monasteries looking for another spiritual master....
>
> In his audience [with the Dalai Lama], according to Dora [M.], Seagal felt that something "unique" had transpired between him and the Dalai Lama. "He claimed that His Holiness bent down and kissed his feet," she said. "And Seagal took that to mean that the Dalai Lama was proclaiming him a deity" (Schell, 2000).

In June of 1997, the deified god-man Seagal was formally recognized as the reincarnation of Chungdrag Dorje—the founder of the Nyingma school of Tibetan Buddhism—by Penor Rinpoche.

> Penor was in the process of setting up dharma centers around the world when Seagal invited him to L.A. and reportedly made a substantial [monetary] contribution to ... his "seat in the West"....
>
> The editor of the Buddhist journal *Tricycle,* Helen Twerkov [*sic*], was blunt about her suspicions: "It's a difficult situation, because no one who knows Steven Seagal—who's been around him—seems to think he demonstrates any elevated spiritual wisdom" (Schell, 2000).

Such apparent dearth of spirituality, however, has evidently not dampened Seagal's enthusiasm for the numerous daft superstitions inherent in the Tibetan Buddhist path:

> [A]ctor Steven Segal [*sic*] declared, "My chakras began spinning and then went into balance after putting on my [Shaolin] Wheel [of Life pendant]" (Randi, 2003).

In any case, the aforementioned Penor Rinpoche is the same one who has expressed deep appreciation for Andrew Cohen's work. It is also the same Penor Rinpoche—now head of the Nyingma lineage—of whom Ken Wilber himself (2000a) has spoken approvingly:

> Although I have been meditating for around twenty-five years—and have tried dozens of different spiritual practices—most of those that I do at this time were received at the Longchen Nyingthig given by His Holiness Pema Norbu (Penor) Rinpoche.

Further, this is also the very same Penor Rinpoche who, in 1986, recognized one Catharine Burroughs as the first female American *tulku,* saying that "the very fabric of her mind was the Dharma" (Sherrill, 2000). Dilgo Khyentse Rinpoche later confirmed that reincarnation, i.e., of a sixteenth-century Tibetan saint, Genyenma Ahkön Lhamo—co-founder of the Palyul tradition of Tibetan Buddhism within the Nyingma School—as Burroughs. (Khyentse was the Dzogchen teacher of the Dalai Lama. He was also, of course, the same sage who reassured Trungpa's and Tendzin's followers that those gurus had given them authentic dharma, *after* Tendzin had already given some of them AIDS.) Burroughs herself, renamed as Jetsunma Ahkön Norbu Lhamo, went on to accumulate around a hundred followers—well short of the fifteen hundred which Penor Rinpoche had predicted would come. She also founded the largest Tibetan Buddhist monastery in the United States, located outside Washington, DC.

The great, recognized female *tulku* had reportedly earlier claimed to be the reincarnation of one of Jesus' female disciples, entrusted in those earlier times with the passing-down of Gnostic texts. She had further apparently told her future third husband, in channeled sessions, that the two of them had ruled ancient, unrecorded civilizations on Earth. They had also supposedly governed galaxies in previous lifetimes together (Sherrill, 2000).

That, of course, could account for Jetsunma's fondness for *Star Trek* and science fiction movies in general.

In any case, the responsibilities given to the *tulku* in this present life were only slightly less impressive than galactic leadership:

> "The future of Dharma in the West is riding on us," she told her students (Sherrill, 2000).

Nor was the Dharma everything to wind up "riding on" the former Brooklyn housewife. For, as her androgynously appealing, strong body of a triathlete, female personal trainer (Teri) was to reportedly discover, in the midst of a "very personal" relationship:

> While Buddhists aren't really supposed to proselytize, lamas are known to be very crafty, and they use all kinds of techniques—flattery, promises, even lies—to expose a student to the Dharma. And it is thought to be an enormous blessing if a lama chooses to have sex with you (Sherrill, 2000).

Oral sex and masturbation, out. Lesbian sex, in.

"Enormous blessings."

Thence followed much additional reported financial and personal nonsense—including the forty-plus Jetsunma dropping Teri and instead taking one of her twenty-something male disciples as a "consort." The latter was, however, himself apparently cut loose a year later. He was further unbelievably talked into becoming a monk in order to "keep the blessing" conferred upon him in having had sex with his lama/guru, by never again sleeping with an "ordinary woman."

Soon thereafter, the space-age Jetson-ma, ruler of remote galaxies, became engaged to another male disciple, two decades her junior. (Her mid-life tastes in clothing correspondingly began to gravitate toward skin-tight jeans, black leather boots and alleged frequent Victoria's Secret catalog purchases. Those were apparently paid for out of a six-figure annual personal allowance which reportedly amounted to half of the perpetually struggling ashram's operating expenses [Sherrill, 2000].) That latest, vacillating follower separated from Jetsunma in 1996, reunited in 1997, separated again in early 1998 and reunited once more later that year, then separated again in 1999.

At the start of her "personal involvement" with the bisexual Teri, Jetsunma had been married to her third husband, in a relationship dating back to when she was near-completely unknown.

In what must surely be one of the odder divorce settlements ever negotiated, that former, embittered husband received $2500 in cash and a "large crystal ball"—presumably to aid himself in not getting involved with any comparably mixed-up women in the future. The same man apparently later worked in public relations for the Naropa Institute for several years (Sherrill, 2000).

Well, "better the Mara you know," etc.

In terms of contextual comparison, Jetsunma predictably fares no better than any of the other "sages" whom we have previously seen:

> [Jetsunma's husband at the time] felt her distance, and he felt her growing contempt for him—and for her students. At dinner she would imitate them, make jokes about them (Sherrill, 2000).

Such reported private imitations and jokes about disciples whose primary failing was to consider their guru-figure to be a great and holy being could, of course, have been indulged in for no one's spiritual or psychological benefit but her own.

Jetsunma's monastery exhibited a ratio of four nuns to every monk. Thus, the reported problems with her and within that community cannot be blamed on any mere "patriarchal" or "male" considerations. Further, to charitably regard her (and her ilk) as being innocent victims, who have simply been "corrupted by the [existing] patriarchy" (cf. Harvey, 2000), would not likely pass muster with the more courageous Tenzin Palmo, for one. For, all indications are that Jetsunma went voluntarily into the Tibetan Buddhist system, knowingly increasing *her own* power at every step. In fact, she allegedly explicitly pressured Penor Rinpoche for his recognition of her as an incarnation, before he wanted to give it. Indeed, she was further reportedly initially openly disappointed when that reincarnation turned out to be of an "unknown" saint. At the time when she first met Rinpoche, well prior to the formal recognition, she and her husband apparently almost didn't even know what Buddhism *was* (Sherrill, 2000). Nor would they likely have been so eager to learn, one suspects, had doing so not increased their own stature in the world.

Jetsunma and many of her followers moved in the late '90s from coastal Maryland to higher ground in Arizona. That was done in anticipation of the fulfillment of apocalyptic Hopi prophecies—her new boyfriend at the time was an American Indian shaman—

that earthquakes, floods and famine would strike the United States in 1999 (Sherrill, 2000).

As of this writing, however, the U.S. thankfully remains very much geologically intact, with no excess of flood water and no shortage of food. And if you've "felt the earth move" recently, it probably didn't register on the Richter scale.

After all that, Penor Rinpoche could reasonably be feeling somewhat burned by his experiences with Jetsunma and Steven Seagal—the latter of whose purported "divinity" was not welcomed by many Buddhists. Indeed, in an interview with Martha Sherrill in 1997, Penor declared that he "would not be recognizing any more Americans as *tulkus.*"

So it looks like Richard Gere's out of luck.

* * *

The *tulku* phenomenon itself has an interesting, and very human, history.

The system of recognizing reincarnations was established at the beginning of the thirteenth century by the followers of Dusum Khyenpa, the first Karmapa Lama. As the religious influence of Tibet's lamas came to be adapted for political purposes through the centuries, internally and via influence from China, the process of recognizing new *tulkus* was rather predictably affected.

> The traditional method of scrutiny whereby the young hopefuls had to identify objects belonging to their past incarnation was often neglected.... It wasn't at all uncommon to have two or more candidates—each backed by a powerful faction—openly *and violently* [italics added] challenging one well-known *tulku* seat (Lehnert, 1998).

Such intrigues are by no means buried merely in the dim and distant past. For, when it came time to recognize a new (Seventeenth) Karmapa Lama in the 1980s and '90s, that allegedly entailed:

- An attempt to steal (literally) the previous Karmapa's heart during his 1981 cremation ceremony
- A short-lived claim by a Woodstock, NY, *tulku* that his wife was about to give birth to the reincarnated Karmapa, discounted when she delivered a baby girl, as opposed to the expected male reincarnation

- Billions of mantra repetitions (as a probable delaying tactic) enjoindered on devoted followers to allegedly "remove massive obstacles" before the new incarnation could be revealed
- An attempted *coup d'état* for the leadership of the Karmapa lineage, with written replies to it being initially smartly given on (unused) toilet paper
- Reported naïve back-room deals with the calculating Chinese government on the part of one of the four "highly evolved" lineage holders responsible for collectively recognizing the next Karmapa. The involved lama had as his emissary to China one Akong Tulku—Chögyam's old nemesis—who came to be regarded as "the main felon splitting the lineage" (Lehnert, 1998)
- Alleged "forgery, deceit, and a looming fight right at the top of the lineage," with the high-ranking lamas there reportedly displaying "greed, pride, and lust for power": "People were being intimidated, forced to sign petitions; some had been beaten." Against that was heard the voice of one (European) Lama Ole Nydahl (Lehnert, 1998).

  Interestingly, Trungpa himself, in 1984, had Osel Tendzin write to Vajradhatu members, warning them against Nydahl. Indeed, in that missive, Nydahl's teaching style was described as being "contrary to everything we have been taught and have come to recognize as genuine." Trungpa was further of the opinion that "there is some real perversion of the buddhadharma taking place by Mr. Nydahl" (Rawlinson, 1997).

  Pot. Kettle. Tibetan Buddhist. Black
- Finally, two different children, each being touted as the Karmapa by different factions within the global Tibetan Buddhist community. One had the support of the politically manipulative Chinese government and of the duped Dalai Lama. (The latter, having too-quickly given informal approval to the recognition on the basis of reportedly false evidence, could not backtrack and admit that he was wrong.) The other was recognized after a more sincere search

Updates to that continuing dispute exist at www.karmapa-controversy.org.

Interestingly, one of the aforementioned four lineage holders claims to have found the reincarnated Trungpa in eastern Tibet. That same holder, however, was not only apparently making deals with the government of China, but had also recognized over three hundred other *tulkus* within the space of a mere few years previously.

The fact that most of those came from an area bordering his own primary seat in Tibet (Lehnert, 1998), however, casts a certain doubt....

Still, if Trungpa's really back in circulation, "Let's party!"

* * *

It is not only "avant-garde" lamas who have "bent" the rules which one would otherwise have reasonably assumed were governing their behaviors. Rather, as June Campbell (1996) has noted from her own experience:

> [I]n the 1970s, I traveled throughout Europe and North America as a Tibetan interpreter, providing the link, through language, between my lama-guru [Kalu Rinpoche, 1905 – 1989] and his many students. Subsequently he requested that I become his sexual consort, and take part in secret activities with him, despite the fact that to outsiders he was a very high-ranking yogi-lama of the Kagya lineage who, as abbot of his own monastery, had taken vows of celibacy. Given that he was one of the oldest lamas in exile at that time, had personally spent fourteen years in solitary retreat, and counted amongst his students the highest ranking lamas in Tibet, his own status was unquestioned in the Tibetan community, and his holiness attested to by all....
>
> [I]t was plainly emphasized that any indiscretion [on my part] in maintaining silence over our affair might lead to madness, trouble, *or even death* [e.g., via magical curses placed upon the indiscreet one].

And how did the compassionate, bodhisattva-filled Tibetan Buddhist community react to such allegations?

> *[M]any rejected out of hand Campbell's claims as sheer fabrication* coming from somebody eager to gain fame at the expense of a deceased lama (Lehnert, 1998; italics added).

* * *

Well, enough of Buddhist sex. How about some Buddhist violence?

More specifically, in keeping with such extreme contemporary brutality as is regularly portrayed in *tulku* Steven Seagal's movies, it has been whispered that

> in old Tibet ... the lamas were the allies of feudalism and unsmilingly inflicted medieval punishments such as blinding and flogging unto death (Hitchens, 1998).

> Visiting the Lhasa [Tibet] museum, [journalist Alain Jacob] saw "dried and tanned children's skins, various amputated human limbs, either dried or preserved, and numerous instruments of torture that were in use until a few decades ago"....
>
> These were the souvenirs and instruments of the vanished lamas, proof, Jacob notes, that under the Buddhist religious rule in Tibet "there survived into the middle of the twentieth century feudal practices which, while serving a well-established purpose, were nonetheless chillingly cruel."
>
> The "well-established purpose"? Maintaining social order in a church-state (Clark, 1980).

The early twentieth-century, Viennese-born explorer Joseph Rock minced even fewer words:

> "One must take for granted that every Tibetan, at least in this part of the world, was a robber sometime in his life," he sardonically observed of the Goloks [tribe]. "Even the lamas are not averse to cutting one's throat, although they would be horrified at killing a dog, or perhaps even a vermin" (Schell, 2000).

The caliber of monks today has not, it seems, radically improved:

> [O]ver 90% of those who wear the robes [in India, and elsewhere] are "frauds" in the sense the questioners would connote by "fraud." The idea that the monk is more perfect than the non-monk is inveterate, and it is *kindled by the monks themselves*. If perfection is to mean greater dedication to the search for spiritual emancipation, then there is undoubtedly more of it among the monks. But in terms of human morality and of human intellect, monks are *nowhere* more perfect than lay people (Bharati, 1980; italics added).

> Far too many men become Buddhist monks, because it's a good life and they have devotion. The Dalai Lama has publicly stated that only ten out of one hundred monks are true candidates (Mackenzie, 1999).

Likewise for Japanese Zen:

> It seemed to me that most of the monks [at Suienji] were proud of their position, lazy, stupid, greedy, angry, confused, or some combination. Mainly they were the sons of temple priests putting in their obligatory training time so that they could follow in daddy's footsteps. They listened to radios, drank at night and had pinups on the wall.
>
> What they were really into, though, was power trips. It's what got them off.... The senior monks were always pushing around the junior monks, who in turn were pushing around the ones that came after them (in Chadwick, 1994).

The observations of a Thai Buddhist monk, in Ward (1998), at a monastery run by Ajahn Chah, are no more flattering:

> The *farang* [Westerners] at this *wat* [monastery] who call themselves monks are nothing but a bunch of social rejects who have found a place where they can get free food, free shelter and free respect. They are complacent and their only concern is their perks at the top end of the hierarchy.

For more of the inside story on Tibetan Buddhism, consult Trimondi and Trimondi's (2003) *The Shadow of the Dalai Lama: Sexuality, Magic and Politics in Tibetan Buddhism.*

* * *

No discussion of Tibetan Buddhism would be complete without mention of T. Lobsang Rampa (d. 1981).

Rampa was the author, in the 1950s and '60s, of more than a dozen popular books concerning his claimed experiences growing up as a lama in Tibet. Among them, we find 1956's best-selling *The Third Eye,* concerning an operation allegedly undergone by Rampa to open up his clairvoyant faculties.

In the midst of that literary success, however, it was discovered that Rampa was in fact none other than a pen name for the Irish "son of a plumber," Cyril Hoskins (Bharati, 1974).

Hoskins himself had never been to Tibet.

But then, the average Tibetan, in Hoskins' day at least, had never seen indoor plumbing.

So perhaps it all evens out.

* * *

As might be expected, radically enlightened practitioners of Tibetan Buddhism counted through the ages and today are as rare as they are on any other path.

> When I asked an old lama from Tibet about whether these ten stages [of awakening to Buddha Nature, i.e., *bhumis*] are in fact a part of the practice, he said, "Of course they really exist." But when I inquired who in his tradition had attained them, he replied wistfully, "In these difficult times I cannot name a single lama who has mastered even the second stage" (Kornfield, 2000).

Undaunted, the current Dalai Lama himself keeps to a busy schedule of spiritually enlightening meditation—six hours per day. He also continues the non-violent political activities which brought him the Nobel Peace Prize in 1989.

Of course, having so little spare time would undoubtedly help to force the proper prioritization of one's activities. Nevertheless:

> Repeated attempts to get a response to this [critical] article from His Holiness through his New York media representative were met with a "too busy" response. Yet the *New York Times* reported that the Tibetan leader somehow found time for a photo op with pop star Ricky Martin (Zupp, 2003).

So it goes, when one is "Livin' La Vida Lama."

Regardless, His Holiness has left us with at least one eminently good idea to live by, in sloughing through the sorry state of affairs that calls itself "spirituality" in this world:

> "Whenever exploitation, sexual abuse or money abuse happen," the Dalai Lama says, "make them public" (Leonard, 2001).

In the next chapter we will meet a group of courageous people who did exactly that, and more.

CHAPTER XXIII

UP THE *ASANA*

(YOGI AMRIT DESAI)

Yogi Desai is an enlightened Master with penetrating insight and intuition (in Desai, 1981; self-published).

YOGI AMRIT DESAI IS THE ORIGINATOR of Kripalu Yoga, and *formerly* the head of the Kripalu Center in Lenox, Massachusetts—by now, the "largest and most established yoga retreat in North America." How he came to found that center, and then be reportedly forced to leave by his own students, we shall soon see.

Desai grew up in India, meeting his guru, Swami Kripalvanandji—a claimed kundalini yoga master—there in 1948, at the age of sixteen. Kripalvananda's guru, in turn, was mythologically believed to be "Lord Lakulish, the twenty-eighth incarnation of Lord Shiva" (Cope, 2000). Interestingly, Kripalvananda is said to have practiced "yogic masturbation," i.e., masturbation in the context of meditation, for the purpose of raising energies up the spine (Elias, 2002).

Amrit himself came to America as an art student in 1960, and described (1981) his discovery of Kripalu Yoga, while married and living in Philadelphia in 1970, as follows:

> [D]uring my routine practice of hatha yoga postures I found my body moving spontaneously and effortlessly while at the same time I was being drawn into the deepest meditation I had ever experienced. The power and intelligence that guided me through this seemingly paradoxical experience of meditation and motion left me in awe and bliss. That morning my body moved of its own volition, without my direction, automatically performing an elaborate series of flowing motions. Many of these "postures" [i.e., *asanas*] I had never seen even in any yoga book before.

As Swami Kripalvananda explained it (in Desai, 1981):

> [A]ll of these innumerable postures, movements, and *mudras* [hand gestures] ... occur automatically when the evolutionary energy of *prana* has been awakened in the body of a yogi.... This is an integral part of the awakening of kundalini.

Desai gave the name "Kripalu" to the system of yoga which he elaborated from his initial experience and others following it. The name was bestowed in honor of his guru, whose special grace Amrit considered to be responsible for that discovery.

Following that awakening, Desai founded his first ashram in 1970, and established a second one in Pennsylvania in 1975. The Kripalu Center for Yoga and Health was created in Massachusetts in 1983, with branches in North America, Europe and India.

From those centers, Yogi Desai (or "Gurudev") dispensed both discipline and wisdom, for the spiritual benefit of his followers:

> As often as possible tell yourself, "I want nothing. I want to be nothing. I brought nothing with me, nor will I take anything when I go. I want to accomplish nothing for myself. I give my life to God and my guru"....
>
> [A]ll the guru wants is your happiness and growth (Desai, 1985).

Amrit's disciple Rajendra (1976) further explained the details of life in the community:

> Gurudev in no way censures sexual love—only the abuse of it. Married couples at the ashram may have a moderate sex life without diverting the course of their *sadhana*. Unmarried persons are asked to refrain.

In the face of those and other restrictions and assurances, loyal ashram leaders still reluctantly allowed that

> [i]n a moment of paranoid self-indulgence [an ashram resident] may question the guru's honorable spiritual intentions (Rajendra, 1976).

Indeed. As they say, however, "Just because you're paranoid doesn't mean they're not out to get you."

Thus, a decade after his founding of Kripalu, still married and encouraging strict celibacy for his unmarried disciples, Desai found himself caught in a scandal. Such controversy was of his own making, and indeed arose from the discovery that he had secretly been demonstrating his "penetrating insight" ... to the receptive vessels of three of his female students (Carlson, 2002a). In the wake of that, he resigned as spiritual director of Kripalu in 1994. Or, more accurately, he was reportedly *forced to leave* by the residents of the ashram which he himself had founded.

Bravo!!

Following that departure, Kripalu restructured its organization to be led by a professional management team, "several of whom are former ashram residents." It has thereby become "the first traditional yoga ashram founded on the guru-disciple model to transition to a new paradigm of spiritual education" (Kripalu, 2003).

Of course, anyone who has ever worked under "professional management teams" knows that they, too, are far from perfect, at times to the point of obvious pathology. But at least it's a step in the right direction.

* * *

Kripalu, wisely sans Desai, now serves over 15,000 guests per year.

As to Yogi Amrit himself, after a period of retirement he resumed teaching, and was recently invited to be the "leading spiritual teacher at a new ashram" to be founded by Deepak Chopra (Cohen, 2000a). He presently teaches in Salt Springs, Florida.

Not surprisingly, Desai's current bio at www.amrityoga.com makes no mention of the Kripalu Center connection or scandal. (Likewise, there is no word within the History section at www.kripalu.org as to *why* Desai left them.) Indeed, on that new site he is referred to with deep respect as "Gurudev"—i.e., "beloved teacher" or "divine guru"—as he was at Kripalu during his heyday.

And thereby are the next generation of fresh-faced, idealistic young spiritual seekers served old, vinegary wine in new bottles—unaware, more often than not, of the history of that sour vintage.

CHAPTER XXIV

SODOMY AND GOMORRAH

> Whenever you have an individual who claims a direct pipeline with God and has no accountability, if you don't have a [so-called] cult today, you will have one tomorrow (Geisler, 1991).

> A [so-called] destructive cult distinguishes itself from a normal social or religious group by subjecting its members to persuasion or other damaging influences to keep them in the group....
>
> Members are thoroughly indoctrinated with the belief that if they ever do leave, terrible consequences will befall them (Hassan, 1990).

CHARACTERISTICS COMMONLY SEEN in so-called cults include the presence of an infallible leader, and a prohibition on questioning the teachings. Hypnotic chanting or the like is frequently fingered as a means of inducing a suggestible, trance-like state, and thus of controlling the minds of the followers. Further, one often finds a "hidden agenda," whereby it is not fully explained to prospective members of the group as to what they may be asked to do, should they choose to join.

In addition, residents of the community will often lead minutely regulated existences—even to the point of control of their sex lives—their hours being filled with organization-related activities, with no time for reflection as to the morality of their actions. ("Keep members so busy they don't have time to think and check things out" [Hassan, 2000].) Plus, not infrequently, devotees have feelings of persecution, and associated beliefs that "the world is out to get them," via conspiracies to destroy the organization. They may also be required to report or confess their "thoughts, feelings and activities" to their superiors.

Also, one regularly finds a lack of proper medical care for even the most devoted members, and indoctrinated phobias to prevent followers from leaving. Plus, we see the suppression of information harmful to the group, and the presence of apocalyptic teachings, with only the members of the sect being "saved" from eternal damnation. The group, that is, is the "one, true Way," allowing its members to conceive of no happiness outside of itself, and keeping them in sway via the fear of losing their salvation should they consider leaving. Conversely, followers who breach the rigid rules and regulations of the organization or ask critical questions of the leader are at risk of being kicked out of the group, or "excommunicated."

Speaking of the Roman Catholic Church....

> [U]nlike Judaism, Catholicism embraces and espouses the belief that it is the one and only true faith (Bruni and Burkett, 2002).

And of its divinely inspired leader, then:

> A pope ... believes, along with many hundreds of millions of the faithful, that he is God's representative on Earth....
>
> The theologian John Henry Newman, Britain's most famous convert to Catholicism in the nineteenth century, delivered a devastating verdict ... : "[A long-lived pope] becomes a god, has no one to contradict him, does not know facts, and does cruel things without meaning it" (Cornwell, 1999).

Even for that "god's" underlings or inner circle, though, the distance from God, in the eyes of their flock, is hardly any greater:

> We were taught [that Catholic priests] were Christ's representatives on Earth (in Boston Globe, 2003).

Papal infallibility (on matters of doctrine, faith and morals) was decreed by Pope Pius IX in 1870. The relatively recent nature of that "perfection" may perhaps allow us to more easily understand the behaviors of at least one of his forebears:

> In the tenth century a dissolute teenager could be elected pope (John XII) because of his family connections and die a decade later in the bed of a married woman (Wills, 2000).

Died happy, though....

> John XII was so enthralled by one of his concubines, Rainera, that he entrusted her with much of the administration of the Holy See (Allen, 2004).

"*One* of his concubines." Among how many?

Some popes have all the luck.

Saint Augustine, too, fathered a child out of wedlock as a teenager, living with its mother for fifteen years, and practicing contraception as a Manichean during that time (Wills, 2000). He further never went to confession—a sacrament given only once in a lifetime, in those bygone days (Wills, 1972). Priestly celibacy was likewise only a medieval demand, enjoindered to ensure that Church properties did not fall into the hands of offspring, as inheritance:

> [I]n the beginning [of the Church], there was no mandatory celibacy. Saint Peter, the first pope, was married. Pope Anastasius I was the father of Pope Innocent, Pope Sergius III begat Pope John XI and Pope Theodore I was the son of a bishop (Bruni and Burkett, 2002).

More recently, a survey was conducted in 1980 by one Richard Wagner. It covered fifty ostensibly celibate priestly respondents—half of whom "knew they were gay before ordination." The survey found that those holy men "averaged 226 partners in sex, a number reached only because 22% of them had over 500" (Wills, 2000).

Surprised? Or: Think of how many partners they might have had if they *weren't* celibate and chaste!

In any case, the altar boys groped, seduced and sodomized by various Catholic priests certainly did not have everything they might be asked to do for the Church explained to them up front.

Nor behind.

Proper medical care for those who have given their lives to the cause? Not if you're Thérèse of Lisieux (1873 – 1897), whose power-enjoying, vindictive prioress delayed sending for crisis medical help. She further restricted one doctor's visits from his suggestion that he come every day to three times in total, and forbade injections of morphia as Thérèse lay dying of tuberculosis (Furlong, 1987).

More recently, in the 1930s, a girl placed in an industrial school in Ireland run by the so-called Sisters of Mercy told her story:

> I had a lot of abscesses.... I couldn't walk at one stage. I kept passing out, particularly at Mass in the mornings. When I was about nine, I was very sick—I had a big lump under my arm, and they had to put poultices on it. They wouldn't call a doctor, because they'd have had to pay for that (in Raftery and O'Sullivan, 2001).

Likewise for the life of nuns in Massachusetts, as one lay member recorded:

> I'd see priests driving around in Cadillacs. I remember reading a story about how nuns didn't have full health insurance and was just infuriated by the injustice in that (in Boston Globe, 2003).

The free exchange of information, beyond the boundaries of the organization, for petitioners to receive honest answers to even embarrassing questions? Not divinely likely:

> Cardinals take an oath to the pope to safeguard the church from scandal—to *prevent bad information from becoming public* (Berry and Renner, 2004; italics added).

> Honest mistakes, incompetence, negligence and intentional wrongdoing are all abhorrent to the higher leadership [of the Roman Catholic Church]. All are denied, covered up and rationalized with equal zeal. The clerical world truly believes that it has been established by God and that its members are

> singled out and favored by the Almighty.... Higher authority figures are regarded with a mixture of fear and awe by all below them. The circles of power are closed, the tightest being among those existing among bishops.... Secrecy provides a layer of insulation between the one in authority and anyone who might be tempted to question its exercise (Doyle, 2003).
>
> Freedom to question the teachings? *Please.*
>
> The French Jesuit Pierre Teilhard de Chardin was so reviled by the Holy Office for his vision of a spirituality in harmony with human evolution that his major works, which have reached millions of readers, were suppressed in his lifetime. Karl Rahner, who argued that theology should develop in the spirit of a time, and Yves Congar, who emphasized the role of laypeople in an evolving church, were marginalized in the 1950s by Pius XII, who had no use for their views (Berry and Renner, 2004).

Under the same intellectual oppression, de Chardin was actually given the choice of either being exiled to the United States, or living under surveillance in a retreat house; he chose the former. One American Jesuit compared that treatment of Teilhard, and of others who had been influenced by his work, to a "Stalinist purge" (Cornwell, 1999).

> By doctrine, it was still [in the 1950s and early '60s, prior to the Vatican II council] a sin to read any book on the [*Index Librorum Prohibitorum*] list, including Voltaire, Rousseau, Kant, and especially Darwin (Sennott, 1992).
>
> [T]he Anti-Modernist Oath, [enacted by Pope Pius X in 1910 and] sworn to this day in modified form by Catholic ordinands ... required acceptance of all papal teaching, and acquiescence at all times to the meaning and sense of such teaching as dictated by the pope.... There was no possibility of any form of dissent, even interior. The conscience of the person taking the oath was forced to accept not only what Rome proposed, but even the sense in which Rome interpreted it. Not only was this contrary to the traditional Catholic understanding of the role of conscience, but it was a form of *thought control* that was unrivalled even under fascist and communist regimes (Cornwell, 1999; italics added).

Nor has the situation improved in more recent years:

> In the first year of his papacy, [John Paul II, Karol Wojtyla] revoked the teaching license of Father Hans Küng, the Swiss theologian who has challenged papal infallibility.... In 1997 Wojtyla excommunicated the Sri Lankan writer-priest Tissa Balasuriya for diluting Roman doctrinal orthodoxy: Balasuriya's writing had cast doubts on the doctrines of original sin and the virginity of the Mother of God (Cornwell, 1999).

By contrast:

> Rome never put Hitler's writings on the Index; the Führer until the end of his reign was allowed to remain a member of the Church, i.e., he was not excommunicated (Lewy, 2000).

Interested in having the truth be known at all costs? *Right....*

> Two ladies, worried about their pastor's overtures to teenage boys, discovered that he had come to their town from a treatment center after a plea bargain. A boy he had molested in a previous parish cut off a finger and received a settlement. When the ladies asked that Father be removed, the bishop not only refused their request but threatened a slander suit if they made a public issue of it (Berry, 1992).

Or, as the journalist Michael Harris (1991) confided to a victim of alleged clergy sexual abuse who was about to go public with his story, in cautioning the latter about the associated police- and government-aided cover-up around the Christian Brothers' Mount Cashel Orphanage in Newfoundland:

> [T]here are powerful forces involved in this story, for whom the last thing that is wanted is the truth. I don't believe that many people will be congratulating either you or me for bringing this sordid affair into the public eye.

> In an interview [in May of 2002] Cardinal Oscar Rodriguez Maradiaga of Honduras, widely seen as a leading candidate to be the next pope, addressed the American [pedophilia] crisis. He blamed the American press for "persecution" of the Church.... "Only in this fashion can I explain the ferocity [of attacks on the esteem of the Catholic Church] that reminds

> me of the times of Nero and Diocletian, and more recently, of Stalin and Hitler" [he said]....
>
> Cardinal Norberto Rivera Carrera of Mexico City ... echoed Rodriguez's comments on the American crisis. "Not only in the United States but also in other parts of the world, one can see underway an orchestrated plan for striking at the prestige of the Church. Not a few journalists have confirmed for me the existence of this organized campaign," he said (Allen, 2004).

Archbishop Daniel Pilarczyk of Cincinnati had earlier characterized the media exposure of Catholic clergy abuse as deriving from a "corporate vendetta" against the Church. Father Charles Fiore, meanwhile, suggested that pedophiles had been planted in the priestly ranks by liberals determined to undermine Christianity. Conversely, he expressed the belief that a purge of communists would stop the conspiracy against his holy organization (Bruni and Burkett, 2002). And as late as 2002, Cardinal Joseph Ratzinger (now Pope Benedict XVI) weighed in with his own, equally facile "conspiracy theory," of there allegedly being a "planned campaign" to discredit the Roman Catholics.

> [Vatican affairs writer Orazio] Petrosillo indicated three groups in the United States that may have inspired such a campaign: "Masonic lodges," "Jewish lobbies," and "groups of free thought and free morals" such as gays (Allen, 2004).

But "impure," menstruating women too though, right? Why stop at gays and Jews—not to mention (gasp!) "free thinkers"—when you're desperately searching for scapegoats to blame for your own family's cruel sins and inexcusable indifference to the suffering of others? When even the crusading, witch-hunting, Inquisitioning Catholic Church is, in its own mind, a "victim," you know you are living in a strange world indeed.

In reality, even a minimal awareness of the extant media exposés of Eastern guru-figures would have sufficed to demonstrate that both the "God-inspired Church" and its "demonic" competitors are being exposed in direct proportion to the sheer quantity of their alleged abuses. The Freemasons, Jews and gays—"surprisingly"—cannot be blamed for that, any more than an "anti-Asian" bias could be asserted to be the source of any "conspiracy" to expose the alleged abuses of our world's gurus!

(Note: Even without any conscious effort on my own part, it turns out that around 45% of the figures covered at any depth in this book are Westerners. "Authentic spirituality" typically involves *Eastern* philosophy. And the guru-disciple phenomenon, in general, comes to the West from the East. Thus, a greater percentage of the "best" of its practitioners are predictably going to be from the East than from the West. One therefore cannot reasonably hope for a split closer to 50/50 than this book represents. Were I aware of any comparable exposés of misbehaviors within guru-disciple-like relationships among Freemasons, Jews, gays or hermaphrodites [cf. Sai Baba], where the guru-figures were widely viewed as purveying "authentic, transformative spirituality" and as being among the "best" in their respective paths, I would happily have included them.)

Nor though, with regard to alleged biases, can recent exposés of the inhumane conditions faced by animals in kosher slaughterhouses be rationally viewed as an "anti-Semitic attack" on Jewish religious practices (in Simon, 2004) ... oy *vey!*

Further, regarding the convenient claim that Judaism avoids the "cultist" tendencies of, for example, the Roman Catholic Church, by not claiming to be "the one and only true faith," thus allegedly allowing followers to leave the religion without penalty:

> In the Olam Ha-Ba [i.e., the Messianic Age], the whole world will recognize the Jewish G-d as the only true G-d, and the Jewish religion as the only true religion (Rich, 2001).

Could one have expected any less, though, given the "chosen group" complex of the entire tradition? Of *course* it's "the one true religion"! How could they be the "Chosen People" if it wasn't?

By stark contrast to such prevailing foolishness, blame-mongering and paranoia as the above, Chapter 2 of Bruni and Burkett's (2002) *A Gospel of Shame* offers a wonderfully coherent and insightful analysis of why the reluctantly apologetic Catholic Church has justifiably fared so poorly in media presentations of its wide-ranging sins. The same book offers by far the best explanation I have found of the various sexual and social factors most likely to play a role in creating the pedophilic orientation. It also contains the best documentation of the initial deferential underreporting of Catholic clergy abuse by the North American media, showing claims of "anti-Catholic bias" in the same media to be wholly unfounded.

For the centuried misogyny, calculated power-grabs, general "stubborn resistance to the truth" and associated widespread deceit in the Catholic Church, consult Garry Wills' (2000) surprising *Papal Sin*. For the shameful history of anti-Semitism in the same organization, from its highest leaders on down, see Cornwell's (1999) *Hitler's Pope* and Lewy's (2000) *The Catholic Church and Nazi Germany*. For the connection between the Vatican and post-WWII "Nazi smuggling" in the fight against communism, refer to Aarons and Loftus' (1998) *Unholy Trinity:*

> [Ante] Pavelić ... had been the Poglavnik of "independent" Croatia, exercising comparable powers to the Führer in Germany. He had even managed to keep the death machine operating almost until the end, while the Germans were frantically dismantling theirs....
>
> In a strange reversal of roles, [Pavelić] castigated the Führer about the "lenient" treatment of German Jews, boasting that in comparison he had completely solved the Jewish question in Croatia while some remained alive in the Third Reich....
>
> The pope's own attitude towards the murderous Ustashi [terrorist network] leader was more than benign neglect.... Pius [XII] himself promised to give Pavelić his personal blessing again. By this time, the Holy See possessed abundant evidence of the atrocities committed by his regime.

Nor were other aspects of that pope's silent conduct during the time of Hitler any more praiseworthy:

> It seems beyond any doubt ... that if the churches had opposed the killing and the persecution of the Jews, as they opposed the killing of the congenitally insane and the sick, there would have been no Final Solution (in Cornwell, 1999).

> If [Pius XII] is to take credit for the use of Vatican extraterritorial religious buildings as safe houses for Jews during Germany's occupation of Rome, then he should equally take blame for the use of the same buildings as safe houses for Nazi and Ustash[i] criminals (Cornwell, 1999).

Or, as Settimia Spizzichino, the sole survivor of the German roundup and deportation of Rome's Jews, put it in a 1995 interview with the BBC:

> I came back from Auschwitz on my own. I lost my mother, two sisters, a niece, and one brother. Pius XII could have warned us about what was going to happen. We might have escaped from Rome and joined the partisans. He played right into the Germans' hands. It all happened right under his nose. But he was an anti-Semitic pope, a pro-German pope. He didn't take a single risk. And when they say the pope is like Jesus Christ, it is not true. He did not save a single child. Nothing.

Of course, when "Satan" is thus attacking holy men—as in the current pedophilia crisis—for doing "God's work," there is a surefire defense for any believer. The same defense could, indeed, be directed equally ineffectually against the present book and author as well:

> [W]e call down God's power on the [anti-Catholic] media (Cardinal Bernard Law, in [Boston Globe, 2003]).

Controlling their followers' sex lives? Injunctions against contraception and the regard for fornication, contraception and homosexual activity as "mortal sins" will certainly do that.

> Many priests were disillusioned by celibacy, which they saw as a mechanism of control, much akin to [the Church's] authoritarian attitude toward lay people's sex lives (Berry, 1992).

> Pius XII ... made the condemnation of birth control resonate ceaselessly from classrooms, pamphlets, confessionals, with a kind of hysterical insistence. Contraception was a mortal sin. Its unrepenting practitioners were going to hell (Wills, 2000).

> Not only were oral and anal intercourse forbidden, but all varieties of stimulation or position were counted unnatural except the man-on-top performance. The act with a single goal [i.e., impregnation] was to have but a single mode of execution (Wills, 1972).

Nor was it necessary to thus "execute" improperly—in "Catholic roulette" (i.e., sex without contraception) or otherwise—in order for one to run afoul of the God of Law:

> [B]ack in the 1950s if you ate meat on Friday, did not wear a hat or veil to church, or ate breakfast before Communion, you could burn in hell for these sins (in Boston Globe, 2003).

Oral sex and "eating meat," out. Hats on, and thou shalt not spill thy seed upon the ground. And yet—

> Dr. William Masters found that ninety-eight out of the hundred priests he surveyed were masturbating (Wills, 2000).

And you just *know* they're sneaking food before Communion, too!

> [A]ll sensual indulgence was lumped together [in the Decalogue, i.e., the Ten Commandments] under the prohibition against "coveting thy neighbor's wife," an approach which made gluttony, laziness, and drunkenness directly sexual offenses—offenses where, according to Catholic moralists of the old school ... all sins were automatically grave or "mortal." I knew a scrupulous young man who was literally driven mad by this line of thought (Wills, 1972).

Are the lives of residents further being wholly given over to the organization? Do they work long days with no time left over to question the teachings or reflect on the consequences of their own actions, having little contact with outside ideas? Evidently so:

> The nuns lived minutely regulated lives, their waking hours crammed with communal prayers, devotional exercises, care of the convent and sacristy, a heavy teaching load, the training of children for first communion (or May procession, or confirmation), rehearsing of the choir and coaching of altar boys.... They were not often allowed out of the convent—not even to visit libraries (Wills, 1972).

Repetitive, hypnotic chanting? Yes, yes, yes:

> [Church] rites have great authority; they hypnotize. Not least by their Latinity. It is not certain, philologists say, that "hocus-pocus" is derived from *"Hoc est Corpus"* in the Mass; but the Latin phrases, often rhythmed, said in litanies and lists of saints' names, replicated, coming at us in antiphonies and triple cries *(Sanctus, Sanctus, Sanctus),* had a witchery in them, to hush or compel us as by incantation (Wills, 1972).

Apocalyptic beliefs? Let me count the Horsemen.

You are free, of course, to leave the Church, along with its Masses, Communion and confessionals, at any time ... provided that you can face the indoctrinated phobia of eternal damnation for your soul, in dying with "mortal sins" unabsolved. In no way, that is, could you leave that group and yet be happy and fulfilled, if any of what you had been taught were true.

Harassment and ostracism of those who dare to expose the corruption of the sacred Church? Naturally:

> The [Patty Hanson] family filed a lawsuit against the Diocese of Phoenix [for the alleged sexual abuse of their children at the hands of their Father]. They got nasty letters saying they were ruthless liars peddling trumped-up accusations and exaggerated suffering for a little limelight and a lot of cash. They got harassing phone calls at 3 a.m. and anonymous death threats (Bruni and Burkett, 2002).

All of which is to say that the closer one looks at alleged "cults" versus "legitimate" religions, the less difference one can find between them. (Cf. "We define 'cult' as a group where the leader is unchallengeable and considered infallible" [Kramer and Alstad, 1993]. Also compare Robert Lifton's [1989] eight characteristics of any totalistic group. Then judge for yourself whether or not the Catholic Church *fits every one of them.* Even with regard to the "loading of language," it is obvious that the Catholic definitions of "confession" and "communion" differ significantly from how the words are used outside of the religion. That is so, just as surely as Scientology's definitions of its key words differ from how the same terms are used outside that organization. Further, when the confession of mortal sins, as a means of ensuring one's salvation, extends down to masturbation, there is nothing healthy about that claimed need for disclosure, any more than writing up self-reports for one's superiors to read in any so-called cult could be healthy.) That elusive difference is even aside from Pope John Paul's explicit endorsement of Mexico's Father Maciel and his allegedly sexually abusive Legionaries of Christ organization. For there, to exit that group—not merely to leave the religion in general—was explicitly to lose one's salvation. Yet reportedly, in the same environment:

> Maciel's ruse about getting permission for his sexual urges from Pope Pius XII was [told] to bewildered seminarians,

> some barely past puberty, in order to sexually abuse them and satisfy himself (Berry and Renner, 2004).

Or, closer to home, as a Cajun Catholic woman alleged of her experiences at the hands of her own parish priest:

> I was told [by Father John] that I had been chosen by God to help him with his studies of sex because *he* was responsible for helping adults and he didn't know anything about it (in Berry, 1992).

> [Tim] said nothing when Father Jay took him into the bathroom at his parents' house and asked him to perform oral sex....
>
> Father Jay told the boy: "This is between you and me. This is something special. God would approve." And Tim believed him (Bruni and Burkett, 2002).

Comparable "chosen by God" lines have, of course, been used by many a guru-figure on his (or her) own bewildered disciples, to get them to put out. As has, perhaps, the trusted, "unimpeachable character" of other "men of God":

> [Father Bruce] Ritter was ... America's answer to Mother Teresa....
>
> When Father Bruce turned his attention to one of [his helpers at the misled Covenant House mission for street kids —the "McDonald's of child care"], they often described feeling a kind of "glow" or "warm light." In many ways, their religious devotion was not only to God but to Father Bruce—a cult of personality around the man whose mission they carried out (Sennott, 1992).

"America's answer to Mother Teresa" was later accused of "sexually abusing or sexually approaching" more than a dozen of the boys in his care—a charge he denies.

Other respected Catholic holy men, however, have been able to counter less of their own alleged indiscretions:

> The priest engaged in anal intercourse, oral sex, group sex with two boys at a time, plied them with pot, had a dog lick their genitals (Berry, 1992).

Elsewhere, too:

> Nearly two hundred people [one of them just four years old at the time] who say they were raped or fondled by [the now-deceased Rev. John J.] Geoghan have filed claims against him and his supervisors in the last several years. Experts believe he probably molested three to four times as many people as have come forward....
>
> By most accounts at least fifteen hundred priests [by now, over four thousand (Zoll, 2005)] have faced public accusations of sexual misconduct with minors since the mid-1980s (Boston Globe, 2003).

> Father Anthony Corbin ... confessed to having had sex with an eighth-grade boy. Corbin dressed his victim in a loincloth to resemble Christ headed for the crucifix[ion] (Bruni and Burkett, 2002).

> Some of what was done [by the Catholic Christian Brothers and the Sisters of Mercy] was of a quite exceptional depravity, so that terms like "sexual abuse" are too weak to convey it. For example ... the account of a man who as a boy was a particular favorite of some Christian Brothers at Tardun [Australia] who competed as to who could rape him one hundred times first, his account of being in terrible pain, bleeding and bewildered (Raftery and O'Sullivan, 2001).

With "holiness" and "purity" like that, who needs obscenity? With conscienceless "saints" and "representatives of God on Earth" like these, who needs demonic sinners?

The family-incest-like attempted cover-ups of alleged Catholic clergy sexual abuse further show quite brutally how little the supposed "checks and balances" within that same system actually work. So, too, do the related and utterly cruel attempts to discredit the victims, and the closing of the upper clerical ranks against the latter. (Thomas Doyle characterized the Church's response to that reported abuse as involving "a defrauding, a stonewalling, and outright lying to the people" [in Berry and Renner, 2004].) For there, offending priests, even those with known and extensive histories of sexual abuse, were more likely to simply be transferred to another parish—if not simultaneously promoted, suspended *with pay,* or retired with pension—than to be meaningfully censured. That was done even after the violated families had been explicitly guaranteed by religious superiors that specific, appropriate steps would be taken to ensure that the abuse would never happen again. (The same promises were, of course, later grossly broken.)

> Many argued that the hierarchy's handling of abusive priests revealed systemic problems with their Church. "It isn't just the cardinal; it's the way we operate.... There are structural issues. What is it that has made us priests be so [unwilling to] speak out when something awful is happening, and not to cover up?" (Boston Globe, 2003).

Amazingly, even after the Inquisition, even after the wanton burning of witches at the stake, even after countless holy wars and crusades, the depths of cruelty and evil perpetrated by our world's "safe," traditional religions—never mind its potentially harmful nontraditional groups—still surprises us. Yet, there is nothing whatsoever "new" in something like the recent Catholic scandals. That is so, first when compared with the fear-ridden constraints and "skillful" cruelties of the centuried guru game, and the rampant alleged sexual abuse by "divine" gurus of their own disciples, in "compassionate, tolerant" Buddhism and elsewhere. It is also true when viewed in terms of the Church's own millennia of canonical laws directed toward (and thus admitting the existence of) pedophilia among their clergy.

> When Pope Alexander VI [d. 1503] marked the final victory of Catholic Spain over the Moors, he did so not with a Mass at St. Peter's but with a party in the piazza in front of the church. Flagons of wine flowed among the honored guests, women from Rome's most elegant brothels offered their services and children were passed freely among bishops and priests celebrating Catholicism's latest triumph with a sexual bacchanalia (Bruni and Burkett, 2002).

If we have learned one thing specifically from the Catholic Church, though, it is that there is no hope whatsoever of our world's religions changing for the better, without their evils being publicly exposed:

> No problem is ever solved discreetly any more, especially in the Catholic Church. The problems are only solved when the Catholic people say out loud and on the record what a lot of them are thinking privately, and aim their message directly

> at the religious leadership (Andrew Greeley, in [Berry, 1992]).

And even then, the scandals which had first surfaced in the late 1980s and early '90s raised their heads again around the turn of the century, in a new wave of accusations of clergy sexual abuse, substantially identical to those which were thought to have been properly addressed by that revered leadership a decade earlier. And both of those waves, sadly, have only gone to show how these "holy" organizations will typically close ranks and fight tooth and nail, in an "ordeal by litigation" directed at their already shattered victims. For they must, above all, protect the virginal public reputation of their "divine institution," through which God speaks so uniquely.

Conversely:

> If there are any heroes in this squalid tale, they are the victims, who found their voice, who found the courage, after years of suffering in silence and isolation, to step into the light and say, as one did, "This happened to me, and this is wrong" (Boston Globe, 2003).

And not only is it wrong, but it must stop.

CHAPTER XXV

OF CABBAGES AND NATURE SPRITES

(FINDHORN COMMUNITY:
PETER AND EILEEN CADDY)

"The time has come," the Caddys said
"To channel many thoughts:
Of Moray Firth—and trailer parks
Of tiny elves—and Scots—
Of why the cabbages grow large—
And whether Swedes are hot"

IN NOVEMBER OF 1962, Peter and Eileen Caddy settled with their three young sons and a friend, Dorothy Maclean, near the coast of the Moray Firth in northeast Scotland. There they lived, down the road from Aberdeen and Inverness, in a house trailer on a parcel of land destined to become the first seed of the Findhorn Community.

Prior to that, Peter, a former military officer, had followed his own guru-figure for five years—a woman who was also his second wife, Sheena. To join them as a disciple, Eileen had left her own husband and children. Soon after that departure, "stricken with guilt and remorse," she began hearing voices, i.e., "guidance." The believed source of those voices is obvious in the title of Eileen's first book: *God Spoke to Me*. Later presumed channelings by her included "transmissions from Saint-Germain [and] Sir Francis Bacon" (Hawken, 1976).

Peter and Eileen later split from Sheena and, by 1957, were managing a hotel in Forres, Scotland, which building was later to become part of the Findhorn community.

They were then transferred from there to another ailing hotel to resurrect it. And, having been suddenly terminated from that position, made their new home in the Findhorn Bay Caravan (i.e., Trailer) Park, adjacent to a garbage dump.

In accord with Eileen's inner guidance, the pioneers established a small garden in the "sand and scrub" of the trailer park in 1965.

> [T]o the astonishment of experts, their results were phenomenal, producing plants whose variety and vigor could not be conventionally explained (Findhorn, 1980).

That "unconventional" success was indeed soon revealed to be ostensibly due to the ability of community members, and Dorothy in particular, to "talk to the plants" and nature spirits/devas. Additional gardening advice came from an Edinburgh man who "had experiences of nature beings, which took the form of elves and fauns, and ... Pan himself" (Riddell, 1990).

The outcome of all that was the forty-pound cabbages for which the community first became famous.

By the mid-'70s, however, when Peter stopped working in the garden, many of the phenomenal aspects of the vegetation disappeared.

> The growth here was fantastic to demonstrate to Peter Caddy and to others that it was possible. Now we know it is possible to work with the Nature Kingdom, but we no longer have the need to produce a plant where it won't normally grow (in Hawken, 1976).

The contemporary American laying-on-of-hands healer Barbara Ann Brennan describes (1993) relevant aspects of her own later extended stay in the Findhorn Community:

> When I was there, I stood on a nature power point called Randolph's Leap, a place near Findhorn where the Druids are supposed to have worshiped and communed with nature spirits. I asked to have access to the nature spirits.
>
> [After] about a month ... I started seeing little nature spirits [or sprites] everywhere I went. They would follow me as I walked around the property. They were always a bit shy and would stay a few feet behind me, giggling.

Ancillary attempts, outside the main development of the community, were also made to contact UFOs and "space beings."

In 1969, Findhorn attracted six hundred visitors ... all of them from our own planet.

David Spangler and his female partner arrived in the early 1970s to live at Findhorn for three years, as the last of the "founding figures" there, lecturing and giving channeled guidance. Their arrival brought the community population into double digits, growing to forty-five by the end of the year.

In those early days, until around 1972,

> Peter would stride around finding fault with everyone. There was nothing but endless work, from early in the morning until late at night.... Young freaks escaping burnt-out lives in London were verbally thrashed by Peter for the slightest deviation from the rigid order and structure of the community (Hawken, 1976).

In 1973, the sixty-ish Peter's heart opened ... to a young, Swedish woman living in the community, with the ensuing reaction from Eileen having the effect of throwing Findhorn into a period of uncertainty. Though the potential extramarital relationship was never consummated, Peter and Eileen grew farther apart as the years passed. The former eventually left the community in 1979.

One female member of the populace described the mid-'70s in the Findhorn Community this way:

> The energy level was very high, and a lot of music came out of that time.... There was this universal energy of love, and all of a sudden it could hit you with somebody else's partner. Because there was an openness towards anything that God sends in one's direction, some people would then ... dive into

> these relationships, and would find themselves in a tangle with no clear way of handling the complications.
>
> It was like an epidemic.... It really rocked the community (Findhorn, 1980).

In spite of—or perhaps *because of*—such "love in the time of cabbages," by 1980 over three hundred people had been drawn to the Findhorn Caravan Park.

Or the rocking "Findstock," if you prefer.

Through all of that, Eileen's guidance slowly disclosed the long-term plans for the community:

> I want you to see this center of light [i.e., Findhorn] as an ever-growing cell of light. It started as a family group; it is now a community; it will grow into a village, then a town and finally into a vast city of light (Caddy, 1976).

Nor was the scope of that undertaking lost on the early founders, or on those who have come since them:

> In one form or another there has been a deep awareness that what was being worked out [at Findhorn] was of supreme importance to the whole world.
>
> This could of course be just an inflated ego on the part of those at Findhorn—or it could be a most daring and glorious act of faith, that God had a vast plan for mankind which, if known and followed, could lead to a new age, and that Findhorn was a key point in that plan (Caddy, 1976).

> The Findhorn Community plays a significant part in a revolution that is gently changing the world.... This revolution does not "do" anything. It does not normally make headlines in any of the news media, but it creates the conditions in which [love, spirituality, cooperation and harmony] can flourish among human beings. Perhaps it is responsible for the rather extraordinary changes that, at the close of the '80s, have laid the basis for the end of the Cold War and the transformation of Eastern Europe. But it has much more still to do (Riddell, 1990).

* * *

The present Findhorn community includes an independent Steiner (i.e., "Waldorf") school, providing additional alternative education for the children there. Students are encouraged to learn at their own rate, in a close relationship to a teacher who continues with a class from one year to the next. By itself, that is undoubtedly a wonderful way to structure an educational program. The "Intimidation of the Waldorf Kind" article by Arno Frank (2000), however, raises serious concerns about those schools in general, as does the information presented at www.waldorfcritics.org:

> Parents should be told that the science and history curriculum will be based on Steiner's reading of the *"akashic* record," according to which the "ancients" had clairvoyant powers which Anthroposophic initiation may help students attain some day. They should be told that loyal Steiner followers believe humans once lived on the lost continent of Atlantis.... They should be told that teachers study a medieval scheme in which race, blood, and the "four temperaments" will help them understand their students' development (PLANS, 2004).

Steiner's first Atlantean sub-race was named the Rmoahals.

> When a Rmoahals man pronounced a word, this word developed a power similar to that of the object it designated. Because of this, words at that time were curative; they could advance the growth of plants, tame the rage of animals, and perform other similar functions (Steiner, 1959).

Rudolf Steiner himself (1861 – 1925), in his *Atlantis and Lemuria* (1963), expounded on the details of our imagined lost history, crediting the terrestrial atmosphere in the time of Atlantis as being much more dense at that time, than it is at present.

> The above-mentioned density of air is as certain for occult experience as any fact of today given by the senses can be.
>
> Equally certain however is the fact, perhaps even more inexplicable for contemporary physics and chemistry, that at that time the *water* on the whole Earth was much *thinner* than today....
>
> [I]n the Lemurian and even in the Atlantean period, stones and metals were much softer than later (Steiner, 1959).

> We need not raise the question now as to whether such a condition of density is compatible with the opinion held by modern science, for science and logical thought can ... never say the final word as to what is possible (Steiner, 1963).

Having thus disposed of physics in his pursuit of a denser, thinner and softer metaphysics, Steiner (1963) continued:

> [T]he human body had been provided with an eye that now no longer exists, but we have a reminder of this erstwhile condition in the myth of the One-Eyed Cyclops.

Nor was that the only discrepancy to be found between our known world and the bodies of yore:

> The forms of [the first] animals would, in the present day, strike us as fabulous monsters, for their bodies (and this must be carefully kept in mind) were of the nature of air....
>
> Another group of physical beings had bodies which consisted of air-ether, light-ether and water, and these were plant-like beings....

"If I could talk to the plantimals...." Or be one:

> [M]an lived as a plant being in the Sun itself (Steiner, 1959).

Steiner further claimed of Lemurian women:

> Everything was animated for them and showed itself to them in soul powers and apparitions.... That which impelled them to their reaction were "inner voices," or what plants, animals, stones, wind and clouds, the whispering of the trees, and so on, told them....
>
> If with his consciousness man could raise himself into [the] supersensible world, he would be able to greet the "ant or bee spirit" there in full consciousness as his sister being. *The seer can actually do this.*

Rudolf himself was the head of the German branch of the Theosophical Society until being expelled from that in 1913 for "illegal" (according to the rules of the Society) activities. From that split, he founded his own Anthroposophical Society, beginning with fifty-five ex-members of the TS, from which the Waldorf phenomenon in general has grown.

> Steiner had encountered Theosophy in the 1880s through the writings of Sinnett and Blavatsky, most of which he later rejected—with the exception of *The Secret Doctrine,* which he regarded as the most remarkable esoteric text (apart from his own) published in modern times....
>
> The audiences for [Steiner's theosophical lectures] were at first very small. Happily, Steiner showed no concern, claiming that the audience was swelled by invisible spiritual beings and the dead, eager for the occult knowledge they could not, apparently, acquire in the Other World (Washington, 1995).

The Secret Doctrine was Madame Blavatsky's anti-Darwinian explanation of the origins of life on Earth, via a number (seven) of "root races" purportedly descended from spiritual beings from the moon. The book was presented as an explication of stanzas from the little-known *Book of Dzyan*—itself written in the unknown-to-any-linguist language of Senzar.

Steiner, meanwhile, taught the existence of a Lord of the Dark Face, an evil entity by the name of Ahriman—the spirit of materialism. That disruptive being, he felt, "had been making trouble in the world since 1879 when the Archangel Michael took over the divine guidance of mankind and began a cosmic process of enlightenment" (Washington, 1995).

Steiner (1947) further described the progressing student's "ascent into the higher worlds" as involving a meeting with the "Guardian of the Threshold":

> [T]he Guardian of the Threshold is an (astral) figure, revealing itself to the student's awakened higher sight.... It is a lower magical process to make the Guardian of the Threshold physically visible also. That was attained by producing a cloud of fine substance, a kind of frankincense resulting from a particular mixture of a number of substances. The developed power of the magician is then able to mould the frankincense into shape, animating it with the still unredeemed karma of the individual....
>
> What is here indicated in narrative form must not be understood in the sense of an allegory, but as an experience of the highest possible reality befalling the esoteric student.

On a more personal level, Rudolf averred:

> The clairvoyant ... can describe, for every mode of thought and for every law of nature, a form which expresses them. A revengeful thought, for example, assumes an arrow-like, pronged form, while a kindly thought is often formed like an opening flower, and so on. Clear-cut, significant thoughts are regular and symmetrical in form, while confused thoughts have wavy outlines.

And speaking of "wavy outlines":

> Anthroposophical medicine seems to be based partly on magical theories of correspondence—for example cholera is a punishment for insufficient self-confidence and the pox for lack of affection. Today the Anthroposophists run clinics, a mental hospital, and a factory for medicines which has marketed a cancer cure (Webb, 1976).

As to Steiner's overall caliber of thought, then, Storr (1996) summarizes:

> His belief system is so eccentric, so unsupported by evidence, so manifestly bizarre, that rational skeptics are bound to consider it delusional....
>
> [H]is so-called thinking, his supposed power of supersensible perception, led to a vision of the world, the universe, and of cosmic history which is entirely unsupported by any evidence, which is at odds with practically everything which modern physics and astronomy have revealed, and which is more like science fiction than anything else.

In a somewhat gentler vein, Robert Carroll (2004d) concluded:

> There is no question that Steiner made contributions in many fields, but as a philosopher, scientist, and artist he rarely rises above mediocrity and is singularly unoriginal.

Ken Wilber (2000b), however, expressed his own, more positive evaluation of poor Rudolf, in this way:

> [Steiner] was an extraordinary pioneer ... and one of the most comprehensive psychological and philosophical visionaries of his time.

Indeed, Steiner's credulous followers similarly believe him to have been "a genius in twelve fields" (McDermott, 1984).

To be fair, Rudolf's grounded philosophizing, as presented in the first half of McDermott's very selectively chosen ("veneer of academia," etc.) *Essential Steiner,* is much more coherent than are his farther flights of fancy. (McDermott himself was president of the California Institute of Integral Studies [www.ciis.edu] for many years. For the catty relationship between himself and the allegedly "evil, hated" kw, see Wilber [2001].)

Still, even given that limited coherence, one cannot help but notice that Wilber, in Chart 4B of his (2000b) *Integral Psychology,* presents a mapping of Steiner's nine levels of reality to the "correlative basic structures" of psychology in his own Four-Quadrant "Theory of Everything." (That same book is intended as a "textbook of transpersonal psychology." Its mapped levels include astral bodies and the like.) Yet, the perception of auras, if real, would come via the same clairvoyant faculties and subtle bodies as would be used to read the *akashic* records. Did Steiner then see auras clearly, but hallucinate his purported *akashic* readings? Or was he equally imagining both? Either way, how does Wilber justify mapping Steiner's levels of reality to his own theories, while ignoring the remainder of what Steiner devoutly claims to have experienced through the *same* purported means?

Regardless, Velikovsky would surely be proud. For, Wilber's endorsement of Steiner means either that he has read so little of Rudolf's work that he is unaware of the "farther reaches" of it ... or that he is aware of those fantasies-presented-as-fact, but still considers the man to be an insightful "visionary" and "extraordinary pioneer" in (clairvoyance-based) psychology and philosophy.

Given Wilber's history with Da's coronas and shabd yoga, those two options seem equally plausible. (Wilber has evidently hardly read into the latter yoga at all, yet still presents himself as an expert, fit to determine who the top yogis of that path are [see Lane, 1996].)

And note again how kw's complimentary appraisal of Steiner is, as usual, offered as no mere opinion, but is rather given as if it were an indisputable fact—"Thus spake the Oracle of Boulder." In reality, however, it is emphatically No Such Thing, especially with regard to Steiner's philosophy.

If you're going to be an oracle, it behooves you to *get it right.*

* * *

The continual buzz of activity throughout a community such as Findhorn could, of course, easily detract from one's meditations. Not one to be thus distracted, Eileen Caddy sought guidance for herself as to where to find a small, quiet place, away from the crowded living conditions.

> [S]he asked within and the voice, in a joyous piece of guidance, replied: "Why don't you go down to the public toilets? You will find perfect peace there."
>
> The little toilet block referred to has been preserved and is now a herbal apothecary and wholefood café (Riddell, 1990).

If such preservation seems to be excessively reverential, note that traditional Tibetan medicine goes even further, at times containing small amounts of lama (not llama) ... um....

> [Seventeenth-century Austrian Jesuit cleric Johann] Grueber was particularly repulsed by the custom of the laity's eating "curative pills" containing the Dalai Lama's excrement (Schell, 2001).

Or, in the vernacular: "holy shit."

> A hundred years ago, rumors that the feces of the Dalai Lama—the spiritual leader of Tibetan Buddhists—had beneficial properties prompted the UK's Surgeon General to analyze them in the interests of science. They contained nothing remarkable, he concluded. Just as well: According to a spokesperson at the UK-based Tibet Foundation, "These days you can't even buy the Dalai Lama's used clothes, never mind his excrement" (Toscani, 2000).

And they call that progress!

> When the doctor [treating David Bohm—the Dalai Lama's "physics teacher"—for "thick blood" in Switzerland] indicated that he would send to Dharamsala for medication, the Dalai Lama insisted that the treatment should begin immediately. He took Precious Tablets, wrapped in silk, from a pouch in his room and instructed Saral [Bohm's wife] on how they

> should be prepared. Bohm found their taste revolting (Peat, 1997).

"Nityananda the Poo," however, would surely have approved—and perhaps even grabbed a mouthful.

Along those same lines, in later years Findhorn experienced a sewage backup, flooding the toilets and bathtubs of the Caddys' former hotel in Cluny Hills, now owned and operated by the Findhorn Foundation as a community residence. Residents spent two weeks attempting to find the relevant sewage lines—including, in desperation, searching via the use of divining rods and pendulums. That ardent pursuit, however, failed to disclose the source of the obstruction.

> It became increasingly clear that the sewer blockage was a symbolic way of showing us something about our life.
>
> A channeling was received. It told us we had become too concerned with outer forms, neglecting our spiritual connection. The sewage began to flood the garden. [Hence, "love in the time of cabbages *and cholera.*"] We organized a meeting and agreed that each member would make a personal commitment to their own spiritual development. In the afternoon we shared what we had individually decided. At 4 p.m., when the meeting ended, the sewers were unblocked. They had unblocked themselves! (Riddell, 1990).

Verily, "the Lord doth work in mysterious ways," etc. As do His "avatars":

> To see if he had become proud after becoming a big guru, Ramakrishna went to slum areas and washed the toilets with his hair (Satchidananda, in [Mandelkorn, 1978]).

* * *

> As time went on, it became ever clearer to Eileen and Peter that they were ... the spearhead of a new age. They were pioneering a new way of living which would spread throughout the world and give new hope for the future. People would come from every land to learn this new way and then go back to live it out wherever they might be....
>
> Gradually the greatness of the task they had undertaken became clearer to Peter and Eileen and those who

> were with them. Findhorn was nothing less than the growing tip of humanity (Caddy, 1976).

To keep one's perspective in the midst of such pioneering, "growing tip of humanity" excitement, however, is no easy task ... as every other community which has ever harbored a similarly grandiose mission could testify.

W. Brugh Joy, author of *Joy's Way,* was then invited to give a talk at Findhorn in 1980, about what he "sensed was ahead for the community as a whole," to a group of participants preparing to enter communal life there. Not surprisingly, the urge to address those unspoken issues proved too strong to resist:

> I talked about the consequences of feeling "special" and how doing battle against the "evils of the world" not only creates the "enemy," but is actually a projection of the darker aspects of the community onto the world screen. Needless to say, the talk was not popular and I was fast falling into the "unwelcome guest" category....
>
> Despite assertions by most partisans of the New Age that they are promoting such virtues as selfless service to the world, New Age beliefs in the specialness and innocence of the New Age are, in my opinion, regressive ... toward the infantile, if not the fetal. Such ideation tends to be self-centered (Joy, 1990).

Some days later, the "community poet" responded, onstage, after some skits and singing, to Joy's earlier talk.

> In venomous poetry, powerful and afire with wrathful righteousness, he unleashed the dark feelings and destructive forces of the community. The objects of his rage were the Americans in general and myself in particular. We were portrayed in terms that would make fecal material seem sunny by comparison. His attack centered around money and power ... the dark side of any endeavor that wears the mask of great good and service. The only thing explicitly missing was sex, except he covered that by using the words "fuck" and "fucking" with an extraordinary frequency (Joy, 1990).

And this was scarcely odd, because....

Of course, such an isolated outburst in no way invalidates the overall good done within and by the community. That is so particularly since the general response to Joy's speech and the poet's counter-attack, at least in public, seems to have been fairly mature. That is, unlike what we might have expected to see from some of the "Rude Boys" in this world, Joy was certainly not run off the property for his comments. Nor was he stripped naked or called a "bottom feeder" by the respected leaders of the community. By contrast, were such criticisms as Joy's directed toward the divine guru-figure or holy ashram of the average disciple, the latter would more often than not consider them to be violently blasphemous.

In a way, though, one could still actually be surprised, overall, by that temperate response. For, considering the grandiose perspective from which the community was founded, coupled with Peter Caddy's authoritarian control during the first decade of its existence, things could have turned out much worse. As it currently stands, however, Findhorn welcomes more than 14,000 guests each year for temporary work retreats or to one of several hundred adult classes taught year-round by New Age personages such as the "spiritual healer" Caroline Myss. It also exists as part of a global network of sustainable "Ecovillages."

Apparently, then, not every foray into spiritually-based community living need end in disaster. Undoubtedly, though, such a diverse group of "believers" as exist in Findhorn would have far less potential for messing up a community than if they were all following the same "sage," i.e., if they all shared and reinforced the same "madness" in each other. After all, a mixed group of people, even if they were each totally conforming to the tenets and expected behaviors of their respective paths, would still effectively create a diverse population of ideas and perspectives.

> A more heterogeneous group of people living together in a community I could not have imagined (Hawken, 1976).

And, as in agriculture, such a varied population is less likely to be devastatingly affected by any specific pathology than is a homogeneous one.

The Findhorn community, further, is a relatively "feel-good, New Age" one. It has thus never placed any primary emphasis on destroying the ego as a means to God-realization. Consequently, it has not sanctioned that easy outlet for sadistic behavior toward others, as if it were "for their own good" as a cover for simply exacting respect and obedience from them, to the degree which one finds in the typical ashram.

Probably of equal or greater importance, though, was the fading-out of the Caddys' influence as the community grew. That was done, surprisingly, in response to Eileen's own received "guidance," in one of the most generous sharings of power that one will ever find in a community, whether spiritual or otherwise.

It will also have helped that Findhorn has never been a monastic environment. For, that freedom itself removes a large part of the potential for suppression, repression/projection, scandals and cover-ups.

There is also a relative absence of both *penalties for leaving* and of a not merely grandiose but spiritually "liberating" benefit to oneself for staying. That is, unlike most of the other communities we have met herein, Findhorn seems to have placed "saving the world"—via the growth of the community into a town, a village, and then a "vast city of light"—ahead of "saving oneself." And one can walk away from the former when the going gets tough, much more easily than one could turn one's back on the latter, for having far less of a personal stake in it. After all, throwing up one's hands and allowing the world to go to hell in a handbasket is one thing; throwing away one's "only chance for enlightenment in this lifetime," through disobedience or abandonment of a spiritual path, is quite another.

All of the above "missing" elements in Findhorn are generally *absolutely central* to any "authentic, spiritually transformative" ashram, as a closed society where "really serious" disciples will remain for the rest of their lives. With stunning irony, then, it is very probably the *lack* of all of those things in Findhorn which have made it into an (according to present indications) "safe" environment. (But, see also Stephen Castro's [1996] *Hypocrisy and Dissent Within the Findhorn Foundation,* for further information in that regard.)

The now relatively democratic management of the community —with feedback and *real* "checks and balances" to keep the rulers accountable to those they rule over—will also have greatly helped.

Of course, even there:

> We have also heard from people who had gone to the community in response to something they had read or heard, only to discover that its reality was not what they had expected. Most of these reports indicated a disappointment

> that, in the minds of these people, Findhorn was not living up to the beautiful ideals which it proclaimed....
>
> [One] young man kept alternating between staying in London and living at Findhorn. Finally, despairing of his ability to adapt to Findhorn, he told us that emotionally it was a worse jungle than London (Findhorn, 1980).

In any case, one cannot help but wonder what might have happened had the already geriatric Peter Caddy had his way with that Swedish girl three decades ago. Or, had he received explicit inner guidance himself—thus qualifying as a guru-figure on top of his existing authoritarian tendencies, and being in a position to inform others of "God's will," particularly as it may have related to the young blond lady. Indeed, in that scenario, there might now be nothing left to mark the spot where Findhorn once stood, nor even a community poet to commemorate the occasion in ribald verse.

Verse, that is, such as the following:

> There once was a Scotsman named Caddy
> A well-nigh impassioned brute laddie
> He spied a young Swede
> Said, "She's got what I need"
> Now he's nine months from being a daddy

CHAPTER XXVI

... TO A NUNNERY

(PARAMAHANSA YOGANANDA)

Nearly everyone is familiar with those three little monkey-figures that depict the maxim, "See no evil, hear no evil, speak no evil." I emphasize the positive approach: "See that which is good, hear that which is good, speak that which is good." And smell, taste, and feel that which is good; think that which is good; love that which is good. Be enthroned in the castle of goodness, and your memories will be like beautiful flowers in a garden of noble dreams (Yogananda, 1986).

For all future time, Paramahansa Yogananda ... will be regarded as one of the very greatest of India's ambassadors of the Higher Culture to the New World (W. Y. Evans-Wentz, in [SRF, 1976]).

PARAMAHANSA YOGANANDA WAS the first yoga master from India to spend the greater part of his life in North America.

Born in northeast India near the Himalayan border in 1893, Yogananda began practicing kriya yoga in his early years, and met his guru, Sri Yukteswar, at age seventeen.

Following a prophetic vision, and at the direction of Yukteswar, Yogananda accepted an invitation to speak at the Congress of Religious Liberals in Boston, in the autumn of 1920. He remained in America following that successful debut, establishing Self-Realization Fellowship (SRF) and its headquarters, now named the "Mother Center," in an abandoned former hotel atop Mount Washington in Los Angeles, in 1925. As a "Church of all Religions," SRF attempts to embrace the "underlying truth of all religions," with particular emphasis on yoga/Hinduism and Christianity. Membership numbers are classified, but reasonable guesses range from 25,000 to 100,000 currently active members.

The enterprising young yogi spent the years from 1925 to 1936 lecturing to capacity crowds in halls throughout America, spreading knowledge of the "holy science" of kriya yoga.

As far as the channels through which one may receive his variant of that particular set of techniques of meditation, Yogananda explained in his (1998) *Autobiography:*

> The actual technique should be learned from an authorized Kriyaban (kriya yogi) of Self-Realization Fellowship (Yogoda Satsanga Society of India).

Earlier versions of the same book, however, within the three editions published while Yogananda was still alive, placed far less restrictions on who may give that initiation:

> The actual technique [of kriya yoga] must be learned from a Kriyaban or kriya yogi (Yogananda, 1946).

More recently, SRF (in Rawlinson, 1997) stated their position regarding the importance of their particular line of gurus in effecting the spiritual progress of the disciple:

> Some take kriya yoga and become fully satisfied and forget about the link of masters—they will never reach God.

The reader may then ponder for him- or herself as to what possible reasons any organization could have for thus restricting, to itself, the dissemination of the techniques of its founder, after the latter's death, when no such restriction was put in place during his life. SRF's position, of course, is that every change to Yogananda's writings since his passing has been made on the basis of instructions given by him while he was still alive, and done simply to "clarify and rephrase" the text. For my own part, I do not find that claim at all convincing. Indeed, the posthumously hamhanded evisceration of his *Whispers From Eternity* poetry alone (see Dakota, 1998)—being subjected to brutal and unnecessary editing which no poetic soul could ever countenance—would cast it in doubt.

Regardless, the kriya yoga technique itself is actually not nearly as "top secret" as SRF presents it as being. Rather, both of the preliminary techniques leading up to kriya proper are widely known in India. Of those, the "Om" technique is essentially just an internally chanted mantra, while the "Hong-Sau" technique/mantra is given in Chapter 7 of Radha's (1978) *Kundalini Yoga for the West.* (Radha herself was a disciple of Satchidananda's guru, Swami Sivananda, and operated an ashram in that lineage in British Columbia, Canada.) Much of the first stage of the kriya technique itself further exists in Chapter 9 of the same book. Yogananda's preliminary "Energization Exercises," too, are very similar to ones given later by Brennan (1987).

Ironically, in spite of their evidently opposite attitudes toward the "secrecy" of those techniques, Sivananda's ashram and SRF have long been friendly with each other.

Swami Sivananda himself (1887 – 1963), in addition to founding the Divine Life Society, wrote over three hundred books. That is hardly surprising, given his exalted spiritual state:

> I have seen God myself. I have negated name and form, and what remains is Existence-Knowledge-Bliss and nothing else. I behold God everywhere. There is no veil. I am one. There is no duality. I rest in my own self. My bliss is beyond description. The World of dream is gone. I alone exist (Sivananda, 1958).

> People consider [Sivananda] to be a Shiva avatar, incarnation (Gyan, 1980).

> Swamiji was a phenomenon. He was described as a "symbol of holiness," a "walking, talking God on Earth" (Ananthanarayanan, 1970).

Of course, no "walking, talking God" would grace this planet without promulgating his own skewed set of unsubstantiated beliefs:

> Swami Sivananda has said that every woman whom a man lures into his bed must in some lifetime become his lawful wife (Radha, 1992).

> The late Swami Sivananda of [Rishikesh], to my mind the most grotesque product of the Hindu Renaissance, advised people to write their "spiritual diaries"; and in oral instructions, he told Indian and Western disciples to write down how often they masturbated.... [O]r, as one male disciple told me, "make a list of number of times when you use hand for pleasure, and check it like double book keeping against number of times when you renounced use of hand" (Bharati, 1976).

And they say accountants don't know how to have fun!

Elsewhere in the same book, Swami Bharati—the highly opinionated monk of the Ramakrishna Order whom we have met earlier in some of his kinder moments—categorized Sivananda as a "pseudo-mystic ... fat and smiling." (Of the Maharishi, by contrast, Bharati stated: "I have no reason to doubt that he is a genuine mystic.... Were it not for the additional claims that Mahesh Yogi and his disciples make for their brand of mini-yoga [regarding 'world peace,' etc.], their product would be just as good as any other yoga discipline well done." So, you see, no one really knows what [if any] is valid and what isn't, even though they all *pretend* to know.)

Further venting his own instructive anger and anguish solely for the compassionate benefit of others, Bharati (1976) offered a comparable opinion of Vivekananda:

> The "four kinds of yoga" notion goes back, entirely, and without any mitigating circumstances, to Swami Vivekananda's four dangerous little booklets entitled *Raja-yoga, Karma-yoga, Jnana-yoga,* and *Bhakti-yoga.* [Those titles and terms refer to "royal," "service," "wisdom" and "devotional" yoga, respectively.] These are incredibly naïve, incredibly short excerpts from Indian literature in translations, rehashed in his talks in America and elsewhere....

> I am certain that Vivekananda has done more harm than good to the seekers of mystical knowledge.... Vivekananda's concept of raja yoga ... is dysfunctional.

Bharati's own contributions to the understanding of mysticism, however, themselves tended toward the insignificant side. Whatever mysticism may be—from psychosis to the valid perception of higher levels of reality than the physical—there is, in my opinion, no measurable chance of it fitting into Bharati's view of things. Even his insistence that the mystical "zero-experience," of the "oneness" of the individual and cosmic soul, must be only temporary and incapacitating, is relatively belied by Wilber's claim to have experienced the One Taste state continuously for half a decade.

Interestingly, Bharati (1974) regarded Yogananda as a "phony," lumping him in with T. Lobsang Rampa and the sorcerer Carlos Castaneda. He simultaneously, though, took Chögyam Trungpa as having taught "authentic Tibetan Buddhism," presumably even in the midst of that guru's penchant for "stripping the disciples." I do not claim to know how to find sense in that position. But then, unlike Bharati and his admired, soporific friend, Herbert V. Guenther, I am not a scholar. And indeed, to devote one's life to becoming an expert in the details of a pile of sanctioned baloney, then trashing anyone who doesn't buy into the same brand of foolishness, strikes me as being one of the most absurd ways in which to waste a life.

At any rate, Paramahansa Yogananda—whether phony or not—slowly accumulated a core of close disciples as the years passed, and thus began a monastic order in his own Swami lineage. One such early "direct disciple," Faye Wright, began following the yogi in the early 1930s, entering the ashrams in her late teens. Now known as Daya Mata, she figures significantly in contemporary SRF culture, as the current lifetime president of Self-Realization Fellowship.

Retiring from his cross-country lecture tours, Yogananda spent much of the 1940s in seclusion in his Encinitas hermitage—adjacent to the famed "Swami's Point" surfing beach there. In that environment, he wrote his *Autobiography of a Yogi,* a perennial "sleeper" best-seller among books on spirituality, generally considered to be among the "Top 100" spiritual books of the twentieth century.

> [The *Autobiography* is] widely regarded as a classic introduction to yoga and Eastern thought (Ram Dass, 1990).

> Few books in spiritual literature compare to Paramahansa Yogananda's *Autobiography of a Yogi*. It is one of those rare works that in a single reading can transform the reader's entire outlook on life. Since its initial printing in 1946, Yogananda's *Autobiography* has continued to enthrall seekers with its fascinating tales of miracles, saints and astral heavens (Lane, 1995).

> *Autobiography of a Yogi* is regarded as an *Upanishad* of the new age.... We in India have watched with wonder and fascination the phenomenal spread of the popularity of this book about India's saints and philosophy. We have felt great satisfaction and pride that the immortal nectar of India's *Sanatan Dharma,* the eternal laws of truth, has been stored in the golden chalice of *Autobiography of a Yogi* (in Ghosh, 1980).

> No book so polarized the West about India and its culture as this one. For those who liked it, their passion went beyond words. For those who found it an incredible mishmash, the high opinions they had been harboring about Indian thought suddenly seemed to have become wobbly (Arya, 2004).

Interestingly, although Yogananda's writings merit only a single quotation in Wilber's (1983) life's work, both Adi Da (1995) and Andrew Cohen were much influenced by the *Autobiography* early in their spiritual careers. Indeed, Cohen obviously derived the title of his (1992) *Autobiography of an Awakening* from Yogananda's earlier life story. For what it's worth.

The *Autobiography* contains numerous claims of miraculous healings, levitation, bilocation and raising of the dead by various members in the SRF line of gurus, and others of Yogananda's acquaintance.

With less of an eye toward the probability of such miracles occurring, however, the Swiss psychologist Carl Jung—who himself spent time in India—had praised the *study* of yoga in general (as distinct from its practical application, which he explicitly discouraged):

> Quite apart from the charm of the new and the fascination of the half-understood, there is good cause for yoga to have

> many adherents. It offers the possibility of controllable experience and thus satisfies the scientific need for "facts"; and, besides this, by reason of its breadth and depth, its venerable age, its doctrine and method, which include every phase of life, it promises undreamed-of possibilities (in Yogananda, 1946).

The phrase "undreamed-of possibilities" has since been adopted by SRF as the title of an introductory booklet distributed in their churches and elsewhere. Jung's attitude toward Yogananda's writings in particular, however, was far less of a marketing department's dream:

> Paramahansa Yogananda's *Autobiography of a Yogi* ... provoked Jung's sarcasm because its cream puff idealism contained not a single practical "antidote to disastrous population explosion and traffic jams and the threat of starvation, [a book] so rich in vitamins that albumen, carbohydrates, and such like banalities become superogatory.... Happy India!" (Paine, 1998).

Jung, though, is an interesting study himself:

> The brilliant thinker Carl Jung's opportunistic support of the Nazis ... is amply documented. In 1933 he became president of the New German Society of Psychotherapy. Soon thereafter, he wrote the following vicious nonsense (seldom mentioned by his admirers nowadays):
>
>> The Jews have this similarity common with women: as the physically weaker one they must aim at the gaps in the opponent's defenses ... the Arian [*sic*] unconscious has a higher potential than the Jewish (Askenasy, 1978).

In any case, the *Autobiography* itself is dedicated to the "American saint" and prodigious horticulturalist Luther Burbank (1849 – 1926). Yogananda began visiting Burbank in 1924, and the latter in return endorsed Paramahansa's ideas on education. (The Burbank potato is named after Luther; Burbank, California, however, is not.) Interestingly, Burbank's mother had gone to school with the girl (Mary Sawyer) upon whose experiences the "Mary Had a Little Lamb" poem is based.

Yogananda (1946; italics added) expressed his positive feelings toward Luther as follows:

> [Burbank's] heart was fathomlessly deep, long acquainted with *humility,* patience, sacrifice.... The *modesty* with which he wore his scientific fame repeatedly reminded me of the trees that bend low with the burden of ripening fruits; it is the barren tree that lifts its head high in an empty boast.

Given that glowing evaluation, however, descriptions of Burbank's character which go contrary to what one might expect from a "humble, modest saint" become very relevant. Thus:

> Conflicting with the independence conferred by his self-esteem was his love of approval by others. Though he would do nothing dishonest to earn such approval (for that would have brought self-condemnation), he eagerly accepted it as no more than his due. "There are striking instances," says [fellow horticulturalist and writer George] Shull, "in which the combination of these two dominant traits produces one instant the most profound modesty and the next instant almost blatant self-praise" (Dreyer, 1975).

Indeed, by 1908, Burbank had come to the immodest conclusion that, having surpassed Darwin in the number of plants he had raised, he was "therefore"

> "the greatest authority on plant life that had ever lived." This being the case, he felt that he was better qualified than anyone else to pronounce on the subject of evolution (Dreyer, 1975).

On that same subject, however: Burbank believed in the inheritance of only *acquired* traits, and was himself actually regarded by the Soviet quack geneticist Lysenko as being one of "the best biologists." Notwithstanding that unfortunate association with such an unscientific protégé of Stalin, Shull (in Dreyer, 1975) offered this opinion of Luther's claims in general:

> [Burbank] had an "exaggeration coefficient" of about ten ... all his figures should be divided by this number to get an approximation of the truth.

Of course, were anyone to display such characteristics as the above *without* having been titled as a "modest, humble saint" by a great yoga master or the like, the same behaviors would be seen as the height of ego. Indeed, a South African customer—H. E. V. Pickstone—who visited Burbank in 1904 and spent the day with him, had this to say:

> I was disappointed with his personality ... I found him too much of an egoist ... I do not think he can be considered a great man from any angle (in Dreyer, 1975).

Regardless, Burbank not only suggested that he had aided the development of his plants by sending them "thoughts of love," but believed himself to be psychic. Indeed, he "insisted that he possessed the ability to heal by a laying-on of hands, citing several cases in which he had employed it" (Dreyer, 1975). Those "healings" were given both to humans and to ailing plants.

Burbank was again famed for introducing between eight hundred and a thousand new plant varieties, over fifty years of effort, including a "spineless" cactus. Yogananda (1986) gives one account of Luther's development of that plant:

> "The secret of improved plant breeding, apart from scientific knowledge, is love." Luther Burbank uttered this wisdom as I walked beside him in his Santa Rosa garden. We halted near a bed of edible cacti.
>
> "While I was conducting experiments to make 'spineless' cacti," he continued, "I often talked to the plants to create a vibration of love. 'You have nothing to fear,' I would tell them. 'You don't need your defensive thorns. I will protect you.' Gradually the useful plant of the desert emerged in a thornless variety."
>
> I was charmed at this miracle.

However, from Dreyer (1975) we learn:

> [Burbank] had assiduously collected varieties of cactus from Mexico, South Africa and other countries until one finally turned up that was without the usual spines on the stalks, and another that lacked spicules on the leaves. These characteristics were combined in a single plant by hybridization after an extensive series of crossings, and a spineless cactus ... was produced. Now and then a spine still occurred on the

> stems.... Burbank demonstrated the harmlessness of his cactus by softly rubbing his cheek against the pads. It was a remarkable achievement. But it was no miracle.

* * *

Regarding the discipline given by Yogananda to his disciples: Durga Mata (1992) relates that at one point in 1948, when Yogananda was in a very high state of *samadhi,* he talked aloud to what he took to be a vision of the Divine Mother. The latter would then answer back in Yogananda's own voice ... laying out the petty flaws of the disciples present and absent, against Yogananda's entreaties not to punish them.

Of course, if Yogananda really was conversing with the cosmic Feminine force underlying all creation, one could hardly find fault with any of that criticism. One cannot, after all, "second guess" God.

If....

God Herself spending time criticizing others who weren't even present, and threatening punishment on the ones who *were* there, for utterly minor exhibitions of selfishness, though, does seem more than a bit odd. It is, indeed, more consistent with Yogananda's own personality than with what one might expect from "God":

> [Shelly Trimmer] spent about a year with [Yogananda] at the SRF headquarters in Los Angeles but then left.... Although he has retained great affection and respect for Yogananda, he also acknowledges his weaknesses. "He loved to order women about—after all he was a Hindu.... He had a violent temper and was a little bit arrogant" (Rawlinson, 1997).

* * *

It is well known that Yogananda took great delight in the technological innovations of his day, including the garbage disposal. Less celebrated are his own alleged contributions to the progress of science and technology, as per Walters (2002):

> I would say that Paramhansa [*sic*] Yogananda was a prophet for the New Age. Monasteries? yes, but far more than that....
>
> In pursuit of universal upliftment [he] spoke, in private conversation with me, of certain inventions he had inspired,

> or in one case discovered among practices in India and elsewhere.... He even said he'd introduced the concept of covers on toilet seats.

It is not easy to know how to react to such a claim. Nor is it easy to know where to rank it in comparison with the scatological inspirations of Eileen Caddy, Bhagawan Nityananda or the Dalai Lama, for example.

Perhaps it is enough to simply say, "Jai, guru. Jai."

* * *

Of course, no guru could have worked for years in Los Angeles without accumulating a few "star" disciples. Famous followers and acquaintances of Yogananda, then, have included Greta Garbo (who also frequented the Ramakrishna-Vivekananda Vedanta Center in Hollywood) and the actor Dennis Weaver (*Gunsmoke*). The latter used to give monthly sermons at the SRF Lake Shrine temple, located where L.A.'s Sunset Boulevard meets the Pacific Ocean, near Malibu.

A stone sarcophagus in that same park-like setting contains the only portion of Mahatma Gandhi's ashes to exist outside of India. (Yogananda claims in the *Autobiography* to have initiated Gandhi into kriya yoga in 1935. There is much reason, however, to question whether the Mahatma actually practiced that technique on any regular basis afterward.) Of course, it is actually against Hindu religious practice to keep the ashes of a departed soul for display, as opposed to scattering them into bodies of water: "When the ashes are kept on the land, the belief is that the soul remains caught on Earth and is never released into the 'afterlife.'" Or, alternatively, to remove any of the ashes of the deceased is regarded as similar to taking a limb from a live individual (Strelley, 1987).

Be that as it may, Supertramp's Roger Hodgson once wrote a song—"Babaji," from 1977's *Even in the Quietest Moments* album—inspired by Yogananda's teachings. In that case, the lyrics were motivated by the Himalayan guru upon whose behest kriya yoga was given to the world, through Yogananda for one. Hodgson further spent time at the northern California "Ananda" ashram of one of Yogananda's direct disciples—J. Donald Walters, a.k.a. Kriyananda. His sister Caroline has resided in the same community. Indeed, Roger met his future wife, Karuna, when the latter was living in a teepee in that very ashram.

George Harrison, although not himself a disciple of Yogananda, was interviewed for SRF's "Lake Shrine" video, quoting there from Sri Yukteswar's (1977) book, *The Holy Science*. (Ravi Shankar was featured in the same film. Shankar introduced George to Yogananda's writings in 1966.) At Harrison's prompting, images of four of the SRF line of gurus—Babaji, Lahiri Mahasaya, Sri Yukteswar and Yogananda—were included on the Beatles' *Sgt. Pepper's* album cover collage. (Jesus was omitted so as to not further aggravate public religious feelings still raw from Lennon's "the Beatles are more popular than Jesus Christ" observation.) References to Yogananda in Harrison's solo work include the songs "Dear One," "Life Itself" and "Fish on the Sand." Harrison's family further donated the U.S. proceeds from the re-release, in early 2002, of his "My Sweet Lord" single, to SRF.

Madonna—yes, *that* Madonna, again—has likewise spoken positively of Yogananda's *Autobiography*. Pamela Anderson (2005) herself has swooned top-heavily over Paramahansa's (1986) *Divine Romance*. And the brilliant comedian/actor Robin Williams—a friend of both George Harrison and Christopher Reeve, having roomed at Juilliard with the latter—actually subscribed to at least part of the *SRF Lessons* series. That, at least, according to a former-Deadhead monk whom I met during my own otherwise-unpleasant stay in the SRF ashrams, which will be detailed later on.

Gary "Dream Weaver" Wright—another friend of Harrison's—has also been rumored to be an SRF member.

The King of Rock and Roll, too, found inspiration in the kriya yoga path:

> Elvis loved material by guru Paramahansa Yogananda, the Hindu founder of the Self-Realization Fellowship (Cloud, 2000).

Following Yogananda's passing, Presley—whom we may dub a *hillolayavatar*, or "incarnation of rock and roll"—actually made numerous phone calls and trips, over a twelve-year period, to see SRF's Daya Mata. (Apparently she reminded him of his deceased mother, as did the Theosophical Society's famously unkempt and grotesquely obese Madame Blavatsky.) Indeed, the Meditation Garden at Graceland—where Elvis came to be buried—is said to have been inspired by SRF's Lake Shrine (Mason, 2003). Elvis actually "took this spiritual inquiry so seriously that he considered devoting the rest of his life to it by becoming a monk" (Hajdu, 2003).

Ironically, as we have seen, had Presley taken such a step, it needn't have negatively impacted his sex life at all.

Elvis was famed for, among other things, his ownership of a pink 1955 Cadillac. And amazingly, it has been reported—though also later disputed, in terms of its (possibly re-painted?) color—that Daya Mata's normal means of transportation to the SRF Mother Center atop Mount Washington in Los Angeles is via a fifteen-minute commute in a "vintage pink Cadillac." (That drive is from a nearby million-dollar "palace in the suburban Himalayas," at 200 South Canon Avenue in Sierra Madre. The house itself is said to have been a 1966 gift from the late billionaire tobacco heiress, Doris Duke [Russell, 2001].)

The present author, however, has no information to suggest that those two are actually the same car. Indeed, it would perhaps be just as well if it wasn't the same vehicle. For, the potential irony of a bunch of nuns driving around in a car full of "good vibrations" from a back seat on which The King must have had his way with *how many* nubile girls—literally a different one every night, in his younger days—is just too delicious to consider.

* * *

No small amount of any sage's "proof" of his divinity invariably comes from his working of purported miracles, even if he may simultaneously downplay their importance as mere "signs and wonders." Thus:

> [Yogananda] said that he knew how to walk on fire, and to go without eating indefinitely, but that God did not want him to perform such feats, for his mission was to teach and bring souls back to God through kriya yoga and love (Mata, 1992).

"Walking on fire," however, is wholly explicable in terms of the known laws of physics. Indeed, according to scientists, it neither requires nor benefits from any advanced "mind over matter" mental preparation or the like. In fact, as early as the 1930s—well within Yogananda's lifetime—the Council for Psychical Research "issued reports stating that religious faith and supernatural powers were unrelated to firewalking." Instead, they ascribed the success in that endeavor to the "low thermal conductivity of the burning wood, and the relatively small amount of time that contact occurs between the hot coals and a participant's feet" (Nisbet, 2000).

> In Fiji, Hawaii, and Japan, a variation of the stunt is performed on lava stone, which also [like hot coals] has very poor conductivity and low specific heat, and is similar to the "heat shield" ceramic used on the outer skin of the space shuttle (Randi, 1995).
>
> One scientific investigation carried out by Chas R. Darling and reported in *Nature,* Sept. 28, 1935, consisted of pressing a thermal junction on to the fire intermittently so as to imitate the period of contact of each foot and the interval between each step. [A] number of separated [*sic*] trials showed a rise of 15 – 20 °C in the junction—conclusive proof that the feet of the performer would not be hot enough for blistering to occur (Edwards, 1994).

For further explanation, see Carroll (2004c), Nixon (2004), Kjernsmo (1997) and Willey (2002).

Still, "don't try it at home."

Regarding the inedia which the portly Yogananda claimed for himself, it is interesting to note that he vouched for a similar talent for the famed Catholic stigmatist Therese Neumann. Indeed, he even credited her a comparable supposed basis to his own, in the purported chakric ingestion of subtle energies.

In support of the yogi's ostensible first-hand knowledge of Neumann's genuineness and metaphysical means of living "by God's light," we learn that Therese's local German bishop

> instigated a surveillance in 1927 that purportedly produced definitive evidence in favor of her claims, but the observations were only for fifteen days. Therese's urine was monitored during this time and for the following fortnight. A study of the results ... is as expected for the period of observation (Nickell, 1998).

However—

> the post-observation data [see Wilson, 1988] were indicative of "a return to normal, suggesting that once Therese was no longer subject to round-the-clock observation, she went back to normal food and drink intake." Magnifying the suspicion

was Therese's subsequent refusal to undergo further surveillance (Nickell, 1998).

Neumann's claimed stigmata fares only marginally better, in spite of Yogananda's (1946) equal certainty as to its validity:

> Therese showed me a little, square, freshly healed wound on each of her palms. On the back of each hand, she pointed out a smaller, crescent-shaped wound, freshly healed. Each wound went straight through the hand. [That must be a mere assumption on Yogananda's part, as he would not have physically verified that the wound was continuous from front to back, by passing anything through it.] The sight brought to my mind distinct recollection of the large square iron nails with crescent-tipped ends, still used in the Orient.

Others less credulous, however, have given additional, uncomplimentary information:

> [A] Professor Martini conducted a surveillance of Therese Neumann and observed that blood would flow from her wounds only on those occasions when he was persuaded to leave the room, as if something "needed to be hidden from observation" [i.e., in manually inflicting superficial wounds on herself]. He added: "It was for the same reason that I disliked her frequent manipulations behind the raised [bed] coverings"....
>
> [The stigmata shifted] from round to rectangular over time, presumably as she learned the true shape of Roman nails (Nickell, 2001).

In another equally impressive attempt at parapsychology, Yogananda (1946) related his encounter with a "Perfume Saint" in India, the latter being credited with the power of manifesting scents on demand:

> I was a few feet away from Gandha Baba; no one else was near enough to contact my body. I extended my hand, which the yogi did not touch.
>
> "What perfume do you want?"
>
> "Rose."
>
> "Be it so."

> To my great surprise, the charming fragrance of rose was wafted strongly from the center of my palm.

The late magician Milbourne Christopher (1975), however, offered a very simple explanation for Paramahansa's reported "miraculous" experience:

> Yogananda, who did not know how the feat was accomplished, erred in saying the yogi did not touch his hand before the rose fragrance came from it. In this presentation the performer secretly breaks the proper pellet [of the requested perfume enclosed in wax, hidden under a fingernail] as soon as a scent is named; the perfume wets the ball of his thumb. Instructing the spectator to extend his hand, the performer reaches across to grasp it with his thumb on the palm and his fingers on the back. As he does this, the performer says, "I want you to turn your hand palm down. I will not touch it." The spectator remembers the words, not the action, of the performer. The performer moves several feet away. While standing at a distance, he tells the spectator to turn his hand palm upward. The scent is not perceptible until the spectator's hand turns and the fragrance rises upward to his nostrils....
>
> With a dozen tiny pellets, an adept showman can convince a skeptical investigator that "any" perfume can be materialized.

Yogananda himself, though, may not have been an innocent stranger to the means behind such "parlor tricks." For, consider the following demonstration of "yogic powers" on his part:

> [Yogananda] interrupted his talk to ask if there were a doctor in the audience. A man stood up and Swamiji asked him to come on the stage. He requested the doctor, "Take my pulse and tell me what you feel." The doctor felt his wrist, looking perplexed at first and then amazed. "There is no pulse," he answered. Swamiji then told him to take the pulse on the other wrist. The doctor's facial expression turned from amazement to incredulity. He said, "Swami Yogananda, this is impossible. Your pulse is pounding at an incredible speed." He quickly tried the other side again and said, "This side is normal." He came down from the stage into the audience shaking his head and mumbling, "Impossible, impossible" (Charlton, 1990).

And yet, as the East Indian rationalist Basava Premanand (2005) has noted:

> [The cessation of the pulse at the wrists] is done by stopping the flow of blood to the hands by keeping a lemon, or a small ball or a rolled handkerchief in the armpits and pressing. Doctors do not in the confusion check the heartbeat but check the pulse and confirm that the pulse is stopped.

In the *SRF Lessons* (Yogananda, 1984), we are further informed of the following metaphysical claim:

> In rare instances ... a person who has lived a very animalistic existence is drawn into the body of an animal, to learn some lesson. This explains the "thinking dogs" and "thinking horses" which have puzzled scientists who have tested them.

The *Lessons* were compiled and edited by Yogananda's direct disciples, under his oversight. Thus, one cannot know whether Paramahansa himself was solely responsible for the above insight, or whether it should rather be credited to members of the current Board of Directors, for example (or to Kriyananda, who also worked on that editing). Either way, though, the "explanation" offered above to scientists—whether puzzled or otherwise—is radically mistaken.

The most famous of the "thinking horses" of the twentieth century were Lady Wonder and Clever Hans.

> Learned professors were convinced that Hans could work out his own solution to mathematical problems and had a better knowledge of world affairs than most fourteen-year-old children (Christopher, 1970).

Lady Wonder was equally feted by the New York *World* in 1927, as allegedly being able to "read minds, predict the future and converse in Chinese." Yet, that did not stop her from being conclusively debunked by Milbourne Christopher in 1956:

> As a test, Christopher gave Lady's trainer, Mrs. Claudia Fonda, a false name, "John Banks".... When Christopher subsequently inquired of Lady, "What is my name?," the mare obligingly nudged the levers [of the horse's large "typewriter"] to spell out B-A-N-K-S....

> Mrs. Fonda gave a "slight movement" of her training rod whenever Lady's head was at the correct letter (Nickell, 2002).

Further experimentation by Christopher disclosed that Fonda had herself been deceptively utilizing the mentalists' trick of "pencil reading"—in visually following the movements of the free end of a pencil, to discern what number had been written down by a questioner. She was then cueing Lady Wonder with that information, thus allowing the horse to fake "telepathy" well enough to fool the credulous parapsychologist J. B. Rhine.

Earlier in the twentieth century, Clever Hans had fared no better when tested by Oskar Pfungst:

> Pfungst's study revealed that the horse could give a correct answer only if the questioner knew it. When Pfungst shielded the eyes of the animal, the hoof remained still. It was reasonable to suppose at this point that [Hans' owner] was cueing Hans subconsciously. Further study ruled out signals by touch or sound. Pfungst now centered his observations on the questioner. He discovered that Hans started stamping when the questioner leaned forward ever so slightly to see the hoof in action. Hans stopped when the man relaxed even a fraction....
>
> Then Pfungst played horse himself. He rapped with his right hand as friends posed queries. Twenty-three out of twenty-five questioners gave the starting and stopping cue without realizing it. Pfungst's answers were as baffling to them as the horse's had been (Christopher, 1970).

"Not so clever *now,* eh, Hans?" Nor such a Clever Parama-*hansa*. For, while "thinking" dogs, pigs, goats and geese have all been exhibited over the course of the past few centuries, ordinary training and conscious or subconscious cueing can account for all of their celebrated behaviors. Thus, independent of whether or not reincarnation exists, there is no rational reason to believe that it has anything to do with such "thinking."

Note, further, how similar cues to those given unconsciously by the questioners of Clever Hans would have to be present and relevant in the search for *tulkus*. For, the latter are again children who are asked to identify the possessions of their "previous incarnation," from among a set of objects ... where others in the room with the child *know what the right answer is.* A suitably sensitive or crafty child, even if only a few years old, might well be able to pick up on such inadvertent cues, just as a relatively dumb horse can. Voilà! an "incarnation," who will very quickly have additional "miraculous" events incorporated into the myth of his "recognition." And thereby do utterly normal rainbows, coincidental dreams, and otherwise-irrelevant pails full of forgotten milk become "signs."

Of course, such searches are typically initially motivated by a lama's dream of a particular house, or of a family with specific characteristics, living in a certain direction, etc. But even there, "seek and—statistically—ye shall find." That is so, even without later "revisionist histories" as to the details of the original events, to emphasize particular attributes of the dream. For, it is unavoidable that elements of the dream which, at the time of dreaming, were no more important than any others, will assume purported significance when a promising family is found, which matches some of the selectively chosen "facts" revealed in the dream, but misses completely on others—as it invariably will. With equal certainty, those "misses" will not be mentioned in later recountings of the "recognition" myth.

Seen in that light, the reported poor behaviors, in sex and violence, of contemporary and past *tulkus* and Dalai Lamas become very understandable. For, those "reincarnated sages" are, after all, very ordinary people, who were simply placed into extraordinary circumstances from childhood onward. And even an otherwise-average person could "play holy," as they do publicly, if that was all he had ever been taught how to do. (Cf. Krishnamurti. Yogananda, too, was trained from earliest childhood to be a "spiritual engine," destined to bring others to God.)

* * *

Yogananda (in Kriyananda, 1974) offered numerous predictions for the future, prior to his passing in the early 1950s. Included among those were an anticipated "revolution" in America against governmental interference; the end of England as a world power; and the prophecy that China would "end up absorbing Japan." The yogi further foresaw a Third World War, around the 1970s, to spread communism throughout "much of the free world." Following that would be a fourth such war, "toward the last decade" of the twentieth century. That conflict was fated to devastate Europe, annihilate (communist) Russia, and leave America victorious, ushering in a new age of peace for hundreds of years.

In addition:

> A terrible [economic] depression is coming, *far worse than the last one!....*
>
> In the next century Boston will have a tropical climate, and the people there will be brown skinned (in Kriyananda, 1974).

We shall have to see, of course, what becomes of the Bostonian climate in the future, what with global warming and all.

In any case, the booklet in which all of the above wildly wrong predictions were preserved by Yogananda's schismatic direct disciple Kriyananda is by now, understandably, long out of print. (The above are not merely the most-wrong of Paramahansa's predictions in that book, but are rather a concise summary of his prognostications. Were there any non-obvious and correct prophecies therein, I would happily have included them here. There are not.)

* * *

Yogananda himself claimed to have lived at Stonehenge around 1500 BC in a previous incarnation, and asserted that Winston Churchill was the reincarnation of Napoleon. (Churchill's [1874 – 1965] life, however, overlapped with Aurobindo's, with the latter, too, again claiming to be the reincarnation of Monsieur Bonaparte.) Also according to Yogananda, Hitler was Alexander the Great. In the same vein, Kriyananda (1977) relates Paramahansa's declaration that Benito Mussolini was Marc Anthony; Kaiser Wilhelm was Julius Caesar; Stalin was Genghis Khan; Charles Lindbergh was Abraham Lincoln; and Therese Neumann was Mary Magdalene. (Neumann died in 1962; Rajneesh's Vivek, claiming the same reincarnation, was born before then; etc.)

Among the SRF gurus, Lahiri Mahasaya was, according to the same source, both King Janaka and the poet Kabir. Likewise, Babaji (as with Aurobindo) was believed to be the reincarnation of Krishna—with Yogananda himself being the Bhagavad Gita's Arjuna, Krishna's most beloved disciple. As he himself explained parts of that:

> [Rajasi Janakananda—James J. Lynn, Yogananda's most advanced male disciple—was] one of the [Bhagavad Gita's] twins, the positive one, Nakula. He was my favorite brother and I loved him more than anyone else. I was also his Guru then too. Krishna was my guru and Babaji, being Krishna, is still my guru, Sri Yukteswarji was my guru by proxy for Babaji (in Mata, 1992).

Yogananda further said that he himself would reincarnate in a few hundred years, "just to sit in back and meditate."

All of the gurus in the SRF lineage (i.e., Krishna, Jesus, Babaji, Lahiri Mahasaya and Sri Yukteswar) are additionally believed to be avatars. Yukteswar is also held to have been the reincarnation of the stigmatist Saint Francis of Assisi.

> "Sir," I asked Master [i.e., Yogananda] one day at his desert retreat, "are *you* an avatar?"
>
> With quiet simplicity he replied, "A work of this importance would have to be started by such a one" (Kriyananda, 1979).

Indeed, Yogananda often said of SRF and kriya yoga, "This work is a special dispensation of God" (Kriyananda, 1979). He further prophesied that it would sweep the world "like wildfire" over the coming millennia, to the point where "millions would come."

As expected, there is an asserted connection with Jesus as well:

> "Babaji, Lahiri Mahasaya, and Sri Yukteswar," [Yogananda] announced, "were the three wise men who came to visit the Christ child in the manger" (Kriyananda, 1979).

Others (e.g., Burke, 1994) have suggested that Yogananda was also previously John the Beloved (i.e., Jesus' apostle, John).

Yogananda himself claimed, on other occasions, to be the reincarnation of William the Conqueror. The latter king, being the illegitimate son of Robert I, Duke of Normandy, and a tanner's daughter, was also known as William the Bastard. He was actually reputed to be able to heal scrofula (a kind of tuberculosis) with a mere "king's touch."

> In later years Yogananda revealed to me why he called me his "giant returned." Yogananda in a past existence had been William the Conqueror.
>
> I experienced in a vision the Battle of Hastings as King William conquered England. I was beside him in this battle, and was of such stature I could look him straight in the eyes while standing beside him as he sat astride his horse. I carried a gigantic battle axe which in effect allowed no harm to come to his person (Paulsen, 1984).

However: Even a very small war horse of, say, fourteen hands at the shoulder, with the nearly six-foot tall William ensconced in its saddle, would dictate a standing "giant" around an unbelievable eight and a half feet tall, for their eyes to be at the same level.

Yogananda (1986) continues:

> Quite a few people have heard me mention a previous life in which I lived for many years in England. Experiences of that life come clearly to my mind. There were certain details about the Tower of London [a historic fortress, originally a royal palace built by William the Conqueror after the Battle of Hastings, and today displaying the Crown Jewels] that I remembered very well, and when I went there in 1935 I saw that those places were exactly as I had seen them within.

Or, as Kriyananda/Walters (2002) relates it:

> Master had told Daya that she was one of his daughters when he was William the Conqueror. One couldn't help feeling that there was a certain regal quality about Daya Mata, as also about Virginia, her sister, who now bears the name Ananda Mata, and who also was closely related to Master during that lifetime. I came to believe, though Master had never told me so, that I was Daya's youngest brother, Master's son, in that incarnation.

Yogananda further said of one of Durga Mata's brothers:

> [H]e was with me in a previous life. If you will recall, when William the Conqueror fell upon landing in England, one of his men [i.e., the current brother] told William, "This fall is a bad omen, let us turn back" (Mata, 1992).

William himself, however, seems to have exhibited somewhat less than the "omnipresent divine love" with which Yogananda has since been credited:

> When William was in his early twenties he asked Count Baldwin V of Flanders for his daughter Matilda's hand in marriage. [Matilda was a diminutive 4' 2", or half the height of Paulsen's alleged gigantic incarnation.] But Matilda was already in love with an Englishman named Brihtric. She supposedly proclaimed that she would rather become a nun than the wife of a bastard, which made William so angry that he attacked her in the street as she left church one day. He slapped her, tore her clothes, threw her to the ground, and rode off (Royalty, 2003).

William and Matilda were actually distant cousins, causing the pope to object to their eventual marriage on grounds of incest. Indeed, His Holiness went so far as to excommunicate the "happy couple"—and everyone else in Normandy—for several years; relenting only at William's promised building of two new abbeys.

In later years, in search of greater conquests,

> William gathered together a great army in Normandy, and had many men, and sufficient transport-shipping. The day that he rode out of the castle to his ships, and had mounted his horse, his wife came to him, and wanted to speak with him; but when he saw her he struck at her with his heel, and set his spurs so deep into her breast that she fell down dead; and the earl rode on to his ships, and went with his ships over to England (Sturlson, 1997).

> [H]e was merciless in the suppression of political opposition. In fact, so merciless was he that he introduced the act of beheading to England in 1076 (Silverman, 2003).

To be fair, however, William B. was said to have been "obsessed by guilt over his treatment of Waltheof [the first Saxon to lose his head, while all around were keeping theirs] until his own death a decade later" (BBC, 2003). And that, from a man who had a lot to feel guilty about:

> William loved gold too much ... he had a passion for hunting and protected his game by savage laws which made beasts more valuable than men (Walker, 1968).

And at other times, when on the warpath:

> Twenty-six unfortunate citizens [from the town of Alençon] were lined up and their hands and feet were cut off, partly for vengeance, partly to terrify the garrison. The savagery was successful. William was rarely driven to that point of anger again (Walker, 1968).

"Rarely"? How often is "rarely"?

The chronically obese bastard himself sadly met with a somewhat unsavory end. For, while on horseback fighting the French at the Battle of Mantes, William's intestines were ruptured in his being thrown violently against the iron pommel of his saddle. From the internal pollution of that injury peritonitis quickly set in, resulting in his slow death, over a five-week period, in 1087 at age sixty.

During the ensuing funeral procession, mourners were forced to leave his coffin in the hot sun while fighting a nearby fire. From that heat, William's pus- and waste-filled intestinal abscess swelled. Further, the prepared sarcophagus into which dear William was to be placed for all eternity had, alas, been built too short to accommodate the full height of the ex-king.

Attempting to squeeze him into that planned stone resting place, the overly enthusiastic undertakers finally pushed on William's swelled abdomen to the point where the body burst. That error drenched his burial garb with pus, filling the St. Stephen's abbey with that stench and sending the nauseous, overheated mourners racing for the church doors.

He was thenceforth quickly buried, and allowed to rest in peace ... until 1522, when the body was exhumed, examined, and re-interred. From that point, it was left alone "until 1562 when the [Calvinist] Huguenots dug him up and threw his bones all over the courtyard" (Silverman, 2003). In the process, they trashed the gold, silver and precious-jewel monument marking the tomb.

> Only a single thigh bone survived, which was preserved and reburied under a new monument in 1642. But even this was destroyed during the French Revolution (Grout, 2003).

Perhaps not fully aware of the relevant karmic history, SRF in the late 1990s set plans in motion to have Yogananda's body moved. That is, they intended to relocate it from the Forest Lawn (Glendale, California) cemeteries wherein it had rested since his passing—down the hall from the tomb of Hopalong Cassidy—to a planned shrine atop Mount Washington in Los Angeles (Russell, 1999).

Arguably best for everyone concerned, the plan was later dropped in the face of intense public opposition.

In addition to his life as William the Conqueror, Yogananda also claimed to be the reincarnation of William Shakespeare. There is, indeed, a vague facial resemblance between the two of them, as between Paramahansa and professed likenesses of William the Conqueror. And Yogananda's *Autobiography of a Yogi* is inarguably the work of a masterful author(s)—whether one regards its stories as factual or fictional. Further, Yogananda (1982) explicitly encouraged his followers to study the Bard in particular:

> Read Shakespeare and other classics, and suitable portions from practical books on such subjects as chemistry, physics, physiology, history of Oriental and Western philosophy, comparative religion, ethics and psychology.

Of course, having thus himself allegedly written all of William Shakespeare's plays in that previous life, none of the following, well-known bawdy aspects embedded in those same works of art could have surprised Yogananda:

- In *Othello,* Cassio's love-interest (aside from the wife of Othello himself, Desdemona) is the prostitute Bianca
- Significant parts of *Pericles* take place in and around a brothel
- *The Taming of the Shrew* has Gremio referring to Kate as a prostitute by offering to "cart" her through the streets—a punishment for whores—instead of to court her. In the opening "wooing scene" of Act II of the same play, Petruchio speaks of having his tongue in Kate's "tail."

> *Tail,* in Shakespearean slang, denotes the female sexual organ just about as often as the male, so there need be no doubt that Petruchio, in his crudely flirta-

tious way, is trying to interest Katherina in the proposition of cunnilingus (Colman, 1974)

- The "playhouse poultry" in *Bartholomew Fair* are prostitutes
- In Mercutio's "Queen Mab" speech from *Romeo and Juliet,* the name "Mab" itself was an insult, being synonymous with "prostitute" in Shakespeare's time
- *Measure for Measure* has a brothel run by a "Mistress Overdone," along with whores lazily whipping transvestite men. Also, the pimp Pompey plays comically sadistic games with his fellow prisoners. The lascivious Lucio in the same script is finally punished by the restored Duke Vincentio by being forced to marry a prostitute
- In *Love's Labour's Lost,* "Boyet's line 'An if my hand be out, then belike your hand is in' is accusing Maria of masturbation" (Colman, 1974)
- In *Henry IV,* if "as seems probable, Falstaff's 'neither fish nor flesh' implies 'neither male nor female,' then the corollary 'a man knows not where to have her' becomes one of Shakespeare's very few references to anal intercourse" (Colman, 1974)
- When Juliet's Nurse demands of Romeo, "Why should you fall into so deep an O?" the letter *O* [cf. nothing/nought/naught/naughty] probably "carries the bawdy implication of *vulva"* (Colman, 1974)
- Likewise with *Hamlet:*

  HAMLET: Do you think I meant country matters?
  OPHELIA: I think nothing, my lord.
  HAMLET: That's a fair thought to lie between maids' legs.
  OPHELIA: What is, my lord?
  HAMLET: Nothing.

  After the pun in *country* [i.e., "cunt'ry"], we need not doubt that Hamlet is making a further bawdy joke with "Nothing" (Colman, 1974)

- Finally, in *Twelfth Night,* Malvolio accepts Maria's forged letter as follows: "By my life, this is my lady's hand. These be her very C's, her U's and her T's; and thus makes she her great P's."

> Helge Kökeritz ... explained this C-U-T not as a jingle on *cunt* but as *cut* itself, a word which, I am told, still occurs in English as a slang term for *vulva.* Kökeritz also proposed that, following this, Malvolio's phrase "her great P's" implies urination (Colman, 1974)

We find additional puns on four-letter "focative" and "genitive" cases; carets/carrots as "good roots"/penises; and "two stones" as probable testicles. Also, numerous references, both humorous and serious, to syphilis, the "malady of France" ... which, ironically, brings us full circle to the Norman Conquest under King William, the bastard.

All of that would, of course, make Yogananda's strong emphasis, a few hundred years later, on celibacy and purity of thought for his own followers, a tad incongruous. ("But Sir, we were just discussing your writings!")

Shakespeare himself passed away on his 52nd birthday in 1616, and remains buried in the Church of the Holy Trinity in Stratford-on-Avon. Having perhaps learned a lesson from previously disruptive post-mortem experiences, the (modernized) inscription on a sculpture of him there reads:

> Good friend, for Jesus' sake forbear
> To dig the dust enclosed here
> Blest be the man that spares these stones
> And curst be he that moves my bones

* * *

Yogananda "shuffled off the mortal coil" for the final time—i.e., entered *mahasamadhi*—in 1952. Immediately thereafter, SRF has since widely claimed, his untenanted body began manifesting a "divine incorruptibility."

> A notarized statement signed by the director of Forest Lawn Memorial-Park testified: "No physical disintegration was visible in his body even twenty days after death.... This state

of perfect preservation of a body is, so far as we know from mortuary annals, an unparalleled one.... Yogananda's body was apparently in a phenomenal state of immutability" (in Yogananda, 1998).

The editors at Self-Realization Fellowship (in SRF, 1976) then waxed eloquent:

> This is as it should be. Paramahansa, flawlessly perfect soul that he was, could not possibly have chosen for tenement a body that was not in pre-established harmony with the purest conceivable soul.

And yet, as Robert Carroll (2004b) has noted:

> The statement [quoted by SRF] of the director of Forest Lawn, Harry T. Rowe, is accurate, but incomplete. Mr. Rowe also mentioned that he observed a brown spot on Yogananda's nose after twenty days, a sign that the body was not "perfectly" preserved. In any case, the SRF's claim that lack of physical disintegration is "an extraordinary phenomenon" is misleading.... The state of the yogi's body is not unparalleled, but common. A typical embalmed body will show no notable desiccation for one to five months after burial without the use of refrigeration or creams to mask odors.... Some bodies are well-preserved for years after burial.

And indeed, with regard to embalming, in the full text of Mr. Rowe's letter, reprinted in the SRF-published (1976) *Paramahansa Yogananda, In Memoriam,* we find:

> Paramahansa Yogananda's body was embalmed on the night of March 8th, with that quantity of fluid which is customarily used in any body of similar size.

And the "miracle" then was ... what, exactly? Apparently, only that the body was relatively well preserved even with the funeral home having used no creams to prevent mold, in addition to the embalming. Yet even there, Harry Edwards' (1995) research in soliciting the opinions of a pair of independent, licensed embalmers, disclosed the following experience on their parts:

> "I'm sure we've had bodies for two or three months with good preservation. This is not unusual. Creams are not necessary"

> ... "preservation for twenty days through embalming is not unusual. We can keep a body a month or two without interral ... an embalming fluid with a lanolin base will have humecant which prevents dehydration, which is the major concern."

As Edwards' embalmers further noted, the circulation of air around Yogananda's body would have been largely prevented by the casket's heavy glass lid, with that too impeding the desiccation of the body.

So the "miracle" then was ... what, exactly? Perhaps only that SRF has gotten away, for over fifty years, with presenting a phenomenon which is perfectly ordinary, as if it was some kind of "sign" to prove the divinity of their eminently human founder.

* * *

> Master had told some of us: "You need never concern yourselves about the leadership of our Society. Babaji has already selected those who are destined to lead this work" (Mata, 1971).

Following Yogananda's passing, the presidency of SRF was assumed by his foremost disciple, James J. Lynn (Rajarsi/Rajasi Janakananda), a wealthy Kansas City businessman. At Yogananda's prompting, Lynn had reportedly endowed SRF with up to six million dollars worth of cash, land and bonds.

Mr. Lynn himself was possessed of the following interesting characteristics:

> Little Jimmy wore dresses and long hair up to the age of six....
>
> Rajasi did not like ugliness in any form. For instance, if he dropped something on the floor and spilled its contents, he disgustingly [*sic*] walked out of the room as fast as he could so he would not have to see it (Mata, 1992).

Since Lynn's passing in 1955, Self-Realization Fellowship has carried on with Daya Mata at the helm, after Durga Mata had declined the leadership offer owing to her own poor health and age (Mata, 1992).

A long-time friend of Durga's later offered her opinion of Daya's character, in Russell (1999), as being "weak and idealistic" in her younger days, but then getting "a taste of power" in India.

One interesting change made by SRF, soon after Rajasi's passing and Daya Mata's corresponding ascension into power, was in the very spelling of their founder's name.

> Yogananda wrote his title, *Paramhansa,* without the additional *a* in the middle. This is, in fact, how the word is commonly pronounced in India. The addition of that letter was made years later, on the advice of scholars in India, according to whom *Paramahansa* without the *a,* though phonetically true, was grammatically incorrect (Kriyananda, 1979).

That change was apparently made in 1958, coinciding with the SRF-sponsored visit of His Holiness Jagadguru ("World Teacher") Sri Shankaracharya Bharati Krishna Tirtha to America. Tirtha himself was the "ecclesiastical head of most of Hindu India and the apostolic successor of the first Shankaracharya."

Personally, I would never have followed Yogananda in the first place if I thought that he didn't know how to spell his own name. (Similar issues to the above surround the past "Rajasi" versus current "Rajarsi" spellings of Lynn's monastic name [Dakota, 1998].)

In any case, under Daya Mata's governance SRF has weathered several recent scandals, including one involving the alleged sexual activities of a highly placed male monastic minister who was reportedly ultimately forced to leave the order. The handling of that difficulty allegedly included nearly one-third of a million dollars in compensation paid to the unfortunate woman involved. In that same context, however:

> [Persons familiar with the details] contend that several top SRF leaders—including Daya Mata—not only turned a deaf ear to [the woman in question] after she sought help while still involved with the monk, but that those leaders attempted to ruin her reputation within the church even as they sought to preserve [the monk's] monastic career.... "They [the church leadership] pretty much destroyed [the involved woman's] faith and ruined her life" [a friend said] (Russell, 1999).

That is all the more disappointing, given the alleged "perfected being" nature of SRF's leadership and its Board of Directors:

> The people running [SRF] are supposedly enlightened *siddhas,* which makes it even more confusing, because how dare lay devotees question, or worse, challenge, what they have done? But then how can we swallow what's being done (radical editing, photo alteration, and the rest of it [see Dakota, 1998])? (Kriya Yoga Discussion Board, 2001).

> In a letter to me, SRF defined a *siddha* as one who is "unconditionally one with God, partaking of all God's attributes, including those of omniscience, omnipresence and omnipotence" (Rawlinson, 1997).

Such beings would ostensibly never make mistakes. Yogananda himself essentially confirmed as much:

> The actions of true masters, though not easily understood by worldly people, are always wisdom-guided, never whimsical (in Kriyananda, 1979).

> A master's word cannot be falsified; it is not lightly given (Yogananda, 1946).

Regarding "mistakes" and the like in Yogananda's own life, however: It has been asserted that, in the February 1934 issue of the SRF-published *East-West* magazine, he had praised the Italian fascist leader Mussolini as being a "master brain," who had been sent to Earth by God to serve as a role model for humanity. (I have not been able to obtain a copy of that issue myself, and so cannot corroborate that claim. Significantly, though, an earlier issue of *East-West* had approvingly included a short piece by Mussolini [1927] himself, on "Science and Religion.") A mere year later, however, the same dictator invaded Abyssinia (Ethiopia), in what has been viewed as the opening round of WWII.

Of course, that a guru would sympathize with a totalitarian dictator should really not be so surprising: There is, after all, very little actual difference between the two positions. (Interestingly, Pope Pius XI, too, "spoke of Mussolini as 'a man sent by Providence'" [Cornwell, 1999].) That is so, even down to both sets of societies beginning, in the most generous reading, with the best of intentions for all, prior to their leaders becoming utterly corrupted in their exercise of power.

Nor, given the history of violence and suppression in our world's secular totalitarian states, should we be surprised to find exactly the same intolerance for discontent being reportedly exhibited regularly on behalf of our gurus and other "infallible" beings. Excommunications and threats of eternal damnation for disloyalty, after all, serve to quell dissenting or independent viewpoints, and preserve the welfare of those in absolute power, just as well as politically motivated murders and bloody purges do.

* * *

A number of other kriya yogis have contributed colorful storylines to the history of yoga and Yogananda, while working both inside and outside of SRF itself.

One of those, Swami Kriyananda (J. Donald Walters), was unanimously elected by the SRF Board of Directors as vice president of Self-Realization Fellowship in 1960. (That board is of course the same "omniscient" group that had earlier elected Daya Mata as president.) Prior to that, he had worked, organized and lectured within SRF since 1948, upon entering the SRF monasteries at age twenty-two. On returning from India on SRF business in 1962, however, he was forced to leave the organization, despite his own entreaties to be allowed to stay and do anything except wash dishes there.

In relating his own side of that story, Walters (2002) regards the reasons for that that split as being "essentially political" in their nature.

That position, however, differs somewhat from what the Ananda Awareness Network website (www.anandainfo.com) has to say. For there, a number of "sexual indiscretion" reasons are alleged for that forced departure.

Whatever the specific grounds may have been for his expulsion, Walters had recovered enough by 1967 to purchase the first of the lands for his own "world brotherhood colony" or spiritual community, the Ananda Cooperative Village, near Nevada City in northern California. That 900-acre village currently hosts a population of around three hundred disciples of Yogananda, their devotion being filtered through Walters' specific emphasis on "service," in his casting of himself as a "channel" for Yogananda's blessings.

Worldwide, the Ananda group numbers around 2500 members; I myself was once officially among them.

The original land—now utilized only as a remote retreat—for that colony was acquired in a six-investor deal involving Allen Ginsberg and Gary Snyder. Also participating in that land deal was Richard Baker of the San Francisco Zen Center, a friend of Walters since 1967.

Walters' motivations for founding the Ananda colony, and various subsequent satellites to it, included Yogananda's (1946) explicit mission statement in the "Aims and Ideals of Self-Realization Fellowship":

> To spread a spirit of brotherhood among all peoples; and to aid in establishing, in many countries, self-sustaining world-brotherhood colonies for plain living and high thinking.

That goal has since been removed from the "Aims and Ideals" printed at the back of every copy of the *Autobiography of a Yogi*. The reader can easily confirm, however, via any reasonably comprehensive public library, that it was present in earlier editions. (Any version with a copyright in the 1940s or early '50s should have it.) Yogananda voiced the wish for the establishing of those colonies in public lectures as well, encouraging

> thousands of youths ... to cover the Earth with little colonies, demonstrating that simplicity of living plus high thinking lead to the greatest happiness (Kriyananda, 1979).

Or, as one of Yogananda's other direct disciples, Kamala (1964), put it:

> Master spoke to me about the value of SRF Colonies. He referred to the forming of groups within a city or a rural area in the manner of hermitage life, among members who do not desire to become renunciates, or cannot do so because of certain obligations. Such a life would enable each one to be in daily association with those who share the same spiritual goal. He described such Colonies as made up of married couples and their families, as well as single people, who have the will to serve, and to live in harmony with one another. Master envisioned the idea as one in which all may work together in a self-supporting group wherein each one is dedicated to God.

With his colony in place and growing, thence followed several marriages of Kriyananda in the 1980s to female devotees at Ananda. (Walters apparently still goes by the monastic "Swami Kriyananda" title when interacting with his students, for example.) More recently, allegations of sexual improprieties with other female followers have surfaced. Indeed, expert witness Pamela Cooper White reportedly told a California court in 1998 that, in her opinion,

> Walters clearly fell within the profile of a clergy sex offender. She added that he was on the "most destructive, predatory end of that spectrum, that of the multiple repeat offender who deliberately seeks vulnerable women to exploit for his own sexual gratification" (Sullivan, 2003).

The same article lists no less than eight women accusing Walters of sex-related infractions, ranging from indecent exposure to sexual slavery.

Walters himself, however, has a different perspective on those alleged sexual encounters. Thus, in a court deposition (Walters, 1995; italics added), in response to the accusations of one of the women whom he reportedly admitted had massaged and masturbated him on eight separate occasions in early 1982, he apparently stated:

> Let me repeat that it was not a romantic or passionate feeling, but it was a *friendly feeling*. I was not using [woman #2]. I did not feel that I was using her.
>
> Her statements many years after the fact are not corroborated by my memory of her action then, which was in fact to *thrust herself upon me, against my pleas to the contrary....*
>
> I was trying to be in seclusion. She and (woman #1) came down repeatedly to my house. And I said, please, leave me be. I want to be quiet, and I want to meditate and understand this confusion that I'm going through with (woman #7)'s departure. I was in a state of emotional shock, confusion and trauma, but I did not in any way notice at the time that she was being upset, hostile, resistant. Rather, quite the contrary, she was thrusting herself on me.

The woman (#2) in question was a twenty-something ex-student, just out of university, at the time; Walters was in his late fifties, balding and overweight.

In any case, judging from Walters' other (e.g., 2002) writings, unwanted attempts at seduction seem to be a recurring problem:

> Many women, not unnaturally, saw in me their natural "prey" .... I remember one attractive lady emerging into the living room of her home from its inner apartment during my visit there. Completely naked, she chased me about the room until I finally managed to make good my escape!

Whew! That was a close one!

The hunter and the hunted—"the hungry, attractive lioness stalks her unsuspecting, innocent prey," etc.

"There but for the grace of God...."

Some monks have all the luck. But then, some monks apparently have all the "realization," too:

> At one point, Swami [Kriyananda] told me that he was greater than Gandhi and Sai Baba, that no one had the spiritual power he had (Woman #2, 1995).

The choice of Sai Baba for comparison was, of course, a singularly unfortunate one: the average housecat has more spiritual power than Sai Baba.

* * *

Norman Paulsen, founder of Santa Barbara's Brotherhood of the Sun community, is another direct disciple of Yogananda. He resided in the SRF ashrams for four and a half years, from May of 1947 to November, 1951.

> Norman had a heart almost as big as his body.... Not at all interested in the theoretical aspects of the path, he understood everything in terms of devotion....
>
> "I don't know any of those things!" he would exclaim with a gentle smile whenever I raised some philosophical conundrum. "I just know that I love God." How I envied him his child-like devotion! (Kriyananda, 1979).

Obvious problems, however, can easily arise from such a simple perspective. Thus, in a plot worthy of George Lucas or Steven Spielberg, Paulsen regards human beings as having been created in the "lost lands of Mu" by "The Builders." That is, created by peace-loving space refugees "from other worlds that had been destroyed by [their] evil conquerors [or 'Fallen Angels']" in a distant part of the galaxy. Such Builders were believed to have outrun their pursuers, half a million years ago, at speeds exceeding that of light. In that view, human beings are a genetic cross between The Builders' own species and *homo erectus*.

The aforementioned "lost lands" were now-sunken island continents near to (and including) Australia, allegedly destroyed twelve thousand years ago by huge meteorites sent by the Fallen Angels, thus being "literally blasted out of the Earth's crust" by those collisions. Fiji and many of the other islands between Australia and Hawaii, Paulsen claims, are simply the peaks of mountains from those submerged continents.

The "prequel" as to how those Fallen Angels came into being boils down to a group of unduly intrepid early Builders venturing into a forbidden area of the galaxy. There, they became trapped within a violent magnetic storm, and were predictably adversely affected by the negative energies of that region. Marooned on a (logically) "Forbidden Planet" in the same zone, "dark and sinister" forces so moved the physical bodies and minds of these unfortunate souls that

> [s]uddenly the fallen Builders felt the urge emanating from within them to conquer and enslave the entire galaxy (Paulsen, 1984).

Their—and our—story continues following the refugee Builders' creation of the human species, with their (Builders) having been discovered here 350,000 years ago by their pursuers.

> The Builders finally lost the war to defend the Earth against their fallen brethren, the Dark Angels, twelve thousand years ago. However, after their defeat, they vowed to return and take the Earth from the evil darkness of the Fallen Angels who now possess it. That vow is beginning to manifest itself today [via UFO encounters] (Paulsen, 1984).

Those insights are based on Paulsen's own numerous meditative experiences/revelations. Indeed, in his view Jesus was "a Builder returned" to Earth. So too was the late shabd yogi Kirpal Singh. Further, the man himself claims to have been abducted by a UFO piloted by Builders from Jupiter. (Another "believer" with him, however, could not see that craft, when it later reappeared to Paulsen's vision.) Also, to have constructed a "free energy" (i.e., perpetual motion) machine based on one-half of that abducting ship's drive systems. And to have destroyed Lucifer himself in an astral battle.

Ah well, even the wise Yoda was never more than one letter removed from "yoga" anyway; just as the "Force," or subtle means by which Aurobindo allegedly influenced world events, appears equally well in George Lucas' world. (Lama Serkong Rinpoche's "furrowed face and large, pointy ears had supposedly been the model for Yoda in the film *Star Wars*" [Mackenzie, 1995].)

Of course, one would not attempt to hold Yogananda or SRF responsible for every idea purveyed by disciples who have since left the organization. Nevertheless, when it comes to UFOs one cannot help but draw a connecting link. For, according to one of the respected and loyal direct disciples of Yogananda whom the present author personally met at the SRF Hidden Valley ashram, Paramahansa himself predicted that "if America were ever at war and losing, space aliens from UFOs would intervene."

Well, let us pray it never comes to that.

* * *

On top of all that, we further have Roy Eugene Davis (2000; italics added), another direct disciple of Yogananda, who rushes in where the mere "channel," Kriyananda, fears to tread:

> [A]lmost all of Paramahansaji's disciples have passed from this world. Of the few who remain, *I am his only guru-successor*. A few of his disciples teach the philosophical principles and practices of kriya yoga; I speak for, serve, and represent the tradition. It is my mission, which my guru confirmed.

One might be more inclined to take that seriously, had Yogananda not explicitly stated elsewhere that he was to be the last in the SRF line of gurus. Even Rajasi, like Daya Mata, was only the administrative president of SRF, not Yogananda's "spiritual successor." Were that not the case, one can hardly imagine other direct disciples presenting themselves as mere "channels" of Yogananda, as opposed to claiming explicit guru status for themselves. Even as it stands, that boundary is regularly pushed as far as it can go:

> "It is generally understood, now, that the wisdom in Master's teachings resides primarily in those who have been disciples for many years," [J. Donald Walters] wrote in a recent open letter to the Ananda community. "It is also vitally important at Ananda that other energies not be allowed to intrude themselves, as if to bypass Kriyananda and go straight to our gurus for guidance and inspiration" (Goa, 1999).

Or, as the self-published Ananda Cooperative Village Membership Guidelines of 1976 (in Nordquist, 1978) put it:

> Each prospective member should understand that joining Ananda ... means, too, following the leadership and personal guidance of Ananda's founder, Swami Kriyananda, as the instrument for Yoganandaji's direction.

* * *

In early versions of his *Autobiography* (1946), Yogananda had given the following information regarding one of his disciples:

> The Washington leader is Swami Premananda, educated at the Ranchi school and Calcutta University. I had summoned him in 1928 to assume leadership of the Washington Self-Realization Fellowship center.
>
> "Premananda," I told him during a visit to his new temple, "this Eastern headquarters is a memorial in stone to your tireless devotion. Here in the nation's capital you have held aloft the light of Lahiri Mahasaya's ideals."

The same Premananda soon became Paul Twitchell's first spiritual teacher—initiating him into kriya yoga—around 1950, before the latter's leaving to follow Kirpal Singh. Twitchell went on to found the Eckankar movement, with "tens of thousands of followers through the Western world" (Rawlinson, 1997). His authorized biography was later penned by the prolific New Age author Brad Steiger.

For the startling, near word-for-word similarities between numerous paragraphs in Twitchell's writings and earlier-published texts, see David Lane's www.neuralsurfer.com website, and his (1983) *The Making of a Spiritual Movement.* The inconsistencies between the various biographies of Twitchell are laid bare in the same latter book.

Twitchell passed away of a heart attack in 1971, "only months after predicting that he would live at least another five years."

Premananda's name and image have since been excised from SRF materials, including the *Autobiography,* apparently at Yogananda's behest, following disloyal actions on the part of the former.

* * *

Of course, not every aspect of Babaji's kriya yoga mission is executed through SRF. There are, indeed, numerous independent groups tracing their lineage to the same great guru.

A highly placed member of one of those ancillary parties has described his own ashram life, under a guru (Yogi Ramaiah, a.k.a. Yogiyar) who was himself a disciple of the immortal Babaji:

> In late January 1971, Yogiyar met with both Cher [no, not *that* Cher—different one; although the *real* Cher's son is a non-celibate Hare Krishna] and the author together and informed them that despite all of the efforts they as a couple had made, the relationship should end, because the genuine love which the author had for Cher was no longer reciprocated by her. If the relationship were to continue, Cher would soon feel forced not only to leave the author, but kriya yoga as well. It was painful for the author because of the expectations he had for a long-term relationship with Cher. But he wanted Cher to be happy. Yogiyar also held out another route for her as an "ashramite," wherein she would live in close proximity to him, and receive a higher level of training (Govindan, 1997).

Such "high-level, close-proximity training" of the woman appears to have worked wonders for her spiritual development:

> Cher dedicated herself to kriya yoga and soon conceived a son, "Annamalai," with Yogiyar (Govindan, 1997).

"I got you, babe."

* * *

If one cares to step just a little further off this already infirm ledge into the truly wild unknown, one can easily find additional tales involving the Himalayan Babaji. Stories such as the following:

> Babaji has had many bodies throughout human history. He can appear to you in any of them, or *all of them at the same time*. I have friends to whom Babaji appeared in many bodies as a parade. This appearance enlightened them. Since meeting Babaji in Herakhan in 1977, Babaji has appeared to me in many forms—as a woman on a bicycle in Poland, as a bum in Washington DC, as a bird, as a snake....
>
> Babaji is the Father of Jesus Christ (Leonard Orr, in [Churchill, 1996]; italics added).

Orr was a pioneer in the development of Rebirthing therapy—a deep-breathing means of releasing psychological blockages and ostensible past-life traumas (Garden, 1988).

Louise Valpied (in Churchill, 1996) likewise relates:

> One experience was when my dog friend, Rafike, was seriously ill after being poisoned by a paralysis tick. I left the vet surgery not knowing whether I'd see her alive again. As I walked out the door, there was a little bird of a type I've never seen before, dancing from foot to foot. Without thinking, I knew it was Babaji saying, "Don't worry, I am here, she's fine."
>
> This is one of the times recently Babaji has communicated with me through a bird. This is happening more frequently.

* * *

Not to be outdone, Yogananda's younger brother Bishnu claims a disciple, Bikram Choudhury. The latter has (literally) trademarked many aspects and *asanas* of his own "heat yoga," so popular in Hollywood these halcyon days. Of that disciple-turned-teacher—who had George Harrison as a student back in '69—it is said:

> Bikram brags about his mansion with servants in Beverly Hills and his thirty classic cars, from Rolls-Royces to Bent-

> leys. He also claims to have cured every disease known to humankind and compares himself to Jesus Christ and Buddha. Requiring neither food nor sleep, he says, "I'm beyond Superman" (Keegan, 2002).

The Über-"Man of Steel" himself then apparently asserts that he has been the subject of blackmail threats on the part of his female students:

> "What happens when they say they will commit suicide unless you sleep with them?" he asks. "What am I supposed to do? Sometimes having an affair is the only way to save someone's life" (Carlson, 2002a).

Again, "there but for the grace of God...."

* * *

My own wholly non-humorous experiences with Self-Realization Fellowship included nine months spent as a resident volunteer at the men-only Hidden Valley ashram/hermitage outside Escondido, California. That occurred from October of 1998 to July of 1999, after I had been a loyal member of SRF for over a decade. While the emphasis there was never on "crazy wisdom"—indeed, the environment was fairly bereft of *any* kind of wisdom—that still left plenty to be concerned about.

- Before being officially accepted to live at Hidden Valley (HV) as a resident volunteer, the applicant is required to sign a pledge affirming that he will regard his supervisors at the ashram as vehicles of God and Guru, and obey their instructions accordingly. That boils down to being an interesting way for the monks in supervisory positions there to allow themselves to feel that their actions are divinely inspired. Further, anyone who disputes their instructions is being a "bad disciple," whose insubordination they will undoubtedly publicly quietly tolerate, but privately discuss and disdain.

  One is also required to disclose his sexual orientation, and whether or not he has ever had any homosexual experiences.

  For the record, I myself am "straight as an arrow," nearly to the point of being a ***hetero*** *sapien,* and consequently have not had any such experiences. The point here is not that I was uncomfortable answering that question—I was not. Rather, it is simply a sad day when our world's "don't ask, don't tell" militaries are more progressive in their thinking than are the same world's "God-centered" ashrams

- The late Tara Mata (i.e., Ms. Laurie Pratt, editor of Yogananda's *Autobiography,* and former senior vice president of SRF) is claimed to have been the reincarnation of Leonardo da Vinci. Her own published writings, however, show none of da Vinci's fertile genius. (Those articles are printed in old SRF magazines, and sometimes available in photocopy to lucky devotees behind the scenes.) Instead, those writings bristle with biting and petty condemnations of anyone who failed to agree with her yogic point of view. In particular, she expends ridiculous amounts of energy trashing H. G. Wells and others who endorsed the standard view of evolution and human cultural development.

  The "logical force" of Tara's arguments, however, comes down to nothing more than a repetitive mongering of the fact that such a view is opposed to the Hindu idea of cyclic spiritual development on the planet, and is therefore "wrong." In particular, she predictably trumpeted Yogananda's (1946) reading of those cycles as occurring within a 24,000-year period, which he associated with the "precession of the equinoxes"—a circular motion of the Earth's rotational axis with respect to the "fixed" stars. He (via Yukteswar's [1977] *The Holy Science*) further regarded that precession as arising from our sun being part of a binary star system—that supposedly accounting for the movement of the stars in the heavens through that cycle. In connection with that presumed rhythm, other SRF monks have suggested that "in the Kali Yuga [i.e., the 'Iron Age'], the average height of humans is four feet; in Dwapara ['Bronze'], six; in Treta ['Silver'], eight; and in Satya ['Gold'], ten."

  As ridiculous as that idea may be, it has a storied history, being endorsed also by Sri Aurobindo's path:

  > The Puranas state that the duration of each yuga is in direct proportion to the diminishing Truth. As a

> result, man's life-span diminishes also. In addition, they say that with the declining Truth man's stature too declines. Man's height, which is fourteen cubits in Treta, is reduced to seven cubits in Dwapara, and goes down to four and a half cubits in Kali (Nahar, 1989).

Notwithstanding all that, the real explanation for the (25,800-year) equinoctial precession is a problem in sophomore classical mechanics. It is, indeed, based upon the same principles as those which cause the axis of rotation of a gyroscope or spinning top to precess or wobble. (Our sun may yet have a binary companion, though, if the research done at the Binary Research Institute is valid.)

Those errors are thus particularly odd, since Tara Mata, like Yogananda, was reputed to have been able to remember her own prior incarnations in those very same previous "world cycles," aeons ago. She should therefore have been in a unique position to bolster her arguments via that supposed directly remembered experience.

It has further been convincingly claimed that the astrologist Tara relied on Edgar Cayce for predictive readings, being Cayce's subject #778. (In Edgar's view, Tara was one of his Egyptian followers, when he himself was an ancient priest there.) Cayce's own work, however, has been thoroughly debunked in Randi's (1982) *Flim-Flam!* and Gardner's (1957) *Fads and Fallacies*. For a comparable deflation of astrology, see Susan Blackmore's (1986) *The Adventures of a Parapsychologist*.

Of course, we have already seen that Aurobindo (1872 – 1950) made the same (da Vinci) reincarnational claim as did Tara Mata (overlapping, at 1900 – 1971). Da Vinci himself, interestingly, was actually homosexual (Wilber, 1998). As to whether he would then have been allowed into the ashrams....

In any case, in a third-person pamphlet narrative, Tara Mata actually styled herself as being an evolved "Forerunner of the New Race," on the basis of her own kundalini awakening. Abbot George Burke (1994), however, related a contrasting perspective on Tara:

> Since she claimed that even before meeting the Master she had fully attained cosmic consciousness, she doubtless believed herself qualified to censor his words.
>
> So great was Laurie Pratt's confidence in her perfected consciousness that she purchased some books on Hindi, read through them, and proceeded to "translate" the entire *Autobiography of a Yogi* into that language—or rather into several hundred pages of gibberish that her illumined intelligence told her was Hindi. When the vice president of SRF, Swami Kriyananda (who could speak and write Hindi), notified the officials of SRF that her manuscript which had been sent to India for printing was utter gobbledygook, he was verbally rapped on the knuckles and told to go ahead and get it printed. Only when he took Daya Mata and other board members to the publishers (at the publisher's insistence), who proved to them that the manuscript (which had been set up at the board's insistence at great expense) was nothing but a string of nonsense syllables, was it finally agreed to not have it printed!

Tara herself was the granddaughter of the Mormon rationalist Orson Pratt. The latter's responsibilities included attempting to explain the curious similarities between founder Joseph Smith's claimed channelings of their scriptures and some lesser-known parts of the Bible

- The late Dr. M. W. Lewis—Yogananda's first American disciple—is likewise believed to have been the reincarnation of Sir Francis Bacon, a primary compiler of the King James version of the Bible. (These questions regarding previous incarnations are not openly touted by Self-Realization Fellowship, but they are well-known behind the scenes, and never directly denied by SRF ministers.)

However:

> [King] James I himself was said to be homosexually inclined, as also was his eventual Lord Chancellor, Francis Bacon (Colman, 1974).

King James was also known to his friends as "Queen James." Seriously.

Of course, Oscar Wilde—who spent time around the Theosophical Society—himself believed Shakespeare, too, to have been gay (Partridge, 1947). He had, however, little evidence for that belief other than wishful thinking. ("Either those curtains go into *samadhi,* or I do")

- In one (question-and-answer session) *satsanga,* the administrator at Hidden Valley "guaranteed" that an unspecified number of the members of SRF's Board of Directors will have been rulers/pharaohs in ancient Egypt
- In a Voluntary League (financial) Appeal newsletter sent to their members in the spring of 1989, SRF disclosed that the city of Los Angeles had been considering a public transit plan which would have disrupted their Hollywood Temple. City council, however, had thankfully been persuaded not to proceed with that in part because of SRF's protests that the site was considered a holy place of pilgrimage by their devotees around the world. ("Shrine" was the actual word they used in the VL Appeal letter.) Amazingly, however, in 1966 SRF had reportedly filed a plan with the city calling for tearing down their Mount Washington Hotel headquarters (Dakota, 1998). That building is considered by devotees to be much more holy than the Hollywood Temple, as Yogananda lived for an extended time in the former historic building. Evidently, then, the holiness of a place depends upon who exactly is planning on tearing it down. ("There's still no room at the inn, Sir, but if we razed it and put up a high-rise instead"...)
- Already back in 1999, according to the HV ashram administrator in a *satsanga,* SRF had hired an image consultant. The relayed recommendation of that expert was that SRF should work toward becoming known as "the spiritual organization which lives up to its ideals more than any other." In light of SRF's reported poor behavior (CANDER, 2001) in their attempted Mount Washington expansion, however, the irony there cannot be missed.

Indeed, the unhappiness generated in the surrounding community through that undertaking included allegations of stacked neighborhood meetings. Those were occurring for an attempted expansion which was compared to the development of "four and a half Home Depot stores" in that ecologically sensitive residential area. In return, "[F]ellowship supporters have compared church opponents to Nazis" (Russell, 1999)

- Midway through my stay at Hidden Valley, a fellow devotee left the ashram to join the Peace Corps. Within a few weeks of that departure, the head monk led a *satsanga*. There, we were told that anyone who leaves the ashram to work for world peace would have been doing more good if he had stayed and done "Gurudeva's work" at the monastery
- In related matters, the nearly functionally illiterate ashram administrator, possessing a mere sixth-grade reading level, once opined in a *satsanga* that "scientists who use their intelligence to 'get famous,' rather than for seeking God, are misusing that intelligence." A former administrator had similarly asserted that "Einstein's intuition failed him in his later years," in that the great scientist allegedly "wasn't able to see" that the accepted indeterministic quantum theory was right. (That formulation is indeed *not* "the last word," as David Bohm's Nobel-caliber work has shown [see Bohm and Hiley, 1993]. Thus, "Einstein's intuition" was *right,* where these ochre-robed administrators, and many of today's physicists, are confidently wrong.)

The certainty in that regard presumably stemmed from the purported "wholistic" correspondences between indeterministic quantum theory and Eastern religion/meditation. Those have been espoused only since the mid-'70s by misled authors such as Fritjof Capra and Amit Goswami, and quoted approvingly in some of SRF's publications. Goswami in turn once wrote a complimentary letter to SRF, praising Yogananda's writings. Amit's non-fiction musings on "quantum consciousness," though, would have been better published as explicit science fiction. For, in reality, such "correspondences" are at best fortuitous, and can more reasonably be regarded as arising from mere wishful thinking, on the part of individuals having next to no understanding of metaphysics.

In any case, how does one best use one's intelligence "for God"? By entering the ashrams and willingly doing what one is told to do by one's spiritual superiors, of course

- At a monks-only gathering at the SRF headquarters around Christmas of 1998, one of the maternal members of the Board of Directors was said to have favored those assembled with a joke: "What is an atheist? A member of a non-prophet religion." The clever riddle was proudly retold in the ashram at a *satsanga,* as a "Christmas gift" from those holy, wise and "spiritually advanced" mother-figures. And all gathered there laughed dutifully, not realizing that the line itself is simply a bastardization of a classic George Carlin observation, i.e., that "atheism is a non-prophet organization"
- One evening, the monk who runs the SRF postulant (i.e., "new monk") ashram graced HV as a guest speaker. One of the points that he brought up, from his unique perspective as head of that monastery, was that "the people most likely to leave the ashram after taking some degree of monastic vows are those who are the most independent." While that is undoubtedly true, the clear implication was that independence and the ability to think for oneself are bad things, when in reality they are the only way of doing anything original in this world. Worse, suffocating attitudes such as that allergy to independence turn the unthinking following of other people's blind guesses and bad advice into an "ego-killing" virtue. They further paint the inability to so blindly follow, against one's own better judgment, what one knows to be wrong, as being a sin
- Each one of the SRF line of leaders/gurus—their "popes"—from Daya Mata back to Krishna, are regarded by obedient SRF devotees as being infallible, and simply "working in mysterious ways" when it comes to any seemingly questionable actions on their parts. I, too, once foolishly viewed them thusly. For, such regard is simply what I had been *taught* was correct, by persons who I assumed would never deliberately mislead me, as I would never have lied to them.

As Margery Wakefield (1993) noted of her own and others' involvement in Scientology:

> I had made the fatal unconscious assumption that since I was honest and had good motives, then others must be too

- James J. Lynn, personally chosen by Yogananda to be SRF's second president, was a married man. That is, married before, during and after Yogananda gave him the title of Rajasi Janakananda. (His wife, however, was "both mentally and physically unwell," and was not supportive of his connection with Self-Realization Fellowship [Mata, 1992].) That fact, however, is conspicuously absent from the relevant literature, e.g., from the SRF-published biography of Lynn's life.

  That anomaly was brought up by one of the HV residents in a *satsanga* period. The justification which the ashram administrator provided for the lack of publication of that information was simply, and predictably, that "that's the way the Board of Directors and Daya Mata want it done"
- The degree to which one is expected to "respect one's elders" as a good and obedient devotee of SRF was underscored by the following (real) exchange, quoted during a sermon at Hidden Valley:

  > Elder: "How are you?"
  > Youthful Inferior: "I'm fine. How are you?"
  > Elder (disgusted at the impudence): "Are you a doctor?"

- Or, consider the changes made to the proffered definitions of *pronam/pranam* over the years, in Chapter 40 of the *Autobiography:*

  > [*pronam:*] Literally, "holy name," a word of greeting among Hindus, accompanied by palm-folded hands lifted from the heart to the forehead in salutation. A *pronam* in India takes the place of the Western greeting by handshaking (Yogananda, 1946).

  More recently, however, the meaning of the (substituted) word has shifted to something more indicative of the respect due the ochre robe:

  > [*pranam:*] Lit., "complete salutation," from Sanskrit root *nam,* to salute or bow down; and the prefix *pra,* completely. A *pranam* salutation is made chiefly be-

fore monks and other respected persons (Yogananda, 1998)

- Further, the extent to which questioning is discouraged in the ashrams is demonstrated by the following example: Early in my own stay at Hidden Valley, our Thanksgiving meal centered on a soy-based turkey substitute. Following that feast, one resident pointed out in a written *satsanga* question that that food was loaded with MSG, which many people are allergic to, or develop headaches from. He also informed us that non-MSG turkey substitutes are readily available, and requested that the ashram use those instead in the future.

  The ashram administrator's response to that request was to relate the story of how, in the early days of SRF, the nuns used to work "all night" (in shifts), manually preparing gluten-based meat substitutes for their festive occasions. He concluded by saying that he didn't want the kitchen at HV to have to work all night in similar preparations (not that they would have had to, but anyway). Thus, the ashram would continue serving the MSG-laced products.

  And all assembled smiled knowingly, that anyone would so foolishly try to improve the ashram, and "resist what God and Guru had given us" there

- At other times, the HV administrator related his own experience of having entered the ashrams in the 1950s as a "health nut," and of being concerned with the poor food being served there. Upon bringing that up with a senior monk, the latter's response was simply, "What Master gives, you take." That advice sounds relatively fine, until one considers that over Easter (in 1996, when I first spent a month at Hidden Valley), "Master/God gave us"—a group of steadfast vegetarians—a box of donuts containing lard.

  Amazingly, although Yogananda very explicitly taught that the consumption of white flour and white sugar is unhealthy, both of those are staples in the ashram diet. Indeed, sugar was sometimes even added to freshly squeezed orange juice, and whole wheat flour was all but entirely absent. The explanation which the ashram administrator gave regarding that discrepancy was that Yogananda's advice on diet was allegedly meant to apply only to the specific group of people to which he had been speaking at the time. Personally, I think that's nonsense: Yogananda regularly encouraged his followers to eat only "unsulphured" fruit, for example. Today, that would equate to it being certified organic. Yet one will find (to my knowledge) no examples of that in the HV cafeteria (other than the produce which they grow themselves, which is close to being organic).

The Hidden Valley menu, inconsistent with Yogananda's teachings, is just the product of a cultural lowest common denominator among their kitchen staff. It is not "what Master gives them," nor did Yogananda's dietary advice apply only to "meat and potatoes" people fifty years ago

- One of SRF's respected monastic brothers will typically put up to eighty hours of rehearsal into a Convocation speech—even to the point of practicing facial expressions and hand gestures, according to the head monk at Hidden Valley. There is nothing wrong with such preparedness, of course. The majority of the audience at those events, however, undoubtedly assumes that those lectures are given "from intuition," with little or no preparation—on the basis of the monk's fifty-plus years of meditation—as Yogananda explicitly taught and practiced. SRF's questionable billing (in their Convocation literature and tapes) of those as "informal talks," when in reality they are highly scripted, does nothing to discourage that perception
- The same monk praised the devotional "receptivity" or "absorptive listening" of audiences in India, in contrast to the "intellectual inquisitiveness/weighing" and analysis which Western audiences give to the words of saints and sages. (By contrast, Arthur Koestler's [1960] *The Lotus and the Robot,* Gita Mehta's [1979] *Karma Cola* and Sarah Macdonald's delightful [2003] *Holy Cow* all offer stunning revelations about what life in India, both inside and outside of her ashrams, is really like, from a skeptical perspective. Strelley's [1987] *The Ultimate Game* does the same, from a less jaundiced view.) As Radha (1978) dangerously expressed it:

> The Eastern mind does not make the clear distinction between intuition and intellect as the Western

> mind tends to do. The difficulty comes for the Westerner when there is an over-emphasis upon the intellect at the cost of the intuition. The simple person who is unencumbered by intellectual concepts is more receptive. What can be done to remain receptive and not to have the intellect continually interfering? Stop intellectualizing and just receive.

There are, however, other possible explanations for such Eastern "non-intellectual receptivity":

> The person buying [*pan*] puts it in his cheek, like a wad of chewing tobacco. It's said to have speed in it, which gives the user a slightly glazed look and, after an initial burst of energy, a sluggishness and a swaying walk.
>
> Over the years it amused me that many freshly-arrived Westerners would refer to the "meditative" look on the Indians they saw, when, in reality, what they were seeing more often than not was the result of chewing this narcotic (Strelley, 1987).

Strelley herself, prior to entering Rajneesh's ashrams, ran drugs for a living; she knows what she is talking about.

One is, of course, always free to glorify the effects of one's preferred narcotics. One is not equally free, however, to confuse widespread, drug-induced stupor with meditative spirituality, celebrating the former in the guise of the latter. Nor may one then lament how "the West" too often lacks the same "Cheech and Chong"-like receptivity! And let's not even get started on the hallucinogenic use of peyote (Das, 1997) and magic mushrooms (Allegro, 1970) in religious rites, in both East and West.

Not unrelated to the (non-narcotic) "mindless devotion" found in the East is I. K. Taimni's native observation that the bane of (conformist psychology) East Indian thought has always been the tendency to accept anything when it has been stated by an authority, without further questioning.

In any case, the attempt to intellectually understand and "separate the wheat from the chaff" is absolutely necessary if one is to retain any ability to think for oneself, or avoid swallowing whole every anecdotal tall tale told "in the name of God."

> Devotion [to the guru] is valued in Vajrayana [i.e., Tantric Buddhism] as a means to destroy doubt. Considered a refuge of ego, doubt is no longer coddled—it has to be crushed. But if a choice must be made between doubt and devotion, I think we are better off to prefer doubt. It is essential to sanity, and therefore to enlightenment; absolutely nothing in the path should be shielded from skeptical scrutiny, especially not devotion (Butterfield, 1994)

- Yogananda founded separate uniformed schools for boys and girls in India. Hidden Valley's administrator once publicly voiced the opinion that Paramahansa would definitely have wanted the same setup implemented in America as well, had he founded schools here.

  Such separation of the sexes, of course, could do nothing to decrease SRF's concern over homosexual activities, given that residential boys' schools are widely renowned for exactly the latter.

> It is not surprising that proportionally more gays would be active in the world of the [Catholic] seminary and rectory.... That is true for any exclusively male situation—in the army, the non-coed school, the Boy Scouts (Wills, 2000)

- SRF's emphasis on the conservation and transmutation of sexual energy as a means toward effecting spiritual (kundalini) awakenings leads readily to a Catholic-like, guilt-ridden attitude toward sex on the part of its devout members. For, if the choice is between sex and spiritual advancement—i.e., if sexual activity leads one away from God—how could one not feel guilty about indulging in it? Notwithstanding that, in response to a *satsanga* question, the HV ashram administrator once explicitly recommended that anyone who decides against entering a monastic order for life should get married, so that his/her ego won't be strengthened by "being able to do whatever he wants, whenever he wants." (As if the "real world" is so lenient and flexible to one's desires! and as if there were a stupider reason to fall in love.) That leads to the obvious conclusion that, unless one is going to become part of the official monastic in-group, he shouldn't even try to live a hermitic lifestyle, lest he be guilty of being "egoic and selfish"

- The same administrator asserted in a *satsanga* that SRF members shouldn't even live together before marriage, as it would "set a bad example" for others' perceptions of persons on the spiritual path. As to how a piece of paper called a marriage license makes cohabitation more acceptable in the eyes of God, that was never really explained.

One can, however, fairly easily track down the source for that fossilized position. For, all of it is simply a repetition of views expressed by SRF's Brother Anandamoy (1995) in a recorded talk, in essentially the same words.

Conservative behavior and conformity, then, would appear to be the order of the day, lest one offend others by even *appearing* to "do wrong." (Even long hair in the ashrams is taboo, by Daya Mata's decree, except for monks in India. Beards, as I recall, require permission to be sought before they are grown, unless you entered the ashrams with one.) Conversely, even positive social change is left to "less spiritual" others.

"Lost in the '50s," or even the '30s, and proud of it

- Anandamoy (1979) has further said that, owing to the discipline and rules laid down within SRF, "there is no generation gap in our ashram, though the ages range from eighteen to over ninety." That may or may not be true. What can hardly be denied, however, is that there is surely an analogous "respect gap," which keeps people just as far apart. That distance may be based on the length of time one has been in the ashrams, or the position one occupies, or just the color of one's shirt. (Blue = postulant, yellow = *brahmachari,* orange = *sannyasi.)* For, when a blue shirt meets an orange one in the monastic caste system, there is no doubt as to which one is more spiritually advanced, and thus more deserving of being respectfully listened to.

Butterfield (1994) described his own comparable experiences within Trungpa's Buddhist community:

> It is easy to pull rank in an organization where rank is given tremendous importance by practice levels, of-

> fices, and colored pins. When a senior student with a higher rank than your own betrays you emotionally or perpetrates some odious piece of arrogance, at which you express overt resentment and anger, the situation may then go over into the game of one-upmanship. The ranking "elder" calls attention to your resentment as though it were solely the result of an ego problem characteristic of your inferior practice level.

Of course, regarding generation gaps, it would be hard to sustain those in any closed community anyway. For there, indulgence in the varying popular interests which normally separate generations are discouraged. Further, any radical behaviors of the younger generation would be left outside the ashram gates, in the attempt to make the younger ones as conservative as the older, rather than having the older generation meet the younger on the latter's own terms, or (God forbid) learn from them. That is, when closed community life is based around ideas which predate even the "grandfathers" of the community, with all members being expected to conform to those ideals, there is indeed little to separate the generations. One may even rightly credit the restrictive rules of the community for that.

In the "real world," however, it is exactly the relative *absence* of such restrictions that allows for radical social, scientific *and spiritual* change. Put another way: If the "real world" was as conservative, homogeneous and "stuck in the past" as such orthodox spiritual communities are, nothing would ever change for the better.

Even just in terms of spirituality, human understanding has increased tremendously over the past quarter of a century. Those increases, however, have *not* come from the world's ashrams. Rather, they have come from people who were, in general, too independent and creative to tolerate the suffocating rules and discipline, not merely of those closed communities, but even of the far less conservative "real world" itself.

Indeed, radically creative breakthroughs in *any* field are far more likely to come from people who make their own rules. Those who enjoy, too much, living within the confines of other people's discipline, in the misled belief that such a slow and painful death has anything to do with spiritual advancement, are not the ones to make such contributions.

Conversely, the idea that "when you are as great as Gandhi was, you can break the rules, as Gandhi did" has got it exactly backwards. For, one only becomes "great," to whatever degree, by judiciously breaking existing rules—after having first mastered them—to do things which wouldn't have been possible within the accepted constraints. If one hasn't ever broken the rules *wisely,* chances are that one also hasn't ever done anything truly original in life.

As Yogananda (1986) himself put it:

> I follow the rules—as much as I want to, and then I say, "Down with rules!"....
>
> Now there is more attempt than ever before to raise the average human being to a desirable level of culture; but there is always the accompanying danger of cramping the genius in the straitjacket of the mediocre

- Interestingly, some Clint Eastwood "spaghetti western" movies are pre-approved for Hidden Valley ashram viewing by monks and residents on their monthly movie nights. *The Sound of Music,* in contrast, is banned. The reason? In the latter, Julie Andrews' character is contemplating life as a monastic, but then finds "the man of her dreams" and "lives happily ever after." Screening such an idealization of romantic love, however, might "put ideas into the heads" of the people living there.

  Guns, however, are evidently relatively okay

- A resident volunteer at HV once remarked within my range of hearing that "everything you do at Hidden Valley gets talked about behind your back." From my own experiences there, and from hearing my immediate supervisor criticize the ashram administrator, behind his back, as being "long-winded," and offer endless critiques of the ashram food, I know too well that that observation is valid. (The aspect of his sharp eyes directed toward *me* included being critiqued, unsolicited of course, on the length of my hair and the shabbiness of my clothes. As Thoreau once remarked, however: "Beware of enterprises that require new clothes.") That widespread behavior exists among a group of people supposedly concerned with their own self-improvement. In practice, however, they inadvertently make a strong case for defining a yogi as "a person intent on killing everyone's ego except his own."

Indeed, the ashram administrator once stated his view on positive thinking as the idea that "failure flattens one's ego," and is thus supposedly a good thing. Aside from the problem that Yogananda taught *nothing* like that, the obvious converse of that idea is that to succeed too much would interfere with the "killing of one's ego" that ostensibly constitutes spiritual progress. Thus, implicitly, even if an individual is successful, he should not feel too good about those triumphs. It does not take an advanced understanding of human psychology to see that, in the face of those taboos, the easy way to make oneself feel good is by "cutting off the heads of others"—albeit behind their backs, for to do it to their faces would make one a "bad disciple"

- Through my work in assisting with Hidden Valley's attempt at setting up a software programming shop during my stay there, I was further informed that I was "impatient" and possessed a "big head," simply for getting things done faster than they (and God) wanted them done. I was also explicitly told that when I had meditated more and become more spiritually advanced, I wouldn't feel the need to be creative in writing books and music. That is, I would just "serve Master's work" by donating money/labor to it, without presuming to do anything original or truly creative in life.

  Yogananda (1986), of course, taught exactly the opposite:

  > Do some creative work every day. Writing is good for developing creative ability and will power.... I am always seeking to accomplish something new. Being creative is more difficult, of course, than following a mechanical existence, but when your will battles with new ideas it gains more strength.

In contrast to that, but in accord with the attitudes present within today's SRF, Butterfield (1994) observed the following within the context of his own discipleship under Chögyam Trungpa:

> Originality is unwelcome; it is regarded as an impulse of the ego which must be processed out of the mind before enlightenment can occur. "If you find something in my talk that is not in Trungpa's writings," said a program coordinator, "then it's just my ego."

In any case, "big-headed" experiences such as the above have led me to the firm conclusion that most of the "patience of saints" comes from them simply not trying to get anything done on schedule. Or, from them being too dumb to know how inefficiently they're working. In contexts such as those, it would indeed be easy to be "patient," get nothing done, waste other people's donated money, and take that as a virtue

- I left Hidden Valley just after the original exposé ("Return of the Swami": Russell, 1999) of SRF and Ananda was published in the now-defunct *New Times Los Angeles*. That timing was just coincidental, but it did allow me to witness the "sagely" analysis of the story given, unsolicited, by the ashram administrator. That reading, then, consisted simply of his mention in that context of several monks he had known who had "fallen" *due to the temptation of women*. There was, of course, no mention in his analysis of the horrible (alleged) abuse of power on the part of those monks. Nor was there any hint of the despicable reported response to that scandal on the part of the "compassionate, saintly, God-realized" SRF leaders, as quoted earlier.

  The same aforementioned "sage" referred to the newsmagazine in which the above information regarding SRF was printed (i.e., the *New Times L.A.*) as being merely a "smut paper." He further regarded the article in question as being simply an attempt to "dig up dirt" on Self-Realization Fellowship, as a means of thwarting their planned expansion. That is, it was, in his words, "garbage" or "trash," not worth sticking one's nose into, particularly when one has been warned of its nature by someone ostensibly in a position to truthfully judge.

The very same respected monk would, I was later told, deliberately drive away in his golf cart when it came time to take his daily medicine, pretending not to see the herniated ashram resident who was chasing after him with that for his own good

- The Environmental Impact Report required for the physical expansion of the Mount Washington headquarters was similarly and explicitly viewed by that administrator as being just a community stalling tactic. In fact, his response to that obstacle was simply that "people will find a reason to oppose SRF," as if there were no other grounds for that EIR to be done!

Indeed, with regard to one of the relatively recent SRF publications—I believe it was their version of Omar Khayyam's *Rubaiyat*—it had otherwise been noted that one of the artists and SRF members working on the illustrations experienced relevant health problems as the publication date drew near. Those difficulties were explicitly chalked up to Satan trying to thwart the spread of truth through Self-Realization Fellowship. Given that, it would be inconsistent for SRF to not have viewed any opposition to the Mount Washington expansion as being literally devil-inspired. One would expect them to have exactly the same attitude toward the present "evil, demonic smut" book.

> Even as early as the summer of 1951, Master often told me that Rajasi's life was in grave danger and that Satan was trying to destroy his body. When I asked Master why Satan wanted to destroy Rajasi's body he answered, "Because he has and is still doing so much for the work and is helping a lot of souls back to God as His Divine instrument and Satan is trying to destroy it so he won't do any more" (Mata, 1992).

The phrase "paranoid belief system" springs to mind.

Interestingly, the Moonies have a similar view of reality and the influence of Satan as is described immediately above:

> "Martha, I have to whisper [from laryngitis]," I apologized.

> "No, you don't! It's just your concept!"
>
> "I'm sorry, I can hardly talk. I don't mean to be negative."
>
> "It's SATAN controlling you. If you *yell* 'OUT SATAN' all the way to campus, you'll be fine," Martha ordered (Underwood and Underwood, 1979).

Or, as Yogananda (1986) described that same evil force's attack on him:

> I saw the black form of Satan, horrible, with a catlike face and tail. It leaped on my chest, and my heart stopped beating

- Daya Mata herself foretold (1971) the following global trials, as seen by her in vision:

> [The Divine] indicated that all mankind would face a very dark time during which the evil force would seek to engulf the world.... [T]he world ... would ultimately emerge from the threatening dark cloud of karma, but mankind would first have to do its part by turning to God.

The question then came up as to why this and other prophesied catastrophes had not yet come to pass in the decades since their prediction. The catch-all response given was that the world was getting "extensions" to that, based on the meditations of its more spiritually advanced beings (e.g., Daya Mata herself).

Compare:

> The leader [of a small religious group], Mrs. Keech, claimed that she received messages from beings on another planet and that she had been informed that an earthquake and flood would signal the end of the world one day in December. But those who had been committed to Mrs. Keech would be saved by a spaceship the night before. On the appointed night, the followers waited anxiously for the spaceship and of course it didn't come.... The group was highly upset when midnight came and went with no sight of a spaceship. But then Mrs. Keech claimed to have received a message saying that the devotion of her and

> her followers had been sufficient to avert the impending disaster (Winn, 2000).

Or this, via Elizabeth Clare Prophet and the apocalyptic Church Universal and Triumphant:

> Ms. Prophet captured national headlines with her reported prediction that the end of civilization would occur on April 23, 1990. Prophet denies having set the date, but local residents disagree. "She has postponed the date at least four times over the last year," said Richard Meyer, a hardware store owner. "Every time it doesn't happen, she says it is because of church prayers" (Nickell, 1998).

Or this, from an admittedly false former psychic:

> We always gave ourselves an out, of course, in the event that the prophecy didn't materialize. The "vibrations" had changed, we would say, or people's prayers had averted the gloom and doom that we had warned about but that hadn't come to pass (Keene, 1977)

- SRF explicitly prides itself on being a spiritual organization "run according to business principles." Hidden Valley receives the vast majority of its labor freely from volunteers, and provides no extravagances in food or shelter for them. Nevertheless, their business segment was barely breaking even financially, during the time that I spent with them. Yet, all the while they were professing "intuitive" guidance in their managerial decisions, and equating obedience to themselves and to the higher leaders of the organization with obedience to God and Guru.

  Indeed, things were so tight financially toward the end of my stay in the ashram that the head monk and my immediate supervisor there discussed, without my input, having me spend my own money to provide a second computer for myself to work on, in the client/server programming that I was doing for them. (I had already provided one, for $1000 U.S., prior to that.) Learning of that, I informed that oppressively negative, short-tempered and visibly neurotic immediate supervisor that I wasn't in a financial position to absorb that expense.

That micromanaging misfit's favorite expression, in the midst of Yogananda's positive-thinking teachings, was "Life sucks, and then you die." Indeed, in his presence of undreamed-of-negativity it was not safe to voice even guarded optimism. Toward the end of my stay there, on more than one occasion when I would see that defective little gentleman coming across the ashram grounds to accost me with one aspect or another of his endless pessimism, I literally felt the urge to vomit. I have still not recovered from what he put me through. In all seriousness, I have never encountered a *less* spiritual environment than I was forced to deal with during my six months working under that particular *monk*.

In any case, with regard to him and the head monk "helping" me to spend my own money for the ashram's good, I further suggested to the former that if money was that tight for them, then the three of us should get together and talk about the possibility of me loaning the ashram several hundred dollars from my own meager savings, to be repaid when I left.

Amazingly, the same weasel stopped me later that day, to inform me that he and the head monk had discussed the situation—again without me, of course!—and might just ask me to provide a computer monitor instead! (I would then take that heavy item back with me to Canada when I left, according to their autocratic plans.)

All of that transpired while I was already providing sixty hours a week of extremely efficiently done, professional-level programming, in return for only a $30 U.S. per month allowance.

(The required ashram work week was actually less than thirty-five hours. I put in the extra time, in spite of my immediate supervisor's unsolicited discouraging of me from doing that, simply because [i] I enjoyed the work, [ii] it desperately needed to be done, and [iii] the sooner I completed the training projects there, the sooner I could get the hell away from that oppressive, micromanaging jackass. Have you ever had someone literally looking over your shoulder, for minutes/aeons at a time, while you were trying to write code? Thanks to Hidden Valley, I have lived that dysfunctional "Dilbert Zone.")

In all fairness, though, the $30 allowance was still better than average. By contrast, most ashrams—e.g., Radha's Yasodhara, Rama's Himalayan International Institute, Ananda and Findhorn—charge *you* significant amounts of money (currently up to $300 per month, in HI's case) for the privilege of doing menial work for them in "karma yoga" retreats, generally with shared accommodations. (People living in Jetsunma's and Rajneesh's early ashrams likewise supported themselves financially. That was in addition to donating to the organization and paying for Rajneesh's encounter groups, etc.) One of the attractions that many people feel toward SRF is exactly that it evinces less of an explicit focus on money

- In the midst of all that top-heavy yet inadequate management, I was informed—unsolicited—by the non-monastic project manager of that enterprise, that the whole programming venture was sure to succeed. That assurance was given on the basis of the "enlightened" (yet medication-fleeing) ashram administrator's visualizing of "blueprints in the ether" for those plans in his meditations. Compare Daya Mata's (1971) confidence:

  > The blueprint for this work [i.e., SRF] was set in the ether by God; it was founded at His behest, and His love and His will sustain and guide it. I know this beyond doubt.

  "And God will lead the way."

  Indeed, the relevant manager's expectation was that the current project would bring in a thousand hours of work per month. That, at least, is what he explicitly requested from the associated devotee salesman, for an anticipated programming staff of half a dozen people. The contract I signed further specified that I would be paid $30 U.S. per hour. That works out to over a third of a million dollars of anticipated gross income per year, just to cover the salaries. Plus, the project manager was already building a house near the ashram, with the intention of deriving his full income from the software shop. Thus, with his cut, the annual gross would have had to be around *half a million dollars* for there to be anything left over for the ashram.

Such rosy pictures of the future, however, were not to come to pass.

Not even close.

I spent three months working with the external project manager on that "content management" programming, against the foot-dragging of my immediate supervisor. (By the end of that period, even the hardly brilliant project manager was floating the idea of replacing that defective individual.) After completing that "training in negativity" period at HV, I returned to Canada, and waited for the promised telecommuting work to arrive. And waited. For two full months. With not a single hour of paying work provided.

I was subsequently informed, by the salesman, that the external company which was supposed to have been the liaison with the outside world for providing contracts had "gone under."

Half a million dollars. Zero dollars. "Divinely guided."

"Blueprint, schmueprint."

Again, the Monty Python reference:

> [Eric Idle character:] Minister, may I put the first question to you? In your plan, "A Better Britain for Us," you claimed that you would build eighty-eight thousand million billion houses a year in the Greater London area alone. In fact, you've built only three in the last fifteen years. Are you a bit disappointed with this result?
>
> [Graham Chapman character:] No, no. I'd like to answer this question if I may in two ways. Firstly in my normal voice and then in a kind of silly, high-pitched whine.

After all that, my entry on the Dilbert Zone website for March 22, 2001—"Biggest Promises Broken By Your Boss"—went as follows:

> TRUE: Full-time work, six-figure [Cdn.] salary telecommuting. REALITY: No work in first two months, ended up $1000 away from living on the street.
>
> —The Artist Formerly Known As Bert

> It placed in the top five.
>
> This life is a cosmic motion picture (Yogananda, 1986).
>
> "I laughed. I cried. If you see only one guru this year...."

- And just when you think it can't get any worse, it turns out that one of Charles Manson's murderous accomplices in the late '60s—still imprisoned to this day—had spent time in the SRF ashrams as a nun:

> During her freshman and sophomore years at Monrovia High School, Leslie [Van Houten] was one of the homecoming princesses. She tried out again her junior year, but this time she didn't make it. Bitter over the rejection, she ran away with [her boyfriend, Bobby] Mackey to Haight-Ashbury. The scene there frightened her, however, and she returned home to finish high school and to complete a year of secretarial training. Mackey, in the meantime, had become a novitiate priest in the Self Realization Fellowship. In an attempt to continue their relationship, Leslie became a novitiate nun, giving up both drugs and sex. She lasted about eight months before breaking with both Mackey and the yoga group (Bugliosi and Gentry, 1975).

The fact that Van Houten—the explicit namesake of *The Simpsons'* Milhouse—was let into the ashrams at all, of course, says nothing positive about the ability of the "advanced souls" at SRF to evaluate others' character, via intuition or otherwise. Indeed, less concern about sexual orientation and blind obedience to an "infallible" dead guru or living mother-figure, and more about character and the many positive aspects of independence, would serve the organization far better

- And just when you think it *really* can't get any worse, you discover the white supremacist Jost (Joseph) Turner (d. 1996), founder of the National Socialist Kindred. For, Turner received kriya initiation from SRF, and then lived for two years in

> a small intentional community in northern California which was founded by one of Yoganandas [*sic*] direct disciples.... He foresaw the importance of Yoganandas [*sic*] cooperative communities, and he realised [*sic*] that it was his mission to fulfill that vision. Today, his intentional community is probably the largest and most successfull [*sic*] in the world (Turner, 2001).

Turner went on to evolve and teach his own version of "Aryan Kriya," claiming guidance and inspiration from Babaji in that endeavor, and regarding Hitler as a "semi-divine religious leader."

> Jost declared that Yogananda was not anti-Hitler and supported the non-interventionist America First Movement during the Second World War. He upheld the Korean War against communism and "foresaw the massive problems" of multiculturalism (Goodrick-Clarke, 2003).

Well, who knows. For someone like Yogananda, who was notably frightened of "Godless" communism and supportive of the "God-fearing" fascist Mussolini ... who knows. He had, in any case, been planning on "visiting" both Hitler and Mussolini in 1936, following his tour of India, at the start of WWII (Inner Culture, 1935)

- Finally, to put one more (though, sadly, not the last) nail in the coffin of Undead Inadequate Management:

> With regar[d] to the first edition of the *Autobiography of a Yogi,* Yogananda had copyrighted this edition in his own name, not SRF's. When SRF renewed the copyright on the first edition, they renewed it in the name of SRF which voided the copyright and put it in the public domain. Now that the original AY is in public domain, it is now on the Internet at http://www.crystalclarity.com/yogananda [this is Kriyananda's publishing house].
>
> The renewal of a copyright is a simple matter of keeping track of when it expires and under what name it was registered. This is an inexcusable blunder (Dakota, 1998).

And so goes the "silly, high-pitched whine" which is all that remains of Yogananda's once-averred "Mighty Cosmic Om" within today's Self-Realization Fellowship.

Imagine the Catholic Church, minus its pedophilia but keeping all of the other problems—surely including ones which haven't yet made it into the news—with just a slightly different set of "original Christianity" beliefs. Right there, you've got a good approximation to today's SRF.

"Everything I ever needed to know about religion I learned," if not in kindergarten, at least from Monty Python's *Life of Brian*.

And yet, Python's John Cleese, ironically, has spoken in support of New Age topics at Esalen, and elsewhere quoted the Russian-American "crazy wisdom" master George Gurdjieff approvingly. (For the debunking of that figure, see Peter Washington's [1995] *Madame Blavatsky's Baboon,* as well as Evans' witty [1973] *Cults of Unreason.*)

* * *

Although I regularly skipped the "mandatory" group meditations at Hidden Valley, the head monk there explicitly invited me, before I left, to come back whenever I wanted to—I did not leave on bad terms with the organization. Indeed, during my stay, several of the office monks there offered, unsolicited, to write letters of recommendation for me, if I ever wanted to apply for a paid position, working at the Mother Center.

It was only after decompressing for several months from the oppressive weight of that experience, and comparing in detail the nonsense I observed there with the relatively benign "evil ways of the real world," that I came to the conclusion that I had never met a complete fool in my life, outside of that setting. (I have since met and worked for half a dozen others, but at least none of them had "God on their side.") Beyond that, it was only in discovering the SRF Walrus (2004) website in late 2001 that I began to understand that I was neither the only nor the first person to regard getting involved with that organization as the worst mistake of my life. (The Cult Busters—SRF Division site has since surpassed the Walrus, in terms of the quality of its postings and their non-censored freedom of expression.)

On the bright side, I did meet a decent, direct descendant of Captain Morgan, the rum-runner, during that same stay. That association has indeed, in recent years, endeared me to some of the Captain's finer pain-numbing products which, ironically, I had never felt any need to consume prior to spending too much time at Hidden Valley.

* * *

In the best of all possible readings, then, naïvely taking Yogananda to be everything that he and his disciples claim him to be, SRF shows how badly a mere two generations of followers, in a short half century, can mess things up. (The gospels were not written down until a comparable amount of time after Jesus' crucifixion. For the Buddha and Ramakrishna, too, the extant stories were not recollected until well after their deaths. No one should then imagine that comparable degrees of distortion as are demonstrably found in SRF do not exist across all of those sanitized scriptures and hagiographies. Conversely, if Ramakrishna and Yogananda were as mixed-up as we have seen, what of the Buddha? Or what of the mischievous, amorous Krishna and his "gopis," assuming that there is actually some factual basis to his mythological life? And what of Lao Tzu and Confucius? Are any of them more worthy of admiration than are the likes of Sai Baba and Adi Da?)

In Yogananda's legacy, we have ashram leaders who, after fifty years of meditation, cannot distinguish between the subconscious and the superconscious mind—teaching that pruning a tree or driving a car (like Zen's view of practiced archery) are acts of intuition, rather than learned skills. And the next generation of lemmings, if they disagree with that or with anything else of what they are being taught, are simply exhibiting "ego."

We also have "perfected" Board of Directors members who work in such "mysterious ways" that they require eighty hours of preparation to give an informal talk, or three years to approve the purchase of a fax machine. (Those, of course, are the same "sages" who will have been "pharaohs in Egypt," etc.) Plus, we have ashrams, run according to "business principles," which can hardly break even financially, even with receiving huge amounts of free labor.

If you "ran Egypt" in a previous life, you would surely be able to make good, common-sense business decisions in operating a simple, nonprofit ashram with free labor, no?

Of course, ashram-run businesses elsewhere are typically equally unsuccessful, for exactly the same reasons. Indeed, failed financial ventures under the far-seeing Jetsunma's leadership reportedly included a typesetting business, much vaunted by her as being a "sure thing," "partly because of the auspicious year of its inception." Also, a microwaveable female hair care device with built-in gel packs, set to retail for $14.95 and fated to sell "millions" of units—according to a dream which Jetsunma had. (When the internal, ashram company producing that product shut down, it was reportedly over half a million dollars in debt.) Finally, a New Age rock group, with the forty-something Jetsunma as its off-key lead singer (Sherrill, 2000).

Hidden Valley, more conservatively, limited itself to growing herbs, vegetables and hibiscus, processing third-party soil analysis numbers, writing software, and manufacturing meditation armrests and portable altars. Of those, the hibiscus, soil analysis and software were all supposed to be "cash cows." (That was the specific phrase which the external project manager used in referring to the anticipated, web-based soil analysis income.) In practice, however, each simply gave support to the classic wag's observation that "we're losing money on every sale, but we'll make it up in volume."

The San Francisco Zen Center's Alaya Stitchery likewise received essentially free labor (in return for room and board, etc.), yet often "lost money month to month, though its deficits went unnoticed for several years ... 'no one seemed to notice that we were essentially paying to sell those clothes'" (Downing, 2001).

In Rajneesh's communities, further:

> Few ashramites worked at the jobs they'd been trained to do, Ph.D.'s collecting garbage, architects working as handymen, filmmakers as shoemakers, and ex-junkies as department heads (Franklin, 1992).

Hidden Valley skillfully incorporated the same principle. That is, they were training accountants who possessed no ability to take creative leaps in thought, to be computer programmers, while they *simultaneously* had established programmers doing office or garden work.

Plaster buddhas or greenhouse hibiscus; hair care or soil analysis; clothing or subsidized restaurants; East coast Poolesville or West coast Escondido, or up north to San Francisco or anything in between—all are equally "divinely guided"; all are equally following "schmueprints in the ether." The frequent failures of those schemes, then, simply get written off under the idea that "99% of what happens in the ashram is just for the [ego-killing] learning experiences of its residents anyway." Or, those flops get blamed on the residents' working off of bad karma, or their "lack of merit." Why worry, then, about turning a profit, even if you're simultaneously bragging that the organization is being run "according to business principles," and that your religion will be the one to save the world from the clutches of Satan and other black cats?

And, to top it all off, there is always unsolicited pressure (at Hidden Valley and elsewhere) to the effect that "the more you meditate, the less you'll feel the need to be creative." In the limit of that, of course, one would be a God-realized vegetable, exhibiting neither independence nor creativity, and fit only to contribute money or free labor to "the Guru's work." (Is it any wonder that these places get called "cults" by people looking in from the outside?)

Further, to resist or question any of that nonsense gets one branded as having a "big head," by persons who themselves have not a creative atom in their bodies.

In such a context, probably the best that one can say, with all possible sarcasm, is: Think of how much worse it might all be if Divine Mother and a lineage of avatar gurus *weren't* guiding their actions!

Of course, the same best-case (reincarnational) scenario would raise additional questions with regard to karma and the overall behavior which one might expect from avatars and their ilk—e.g., in terms of beheading Saxons and Shakespearian bawdy. For, if Yogananda was freed many lifetimes ago, yet was incarnated relatively recently as both William the Conqueror and William Shakespeare, then both of those—as reincarnations of Arjuna, if nothing else—must have been either avatars or very close to such "perfection."

One might yet feebly try to excuse William the Bastard's non-saintly behaviors by suggesting that they were a product of his political position and period of history. That is, if one is willing to neglect his violently ill-tempered behavior toward his wife, which can be given no such absolution.

Fine. And Shakespeare's equally non-saintly bawdiness was then comparably "someone else's fault" ... how? For, the better selections from amongst those "cunt'ry matters" would hardly have been out of place in Dan Savage's syndicated "Savage Love" sex-fetish advice column in the *New Times L.A.* (and elsewhere), which to SRFers was explicitly merely a "smut paper." Yet, "conquering" karma does not transmute to sexual karma except via double entendres. And besides, avatars are not supposed to carry karma from one lifetime to another, much less create new karma in each succeeding "compassionate incarnation," as Daya Mata (1971) herself explained:

> When any soul, even a Christ, descends into the world of duality and takes on a human form, he thereby accepts certain limitations. But taking on the compulsions of the law of karma is not one of them. He still remains above and beyond all karma.

At any rate, getting thee "to a nunnery," whether run by SRF or otherwise is, as we have seen too clearly and too often, sadly more likely to increase one's problems than to offer balm for them. Doth Ophelia's river, then, beckon?

Of course, in Shakespeare's day "nunnery" meant both "brothel" and "monastery." Since Hamlet could not have been telling Ophelia to avoid sex by going to a brothel, however, the monastic meaning was evidently the intended one.

Again, though, with irony—damned irony—probably no one has ever been driven to the madhouse via the whorehouse. (That is, aside from untreated syphilis which, again, is not absent from the holy Shakespeare's plays.) The same claim, however, clearly cannot be made with regard to our world's monasteries and their guru-figures. For they, indeed, have surely contributed to more than one sincere seeker's literal and clinical depression and madness, via psychological binds, alleged spiritually incestuous sexual abuse, crippling negativity and more. All "in the name of God," and for the purported "benefit of all sentient beings."

* * *

What, though—no widespread, hot 'n' heavy sex in the SRF ashrams? Do the monks not sneak out over the Mother Center walls down to Sunset Boulevard on sultry summer nights, their monthly allowance in hand? Do voluptuous young nuns not pair off with each other's holy genitals for much-needed, slap-happy release? Is it really all service, meditation, and sleeping with one's dry monastic hands outside the pure white sheets?

Well, the allegation has actually been made (in Russell, 2001) that Yogananda may have been "screwing everything in sight" when alive. My own reaction to that is probably the reflex of the majority of already disillusioned ex-disciples of their respective "perfect masters." That is, half of me cannot take the allegation seriously, given the many testimonials to his integrity from his disciples. Testimony, that is, such as from one of SRF's most respected monastic brothers, who "speaks joyfully of his guru's overwhelming love, humility and gentleness, his deep respect for others and his boundless desire to serve" (in Watanabe, 1998).

Of course, the brother in question, having entered the ashrams nearly a quarter century after Yogananda's passing, *never actually met* the "avatar." That is, he is simply parroting the party line, speaking what he would *imagine* to be true. But that is par for the course in spirituality.

Regardless, the other half of me would actually *like* for every alleged indiscretion on the part of "the Bastard and the Bard" to be true, for the whole mess to have been pure baloney from the beginning.

As a bottom line, then, SRF in its current state can take a (former) disciple such as myself, who would never have dreamed of being disloyal to the guru or his organization, and turn him into someone who would *like* for the worst accusations against them to be true. That is, if they could change *me* in this way, they could change *anyone*—or, at least, change anyone who was *willing* to see.

Yogananda's claim to be able to walk on fire might only make him a fool, for genuinely believing that his purported spiritual advancement, rather than the laws of physics, were the source of that "yogic power." Likewise for his many wildly wrong prophecies and his endorsements of Therese Neumann and of his "Perfume Saint." His comparable "ability" to stop his pulse in one wrist, however, unless one takes that as a real parapsychological phenomenon—which I do not—makes him something much worse.

Personally, even with that, I still consider Yogananda to have been among the less harmful of the spiritual leaders covered herein, comparable to the Dalai Lama, Aurobindo or Ramana Maharshi if the allegations about his "harem" are false, or somewhere below them if those claims are true. Being the "sanest man in the asylum," however, is hardly something to crow about.

And even in that grouping, one would keep in mind that the claims made by both Aurobindo and Maharshi leave one with *very little* confidence in their respective abilities to distinguish fantasy from reality—plus, there is the significant problem of Maharshi's documented caste bigotry. Further, the Dalai Lama these days is functioning more as a mere moral guide than as a guru or "savior of humankind." That, however, is a good thing, as his reported behavior in the Karmapa Lama controversy has been consistently less than inspiring. Likewise with his reported attitude when faced with allegations of sexual exploitation against Sogyal Rinpoche, best-selling author of the *Tibetan Book of Living and Dying:*

> "The Dalai Lama has known about this for years and done nothing. There is a real code of secrecy and silence," said [Victoria] Barlow (Lattin, 1994).

Interestingly, contemporary disaffected disciples of Yogananda, in spite of their own disillusion, have yet proposed that no one should be informed about the behind-the-scenes issues with SRF until they have been involved with the organization for at least a decade. By that point, it is believed, they may have begun to lose some of their initial idealism on their own, being then more willing to listen to the possibility that the guru and his organization are less than perfect. For my own part, however, I disagree *completely* with that approach. After all, many of the most committed students of any spiritual path will undertake a long-term, residential stay within their first ten years or so. And it is exactly in that context where the real damage is done. I speak from experience on all of those points.

Further, ten years might as well be a hundred if one is only having contact with such a community from "outside," via books, printed lessons, or mere casual and occasional contact. For, all of those have been carefully edited to ensure that nothing uncomplimentary about the organization is ever revealed through them. (Compare simply attending Mass as a lay Catholic, versus being imprisoned in the organization as a sodomized altar boy or a monastic. Indeed, if we have learned one thing from Bette Midler, it is that "from a distance there is harmony" ... even if, up close, the situation is very different.)

One may well not be willing to consider the possibility that any of the reported "dirt" on one's favorite organization could be true during one's initial honeymoon period with it. To suggest, however, that having that dirt swept under the rug is preferable to at least being made aware of it, and thus being in a position to make relatively informed decisions about one's future there, strikes me as ridiculous. When dealing with our world's religious/ spiritual organizations in the long term, such ignorance is not bliss, nor is it a path to anything but pain.

As Bailey and Bailey (2003) put it, when discussing the concerns increasingly surrounding Sai Baba:

> This is an opportunity to become aware of [the reported problems], thus moving into a position enabling informed choice, rather than one coming from ignorance.

Lacking the information on which to base such an informed decision leads to a very predictable end, which another former disciple of Sai Baba suitably noted:

> The intense desire I have to expose him now is directly proportionate to the amount of devotion I gave him (in Brown, 2000).

* * *

Of course, one would not expect to publicize even such relatively lukewarm negative information as all this without causing offense among the "believers." At the very least, as others who have spoken out against the ungodly aspects of their respective paths have discovered, one would have one's motives (in profit, fame, bias, sensationalism, etc.) in doing so questioned. (Even established newspapers which dared to speak out against Catholic clergy abuse in the mid-'80s were accused of "yellow journalism" by less-courageous competitors who could not believe that the stories were true [Berry, 1992]. But as we all know by now, the horrific tales there are, too often, indeed sadly true.) Not surprisingly, then, reactions to elements of the above mild exposé of Hidden Valley have included my being called a "whinner" (*sic*)—by someone who evidently confuses thorough attention to detail (e.g., in spelling) with *whining*—and a "cowered" (*sic*).

Speaking out against what one has found to be wrong with our world's spiritual environments may be a lot of things, but it is *not* the product of cowardice, as anyone who has ever been driven by conscience and anguish to do it knows well. That is so particularly when the objections to the "teaching" are raised with one's name being attached to them, as opposed to being posted anonymously for (justified) fear of retribution. The real cowardice in those situations rather comes from the remaining loyal members of the organization who attempt, anonymously, to intimidate disaffected followers into remaining silent.

And, one need not have suffered every possible mistreatment at the hands of one or another divinely inspired fool or "vehicle of God" to have suffered *enough* that one is more than justified in speaking out against it, both for one's own healing and to warn others.

So "kill the messenger" for all of this, if you must. For, we all have profound, if merely implicit, emotional involvements in having our professional ideas be correct, in maintaining our own self-images, and in preserving our dearest human relationships. None of those cherished investments, however, can compare with the value placed on one's religion and salvation/enlightenment, for anyone deeply committed to those. Conversely, the discomfort felt in the potential loss of any secular perk would surely be minor compared to the panic induced when one's salvation is threatened. The one who would deign to thus "threaten" should then clearly be prepared, with no few deep breaths, to be more hated than loved for his efforts.

In applying that principle to the present author, though, realize that (i) every alleged abuse and ludicrous "divine" claim covered herein, with the sole exception of my own experiences at Hidden Valley, had already been put into print elsewhere; and (ii) I myself have lost my religion through doing this thorough research. That is, when I began this writing, in late 2003, I still believed that Yogananda was all that he claimed to be, and that it was just his followers who had subsequently messed up his organization. Indeed, I still accepted, at that point, that the "enlightenment" attained to by himself and by the likes of Ken Wilber and Ramakrishna, etc., was a goal worth pursuing.

Sadly, I now know much better.

To state another obvious point: When we have, by the monks' own admission, many individuals arriving at Hidden Valley (and elsewhere) believing that every monk there is a "perfected being," then *every imperfection* in those "holy" individuals immediately becomes relevant and worth documenting. To be categorized as a "whinner" or a "cowered" for that is a small price to pay for showing that these people are not what they seem (and happily role-play) to be.

Reactions to my documentation of the shortcomings within Self-Realization Fellowship have also included the unsolicited suggestion that if I was "uncomfortable" answering questions about my sexual orientation, then I should just not have entered the ashram in the first place. The clear implication there, of course, coming from an openly backward SRF member who was explicitly opposed even to having gays in the military, was again that only a person with "something to hide" would consider the organization's "do ask, do tell" policy to be worth mentioning.

That still, however, pales in comparison with what an SRF monk, giving tours of the Mother Center, said to me in the late '80s, when I was in Los Angeles to receive kriya initiation. For some reason the topic of AIDS came up. The voiced opinion on the part of that monk, then, was to the effect that perhaps that scourge was God's and Nature's way of cutting down on sexual promiscuity, and thereby of creating a "holier" world. Yikes. Yet, that attitude is not unique in the spiritual world. For while at Hidden Valley and glancing through a respected yogic magazine, I saw comparably "compassionate" rationalizations expressed there regarding the same illness.

More recently, I received several hundred copies of the following abusive rant, in an attempted "mailbombing" sent first from HiddenValleyLover@FirstReaction.com, and then from fabricated/spoofed web-based email addresses, by one particularly defective, relatively illiterate, obvious member in good standing of SRF:

> I've been seriously itched by your gossipy statements about Hidden Valley I've spend [*sic*] more than 3 years there and it's been the best time of my life so far!You're [*sic*] an ungrateful piece of shit, highly unethical and disturbed.And [*sic*] for your info I've been in SRF 2 times as long as you.
>
> If you want to be able to keep using your email adress,remove [*sic*] the worthless crap about SRF and Hidden Valley(all of it) [*sic*] from your excuse for a website.

Can't ya just "feel the guru's love"?

Or, "What Would Yogananda Do"?

Of course, the above threats could have come from *any* of the spiritual communities in this world, to *anyone* who had left the society and then spoken too accurately of the people or the beloved "God-realized guru" there. Such responses are, indeed, "a dime a dozen," coming from devoted members of organizations which have every reason to fear the details of their alleged behaviors getting out. And so, for them, reality becomes something "from the devil."

Being on the receiving end of the above name-calling does, however, at least bring to mind a comment from the late Canadian prime minister, Pierre Trudeau: "I've been called worse things by better people." On the brighter side, persons who have themselves lived for extended periods on the inside at Hidden Valley, and become as disillusioned as I have with that environment, have corroborated my depiction of life there as being fully accurate.

Further, as far as "gossip" goes: These disclosures regarding Hidden Valley are not trivial, idle talk; and they are given first-hand, not via rumor. By contrast, the respected monk who quietly informed me of the alleged Tara/da Vinci reincarnation put his own position this way: "Don't tell anyone ... or at least don't say that it was *me* who told you."

"Here's a secret everyone would like to know—but don't tell anyone. But if you *do* tell anyone, don't tell them *I* told you."

And *I'm* the gossip?!

Finally, the present author was a lot less "ungrateful," and certainly a *lot* less "disturbed," *before* those nine months of being hurled on peristaltic waves of chronic negativity, *real, trivial* gossip, and independence-robbing, ignorant pseudo-teachings in the bowels of yogic hell. If I could do it over again, I would, in all deadly seriousness, rather live on the street. Conversely, that experience has at least rid me of a great deal of fear: whatever else may come in life, I've already been through worse. (A less positive way of stating that, however, is simply: "There is no one freer than someone who has nothing left to lose.")

But you need not even believe me in any of this. For, other persons who have had comparably disillusioning experiences with SRF have posted their stories, with much additional "dirt" and allegations of disturbing meanness, homophobia and highly questionable actions on the part of the leaders there, on the SRF Walrus (2004) website. Many of those stories are *much* more damning than my own first-hand experiences, even if giving less complete portraits of what daily life within the Hidden Valley ashram is like for anyone who hasn't checked his brain and independence at the door.

So: Yogananda was the "Smut Merchant of Venice." *And* he introduced the act of beheading to England *and* he cut off people's hands and feet for vengeance *and* he beat and killed his wife in his "conquering" incarnation. And Tara Mata was the gay da Vinci, and Dr. Lewis was the equally ass-happy Francis Bacon.

Happy now, SRF? Because those problems are simply what happens when the long-documented, inarguable *facts,* which anyone could have researched, meet head-on with what a bunch of aged fools, closing their eyes to reality, just pleasantly *imagine* to be true.

* * *

Prior to my Hidden Valley sojourn, I had worked for a year for a nonprofit, community-owned, politically correct organic food store. There, the Board of Directors effectively had a position reserved for a "competent idealist with business sense," who would invariably resign in disgust within a year, in response to resistance from other power-enjoying board members to doing things intelligently.

Following the "bad trip" at HV in California, I toiled menially for a month at the headquarters of the Canadian branch of UNICEF. There, one former, disenchanted donor sent in a newspaper clipping reporting the inadequate auditing of a large amount of "missing and poorly spent money" which the UNICEF executives had allegedly touched. (Compare the U.S. Red Cross earmarking monies collected immediately after 9/11 for "other projects." That behavior followed the delays of their Canadian branch in implementing proper AIDS/hepatitis testing in blood donations, in the mid-'80s. The latter shortcomings, in turn, led to their own role in the ensuing front-page "tainted blood scandal.")

In that same (UNICEF) charity, as numerous donors discovered the hard way, requesting to have one's name taken off their periodic mailing list had about as much effect as idly wishing for an end to world hunger on a balmy summer's afternoon, lemonade in hand. Indeed, some of those former donors expressed their disgust with that repeated waste of paper and postage by sending UNICEF *their* junk mail, or other irrelevant materials, in the donation envelopes!

When I left that temp job, the organization was on the verge of moving into a new headquarters in the most expensive rental area of the most expensive city in the country. In response to questions from employees at that time, the move was justified by the management there as being appropriate so as to more appeal to their large donors—as opposed to the trusting "little old lady" contributors, who would in turn express their heart-rending regrets that they couldn't send any/more money because of their own failing health and/or poverty.

I have it on good authority (unrelated to Hidden Valley) that the Peace Corps is no better than any of those, in terms of efficiency.

The nonprofit Habitat for Humanity? Their founder and president was fired in early 2005 amid allegations of sexual harassment. That dismissal further reportedly occurred against the efforts of Jimmy Carter himself to broker a deal to keep the scandal quiet (Cooperman, 2005).

The Boy Scouts? They are currently being investigated by the FBI for having allegedly inflated their membership numbers, to boost their funding from the United Way (Reeves, 2005).

And the respected United Way itself? Well, in the early 1990s, that charitable organization "became embroiled in a highly publicized exposé of its own financial misdeeds" (Sennott, 1992).

After all that, I can honestly say that I have *far* less ideals intact by now than I used to. Yet amazingly, no matter how bad one allows or expects for things to be in the spiritual and secular world, they invariably turn out, upon proper research, to be *much worse.*

One does not ask for perfection in any organization—spiritual, humanitarian or otherwise—knowing that it is run by imperfect human beings. One simply asks for minimal competence, basic integrity/ethical behavior, accountability, and the ability to admit when they are wrong, to be able to correct their course.

One might as well ask for the moon.

Well, you live and learn.

Or, as the late Douglas Adams would say, "At least you live."

CHAPTER XXVII

GURUS AND PRISONERS

AS WE HAVE SEEN, a common set of alleged problems, even expressed in nearly identical words, tend to occur in our world's spiritual communities. Indeed, the reported characteristics observed are essentially independent of the specific beliefs espoused by the community, and of the historical time and place in which the spiritual leader and his disciples have existed.

Why would that be?

A large part of the answer surely comes from well-known research done at Stanford University in the early 1970s. There, Dr. Philip Zimbardo—later, president of the American Psychological Association—was able to inadvertently transform a group of "healthy, intelligent, middle-class" college-age individuals into "fearful, depressed, neurotic, suicidal shadows" in less than a week. He did that simply by arbitrarily assigning them (via the flip of a coin) to guard/prisoner roles in a simulated prison environment *which they all knew was just an experiment.*

The dozen guards were given no specific training, but were rather allowed, within limits, to create their own rules to "maintain law and order" within the prison, and to "command the *respect* of the prisoners" (Zimbardo, 2004; italics added).

Each of the dozen prisoners had been assigned a number in place of his name upon entering, and was referred to only by that number, in a tactic designed to make him feel anonymous and to dissociate him from his pre-incarceration identity. That is, he was not to have that past as a guide for how to behave, or as a reference for what would be appropriate treatment of himself, for instance.

Monks and *sannyasis* are, of course, frequently subjected to a similar change of name. In Rajneesh's ashrams, as an extreme example, that was often effected within mere days (or less) of the individual's acceptance of Bhagwan as a teacher, even for persons not entering into long-term residence there. (Uniforms—e.g., of Rajneesh's saffron-wearing "orange" followers—have the same effect of "deindividuation" on their wearers.)

> Living among strangers who do not know your name or history ... dressed in a uniform exactly like all other prisoners [or monks], not wanting to call attention to one's self because of the unpredictable consequences it might provoke [with those being given as "discipline for one's ego," in the ashram] —all led to a weakening of self-identity among the prisoners (Haney, et al., 1973).

Following a brief rebellion on the second day of the Stanford incarceration, solidarity among the prisoners was broken. That was done via the psychological tactic of designating a "privileged cell" for "good prisoners," whose inhabitants could exercise freedoms which were not given to the inmates of the other cells.

Comparable residence in privileged rooms/houses, or increased access to the guru-figure, is often given in ashrams to disciples who are the most loyal in following the rules set down by their guru and other superiors. Indeed, Milne (1986), Tarlo (1997) and van der Braak (2003) have all described exactly that dynamic, alleged to occur under Rajneesh and Cohen. Comparable promotions and demotions have also been reported in Adi Da's community. In SRF, by comparison, residence in the "power center" of Mount Washington is valued over "banishment" to their ancillary temples in Hollywood, Hidden Valley, or India.

In attempting to break the will of their prisoners, Zimbardo's guards resorted to the non-violent humiliation of them.

In any ashram, the comparable humiliation is done with the stated intention of killing the residents' "unspiritual" egos. In practice, however, it kills their closely related individual wills (i.e., their self-esteem and independence) as well.

After a few days, "parole hearings" were held in the simulated prison. There, prisoners were given the option of being released in return for their forfeiting of the money they had earned. Most of them agreed to that deal ... but then returned to their cells while the parole board considered their requests. That behavior came in spite of the fact that, by simply quitting the experiment, they could have gotten exactly the same financial result.

Why would they have behaved so? In Zimbardo's (2004) explanation, it was because they "felt powerless to resist," being trapped in a "psychological prison" which they could not leave without the approval of the relevant authorities there.

When a disciple attempts to leave an ashram after a long-term stay, or to sever ties with a "divinely guided guru," it is often only after having played the disciple/prisoner role for many years. Psychologically, then, having bought deeply into that role, he cannot leave without the permission or blessing of the guru. The latter is then equivalent to the superintendent and parole board, holding the keys to "salvation" or release from the prison (of the ashram, and of *maya* or delusion.)

To thus depart, further, is typically equated with "falling from the spiritual path." To leave, therefore, is to weakly sell out the reasons why one entered the ashram in the first place. That is, it is to fail at one's own enlightenment, the "only thing that really matters." Or worse:

> I am just temporarily in the throes of my ego, they say, and I shouldn't throw away my one chance in this lifetime for enlightenment (van der Braak, 2003).

> Eckists [i.e., followers of the Eckankar religion] are warned that when they drop out their spiritual growth stops, and they are at the mercy of the Kal, or the negative force of the universe (Bellamy, 1995).

> [P]otential devotees make a binding vow of eternal devotion to Adi Da—before actually being allowed to be in [his] presence.... [Adi Da's followers] claim that breaking the vow will result in far more than seven lifetimes of bad luck (in Bob, 2000).

> We'd been told if you leave Poolesville and Jetsunma, you go to Vajra hell.... You are crushed and burned and chopped up over and over again, it repeats. You are there for eternity (in Sherrill, 2000).

> The Buddhist hell sounds as vicious as the Christian version —with torture by molten iron, fire and disembowelment (Macdonald, 2003).

It is rather shocking to thus discover that Tibetan Buddhism, for one, has fear-based means of keeping its disciples loyally following their gurus, which are every bit as harsh as the Bible Belt visions of hell.

Consider, further, that the Christian view of eternal punishment has long been viewed by psychologists as leading to a rigidity in thought and behavior on the part of the relevant believers. It has also been seen as producing a "missionary zeal," whereby persons concerned about their own salvation would project those fears onto others, and need to convert them in order to allay their own doubts. If that long-asserted dynamic is valid for the Christian view, however, it must apply just as well to the Buddhist perspective. That is, it must produce related behaviors, with "loyalty to the guru" substituted for "faith in Jesus Christ," and a pressure on one's fellow disciples to maintain their own rigid obedience to the master then standing in for the Christian attempt to convert "heathens" and ensure that the converts remain loyal.

Conversely, if Christian blind belief can create an Inquisition, so too equally could the standard Buddhist ("Tibetan Catholic") teachings. For there, the breaking of the savior-disciple bond, as with other "sins," generates punishments to delight the Marquis de Sade.

Thus, the state of mind apparently evinced by the lama in charge of the Karmapa's seat in Tibet, in explaining to Lama Ole Nydahl what the purported effects of his (Nydahl's) breaking of the guru-disciple vow would be, becomes both understandable and completely predictable:

> Although by title a Buddhist teacher, the venerable Drubpoen Dechen sounded as though he had come straight out of the Catholic middle ages. He would have also probably felt quite at home with the Holy Inquisition, since his letter, in

> spirit and context, seemed to have been the product of this notable institution (Lehnert, 1998).

Similarly, from its beginnings, the giving of money and food to begging Buddhist monks, like the indulgence scams of the Roman Catholic Church, was a way for wealthy patrons to purchase merit, redeemable for their own future good (Downing, 2001).

Of course, as always, one could avoid many of the problems arising from such teachings simply by not believing too much of what one has been told in the first place:

> A man, worried about the gruesome Tibetan Buddhist teachings of the hell realms, wants to know what Tenzin Palmo thinks happens after death....
>
> [Palmo:] "I once tackled a lama about it as by his definition I was definitely going there [i.e., to hell]. 'Don't worry about it,' he laughed while slapping me on the back. 'We only say that to get people to behave themselves'" (Mackenzie, 1999).

The fact that Buddhism includes "proof-delivering meditation" in its path is actually irrelevant in all of this. For, that in no way offsets the *blind belief* inherent in the claimed necessity of keeping the guru-disciple vow, where the punishment for breaking that vow is to be cast into Vajra hell or the like. East or West, southern U.S. or northern India/Tibet, agrarian or postindustrial, all makes absolutely no difference. Rather, the fear of long-term punishment will produce *exactly* the same rigid reactions, and inability to walk away from toxic situations, in the East as in the West. The universal nature of known psychological structures and dynamics throughout the human species guarantees this.

> When [alleged] cult leaders tell the public, "Members are free to leave any time they want; the door is open," they give the impression that members have free will and are simply choosing to stay. Actually, members may not have a real choice, because they have been indoctrinated to have a phobia of the outside world. Induced phobias eliminate the psychological possibility of a person choosing to leave the group merely because he is unhappy or wants to do something else (Hassan, 1990).

That is, individuals in so-called cults who have been taught that bad things will happen to them should they leave will be no more "free" to exit those environments than someone who is petrified of the water would be "free" to go swimming.

> Father [i.e., Jim Jones] kept my treasonous thoughts in check by warning us that leaving the church would bring bad karma. He reminded us in his sermons that those who had chosen to join were here because we were on the verge of crossing over to the next plane. Without his help, we would not make it. Those who left or betrayed the Cause in any way would be reincarnated as the lowest life form on Earth and it would take us another hundred thousand years to get to this point again (Layton, 1998).

And that differs from Trungpa's *traditional* "pursuing disasters/furies" how, exactly? Conceptually, and in terms of its effect, it differs not at all.

Further regarding leaving: When one of the subjects (#819) in Zimbardo's study was labeled as a "bad prisoner" by his fellow inmates after being removed from his cell, he broke down into hysterical tears. When Zimbardo suggested that they leave the experimental area, however, the subject refused, explicitly preferring to return to the prison, in spite of feeling sick and even while sobbing uncontrollably, to prove to his compatriots that he was not the bad prisoner they accused him of being. (When Zimbardo pointedly reminded the man that he was a subject in an experiment, not a real prisoner, he quickly stopped crying, and looked up "like a small child awakened from a nightmare.")

Disciples stay in ashrams, in part, exactly for feeling the same need to prove that they are not being bad or disloyal to the guru-figure and his inner circle of "spiritually advanced" beings. No one wants to be a "bad disciple," after all, when "the guru is God."

* * *

An incident from Ken Wilber's life may serve to further drive home the aforementioned difficulty of leaving psychological "prisons."

Wilber's second wife, Treya, suffered her first bout with breast cancer in the mid-1980s. During and following that period, their unspoken resentments toward each other, deriving from that stress, caused their relationship, and Wilber's own life in general, to deteriorate to the point where he was consuming alcohol to the tune of over twenty drinks a day, every day. He was further doing little else but lethargically watching television; and feeling depressed, not caring whether or not he ever wrote another book. At the lowest point of that spite, he actually went out gun-shopping, intending to end his own life (Wilber, 1991).

Rationally, however, Wilber could have walked away from that situation at any time. All that he ever had to do was to get into his car and drive, and never look back. He had his book royalties, his high reputation in transpersonal psychology—starting over without his wife would, rationally, have been so easy. In the absolute worst fallout from that, after all, he would have owed her half of their house and half of his book royalties in a divorce settlement, getting his own life back in return.

To his mindset at that time, however, there was obviously simply "no way out" for him from his misery. Rather, suicide evidently looked "easier" to him than either attempting to fix the problem or simply walking away from that *prison,* from which there was apparently "no escape."

By comparison, disciples more often than not "fall in love" with guru-figures who, in the long run, do nothing but make their lives miserable. The one-sided attempts to untangle the ingrown emotional codependencies as the relationship crashes, then, place even greater constraints on the doubting disciple than for any secular, romantic relationship. Thus, it is in no way easy there to "just leave." Indeed, such abandonment would again be equated not merely with "falling out of love"—a plight for which there is an easy remedy. Rather, one must deal with the guilt of feeling disloyal to the god-man guru, and with the fallout from "leaving the spiritual path"—perhaps for incarnations.

> Most [so-called] cult members feel depressed during the first few months of post-cult life. Some compare the experience to falling head-over-heels in love, only to realize that their lover was two-faced and just using them. Others liken their involvement to a spiritual rape of their soul (Hassan, 2000).

> Losing one's [alleged] cult is like losing the love of one's life. The lover has lied to you, but the lover is oh so seductive and satisfying, and submission is so thrilling (in Bellamy, 1995).

> Belief in a guru, while it persists, entirely overrules rational judgment. Dedicated disciples are as impervious to reason as are infatuated lovers....
>
> [T]he person who becomes a disciple "falls for" a particular guru without being able to distinguish between dross and gold. The process is equivalent to falling in love, or to the occurrence of "transference" in psychotherapy. *None of us is immune to such phenomena* (Storr, 1996; italics added).

> I never questioned Bhagwan's insistence on surrender. One surrenders to a lover joyously, willingly. It's only when the love affair ends that you notice the paunchy jowls and sagging muscles, the cruelties and indifference, and suspicion creeps in (Franklin, 1992).

> Seen from a certain perspective, my time with Andrew [Cohen] was a botched love affair (van der Braak, 2003).

It may be difficult to walk away from a romantic partner who was once "the center of your life," on whom you could rely even when you had nowhere else to turn. Imagine, then, how much harder it would be to walk away from a "god," regardless of how much that figure may be causing you anguish on a daily basis.

> I can't describe the depth of pain I experienced in considering the possibility that the one I had loved absolutely might be less than what a God ought to be (Underwood and Underwood, 1979).

Not surprisingly, then, given all that, numerous former monks have admitted to feeling depressed and suicidal within their ashram/prison cells.

Wilber did later leave for San Francisco, "with or without" his wife, but only after having regretfully hit her in response to an argument they were having. Disciples who have finally, after much soul-searching, walked out of an ashram to end a promised lifelong stay, could frequently point to a similar "can't get any worse" incident, which finally brought them to their senses, and made them realize that simply leaving was a preferable option to suicide.

* * *

Even among lower animals, lacking obeisance to a purported deity-in-the-flesh, the inability to take the simple steps which would lessen their own pain, in exiting from a harmful environment, has long been known. That knowledge has come in large part via Martin Seligman's experiments in the mid-'70s, in which animals were given electric shocks in an environment where they could not escape that mistreatment.

> At first the animals fought, tried to get away, and uttered cries of pain or anger. Then they sank into listlessness and despair. Later on, in a second set of experiments, the same animals were shocked again—only this time, by pressing a certain lever or completing some other simple task, they could stop the electric current. But they made no effort to do so.
>
> The animals had learned to be helpless. Due to their previous experiences, even when a means of escape from the pain was provided, these animals were too defeated, perhaps defeated neurologically, to take the simple action that would end their suffering (Matsakis, 1996).

Being forcibly stripped in public against one's pleas to stop, or coerced into often-violent individual or group sex (with or without a "church's dildo collection"), or into psychologically incestuous sex with the guru-figure, would obviously qualify as shock or trauma by any reasonable definition. So too would Rajneesh's violent humanistic encounter groups, even for people who knew going in that they might suffer broken bones or be raped.

To a more chronic degree, though, much of the emotional violence and psychological abuse reportedly perpetrated in the name of "ego-killing discipline," as a betrayal of trust and widely recognized "spiritual rape," would also qualify as trauma. Indeed, Tarlo's (1997) and van der Braak's (2003) stories of alleged discipline at Cohen's hands are nothing if not descriptions of repeated emotional trauma/shocks, humiliation and degradation. Further, those occurred in an "intimate or bonded relationship" with the guru-figure, which they could not escape without being "bad disciples" or "failures." And wherever there is such inescapable trauma, one will find instances of both "learned helplessness" and Post-Traumatic Stress Disorder. Thus, "crazy wisdom" or "Rude Boy" environments in particular cannot help but be breeding grounds for exactly those ailments.

Further, working efficiently at one's assigned ashram tasks, and taking initiative to coordinate others' activities with that, will alternately get one highly praised for serving "the Guru's work" well, and then severely criticized for overstepping one's bounds and having "a big head." Such an environment—in the tension between serving the guru-figure efficiently, but not "too efficiently/egoically" —is at least halfway to being rife with psychological double binds. For there, one cannot know in advance how to gain the approval of one's guru-figure and other "superiors"—when, as every sad dog knows, securing the approval of the master is all that matters.

> Should there be craftsmen in the monastery, let them exercise their crafts with all humility and reverence, if the Abbot so command. But if one of them grow proud because of the knowledge of his craft, in that he seem to confer some benefit on the monastery, let such a one be taken away from this craft and not practice it again, unless perchance, after he has humbled himself, the Abbot may bid him resume it (Saint Benedict, in [Goffman, 1961]).

Or, as Janja Lalich (2004) described her own experiences in a "political cult":

> Militants were expected to "take initiative," within the bounds of discipline; yet the reality of their everyday lives gave them very little of consequence to make decisions about. Eventually, a militant who thought she was taking initiative would be "reined in" and criticized for "careerism," "grandstanding," "factionalizing," or a variety of other charges that served to stifle further efforts at independent action and to set an example for others.

Thus, one is reduced to simply guessing which course of action one should take, without knowing whether it will garner exultant praise or harsh blame. (Failing to take sufficient initiative would be no escape from that, rather placing one in exactly the same position. That is, for a given set of moderate actions, one might be praised for "knowing one's place" ... or harshly upbraided for not doing one's job.) One possible extreme reaction to such long-term binds is again violent neurosis, from "trying too hard." The other is severe depression in which, since one cannot predict the results of one's actions or find a reliable way to succeed or to win approval, one simply stops trying at all. Thus, one moves about purposelessly and only in response to others' explicit orders (cf. Haney, et al., 1973).

* * *

It is indeed the most independent disciples who are the most likely to leave any ashram, as the SRF postulant ashram administrator noted. For, they will be the quickest to figure out that they need to get the hell out of there, for their own mental and physical health. The independent ones and those with integrity (guided by some clarity of sight, as opposed to the "idiot integrity" we have previously seen) are thus always "evaporating off." Consequently, the concentration of pathology or pollution in the environment will only increase as time goes by. And the long-term dependent/obedient prisoners then get promoted to guard (or inner-circle disciple) status, demanding obedience and respect from all those below them.

Some individuals are indeed able to leave any such closed environment, via independence and/or outside contact, in spite of the fact that neither of those are ever encouraged in our world's ashrams. That, however, again does not in any way mean that the ones who stay have the same choice, and might simply be making a different, equally rational decision.

Ram Dass himself, interestingly,

> compared his own experience [with Joya] to what invariably occurs in [so-called] cults. "Once you are in them, they provide a total reality which has no escape clause," he wrote (Schwartz, 1996).

Any reality with "no escape clause" would obviously not be an easy one to simply walk away from.

> I can't express the amount of relief I feel about being rescued by my parents [from the Moonies]. I know *I could never have left on my own*. It's hard for anybody outside of the experience to understand the depth of that (Underwood and Underwood, 1979; italics added).

Recall, further, the dangerous idea that as long as people entering a "crazy wisdom" environment know what they are getting themselves into, that path may still work to the benefit of the disciples, rather than acting to destroy them. All of the participants in Zimbardo's study, however, believed that they knew exactly what they were getting themselves involved with. Indeed, they signed consent forms which are today posted online, after having been fully informed as to the nature of the study (Zimbardo, 2004). Further, as prisoners, they explicitly expected to have little or no privacy, to be kept under surveillance, and to have their civil rights violated (Haney, et al., 1973).

Nevertheless, that knowledge did not help those peons when faced with their bored and respect-extracting guards. Nor did it make it any easier for them to "just leave" that environment, or even to simply object to the treatment they were receiving from their authority figures:

> In only a few days, [one-third of] our guards became sadistic and our prisoners became depressed and showed signs of extreme stress (Zimbardo, 2004).

Tarlo (1997) described similar behaviors, which she claims to have seen within Cohen's community:

> There was an inappropriate sadistic flavor to these [verbal] attacks on Sarah [as the house scapegoat].

Likewise, in Rajneesh's ashrams:

> [S]omehow the ego bashing [as instructed by Bhagwan's "guard" Sheela, who made no recorded claims to enlightenment] seemed to be getting more severe, almost sadistic (Hamilton, 1998).

Consider also the reported mistreatment of children in Irish Catholic institutional schools, being frequently harshly beaten "for everything and for nothing," without even knowing why they were being hit so mercilessly:

> Survivors describe a wide range of weapons used to beat them on all parts of their bodies—whips, cat-o-nine-tails, leathers, belts, straps, canes, sticks, tree branches, chair legs, hose pipes, rubber tires and hurley sticks. Many of the leathers used had been reinforced by having pieces of metal or lead sown into them.... One former inmate remembers a [monastic] brother who used to freeze his leather in order to make it harder and consequently more painful.... Violence was an intrinsic part of the culture of these institutions—its aim and often its effect was the *systematic and thorough de-*

> *struction of the will of each and every boy and girl* (Raftery and O'Sullivan, 2001; italics added).

A former male resident of St. Joseph's Industrial School in Letterfrack, Ireland, later enlisted in the army and was captured by the Germans in WWII. Yet, he observed that "compared to Letterfrack, the German prisoner of war camp was like a tea party" (Raftery and O'Sullivan, 2001).

In the spiritual world, sadistic or "Rude Boy" mistreatment may be daftly viewed as being a "good thing," for supposedly acting to "kill one's ego." But no one's psychology ever changes magically simply for having passed through the ashram gates. Thus, the long-term negative effects of such reported cruelties are going to be exactly the same in "spiritual" contexts as in the kinder "real world."

* * *

Several days into Zimbardo's study, a standby prisoner (#416) was admitted to the prison, without having experienced the gradual escalation of harassment which the other inmates had.

Following #416's attempts to force his own release, via a hunger strike, from what the "old-timers" assured him was an inescapable "real prison," he was thrown into solitary confinement. Through all that, he was seen not as a hero but rather as a troublemaker by the existing, veteran prisoners. Indeed, most of them preferred to leave him in solitary confinement rather than give up their blankets to secure his release from that punishment, in trade.

That treatment exactly parallels the ostracism which any independent or "disloyal" (i.e., troublemaking) disciple who breaks the rules set by his superiors or guru-figure will face in the ashram environment:

> I'm living proof of why you better not speak out.... The degree to which I was scapegoated publicly was most effective in keeping everyone else quiet (Yvonne Rand, in [Downing, 2001]).

Conversely, a former novice—Patricia Burke Brogan, now a celebrated playwright—in the Irish Catholic Sisters of Mercy noted of her own experience in that congregation:

> What defined you as a good nun [in a hierarchy of senior nuns and novices] was that you obeyed the rules. There were the three vows—poverty, chastity and obedience. But if you were obedient, that covered everything (in Raftery and O'Sullivan, 2001).

A nun in the Franciscan (Catholic) Poor Clare order expressed a comparable attitude (in Goffman, 1961):

> This is another of the marvels of living in obedience. No one is ever doing anything more important than you are, if you are obeying.

Should you fail to obey, though, prepare to be punished, not merely by your superiors but even by your peers:

> If you ... did not obey the rules of the group [in the Moonies], love and approval would be withdrawn (Hassan, 2000).

Or, consider the experiences of a female disciple of Chögyam Trungpa's, who once disobediently dumped a bottle of glue into the guru's hair, in anger.

> She was subsequently ostracized by the Boulder Buddhist community, beaten up by several women of the community, and left to shift for herself and her out-of-wedlock child, she claims (Clark, 1980).

When the same woman left the community, intending to continue practicing the master's teachings, Trungpa fiercely told her: "The lions will come to devour you."

> "I personally found that I was punished when I didn't want to go to bed with Trungpa after he asked me to," she says. The "punishment," apparently, comes in the form of psychological rejection (Clark, 1980).

* * *

By the end of Zimbardo's study, four of his twelve prisoners had experienced "extreme emotional depression, crying, rage and acute anxiety," to the point of needing to be removed from the study for their own good. (Those breakdowns were later interpreted by the experimenters as being a "passive way of demanding attention and help." Still, they were certainly real to the persons experiencing them, regardless of what the subconscious motivations might have been.) A fifth developed a psychosomatic rash on portions of his body (Haney, et al., 1973).

> The prisoners who adapted better to the situation were those who mindlessly followed orders and who allowed the guards to dehumanize and degrade them ever more with each passing day and night (Zimbardo, 2004b).

> Compared with those who had to be released, prisoners who remained in prison until the termination of the study ... scored higher on conformity ("acceptance of society as it is") (Haney, et al., 1973).

> On a psychological test designed to reveal a person's authoritarianism, those prisoners who had the highest scores were best able to function in this authoritarian prison environment (Zimbardo, et al., 1973).

Dr. Zimbardo further characterized the prisoners in general, by the end of the experiment, as simply "hanging on ... much like hospitalized mental patients," blindly obeying the commands of their guards.

Loyal, beaten-down disciples, of course, "hang on" in much the same way. And, as the SRF monk implicitly noted, the ones who stay and adapt the best are, more often than not, exactly the ones who are able to "mindlessly follow orders," being free of the "delusive evil" of independence. Further, as judged by their high authoritarianism scores in Zimbardo's study, those order-following ones *are the very same individuals who most enjoy sitting in authority over others*. Put another way: The ones who send the deepest bows to their own overlords ("divine" or otherwise) also typically crave and insist on the most respect and obedience from others. Even without experimental confirmation, one could easily have discerned that dynamic simply in common sense from one's daily observations of others. That, at least, has been my own experience.

(Interestingly, like the "ashram gossip" which one cannot avoid in such "God-centered" environments, the conversations of Zimbardo's prisoners, too, centered a full 90% of the time on the shortcomings in their prison conditions, without reference to the outside world [Haney, et al., 1973].)

It is equally clear that the prisoners in Zimbardo's study were not capable of giving "adult consent" to anything requested of them by the guards or the superintendent—even though they were perfectly normal, college-age individuals going into the study. That has profound relevance to the idea of sexual relations between guru-figures and their disciples. And that is so, even in addition to any context of "spiritual incest" deriving from the disciples viewing their leader as a "perfect father/mother figure," as we shall see.

Ironically, there is a Hindu story about a lion who was raised among sheep, and grew up to believe that he himself was a sheep—bleating when he should have roared, etc. That behavior lasted until one day when another lion grabbed him, pointed his face into the mirrored surface of a pond, and showed him that he was a mighty lion, not a meek lamb.

The intended point of that story, of course, is that in our soul-natures we are mighty lions, simply behaving as sheep in our earthly lives. (Compare the other tale of the king who went out among his people and forgot who he was, then living as a commoner until awakened from that delusion.) A more poignant application, however, would see that self-confident, relatively independent lions and lionesses become dependent sheep when surrounded by other guarding/guru-ing "sheep in wolves' clothing."

As one final eerie observation regarding the Stanford role-playing: Before the termination of the experiment, the rumor of an impending breakout from the simulated prison had begun to circulate. In response to that, rather than simply recording the transmission of rumors and observing the escape, Zimbardo and his colleagues began planning how to foil it. That is, Zimbardo, as he later admitted, had begun to think and act like the prison superintendent role he was playing, rather than as an impartial, witnessing social psychologist.

The prisoners in that study were initially rounded up by police, de-loused when checking into the prison, and stripped of their prior identities by being given numbers instead of names, etc., in order to make their prison experience as "real" as possible. Likewise, the acute rebellion on the second day of the incarceration will have made the guards' experience more "real." No such "mind games," however, were played with Zimbardo himself. Nor was he at any risk, compared to the guards, of coming to physical harm from the prisoners. Yet his adopting of his self-assigned "role" came just as quickly, and just as intensely.

How much explicit "mind control" or "brainwashing" is then likely to be necessary, over a sufficiently long period of time, to get the people in any context into their roles, and turn their environment toxic? Probably none at all—though that is not at all to say that the use of such techniques would not cause things to get worse, faster, for it certainly would. ("Mind control" is regarded as being effected via techniques which include "sleep deprivation, special diets, controlling information going in and out, peer pressure, extensive indoctrination sessions, such as long hours of chanting, meditating, listening to droning lectures and mild forms of trance induction that ... reduce the person's ability to think clearly" [Lalich, 1997].)

Interestingly, rock stars, too, have at times sought psychological counseling to help them step out of their adopted, onstage personas, when those seeped too far into their private lives.

Comparable to Zimbardo's slipping into the superintendent role, at one point several disciples of the superintendent-guru Rajneesh left his Oregon ashram without warning. Rather than simply observing that with enlightened "choiceless awareness," however, Bhagwan's concern over additional "escapes" is said to have led him to tell his disciples that if anyone else departed in the same manner, he would leave his body permanently. That, of course, would have been the worst thing that any of his devoted disciples could have imagined. And no one wants to be the one who "killed God," or to have to face that guilt either from his own conscience or from the community. Thus, the pressures mobilized by that warning, and the fact that followers needed help in leaving the isolated area, ensured the "security" of that "prison." Indeed, according to Milne (1986), the threat immediately staved off three more already planned "escapes."

After all that, Alexander (2001) summed up the enduring legacy of Zimbardo's study:

> What drives much of the fascination with the experiment is the sense that any individual could become a brutal dictator if given the chance....
>
> "These guys were all peaceniks," [Zimbardo] recalled of the students chosen to be guards. "They became like Nazis"....
>
> "It shows how easy it is for good people to become perpetrators of evil."

Zimbardo's website, at www.prisonexp.org, presents a fuller, online photo/video documentary of that chilling experiment.

* * *

Temporary residents of psychiatric asylums have observed with discomfort how easy it was for them to slip into enjoying having all of their decisions made for them—as to when to eat, bathe, sleep, etc.

It would be naïve to think that a similar dynamic did not apply to a significant proportion of our world's ashram residents. For, they equally have their practical decisions made by the rules of the community, and their moral and metaphysical ones made by the guru-figure. With or without profound energy flows and transmitted bliss/enlightenment, that abdication of independence would appeal to far too many, and provides a very significant additional impediment in attempting to return to the "real world." For in the latter, one must make one's own choices, and be held responsible for the consequences. In the former, by contrast, to yield one's decisions to others is taken as a sign of loyalty and spiritual growth in the loss of ego, and is correspondingly socially rewarded.

> Once you get the rules and the rituals straight, it's easy. No decisions, no choices, nothing to plan. It's ever so much harder to live on your own [than as a Zen monk] (Boehm, 1996).

> Given that all daily needs were taken care of—food, clothing, living arrangements—there were few decisions left for a member [of Heaven's Gate] to make (Lalich, 2004).

> Persons can voluntarily elect to enter a total institution and cease thereafter, to their regret, to be able to make ... important decisions. In other cases, notably the religious, inmates may begin with and sustain a willful desire to be stripped and cleansed of personal will (Goffman, 1961).

> Jetsunma's telephone number was unlisted and kept private, even from most of her students. "Otherwise, I'd get calls all day," she explained later, "people asking me which cereal to buy" (Sherrill, 2000).

Of course, such crippling (co-)dependence is a two-way street: Jetsunma, Cohen, Trungpa, and many others, have all reportedly controlled the personal lives of their followers as well. That governance has typically included the guru-figure setting up, and breaking up, long-term relationships, and suggesting which couples should have children, etc.

As a loyal disciple, one is taking the guru-figure's claims of enlightenment seriously, and regarding his/her teachings as being the shortest route to the end of one's own sorrows in bliss or some other variation of enlightenment. What choice, then, does one have but to follow such "God-given" advice, regardless of how obviously meddling and obsessively controlling it may be? What, other than "ego," would resist?

If "God" tells you to do something, you do it, right?

Such devoted following will further generally and "validly" (in that context) lead you to immerse yourself in the guru-figure's teachings, to the natural exclusion of outside writings or news. In such a scenario, you will probably equally willingly drop your relationships with family and friends outside the ashram, if the resistance or lack of understanding of those outsiders is felt to interfere with your spiritual quest. Conversely, they will just as easily drop *you,* should your new set of beliefs and activities be too "weird" for them to be comfortable with.

> "Call me," [Pam] said. "I hate to see you fuck up your life in a place like this."
>
> "You don't want to be a Hare Krishna. Think about it," Diana added.
>
> Pam sat there, the radio blaring louder than the ritual music from the temple, and then she squealed out of the driveway and roared off into the darkness of Watseka. I watched until the taillights faded. I hoped my friends would come back someday, but feared I'd lost them forever (Muster, 1997).

> After making the decision to stay on at Kripalu, I had settled comfortably into the rhythm of life on campus.... My friends back home had their reactions, of course. Nina stopped talking to me for a while (Cope, 2000).

Georg Feuerstein (1992) related his own comparable episodes in entering, and later leaving, Adi Da's ashram:

> Old friends and colleagues had reacted to my decision to "drop out" of the academic world with incomprehension,

> some even with hostility. Similarly, my former fellow disciples quite failed to understand why I had to leave [the ashram, five years later]. Some even reacted angrily toward me, and a few still harbor ill feelings.

> If you questioned and decided to leave [the Moonies], you would not be worthy of love—to the contrary, you would be worthy of scorn and even hatred (Hassan, 2000).

Or, as Butterfield (1994) summarized the dynamic:

> The hypocrisy of [so-called] cult friendships, typically, is that while they pose as unconditional love, they depend powerfully on loyalty to the [alleged] cult.

All of that follows straightforward from the simple conformist principle of "fit in or be ostracized." And *that* is applied just as much by members of the heterogeneous society outside the ashram gates as it is applied inside the homogeneously believing "cult."

> The push to conform was very strong in Heaven's Gate but in some ways not so different from the norms of conformity found throughout U.S. society. The specifics of this conformity—ideas, appearance, language, deference to Ti [Nettles] and Do [Applewhite]—may seem odd to the outsider, but such conformism is rampant everywhere, as citizens flock to buy the latest fashion or hot product or kowtow to their bosses. It is the very normalcy of that behavior that made it easy for Ti and Do's followers to go along with the program (Lalich, 2004).

* * *

It is just a question of degree or intensity, not a difference in kind, that separates "safe" communities and societies from so-called destructive ones. That is true along a continuum ranging from high school or the business world to the Marines to prison confinement to Jonestown. For, any relatively closed, hierarchical system with an emphasis on respectful obedience to the rules of enlightenment/parole/graduation/promotion, and insufficient checks and balances placed on the leaders to make them accountable to the followers and to the outside world, is a "pathology waiting to happen," regardless of the sexes or ages involved.

Significantly, then, in a 1975 *Psychology Today* article, Zimbardo and his colleague, Craig Haney, observed that, in many important ways, "it's tough to tell a high school from a prison":

> While we do not claim high schools are really prisons, the two environments resemble each other to a remarkable and distressing degree.... Any social institution—a school, hospital, factory, office—can fairly be labeled a prison if it seriously restricts a person's freedom, imprisoning him in regulated and routinized modes of behavior or thought.

Zimbardo and Haney proceeded to sensibly map high school teachers to guards, and students to prisoners. And had they directed their attention to how religious communities are structured, they would surely have found it worth their while to perform a comparable mapping for those. They could further not have been at all surprised, in hindsight at least, to find that *exactly* the same problems are reported to occur in our world's ashrams as manifest in our prisons, "in spite of" the former having a "god in the flesh" as a "superintendent," and close disciples as "guards."

Comparably, even with regard to the relatively safe business world, an anonymous poster on the SRF Walrus website observed:

> It was so awful, working in corporations. I was a computer programmer, so I saw a lot of the inner workings at various levels. The first shocking thing that happens is to be in on an upper management meeting and see how blatantly anti-employee they are, with no apologies. But I came to feel that what was worse was the way the employees bought in to the mistreatment. If you say anything to point out to them how they're being used and abused, you become the troublemaker [cf. Zimbardo's prisoner #416], the boat-rocker. They are desperate to believe the emperor has on the latest and best stylings, and this drove me crazy.

That is, the psychological dynamics, as we could have guessed, are no different from those which occur in so-called cults and prisons, even if not approaching the Jonestown end along that continuum. (In such "cult"/prison environments, inmates can again be sadistically abused, with no regard for their rights, almost as if they were inferior animals rather than equal human beings.) Here, we obviously have executives substituted for guards, peon employees for prisoners, and CEOs for superintendents. The structure into which those fit, however, is as hierarchical as in any prison or ashram. It further contains persuasive (financial) reasons for the underlings to obey their superiors, and equal reasons for them to not "just leave," even when being shat upon. So they instead remain, being "good employees," not rocking the boat, in the hope of receiving reward and recognition/promotion for their obedience to the "much wiser" parent-figure managerial leaders.

Interestingly, similar dynamics can apply even in the smallest of "communities":

> The social convention of marriage ... becomes for many couples a state of imprisonment in which one partner agrees to become prisoner or guard, forcing or allowing the other to play the reciprocal role (Zimbardo, et al., 1973).

Focusing on "patriarchy" as opposed to "hierarchy" in any of those systems, however, only serves to obscure the relevant issues of basic human psychology. It further typically leads to utterly fallacious, frequently misandristic (as opposed to misogynistic) proposed "solutions" to the reported problems we have seen herein.

* * *

Even a pure democracy will naturally and inevitably turn into an authoritarian hierarchy in the face of any one person whom enough people believe to be an infallible "god." Those supporters then defer to his (or her) "omniscient" perception of reality, and collectively enforce that same deference on their peers, against the penalty of ostracism from the community—a fate worse than peonship, even were salvation not at stake. Thereby do they ingratiate themselves and secure their own inner circle status, where they can "bask in the reflected glory" from such close proximity to the "cool sage" above them. In the same positions, they will further receive bowing respect from those below—exacted sadistically, if need be.

(With regard to the spontaneous production and defense of the guru position: Compare the unavoidable—not necessarily good, but unavoidable—presence of "alpha males" and pecking orders even in the animal kingdom. There is neither "patriarchy" nor "too much linear thinking" in such pre-verbal environments; yet the hierarchical orderings occur all the same.)

Spiritual paths as diverse as Roman Catholicism, Tibetan Buddhism and Paramahansa Yogananda's SRF have been grown in cultures ranging from the agrarian East to postmodern America. Yet, they are scarcely distinguishable in their power structures, the behaviors of their members, the penalties for leaving and the reported, spirit-crushing cruelties visited upon those who stay. And given all that, it seems clear by now that not only are the problems with such communities systemic, but the abuse-creating structures themselves are basically unavoidable.

The issues we have seen, then, are the product far less of a few "bad apples," than of the surroundings in which they are contained.

> Prisons [and other authoritarian institutions, e.g., ashrams], where the balance of power is so unequal, tend to be brutal and abusive places unless great effort is made to control the guards' base impulses, [Zimbardo] said. At Stanford and in Iraq [e.g., Abu Ghraib], he added: "It's not that we put bad apples in a good barrel. We put good apples in a bad barrel. The barrel corrupts anything that it touches" (J. Schwartz, 2004).

In Abu Ghraib, "guards were allowed to do what they needed to keep 'order and justice' inside the prison"—an instruction which is obviously wholly comparable to that given to Zimbardo's guards.

David Clohessy, the national director of S.N.A.P. (the Survivors Network of those Abused by Priests), gave a similar analysis of the Catholic Church, in its problems with clergy sexual abuse (in Bruni and Burkett, 2002):

> It's not bad apples. It's the structure of the barrel that the apples are in, and it's the people who are in charge of the barrel, and the people who fill up the barrel [i.e., the bishops, cardinals and pope].

Almost universally, in spiritual communities, there are no meaningful checks and balances on the behaviors of the leaders, to restrict their exercise of "divine" power. That is so, not only in terms of their indulgence in base (e.g., sadistic or sexual) impulses, but also in failing to prevent the *Animal Farm*-like rewriting of the tenets on which the community was originally founded. (Compare SRF's current monopoly on "valid" kriya initiation, etc.) Yet, there is simultaneously no shortage of indoctrination, required deference, ostracism and worse, utilized to keep the followers from even cognizing, much less speaking up about, those power-grabs and rule-changes. And before you know it, the Board of Directors members, for example, have become "more equal" than the people to whom they should be accountable. They will further benefit from there being no shortage of peons eager to prove their loyalty to the cause, and work their way up "toward God," by doubly reinforcing that inequality on anyone who dares to question it.

Profound deference in such spiritual communities will further occur even if all below the "alpha sage" believe that they themselves can *eventually* attain to his or her ostensibly exalted level of wisdom or spiritual realization. For, no small part of the means toward attaining that enlightened wisdom is to "temporarily" defer to its manifestation in the guru-figure. Conversely, to question "God's" wisdom is to suffer one form or another of damnation within the community, just as to obey him unquestioningly is to secure one's own salvation.

> There is in the Indian *tradition* the notion that ... "criticizing the guru" is a thing that the disciples must not tolerate; and they don't (Bharati, 1976; italics added).

> Whatever you do should be done only to please the guru. Without the guru, enlightenment is impossible (Butterfield, 1994).

> You have to do everything your guru says. You must obey (Neem Karoli Baba, in [Das, 1997]).

> [Ramakrishna] once admonished an unsuspecting young man who refused to wash the Master's feet after the latter's toilet: "If I piss standing, you buggers have to do it dancing around. You must do my bidding for your own good" (Sil, 1998).

In the relevant words of Upasani Baba (1978)—a disciple of the original Shirdi Sai Baba—who was himself married, by ancient Vedic custom, to a full twenty-five virgin girls:

> [I]t is never the business of the devotee to *doubt* or interpret in his own way whatever he is spoken to by the Satpurusha [God-realized man]. He cannot understand the real purport

> of Sadguru's [i.e., the true teacher's] talk or action; because his reasoning and thought are never capable of fathoming Guru's thoughts or actions.

Or, as Adi Da (1974) conveniently explained to his own followers:

> If you assume the Guru is less than [living always and consciously in Divine Communion], if you assume what he says is less than Truth, that he is other than the Divine, that he does not live in God in exactly the way that he is asking you to live in God, then you are not living in Satsang with such a one, and you are not doing this *sadhana*.

Or recall Andrew Cohen's reported promise to his disciples: "Anyone who loves me ... is guaranteed enlightenment." But how is such love shown, if not through quick and willing obedience? Could someone who "loved" him still openly question, much less disobey? Not if we are to believe the reports from his former disciples:

> Whoever shows himself to be a loyal student is his friend. Those who are disloyal or unreliable fall out of favor (van der Braak, 2003).

Comparably, from the Tibetan Buddhist tradition, we have this dangerous counsel:

> A courageous disciple, armored with the determination never to displease his teacher *even at the cost of his life,* so stable-minded that he is never shaken by immediate circumstances, who serves his teacher without caring for his own health or survival and obeys his every command without sparing himself at all—such a person will be liberated simply through his devotion (Rinpoche, 1998; italics added).

> Guru-devotion involves both your thoughts and actions. The most important thing is to develop the total conviction that your Guru is a Buddha.... If you doubt your Guru's competence and ability to guide you, your practices will be extremely unstable and you will be unable to make any concrete progress....
>
> If your Guru acts in a seemingly unenlightened manner and you feel it would be hypocritical to think him a Buddha, you should remember that your own opinions are unreliable

> and the apparent faults you see may only be a reflection of your own deluded state of mind. Also you should think that if your Guru acted in a completely perfect manner, he would be inaccessible and you would be unable to relate to him. *It is therefore out of your Guru's great compassion that he may show apparent flaws.* This is part of his use of skillful means in order for him to be able to teach you. *He is mirroring your own faults* (Beru Kyhentze Rinpoche, in [Berzin, 1978]; italics added).

> Once a person has been identified [in India] as a saint, a holy man, nothing he does or does not do can change his title, unless he is caught *in flagrante,* and several times, engaged in disastrous things like sex or forbidden drink. But even in such a case, once his charisma is firmly established, there is a dialectic out of such dilemma: the emancipated person is not bound by social rules, and there is enough scripture to support it (Bharati, 1976).

All of that, of course, is simply manipulative, power-preserving nonsense, presented in the guise of spirituality. And it all, as we have seen, exists just as surely in the traditional, agrarian East as in the postmodern West, by its own admission.

The indefensibly stupid notion that the "real difficulty of 'the strange case of Adi Da' is that the guru principle is neither understood nor accepted by our culture" is clearly part of the same dangerous apologetic. For, it is again obvious that whenever "God" is involved, there *are* no checks and balances: "God" can always do whatever he wants, regardless of the surrounding culture or tradition.

In the face of such traditional instruction, points such as the following, from the Dalai Lama no less, ring utterly hollow:

> Part of the blame lies with the student, because too much obedience, devotion, and blind acceptance spoils a teacher.... Part also lies with the spiritual master because he lacks the integrity to be immune to that kind of vulnerability (in Butler, 1990).

Of course, by parity of argument, one would equally place "part of the blame" on abused women for giving up their power to men, or ridiculously regard too-obedient children as "spoiling" their parents, etc.

Much more sensibly:

> The guru system, the Zen Master system and every other variation on that theme is just as horrible and destructive to folks with amber skin and almond shaped eyes as it is to folks with white skin and blue eyes. It didn't work two thousand years ago in Rishikesh, India any better than it works right now in Racine, Wisconsin (Warner, 2004).

> Charaka, the first-century court physician whose writings help form the basis of ancient Indian medicine, wrote that a student was free to ignore a guru's orders if they jeopardized health or were against the law. One suspects, though, that it would have been difficult for a student so trained in obedience to decide when the time for rebellion had come (Brent, 1972).

* * *

Even if the guru-figure was ever all that he claimed to be, it would take at most a few years for an inner circle of "guards" to accumulate around him or her. Those high-ranking followers will then work roughly within the overall constraints set by the guru/superintendent and immediate culture. They themselves are always looking up to the guru-figure with respect, being at times harshly disciplined by him, and feeling always inferior to him. They will thus exact their own craved measures of respect, obedience and superiority, to re-inflate their own self-esteem, from the only source available, i.e., from those below them in the closed community. And the obedience of the latter can only be unconditional, with no threat of rebellion, when their wills are completely broken. (Absolute power in any context is mutually exclusive with a tolerance for discontent. For, it is exactly the vocalization and acting-out of such dissatisfaction that would show the governing power to be less than absolute.)

> People compensate for their subservience to superiors by exploiting inferiors. They feel entitled (Mike Lew, in [Bruni and Burkett, 2002]).

Or, as Goffman noted in his (1961) study of totalistic institutions, *Asylums:*

> [W]ith the decision that [military] officer training camp has "earned" him rights over enlisted men, the officer trainee becomes an officer. The pain suffered in camp can be used as a justification for the pleasures of command.

As to those "pleasures of command" in the exercise of dominance over others, Zimbardo (1971) further observed:

> [W]e are all subject at some level to being corrupted by power. It may be as children we start off with an unfair power disadvantage where adults tell us [as gurus similarly do later] what to do and we have to do it. Maybe at some level we are seeking to redress that imbalance.

Toward that same wish for redress, in proportion to the experienced imbalance, Haney and Zimbardo (1998) noted:

> [A]s the experiment progressed, more [prisoners] frequently expressed intentions to do harm to others (even as they became increasingly more docile and conforming to the whims of the guards).

When it comes to (bowing) respect, then, it seems that the more we give, the more we crave to get in return—easily slipping into even the sadistic abuse of others in order to secure that.

Of course, in spiritual contexts and elsewhere, the rabid intolerance for disobedience, disrespect and disloyalty in others, and consequent punishment for that, could also be seen as having additional psychological origins. Indeed, one might well take it as involving a projection of one's own unallowed feelings of disloyalty and wishes for disobedience onto them. That is, since one is not permitted to acknowledge disloyalty or disobedience in oneself, one instead sees and punishes it doubly in others.

The guards in Zimbardo's study had further been instructed to maintain order in the prison by an authority-figure. Thus, it is also quite possible that a significant part of their behaviors might be traced to attempts at winning the approval of that authority. If they were going to do their jobs well in the eyes of their own bosses, after all, they could brook no discontent or disrespect from the prisoners.

The extracting of respect and obedience, in any case, will be done via whatever means of psychological and physical manipulation and abuse the upper echelon can get away with. And that will again be done under pretenses (in religious communities) of "killing the egos" of others for their own spiritual benefit. Further, it will be enacted within a group mentality (at all levels of the hierarchy) where to resist what your "elders" are telling you is to invite ostracism from the rest of the community.

* * *

In Zimbardo's study, the early rebellion of the prisoners both created a solidarity among the guards, and reinforced the awareness of the latter that they might actually be in danger. I know of no ashram that has ever had such an acute, concerted rebellion—Kripalu at the end of Desai's rule perhaps comes closest. Nor are the guru-figure or his inner circle ever in any physical danger from their followers. Yet they reportedly behave sadistically all the same, with no more tolerance for disobedience or disloyalty than Zimbardo's guards exhibited. That is, the "steady state" of the environment is remarkably similar even if, in the absence of acute transients, it may have taken longer to get there. (It took all of a few days in Zimbardo's prison study, even though both the guard and prisoner participants in it were perfectly normal and healthy individuals going into that.)

Nor would even a genuine "perfect master" (if there were such a thing, which there absolutely is not) at the head of such a community be able to avoid those problems. For, as much as disciples may transfer their own hopes for perfection onto the guru, no such perfection was ever ascribed to Zimbardo or to his guards. Nor did he or his guards promulgate any "weird" system of beliefs. Nor were those guards intending, at the start, to enact any means of "mind control."

Yet, in spite of those innocent beginnings, Zimbardo's guards actually ended up effecting sleep deprivation and controlling even the bathroom activities and food intake of their prisoners, attempting force-feeding on at least one occasion.

Comparably:

> I wasn't long in the [Irish Sisters of Charity orphanage] and there was a piece of parsnip in my dinner, and it was dirty. I politely put it to one side of my plate, and ate everything else. The nun came down and told me to eat the parsnip. I said no. So she force fed it to me, and I got sick. Then she

> force fed that to me as well. And she started to beat me with her belt (Raftery and O'Sullivan, 2001).

Note, then, how the sadistic behavior is exactly the same whether coming from women or from men. That is, the fact that all of Zimbardo's guards and prisoners were male is not, in practice, relevant. (The mixture of the sexes in Abu Ghraib likewise did not prevent female guards there from allegedly being among the worst abusers of power.)

Zimbardo's "bad" guards enacted their sadistic and controlling behaviors not for having been told to do so by him. Rather, they evolved those means of control on their own. That is, like the Irish nuns above, they behaved thusly not because they were directly told to by an authority figure, but rather just because they were *allowed* to.

Consider further that in Zimbardo's study, the power was divided up more or less evenly among the guards. Had Zimbardo not been there at all (as superintendent), one can easily see that the division of power among the guards would have been just as equal. Yet things could only have gotten worse, faster. The point, then, is that a *group* of people with absolute or near-absolute authority is no better than is a single individual with the same power.

Nor would such a group act to enforce "checks and balances" on each other at their own level. For, Zimbardo's "good" guards, rather than constraining the activities of their "bad" counterparts, simply felt helpless in watching the sadistic behaviors of the latter.

How are we to understand why otherwise-reasonable and healthy men would behave so impotently? First, we may note that it is typical of human behavior that, in witnessing any objectionable activity from within a group of comparable onlookers, we assume that "someone else" will speak up or call the police, if that needs to be done. Indeed, it has actually been shown in controlled studies that we are less likely to intervene if we are surrounded by a group of others than as a sole witness to a crime or emergency (Cialdini [2001]; Zimbardo [2004b]). For, we will naturally take our cues from their outwardly calm, evaluating behaviors, as they take their cues from ours.

As one relevant example of such covert evaluation and subsequent going along with the group, consider the reaction of the guest reporting Ken Wilber's alleged public miming of masturbation and frequent, sophomoric requests there for blowjobs:

> I laughed with everyone else, but at the back of my mind, I realized I was disturbed and disappointed by it.... But other people I talked to weren't bothered by it at all, so maybe he just gauged his audience correctly (in Integral, 2004).

In asking other subjects about whether they were bothered by such behaviors, though, one is effectively inquiring: "Were you disturbed by our emperor's new clothes?" The obvious answer to which is, "No, of course not."

Regardless, having spent sufficient time in silence within a group of onlookers, the first question one would face should one finally openly object would be the embarrassing: Why did you keep quiet for so long, if it was obvious from the beginning that something needed to be done? We therefore have a personal stake in not admitting that we should have done things differently—i.e., that we were wrong to behave thusly. For that reason, and even merely for the sake of socially rewarded consistency, we instead remain silent, allowing the problems to continue. (Institutions such as the Vatican persist in their errors and reported abuses in no small part exactly for being unable to come out and admit that they have been wrong in the past [cf. Wills, 2000].) Plus, for Zimbardo's relatively sensitive "good" guards, for example, to speak out against the activities of their more sadistic counterparts would surely have resulted in their quick ostracism from that sub-community of "alpha guards," who actually *enjoyed* mistreating their prisoners.

> Everyone and everything in the prison was defined by power. To be a guard who did not take advantage of this institutionally sanctioned use of power was to appear "weak," "out of it," "wired up by the prisoners," or simply a deviant from the established norms of appropriate guard behavior (Zimbardo, et al., 1973).

In evaluating the actions of their guards, Zimbardo and his colleagues further noted:

> [T]he behavior of [the] good guards seemed more motivated by a desire to be liked by everyone in the system than by a concern for the inmates' welfare.

Guards who thus want to be "liked by everyone," however, will not only do small favors for the prisoners and avoid punishing them, but will equally shrink from offending their own peers.

Thus, they will again avoid speaking out against the abuses of the latter. (As Zimbardo [1971] himself further noted, allowing those "bad" guards free reign also makes one look "good" by comparison. That is, it casts one's own ego in a positive light, and allows one to feel like a better person in that contrast.)

Whatever the theory behind the ensuing silence may be, though—in broad strokes or in nuances—in practice it is a pervasive feature of human societies, both secular and "sacred":

> It is evident from the testimony of former inmates that by no means all of [the Irish Catholic nuns and monastic brothers] behaved brutally towards the children. But it is a common theme that the "good" nuns and brothers never interfered with or protested about the activities of their more violent colleagues (Raftery and O'Sullivan, 2001).

Zimbardo has more recently (2004a) concluded:

> My research and that of my colleagues has cataloged the conditions for stirring the crucible of human nature in negative directions. Some of the necessary ingredients are ... bystanders who do not intervene, and a setting of power differentials.

"Bystanders who do not intervene": e.g., "good" monks who wonder out loud why their peers and superiors are not behaving with integrity, but who do nothing to stop it. For, to speak up would make them "bad disciples" and open them to retaliation/ostracism from those tougher ones on the same level and above them.

"A setting of power differentials": e.g., guru-figure, inner circle, and peon/newbie disciples.

* * *

No amount of flaws shown by the spiritual teacher will dissuade the truly sincere seeker from becoming involved and deferential. Not, at least, if he places enlightenment/salvation as a high enough goal in his own life, and believes that the holy figure in question can help him get to that state faster than any other route. Thus, as Butterfield (1994) noted in the context of his own initiation into Trungpa's path, with the latter having given that Vajrayana transmission via a rambling, nearly nonsensical, stream-of-consciousness delivery:

> He could have said very little to dissuade me, as long as I remained convinced that he knew what I wanted to learn.

Ponder that point deeply, for it means that the utilization of "deceptive recruiting" as a means of defining what a potentially destructive group is, is far less relevant than one might imagine it to be. For, even without such deception, one may well truly believe (on the basis of "genius" recommendations and the like) that one or another guru-figure is a "great Realizer," and that he can lead you to the same exalted state if you just "surrender completely" to him. And in that case, you will put up with any amount of "Rude Boy" mistreatment in that relationship, and consider it to be for your own benefit, *even if you have been warned about it beforehand.*

Even just in normal human relationships, if someone has something we want—sex, money, etc.—we will tolerate a great deal of grief and mistreatment in order to get it. And being told up-front that the other person is "trouble," or that we will be asked to compromise our principles in the process, won't stop us from going willing into that, if we just want the "prize" badly enough.

So, how badly do you want enlightenment?

> The guru claimed to offer access to profoundly ecstatic spiritual realization, and the only way to gain access to that experience was by playing his game. The better you played the game, by showing your devotion and obedience, the greater your contact with the guru and the more frequent your opportunities for grace (Lowe, 1996).

Interestingly, the Daists have reportedly (Lowe, 1996) attempted to get the "disappointingly" tame *Garbage and the Goddess* out of circulation. Likewise, when an exposé of the "Merwin incident" was published in their local *Boulder Monthly,* Trungpa's followers apparently "scurried about town, trying to keep the magazine off the racks by purchasing several copies at a time" (Schumacher, 1992). Books uncomplimentary toward so-called cults also tend to vanish mysteriously from public libraries. My local city reference library, for example—which allows no books to be taken out —is nevertheless missing its sole copy of David Lane's (1994) *Exposing Cults.* That book itself is notably critical of Da Free John, among numerous other "lesser lights/coronas."

Such reported attempts at covering up questionable behaviors, however, are fairly superfluous. For, the spiritual world is more than screwed up enough for its leading figures to still explicitly encourage you to go along for the "adventure," even years after the reported methods of "Teaching" have been widely publicized.

And, if you can't take the "Rude Boy" discipline, whose fault/ego is that?

Remember: "The greater the offense, the bigger the ego."

Put another way: The expert reassurance of a highly respected hero or "genius" that being disciplined by a God-realized "Rude Boy" is the fastest way toward one's own most-valued realization (or salvation) will easily override any concerns one might have about even a reportedly "problematic" group. It is, after all, very easy to rationalize away the complaints of disaffected former followers as being mere "whining" or "cowardice" on the part of people who "couldn't take the heat," etc. That is so even if the group is prone to literally beating the crap out of its followers, as we have seen. In such a case, the purportedly destructive group could even fully disclose all of its past alleged abuses and plans for future mistreatment to potential members, and new lemmings would still flock to join. (Recall how Zen monks will allow themselves to be literally beaten black and blue *just to get into* the monastery. That is, they go into that environment knowing full well that it is a violently abusive one. They have further in no way been "deceptively recruited" into that.)

In such a realistic scenario, then, seekers absolutely would not merely find themselves involuntarily "recruited" into reportedly destructive groups by any deceptive means. Rather, they would explicitly go looking for those. They sought out Rajneesh's violent humanistic encounter sessions, too, presumably frequently on the recommendations of people they admired, as opposed to going into them without knowing what would likely occur in those groups. Likewise, Yogi Bhajan's (1977) explicit, printed statement that disciples might be required to *steal* on behalf of the guru (e.g., Bhajan himself) was evidently not sufficient to scare off his own reported quarter of a million followers.

> [A]lmost everyone [in Da's community], without exception, was subjected to a number of [alleged] mind-control methods, including non-stop indoctrination, intense overwork, sleep-denial, constant peer pressure and a barrage of demands, to the point where they were effectively robbed of judgment.

> People accepted this mistreatment because ... they believed the promise that it would break down their "resistance" to God in the person of the Guru. People accepted that their "egos" needed to be disciplined and "destroyed," so that the same "spiritual genius" the Guru claimed would awaken in them (Elias, 1999a).

The full extent of the behind-the-scenes dysfunctionality in any religious organization is, of course, never explained to its prospective members up front. (Likewise, it is never disclosed at the beginning of any job or human relationship, nor could one reasonably expect it to be.) Still, if there is "deception" in our world's "authentic, transformative" spiritual organizations, it is more in the guru-figures not living up to their own teachings, or not possessing the spiritual realization which they claim to have—an entirely separate issue. It has little to do with potential followers supposedly not knowing that they would be subjected to extreme "discipline," or required to break the law at the guru-figure's instruction, with the reward of eventually becoming "as great as the guru" themselves.

And, having gone willingly into that "heat," devotees have no easy way out, to save spiritual face. They will therefore soon find themselves bearing the reported abuse willingly and silently, as a purported sign of spiritual development/loyalty/obedience. Further, that will be done in the implicit hope that if they are thus "loyal" and obedient enough, for long enough, the mistreatment will stop, and they will receive nothing but love.

That futile strategy of coping, however, is one which they share with battered wives. Indeed, the latter, like the former disciples, frequently feel unable to leave their abusive spouses in large part for having had their own egos destroyed by being told repeatedly, in one form or another, that they are worthless and incapable. They then behave accordingly, with all due expected helplessness.

> [B]attered women are notoriously loyal to their abusers, and often cling desperately to the hope that everything will change and come out for the best. A primary task of battered woman shelters and support groups is to break through this denial and help the woman face the fact that the abuser is in fact doing what he is doing. From there, recovery is possible.

> The same psychological mechanisms that create loyalty in a battered woman [e.g., by making her "complicit in her own exploitation"—in helplessness and otherwise—from which she "becomes supportive of the exploiter"], deliberately instilled, can make a [so-called] cult victim loyal to the [alleged] cult (Bob Penny, in [Wakefield, 1991]).

It is well known, further, that certain people will knowingly enter into secular sadomasochistic relationships for "getting off" on that pain or humiliation—having psychologically associated it with receiving love. In a like manner, spiritual seekers with sufficiently skewed views of enlightenment, associating pain or extreme discipline/humiliation with realization and spirituality, will only be attracted, not repelled, by the idea of being abused "for their own good" by a realized "god." (Compare even the "suffering as a path to salvation" perspectives of the likes of Thérèse of Lisieux—described by Pius X as "the greatest saint of modern times"—and Mother Teresa in the Catholic Church. Indeed, for a revealing analysis of the probable psychological factors underlying the religious fervor, and eager embrace of suffering and humiliation on the part of the former "Little Flower," see Monica Furlong's [1987] *Thérèse of Lisieux*.)

The ability to put one's own conscience aside and do whatever the guru asks you to is further believed to be essential to God-realization (with that being gained only through the grace of the guru). One might well then even seek out guru-figures who are known to be "amoral." For, what is morality but a product of the same conceptualization which daily blinds us to the Way Things Are? Isn't breaking such arbitrary hang-ups exactly what we need to do if we wish to be free of our dualistic conceptual boundaries? So, a "wild and crazy" guru who will "wisely" place you into situations where you have no choice but to drop your categorizing intellect and culturally molded conscience in "choiceless awareness" would be the best for accelerating your own spiritual evolution, yes? You could further hardly ask up-front for a detailed list of what you might be asked to do in such a community, as that would spoil the spontaneity of the guru's "divine expression," would it not?

There is further, quite clearly, no alleged abuse or breach of conventional morality so gross that it cannot be rationalized away, even by persons outside of the residential group. That is so, particularly for those who desperately want to believe that one or another guru-figure is the "greatest living Realizer" or the like, and that everything he or she does is a "Teaching." And, one need not be "brainwashed" in order to think that such rationalizations "make sense." Rather, one needs only to sincerely believe in the long-touted, if utterly wonky, transpersonal theory.

The voluntary entrance into known (reported) psychologically/physically abusive and amoral environments will then quite naturally follow. For, how else can one prove one's "spiritual machismo" to the heroes who have recommended "complete surrender" to one or another even-"problematic" guru and environment? How else to show that you're serious about becoming as "enlightened" as they are in their spiritual genius, except by "taking the heat"?

Interestingly, Live singer/songwriter Eddie Kowalczyk has expressed his early appreciation for Wilber's (1996) *A Brief History of Everything*. He later visited with Wilber himself in August of 1999. Kowalczyk then blurbed for Da in 2000, crediting him with being "Real God ... incarnate as Avatar Adi Da Samraj."

Coincidence? Or a troubling demonstration of the points above, even with Kowalczyk meeting Da as a "celebrity" either way, and thus necessarily having no real knowledge as to what the "Avatar" and his reportedly dildo-wielding, corona-seeing "pod people" are really like?

* * *

Zimbardo again took two dozen completely normal, physically and mentally healthy college-age individuals. He then confined them, willingly and voluntarily, to a closed environment; stratified the community into guards and prisoners; and simply instructed the higher-ups to exact obedience and respect from the lower ones. He further introduced no charismatic leadership, weird beliefs or claims to divinity on his own part. There was even *no punishment for leaving,* other than the loss of the money the prisoners were to be paid for their full-term participation in the study, and their own subjective feelings of being "bad prisoners" in prematurely exiting. Yet, in less than six days, and quite unintentionally, he created behaviors among the various classes of participants which are indistinguishable from those allegedly found in—as a very reasonable extrapolation from the known, reported data—every ashram and every so-called cult.

It is thus not the charisma or "divine" status *per se* of any leader which creates problems. Rather, the "problematic" nature is again inherent in the power structure of every closed hierarchical community, when that stratification is combined with basic human psychology. Having an "infallible god-man" rather than a merely human superintendent at the helm will make it harder for others to disobey or to leave, but even without that, disobedience and departure will in no way be easy to enact.

Conversely, each one of us is again susceptible to exhibiting docile "cult-follower" behavior in the right/wrong circumstances. Tendencies toward conformity, authoritarianism or blind belief may make it statistically more likely for any given person to be thus fooled, but truly, it could happen to any one of us.

> People believe that "it can never happen to them" because they want to believe they are stronger and better than the millions who have fallen victim to [alleged] cult mind control....
>
> A [so-called] cult will generally target the most educated, active, and capable people it can find. I hear comments such as "I never knew there were so many brilliant people in these types of groups" (Hassan, 1990).

> Such beliefs as, "others could be made to do that but not me" and "others could be swayed by speeches but not me" are dangerous because they set us apart from other people who *are* like ourselves and therefore prevent us from learning from their experience what may be valuable for ourselves (Winn, 2000).

> [O]ur experiences [with the Moonies] could happen to any American family (Underwood and Underwood, 1979).

> [E]ven people who said, "I could never join a cult," would walk in [to Rajneesh's ashrams] as if on a dare and emerge no different from a person who had entered as an eager seeker....
>
> Bhagwan emphatically stated that what we were involved in was *not* a religion, and this appealed to people who would be the first to decry anyone who joined a "cult." As a matter of fact we joined a cult precisely because it *wasn't* a cult (Strelley, 1987).

* * *

Significantly, it was only when an "outsider" objected to the behaviors occurring within Zimbardo's study that it was stopped. (That came, however, only after *fifty* other outside observers had themselves voiced no shock or negative opinion.) Having not previously been involved with the experiment in any capacity, she had thus not participated step-by-step in the "slow descent into madness," instead walking straight into it, unprepared, on the sixth day (Zimbardo, et al., 2000).

That, of course, reminds one eerily of the old experiment/story of the frog placed into water in a saucepan on a stove, with that water then being slowly heated. Lacking any sudden increase in temperature to alert him that all is not well, the frog will allow himself to be slowly cooked, rather than simply jumping out of the water to safety.

A comparable "slow descent," invisible to those who participate in it step-by-step on a daily basis, occurs in our world's ashrams. Indeed, even new members in an already "mad" environment will have that introduction cushioned by having the most questionable aspects of the organization hidden from them until they have demonstrated their loyalty. To find out, first-hand, how bad things really are, then, one must already be "halfway cooked" oneself, via that slow increase in heat.

Consider, further, Stanley Milgram's (1974) obedience experiments. There, a majority (nearly two-thirds, in one experimental version) of ordinary people were induced, in less than an hour, to administer what they thought were potentially lethal shocks to even hysterically protesting others, simply out of their obedience to the minimal authority of an experimenter.

> The most significant aspect of [Milgram's] experiment is that not one participant refuses to continue when the planted subject *first* asks them to stop. It is only later, with a threat of death or grave illness, that people refuse to go on with the shocks. It is always and only the scream that is heeded, and never its antecedent, never the beginnings or first hints of pain [i.e., never the first sensings of the "slow, continual increase in heat"]....
>
> One sees the same thing at work in [so-called] cults: a refusal to recognize in early excesses, early signs, the full implications of what is going on and will follow later. Relinquishing step by step the individualities of conscience, followers are slowly accustomed to one stage of [reported] abuse

> after another, becoming so respectful of the authority that they never quite manage to rebel (Marin, 1995).

Both of those frightening experimental demonstrations (of Zimbardo and Milgram) arise simply from basic human situational psychology, present as much outside our world's ashrams as inside them.

One could, indeed, substitute respect-hungering inner-circle monks for guards, gurus for superintendents, and younger monks for prisoners, repeating Zimbardo's study in any of our world's ashrams, and the results of the experiment would surely not change at all. Likewise, one might substitute elder monks for dial-turning shockers, younger monks for shockee subjects, and gurus for lab-coated experimenters, willing to accept responsibility for the results of the shocks, even unto death/enlightenment. In that case, one would no doubt find the vast majority of "holy, peaceful" monks and nuns just "doing what they were told" in that context, regardless of the consequences to the physical or mental health of their shocked subjects.

Milgram's subjects were not behaving sadistically in raising the voltage with which they shocked their learners, as he showed in additional experiments. They equally, however, were not attempting to exact obedience or respect from the people they were shocking. The difference in both motivation and behavior there is thus quite understandable. For, there is clearly quite a significant contrast in mindset between trying to help someone learn, even as a semi-teacher—the "cover story" for Milgram's obedience experiments—versus explicitly attempting to exact respect and unconditional obedience from them.

It further goes without saying that gurus and their close disciples would not react any more favorably to attempts to "reform" them than Zimbardo's guards could possibly have welcomed that, had the prisoners tried to improve that environment to curtail the sadistic abuse to which they were being subjected, for example. (Compare the one "troublemaker," #416.) Indeed, most of those guards—willingly working overtime, for no extra pay—were *upset* when the study was prematurely ended, in contrast to the prisoners, who were glad it was over. That is, the guards' sadistic behaviors were in no way caused or amplified by them hypothetically "not wanting to be there" and taking that frustration out on the prisoners, or the like.

> There has been much speculation in recent times that perhaps so many of the nuns [running Irish Catholic institutional schools] were cruel to the children in their care because they themselves were frustrated, having possibly even been forced to enter a convent by their families. There is no evidence to support this view. In fact, quite the reverse (Raftery and O'Sullivan, 2001).

All of that is hardly surprising, though. For, as every "Rude Boy" and sadistic guard knows, killing other people's egos or breaking their wills via humiliation, or "beating the crap out of them" for their own good, is such *fun*. With power being such an aphrodisiac, who would want to give up that complete control over another person's life? (See Zimbardo, et al. [1973]; Haney, et al. [1973].)

* * *

William Golding's *Lord of the Flies,* too, offers valuable insights into the dynamics of closed, authoritarian societies. And interestingly, when a movie version of that book was being filmed, the problem which the director encountered was not in getting the child actors into character while the cameras were rolling. Rather, the difficulty was in getting them *out* of character when the shooting was stopped. As Peter Brook explained (in Askenasy, 1978):

> Many of their off-screen relationships completely paralleled the story, and one of our main problems was to encourage them to be uninhibited within the shots but disciplined in between them.... My experience showed me that the only falsification in Golding's fable is the length of time the descent to savagery takes. His action takes about three months. I believe that if the cork of continued adult presence [i.e., of external checks and balances on the group's leaders] were removed from the bottle, the complete catastrophe could occur within a long weekend.

One may, of course, validly compare that with the role-playing in Zimbardo's study—and in each of our real lives—which quickly ceases to be just a conscious "role." And as far as "long weekends" go: The degeneration of character in the simulated Stanford prison happened literally within three days.

In Dittmann (2003), Zimbardo further traces the parallels between the mind-control methods and behaviors utilized by George

Orwell's fictional totalitarian state in *1984,* and Jonestown. Christopher Browning, in his (1998) *Ordinary Men,* performs a comparable mapping for the similarities between Zimbardo's and Milgram's studies, and the Final Solution in Poland. Significantly, the percentage of "cruel and tough," "tough but fair," and "good" soldiers, respectively, in that Solution, "bears an uncanny resemblance" to the comparable split among the guards in Zimbardo's simulated prison.

> [U]nder conditions of terror most people will comply but *some people will not,* just as the lesson of the countries to which the Final Solution was proposed is that "it could happen" in most places but *it did not happen everywhere....*
>
> The trouble with Eichmann was precisely that so many were like him, and that the many were neither perverted nor sadistic, that they were, and still are, terribly and terrifyingly normal (Arendt, 1992).

* * *

All of the subjects in Zimbardo's prison study were men. In practice, however, any minor bias which the study's male-only nature might introduce, as to the exact percentage of guards who turned "bad" and abused their power, or of the specific ways in which they abused that power, or of the percentage of prisoners who broke down emotionally, in no way lessens the applicability of the general mapping to "all humans."

The mixture of the sexes in Abu Ghraib again did not prevent female guards there from being among the worst alleged abusers of power. Nor did it stop nuns from force-feeding other nuns elsewhere, etc. That is, where comparable "experiments" to Zimbardo's have been performed in the real world, they have led to exactly the same toxic environments and sadistic behaviors as were observed in the simulated prison, independent of the sexes involved.

Further, note that the majority of the participants in Zimbardo's study were young, white Americans; there was thus also a "young, white American" bias to their behaviors. Indeed, if one were to follow all such possible claimed biases through, the results of the study could not be relevant to anyone or anywhere except ... yep, to white, healthy, intelligent, middle-class, college-age men in early-'70s Stanford, California. Yet, the elementary principles which led to the breakdown of the simulated prison society into an abusive one are relevant everywhere, in all cultures and times, for women as surely as men: They are just basic human psychology, brought out by power differentials and respect-hungering.

***

As Philip Zimbardo himself noted in the 1970s, high schools share a number of significant characteristics with prisons, in their respective authoritarian power structures. Yet obviously, schools do not have the same degree of isolation from outside perspectives as prisons do. Does that, then, mean that high schools and prisons are indeed different in kind, not merely in degree?

No, not at all. Even prisoners, after all, are not totally isolated: They receive visitors, at designated times. And newly incarcerated prisoners will, for a short time at least, offer real-world perspectives which have otherwise died out in prison life. Conversely, high school students cannot leave during class hours, nor drop out completely before age sixteen.

Further, if a student and a teacher disagree in a matter of discipline, or about which of them is in the wrong in a dispute, who do you think the parents are going to believe 90% of the time? Even if parent-teacher feedback and the legal system (thankfully) constrain teachers' exercise of power, and even if the freedom to go home at night (in *non-residential* schools) allows the students to retain *some* additional outside perspective on that environment, it is again all a question of *degree,* not of kind. And *degree = continuum.* (Plus, guards in real prisons, as in Zimbardo's simulated one, go home at night just as surely as do teachers and students, thus being integrated with their surrounding community, too. Unfortunately, that doesn't stop them from sadistically punishing their prisoners to ensure the unconditional respect of the latter ... just as teachers expect unqualified respect from their students.)

Realistically, basic principles of social psychology ensure that teachers who have been charged, as a condition of their continued employment, not merely with assisting their students in learning (as in Milgram's obedience experiments) but with maintaining the *respect and obedience* of their students (as in Zimbardo's simulated prison), will predictably degenerate into a less-intense version of good/bad prison guards when faced with any challenge to their authority.

The formation of cliques and consequent ostracism of outcastes, and the reaction of those outcastes to being stuck in that "hell on Earth" with "no way out," play a gargantuan role in shaping the behaviors of students, even for those who have ideal home lives. Or would it surprise you to know that the shooters in the Columbine massacre came from completely stable homes, with loving parents, to whom they explicitly apologized on videotape prior to the planned massacre?

At Columbine in 1999, and in other similar shootings, the assassins were not "bringing their dysfunctional home lives into school." Rather, they were reacting to the harassment and humiliation which they experienced from other students and authorities *in school*. That, after all, is why such young mass murderers kill their classmates and teachers, not their parents or neighbors.

And if that is true of the perpetrators of the worst of high-school tragedies, don't you think it might also apply, at lower levels of intensity, even to the bulk of the high-school student population? Of *course* it will.

***

> [I]t seems to me that what went on at Naropa, although more dramatic than what we usually see around us, was simply the lurid equivalent of what endlessly repeats itself in America in most systems of coercive authority, not only those at Naropa....
>
> Trungpa's behavior toward Merwin and Dana was essentially no different—in essence or extent—from what we ordinarily accept without question between doctors and mental patients, or teachers and students, or military authorities [or guards and prisoners]. It is here, where we always think discipline is necessary, that we habituate people to doing what they're told, to acceding to authority, and to accepting without question the ways they are treated (Marin, 1995).

There will always be those who are prone to feeling, especially from a safe distance, that being a subject in ashramic "experiments" comparable to Zimbardo's or Milgram's, with real (psychological) shocks and physical deprivations in closed hierarchical environments, could be spiritually beneficial. (Note, though, that significant concerns have been raised by psychologists regarding the effects on the subjects in both of those classic studies, to the point where neither of them can be repeated today, simply for ethical considerations. And yet, ashram life continues....)

Short of that myopia, however, the rules and behaviors of the open-society "real world," constricting though they may be at times, begin to look relatively benign by comparison. Conversely, if one has been on the inside of our world's ashrams and then left because being there felt like a "prison," that feeling has a very simple explanation. For, structurally and in terms of individual and group psychological dynamics, that is *exactly* what it was.

As Zimbardo himself (1971) put it:

> For me, a prison is any situation in which one person's freedom and liberty are denied by virtue of the arbitrary power exercised by another person or group.

And elsewhere, with his colleagues:

> The *inherently pathological* [italics added] characteristics of the prison situation itself ... were a *sufficient* condition to produce aberrant, anti-social behavior (Haney, et al., 1973).

And, as we have seen, nearly identical characteristics are sufficient to produce the same reported pathological behaviors in the leaders and residents of our world's ashrams and monasteries.

Only three things are really needed in order to begin creating a closed, toxic environment—whether that be a "cult," a bad marriage, a prison or a dictatorship. And those are (i) a significant power differential between the leaders and their followers, (ii) a lack of checks and balances on the leaders to keep them from abusing their existing power and grabbing for more, and (iii) sufficient psychological, financial and/or physical (e.g., locks and bars) constraints to keep the mistreated followers from simply leaving. The increasingly "cult-like" nature of the environment will then follow straightforward, simply via the presence of basic human psychology in both the leaders/guards and their followers/prisoners.

Further, as in Zimbardo's study, the only necessary difference between those two groups is in the roles which they have tacitly agreed to play. That is so, even while the one group invariably turns quickly into a split collection of impotent "good guards/disciples" and sadistic "Nazis," while members of the other set follow docilely or break down emotionally, yet are unable to "just leave."

CHAPTER XXVIII

SPIRITUAL CHOICES

OF COURSE, NOT EVERYONE WOULD AGREE that things are as bad as we have seen with today's spiritual leaders and communities. Indeed, one does not have to search far at all to find psychological professionals who are more than willing to stand up and defend the highly questionable reported actions of our world's guru-figures.

In 1987, for example, Dick Anthony and Ken Wilber, teaming with another of their like-minded associates, published *Spiritual Choices: The Problem of Recognizing Authentic Paths to Inner Transformation.* We will evaluate the worth of that text shortly.

Anthony himself has often served as an expert witness in defense of alternative religious movements accused of "brainwashing" their members, and the like.

> [He] listed some of his clients for the record. That list included the "Unification Church [i.e., the Moonies, whose founder 'was convicted of conspiracy to obstruct justice and conspiracy to file false tax returns and sentenced to a term in federal prison' (Singer, 2003)], the Hare Krishna movement,

The Way International [and] Church of Scientology" (Ross, 2003).

Regarding the Moonies, then:

> [In July of 2002] Moon announced himself as "Savior, Messiah and King of Kings of all humanity." He actually splashed this across newspapers throughout America in full-page ads (Ross, 2002a).

As Moon himself elaborated, in his *Unification News* (for August 24, 2002):

> In early July I spoke in five cities around Korea at rallies held by the Women's Federation for World Peace. There, I declared that my wife ... and I are the True Parents of all humanity. I declared that we are the Savior, the Lord of the Second Advent, the Messiah.

Enough said—except to add that Moon owns the *Washington Times* newspaper. (The Moonies also apparently own the University of Bridgeport, Connecticut [Hassan, 2000].) He has also been reported to be a friend of (and up to $10 million donor to) the George Bush family (Kuncl, 2001), and has had close contact with Mormon U.S. politician Orrin Hatch.

Regarding The Way International: Details as to the allegations of sexual misconduct against leaders at TWI exist online at EmpireNet (2003). And for those who wish to leave that nontraditional Bible group, the following allegations have been made:

> Sharon Bell says Way members told her "it might be necessary to kill anyone who tried to leave the group." Timothy Goodwin was told the devil would kill him if he left (Rudin and Rudin, 1980).

Such organizations as these, then, constitute some of Dick Anthony's reported clients, which he would surely, one assumes, not hesitate to suggest are "not as bad as" the other, genuinely "problematic" groups in the world. Just because they are "nontraditional religions," after all, is no reason to discriminate against them.

Also reportedly on Anthony's list of nontraditional religions, however,

> are the Branch Davidians [of David Koresh fame] ... and he says, "In the United States, the Catholic Church, well it's definitely the largest nontraditional religion" (Ross, 2003).

The idea that the Catholic Church is "nontraditional" is puzzling—leaving one wondering, indeed, what religions might ever qualify as "traditional"—but we may let that pass.

Anthony's religious allegiance belongs to Meher Baba, who in his heyday had "as many as a million devotees ... in India and thousands in the United States" (Manseau and Sharlet, 2004).

When Pete Townshend of the Who embarked on his own spiritual quest in 1968, he too found his guru in the voluntarily mute Meher—the "Baba" in "Baba O'Riley" refers to none other—as did the Small Faces' Ronnie Lane. (In much earlier, silent film days, Hollywood stars Douglas Fairbanks and Mary Pickford once gave a reception in Meher's honor.) Townshend actually ran a "Baba Center" in England for a time. His solo LP, *Who Came First,* further grew out of a planned tribute to the guru, who himself claimed "to have been taken into the council of the gods and to know the future of all mankind" (Brunton, 1935).

As Baba O'Meher himself put it:

> Once I publicly announce myself as a messiah, nothing will be able to withstand my power. I shall openly work miracles in proof of my mission at the same time. Restoring sight to the blind, healing the sick, maimed and crippled, yes, even raising the dead—these things will be child's play to me! (in Brunton, 1935).

Indeed, Meher "Eyesight to the Blind" Baba claimed to be, not merely an avatar, but *the* Avatar for this world age, after having been confirmed as such by Upasani Baba. (Interestingly, Adi Da purported a connection to the same Upasani Baba, if not to his twenty-five virgin wives [Bob, 2000].) He further claimed to have previously manifested as Zoroaster, Rama, Krishna, Buddha, Jesus and Muhammad.

> In response to questions about his spiritual identity, Baba tap-tapped things [on his letter-board] like "I am God in human form. Of course many people say they are God-incarnate, but they are hypocrites" (Manseau and Sharlet, 2004).

Baba further told an illustrative story of a guru who had ordered one of his disciples to kill the latter's own child. Having obediently complied and buried it according to instruction, the sage then told the same disciple to go home, where he would find the child alive, as he soon did.

"And they all lived happily ever after."

> Though an extreme example of the methods a Master may use in order to show his disciples the illusory nature of this phenomenal world, it illustrates the unquestioning faith which a disciple should have for his Master, and how utterly detached and obedient he is expected to be (Adriel, 1947).

That, then, is obviously the degree of obedience which Meher expected from his own followers, in order for them to be regarded as being "loyal" to him—as Adriel was, and presumably Anthony himself still is. (Yogananda told a similar "true story" in his *Autobiography,* regarding a man who threw himself off a Himalayan precipice at Babaji's command, to show his obedience. When subsequently brought back to life after passing that "test," he became one of Babaji's "immortal" band of disciples. As manipulative fairy tales go....) Indeed, the following absurd recommendation from Anthony (et al., 1987; italics added) would seem to support that proposal, regarding loyalty:

> The idea of a master having perfect consciousness is uncomfortable and unwelcome—and therefore not taken seriously —because the perfection implies total faith, surrender, and *obedience to the master, no matter what one is told to do.*

Indeed, as Baba himself (1967) explained:

> It is only possible to gain God-realization by the grace of a Perfect Master.

And such grace is gained, of course, only through unconditional obedience. (Note: Anthony [et al., 1987] *never actually met* Meher in the flesh, and is thus in a uniquely poor position to recommend surrender and total "obedience to the master." Rather than practicing such in-person subservience, he has simply had a few mystical experiences which he precariously takes to have been initiated by the deceased Baba. In such a situation, it would indeed be easy to have "total faith" that one has found a "Perfect Master."

Indeed, that perspective is fully comparable to Wilber's safe distance from Da and Cohen, and his equal recommendation that others surrender themselves to an "adventure" which he himself *has never had.)*

Meher Baba's teachings also included the instruction, "Don't worry. Be happy" (C. Welch, 1995). His ideas in general greatly influenced Townshend in writing his classic rock opera, "Tommy," about a child traumatized into being deaf, dumb and blind, and thereafter receiving his knowledge of the world only through (skin) sensations.

Ironically, Townshend himself went stone deaf within a decade of recording that album, after years of in-concert aural abuse. Along with Baba's silence, then, between the two of them they covered two-thirds of Tommy's disabilities.

If I was Roger Daltrey, I'd be having regular eye checkups. For, Baba's own healing abilities, even while alive, seem to have been markedly less impressive than he and his followers claimed them to be. Indeed, as Paul Brunton (1935) related:

> I have taken the trouble to investigate during my travels the few so-called miracles of healing which [Meher Baba] is alleged to have performed. One is a case of appendicitis, and the sufferer's simple faith in Meher is said to have completely cured him. But strict enquiry shows that the doctor who has attended this man could discover nothing worse than severe indigestion! In another case a nice old gentleman, who has been reported cured overnight of a whole catalog of ailments, seems to have had little more than a swollen ankle!

As further detailed by Brunton, Meher's numerous prophecies concerning upcoming calamitous events fared no more impressively, consistently failing to materialize on time.

Brunton then came to an understandable conclusion:

> Meher Baba, though a good man and one living an ascetic life, is unfortunately suffering from colossal delusions about his own greatness ... a fallible authority, a man subject to constantly changing moods, and an egotist who demands complete enslavement on the part of his brain-stupefied followers.

And what did Meher himself have to say about all of those concerns?

Not much:

> Baba, hailed as a Perfect Spiritual Master [of which there are supposedly exactly fifty-six present on Earth at all times, with the highest of them always being a man (Adriel, 1947)], had taken a vow of silence but he was supposed to reveal all and give his followers "the word" before his death. Unfortunately he died in 1969 before he could utter another sentence (C. Welch, 1995).

A mere half century after Brunton's reasonable conclusions regarding Meher Baba's veracity, Feuerstein (1992; italics added) opined:

> It became evident to *many* that his announcement [of the anticipated silence-breaking] had been meant symbolically, though *some* saw it as an indication that he had, after all, been duping everyone.

All things considered, then, good to be one of the "some" rather than the "many." Although one suspects that, overall, the "many" are probably *far less* in number than the "some."

In any case, it must be quite clear by now that if "idiot compassion" exists, in coddling people rather than judiciously telling them the painful truth for their own benefit, then so too does "idiot tolerance." The latter is indeed exemplified via insufferable apologetics for unrepentant (and not infrequently highly deluded) guru-figures and organizations of which little good can really be said. Further, what meager good can be legitimately claimed about them does not even begin to weigh against the bad. Thus, any "balanced" presentation would still look like an unbalanced one to anyone who had naïvely bought into the scrubbed, public face of the guru-figure or organization.

Those figures and groups invariably have well-oiled PR (or propaganda) departments which have fully succeeded in publicizing the good elements (both real and fabricated) of the spiritual teacher and his/her organization. It is only rarely, however, that the alleged *bad* aspects of each of those make their way into print, often against reported violent attempts at suppression or retribution.

* * *

Incredibly, most of the "enlightened" individuals and ashrams included herein would have been considered to fall close to the "safest" of the categories in the typologies of Dick Anthony (1987), et al., via the *Spiritual Choices* book. That is, nearly all of the spiritual teachers we have met thus far (not including the leaders of the Hare Krishnas, Moonies, or Jim Jones) were:

- Monistic rather than dualistic—i.e., working toward realizing a state of inherent conscious oneness with all things, as opposed to placing God as inexorably separate from creation and approachable only through a unique savior such as Jesus, with the failure to follow the appropriate savior leading to eternal damnation (exceptions: none)
- Multilevel—i.e., having a "distinct hierarchy of spiritual authority," in gnosis versus teachings versus interpretations (unilevel exceptions, which "confuse real and pseudo-transcendence of mundane consciousness," include Findhorn, Scientology, Rajneesh and TM [notwithstanding that the Maharishi's teachings themselves are rooted in the Vedas]), and
- Non-charismatic—i.e., emphasizing techniques of spiritual transformation (e.g., meditation), rather than relying on a personal relationship between disciple and teacher as the means of evolution/enlightenment of the former (exceptions: Ramakrishna, Meher Baba, Neem Karoli Baba, Adi Da, Muktananda, Ma Jaya Sati Bhagavati, Jetsunma, Cohen, and Sai Baba and Chinmoy to lesser degrees)

Trungpa, Satchidananda and Zen Buddhism were all explicitly placed in Anthony's "safest" category—of "multilevel, technical monism." In his second-safest grouping ("multilevel, charismatic monism") we find Meher Baba, Neem Karoli Baba, Muktananda, Chinmoy and Adi Da.

If those are "safe" spiritual leaders and communities, though, one shudders to think what "dangerous" ones might look like. One's jaw drops further to find that, as late as 2003, Wilber has still been recommending *Spiritual Choices* to others as a means of distinguishing "safe" groups from potentially "problematic" ones. That such recommendations are coming years after the central thesis (as documented above) of the text has been wholly discredited in practice, is astounding.

Fooled by the arguments of Anthony, et al., I myself had endorsed *Spiritual Choices* at one point in a previous work. Obviously, however, my opinion of that book and of its authors' ideas has matured significantly since then. Indeed, by this point I very much regret that previous naïvete on my part, particularly when it is coupled with ideas such as the following, from the same group of "experts":

> [Tom] Robbins and [Dick] Anthony's own contribution [to *In Gods We Trust* (1982)] includes a superb introduction—perhaps the best single chapter in the anthology; a complete and devastating critique of the brainwashing model; and an insightful report on the Meher Baba community (Wilber, 1983b).

The relevant meager, twelve-page, utterly simplistic chapter on brainwashing, however, is anything but a "complete" critique, much less a "devastating" one. Whatever one may think of the brainwashing and mind-control debate, how could a five-thousand word treatment of that complex subject possibly be "complete"? Entire books have been written from both sides of the controversy without exhausting it; entire Library of Congress Cataloguing in Publication designations exist for the subject! Even if the short paper in question were the greatest ever written, *it could not possibly be "complete"!*

For myself, I have found the chapter in question to be utterly unimpressive. Indeed, it shows near-zero understanding of the psychological factors influencing one's "voluntary joining," and later difficulty in leaving, such environments. There is nothing whatsoever "devastating" about the text, whether one agrees or disagrees with Anthony's overall perspective.

By stark contrast, for a genuinely *intelligent* and insightful discussion of the brainwashing and mind-control question, consult Chapters 2 and 3 of Michael Langone's (1995) anthology, *Recovery from Cults.* Chapter 13 of the same book offers many chilling examples of previously healthy persons suffering mental breakdowns as an alleged result of various, unspecified, large group awareness training sessions. Child abuse in so-called cults is covered disturbingly well in its Chapter 17.

For a revealing example of Anthony's own dismal attempts at critiquing other scholars' ideas, see Zablocki (2001).

* * *

Zimbardo, for one, had the common sense and compassion to remove the prisoners who weren't psychologically able to leave on their own, from his simulated prison. Religious apologists by contrast, in support of their insistence that brainwashing and mind control don't exist, would more likely simply leave the poor bastards there to suffer. After all, everyone in the ashram/prison entered that totalitarian environment voluntarily, and other people manage to leave on occasion, so what is the problem? Why interfere with that "nontraditional" society, where no one is being *physically* constrained to stay?

> In our view persons have a right to enter totalistic subcultures and have done so voluntarily for centuries (Robbins and Anthony, 1982).

Certainly, we each have the right to enter, and remain in, any subculture in which we wish to participate; that much is blindingly obvious. But it is not difficult to comprehend the dangers inherent in walking naïvely into environments where, if one has bought deeply into the teachings at any point, *it is not easy to leave*. There is thus at least an obligation to warn others as to what they may be getting themselves into, in voluntarily entering such contexts. To fight for the right to enter and "surrender completely" to one or another "holy fool," without in any way comprehending the difficulties involved in leaving, is beyond acceptable human ignorance. It is also absolutely guaranteed to create more pain than it could ever alleviate.

Robbins and Anthony (1982) then give their grossly oversimplified perspective on the constraints binding people into closed communities:

> The psychological and peer group pressures which are mobilized to inhibit leaving [so-called] cults should probably not be equated with armed guards and fences in their capacity to influence attitudes.

But: Tell that to Zimbardo's prisoner #819—the "bad" prisoner who refused to leave the study—for whom those pressures were indeed just as constraining, and *more* psychologically destructive, than any mere "armed guards and fences" could have been. Indeed, whether the constraints take the form of peer pressures, literal fences, or concern about "pursuing furies," they will all have the same effect. That is, they will all make it extremely difficult for one to leave such environments, even having entered them voluntarily to begin with.

> As I later tried to explain to people outside Scientology, I was like a two year old child. I was incapable of leaving home. They owned my soul. The ties binding me to the Org, though invisible, were more powerful than any physical bond could have been. I was in a trap *more powerful than any cage with iron bars and a lock.* Mentally I belonged to them (Wakefield, 1996; italics added).

> [Scientology founder L. Ron Hubbard] controlled our thoughts to such an extent that you couldn't think of leaving without thinking there was something wrong with you (Gerry Armstrong, in [Miller, 1987]).

Without having done in-depth research (particularly in the pre-Internet days), however, such poor souls had *no way of knowing* what they were getting themselves into. Thus, they suffer endlessly, for no greater sin than having "surrendered completely" to one or another "god" in a voluntarily entered totalitarian environment. Meanwhile, our world's unduly respected theoreticians congratulate themselves, and each other, on having composed "devastating critiques" which embody little reference indeed to the spectrum of relevant concerns.

One may further argue endlessly about what constitutes coercive "brainwashing" or relatively subtle "mind control," and whether any given community is guilty of either or both of those. The answer does not really matter here, simply because there are people trapped in every such environment who cannot, psychologically, "just leave," regardless of any "theories" which may say that they shouldn't be thus constrained. Zimbardo demonstrated that with a mere dozen previously healthy individuals *thirty years ago;* as did Wilber himself, inadvertently, at the low, suicidal point of his own second marriage.

One might further be tempted to disparage the intelligence, independence or emotional stability of #819 as a cause for his inability to leave the simulated prison. One would not likely cast the same aspersions on Wilber himself, however, in *his* "inability to leave" a marriage which he had voluntarily and enthusiastically entered, but which came to (at that low point) cause him nothing but distress.

One may well then be free to abandon those who cannot leave any environment, if one's superficial theories say that they *should* be able to leave, since "others are able to." One might even apply that callous idea to individuals ranging from trapped disciples to battered wives who entered their marriages "voluntarily." One is not equally free, however, to lay any claim to bodhisattva-like compassion, while uncaringly turning one's back on others who clearly cannot, in those circumstances, help themselves. Such a "survival of the fittest/rudest" approach, enforced in these contexts, is in no way worthy of the name "spiritual."

* * *

> [So-called cults] clearly differ from such purely authoritarian groups as the military ... and centuries-old Roman Catholic ... orders. These groups, though rigid and controlling, lack a double agenda and are not manipulative or leader-centered (Singer, 2003).

Regarding the military, though:

> [T]he military uses many components of mind control. [S]ome vets have [told me that] their recruiter lied to them [in a "double agenda"] (Hassan, 2000).

Or consider this, from one of Philip Zimbardo's (2004b) correspondents:

> I joined the United States Marine Corps, pursuing a childhood dream. [While there, I was] the victim of repeated illegal physical and mental abuse. An investigation showed I suffered more than forty unprovoked beatings....
>
> The point I am trying to make is that the manner in which your guards carried about their duties and the way that military drill instructors do is unbelievable. I was amazed at all the parallels.

> A body of social science evidence shows that when systematically practiced by state-sanctioned police, *military* or destructive [so-called] cults, mind control can induce false confessions, create converts who willingly torture or kill "invented enemies," engage indoctrinated members to work tirelessly, give up their money—and even their lives—for "the cause" (Zimbardo, 2002; italics added).

In any case, Zimbardo's simulated prison environment, too, had no hidden agenda, and was not leader-centered. (It was "manipulative" only to the degree required to enforce the desired level of obedience and respect from its prisoners—or from its "congregation"—each of whom had again voluntarily entered the study, being in no way deceptively recruited.) Yet, "toxic is as toxic does"—that is, the relevant *effects* on their members are no different, even if one can list a series of differences in the apparent *causes*.

Of course, even the most reportedly destructive group will have aspects which are not "cult-like"—particularly for members who are only participating "from a distance" on Sabbaths or Sunday mornings, not seven days a week. Those attributes can thus be used to argue/theorize that the groups in question are rather "respectable" and "mainline" ones, which might appear to match any definition for what a "cult" is only via "picking and choosing." Yet, a few good points will never outweigh multitudinous shortcomings in other regards.

Further, whether any of those communities are leader-centered or not is essentially irrelevant. For, one can be imprisoned by an infallible, unquestionable ideology—ascribed to relevant prophets and archaic "holy scriptures," which one cannot disobey without suffering severe consequences—just as easily as by an individual charismatic leader.

A prison or a high school or a heartless business corporation or a fundamentalist religious ministry or a frat house during pledging "Hell Week," or a bad marriage or an abusive family, is assuredly not a destructive, sadistic, brainwashing "cult," by any definition of the phrase.

But still ... one cannot help but notice that each of those environments can be highly intolerant of even minor disobedience to its authority-figures. Likewise, each may well offer no "exit clause" whereby one can "just leave" without suffering extreme social or financial penalties, should one be mistreated by one's peers and/or superiors.

> I saw that the structure of most families, businesses and governments were as committed to keeping their members in their places as my [so-called] cult [under Yogi Bhajan] ever had been (K. Khalsa, 1994).

Even in a free and democratic country under siege one can see precisely the same psychological dynamics. For, a populace rallying 'round the flag will treat even the mildest questioning of its leaders' abilities or motives as being near-treasonous—worthy of imprisonment or deportation, if not of literal excommunication. In doing so, they are behaving exactly like the members of any "cult" would, when confronted with even the most gentle suggestion that their "divine, infallible" leader may not actually be fit to lead, or in having the well-being of their "saved" or "best" group be threatened.

And, just as with "brainwashed cult members," such a populace, too, willingly surrenders its hard-won freedoms to even the most bumbling and dishonest authorities, in order to once again feel safe and saved from other "evil, persecuting" outsiders. And, just as a guru-figure and his followers may truly believe that the only reason they are being picked on is because their superior integrity, etc., makes others feel uncomfortable, presidents and entire countries will advance and believe the same foolish arguments. And, the quickest way for both spiritual and political leaders to detract from their own scandalous behaviors and associated attempts at controlling their followers' thoughts is to focus on the "war against Evil," which exists in full force only outside the borders of the community, and cannot be allowed inside ... or, if already inside, must be exterminated (e.g., via witch hunts or genocide).

The complication, of course, arises when the enemy is real, has indeed infiltrated the borders of the community, and is intent on destroying your freedoms and way of life. Such situations rarely arise in the spiritual world, where "Satan" is just a chimera; the political world, unfortunately, is not so simple and harmless.

* * *

The tortures which frat house pledges in particular will voluntarily undergo are further worth giving additional consideration to. For there, prospective house members have been known to willingly endure beatings, drink their own urine, and literally choke to death in attempting to swallow slabs of raw liver (Cialdini, 2001). All of that behavior, of course, is the product of absolutely no "mind control," deceptive recruiting, sleep deprivation or hypnotic chanting, etc. Rather, it is willingly embraced simply in order that one may become a member of an "in" group—"saved" from the "damnation" of being a social outcaste.

The corresponding social dynamic in the world of both nontraditional and traditional religion, with its associated unsaved "spiritual outcastes" is, in my opinion, *grossly* underrated.

Also, consider Solomon Asch's conformity experiments, again showing that, when faced with the choice between being liked versus being right or telling the truth, we frequently choose the former—i.e., on the average, around one-third of the time. That is, we will lie to others, and to ourselves, in order to fit in, to not look foolish, to avoid criticism, and/or for assuming that the group knows better than we do.

Now, simply couple that fact with the idea that if we tell ourselves a lie often enough, we will eventually believe it. (Even in Asch's study, there were subjects who genuinely believed that the obviously wrong, peer-pressured answers they had given in the group, were actually correct [M. Underwood, 2005].)

The question now, though, is not which of several lines is the same length as another. Rather, it is whether Guru X is the most enlightened being around. And the "confederates" vouching for that guru as being the "right answer" have been there longer than you have, and are thus more spiritually advanced than you are—only "ego" would question that, after all. Thus, they know better than you do.

So, in that environment, simply via the pressures of conformity, without any necessary techniques of "mind control" being applied: Who do you think Da Greatest Living Realizer is?

Controlled studies have further shown that the greater the amount of trouble or pain we have to go through in order to get something, the more we will value it later:

> Aronson and Mills [demonstrated] that the severity of an initiation ceremony significantly heightens the newcomer's *commitment* to the group (Cialdini, 2001; italics added).

And, of course, the more committed one is, the more difficult it will be to leave.

The experiences of Zen meditators sitting *zazen* in the lotus posture for hours on end, their knees burning and bodies aching—being hit with "the stick" should they even shift their positions—will unavoidably fall under the sway of exactly the same principle. For, those sitters are effectively "pledging" to be accepted as members of a fraternity of more enlightened, respected and admired individuals than themselves.

Whether there is, or has ever been, any calculation or malice on the part of the spiritual leaders in all that, is irrelevant here. For, the psychological effect is just as certain. That is, when one has gone through extreme pain and humiliation in order to get closer to enlightenment and be "one of the boys," one will thereafter encounter great psychological difficulty in leaving the community, or even in questioning whether "enlightenment" is anything of value.

Any effects of explicit "mind control" (in sleep deprivation, love-bombing, hypnotic induction, etc.) would only be on top of the "baseline" of conformity, and of the commitment (and ensuing difficulty in leaving) involved in "pledging enlightenment." And those baselines, arising from simple and unavoidable human psychology, are already enough to create environments which, were only a little theology to be thrown into the mix, one could hardly avoid calling religious "cults."

"Cult members," at least prior to joining their respective organizations, do not differ significantly in terms of their psychologies and associated mental stability as compared to their counterparts on the "outside," any more than Zimbardo's "Nazi" guards and docile prisoners differed prior to their incarceration. (Again, explicit and recognized psychological tests given prior to that imprisonment documented exactly that homogeneity.) Even more unsettling, however, the closed societies which are composed of those same members differ from our "safe, daily life" only in degree, not in kind.

Indeed, the fact that "problematic" groups partake of exactly the same psychological dynamics and social structures as does our "normal" world, just at a higher level of intensity, is precisely why previously healthy groups of people can degenerate into sadistic "cults" in less than a long weekend, even without a guru to push that devolution along.

So, as far as "spiritual choices" go, the safest thing, really, is to "Just say, 'No.'" Or, failing that, to ignore, as much as you possibly can, the advice of "experts" who search too ardently for reasons to "not worry" and "be happy" about our world's spiritual organizations.

For example:

> When questioned in 1988 [i.e., a full ten years after the Jonestown mass suicides] about the Jim Jones group, [J. Gordon] Melton said, "This wasn't a cult. This was a respectable, mainline Christian group" (Hassan, 2000).

When you are dealing with people—however warm-hearted, kind and considerate they may be in their private lives—with such professional views of reality as to insist that even Jonestown was not a "cult" ... oy vey.

Nor is there, unfortunately, any comfort to be taken in the relative absence of geographic isolation in North America or the like, as compared to Jones' Guyana. That is so, in spite of the claims of long-time "cult" observers such as the late Louis Jolyon West. For, in the immediate aftermath of the Jonestown suicides, Dr. West opined:

> This wouldn't have happened in California. But they lived in total alienation from the rest of the world in a jungle situation in a hostile country (in Cialdini, 2001).

In the years since Jonestown, however, the tragedies involving both David Koresh (in Waco, Texas) and the Heaven's Gate cult (San Diego) have occurred. Indeed, the latter 1997 suicides were enacted even more willingly than those of Jim Jones' followers had been. For, no gun-barrel threats of force at all were required on the part of the leaders of that UFO-related cult. Rather, the suicides were simply part of their members' sincere efforts to get to the "Next Level" of conscious evolution, in actions which *fully "made sense"* within the believed theology of that organization. That is, the Heaven's Gate followers simply did what they took to be necessary to ensure their own salvation—albeit after many years of waiting.

So, how badly do *you* want the form of salvation called "enlightenment"? Are you willing to do whatever it takes—to "face the heat" of Truth, regardless of how bad it may get? To have the crap beaten out of you? To have your ass roasted? To eat barbiturates in applesauce?

> [T]he line that separates religious enthusiasm from [so-called] cult zombiehood is narrower than we commonly pretend ... our own beliefs (or the beliefs of our friends) in angels, UFOs, ESP, Kennedy assassination conspiracies, you name it, differ from the elaborate sci-fi ideologies of groups like Heaven's Gate in degree, not in kind (Futrelle, 1997).

So, assuredly, it could "happen in California." It already has.

The heavily armed Rajneeshpuram could easily have violently and apocalyptically "happened" too—even without mass suicides—had it not been for its fortunate collapse following the guru's "brave retreat" out of the country. Plus, much of Charles Manson's mind-control programming of his own followers, in the late '60s, was effected at the machine-gun fortified Spahn Ranch, outside of Los Angeles (Krassner, 1993).

And all of that is sadly not surprising. For, the issue in all of these cases is the degree of isolation from outside ideas and perspectives, specifically from being able to see how others "like you" are behaving in the real world, to use that as a guide for your own thoughts and actions. And one can be thus isolated and obsessed by apocalyptic fears in the middle of a major city, or in a simulated basement prison at the center of a bustling university campus, just as surely as one can be so in the darkest jungle.

Note: Dick Anthony himself was present at an alternative spirituality-based seminar in the mid-'80s with both Zimbardo and Wilber, along with numerous other highly placed transpersonal psychologists. The footnoted indication of Zimbardo's attendance at that meeting, however—plus two inconsequential questions asked by him of an interviewee (Werner Erhard)—is the only mention of him in Anthony, Ecker and Wilber's (1987) *Spiritual Choices*. That is, not a word is spoken of Zimbardo's (or Milgram's) groundbreaking professional work, while the other contributors to that misled volume occupy themselves with the valiant struggle of determining how to distinguish "safe" guru-figures and organizations (such as Trungpa's and Muktananda's) from reportedly "problematic" ones. Nor, amazingly, have Zimbardo's classic observations even quietly made their way into the confident arguments given there, by people whose lives have been devoted to understanding those issues.

Sad. Very sad.

CHAPTER XXIX

AFTER THE ORDEAL

> I thought this ashram was going to show me the way. No more politics. Only philosophy and salvation. I should get so lucky. There's more politics in one Indian ashram than in the whole of the Western Hemisphere! (in Mehta, 1979).

> Ashrams are often the heaviest, most neurotic, political settings I've ever been in (Dass and Levine, 1977).

Dass himself, recall, was a clinical psychologist at Harvard; his categorization of others' behaviors as "neurotic" is thus an informed, not merely a colloquial, opinion.

> Ashrams, in my experience, are lunatic asylums filled with jealous and needy people.... [M]ost of the ashrams I have known and visited are *not* sacred environments where people progress; they're places in which people regress—to blind adoration, spiritual vanity, sibling rivalry, mirroring and parroting of the so-called master—and in my experience, I have to say, sadly, that I have seen very little real spiritual progress made in them (Harvey, 2000).

> My life was forever altered by my experience in a [so-called] religious cult. Not only did I abandon my passions in life, I spent fifteen years following someone else's path. When I finally awakened from my enchantment, I found myself with near-zero self-esteem, a lot of regret for many wasted years, and plenty of anger at my own naïvete, as well as being furious with my former group. I felt that a gigantic chunk of my real identity had been stolen from me without my conscious consent. At the same time, I felt a euphoric sense of freedom and complete delight that I now had my life back in my own hands (Goldhammer, 1996).

ONE MAY JOIN A SPIRITUAL ORGANIZATION for reasons ranging from the childish search for a substitute parent-figure to the mature hope of achieving liberation or enlightenment in this lifetime. And having thus joined, there is a comparable range of reasons to stay. In that regard, one former ashram resident informally estimated that 85% of monks and nuns he had met were there just for power, control or codependence trips, or for fear of the world. Or, for a feeling of belonging to something larger, and for enjoying the stardust falling on their robes. That is, for adulation in their positions as ashram "rock stars," a respect which they would not receive anywhere else in the world for any reason, much less for so little accomplishment as the color of the robe they are wearing. Or, they were there "just for laziness, for being trapped or were just too 'short' of brains to know any better." (If that estimate of 85% seems excessively harsh, consider that the Dalai Lama himself proposed an even less complimentary figure of 90%. My own independent estimate had been a mere 80%.)

Fond memories of past good times, in one's early "honeymoon" days with the guru-figure, can also play a role in keeping disciples living in the community (Strelley, 1987).

Other reasons for staying typically include financial constraints and atrophied "real world" skills. Indeed, the more that one's life has been positively changed in the very early stages of one's involvement with any spiritual organization, the more likely it is that one will have—*big mistake*—donated all of one's worldly goods to the "God-inspired" work. That noble if naïve commitment, however, makes it *much* harder to leave when the "love" wears off, and you begin to realize what you have gotten yourself into. And then, how to get out of it? For, in the best possible successful outcome, your most recent job reference is still, in the eyes of the business world, from a "cult."

> Doctors who had for years worked as carpenters, cooks, and laborers began [after Rajneeshpuram collapsed] with part-time work in emergency rooms or covering for other *sannyasin* physicians who had never come to live on the ranch. Architects worked as draftsmen and reporters as proofreaders and copy editors. Nurses who had been in charge of whole medical wards before they came to the ranch worked private duty or part time in clinics (Gordon, 1987).

Of course, there are also positive reasons for staying in the ashram environment, including the energies and love which the residents have felt to be emanating from the guru-figure—whether those energies are real or (far more likely) simply imagined. By contrast, however, weigh the following, where there were demonstrably no "divine energies" whatsoever flowing, yet the effect was substantially the same:

> The Beatles [were] such a hit that *Life* magazine showed a picture of people scraping up the earth and saying: "The Beatles walked here," as if these young musicians were Jesus Christ Himself (Radha, 1978).

Indeed, when the Fab Four toured North America, there were girls in the audience not merely fainting, but literally losing bladder control. None of that, though, was from any overwhelming, radiant energies which John, Paul or George—much less Ringo—were giving off, in spite of their best attempts at wearing their fame/divinity well:

> Who could think ill of boys who, smothering inner revulsion, were charming to the chain of handicapped unfortunates wheeled in by credulous minders deluded that a "laying-on of hands" by the four pop deities would bring about a cure? (Clayson, 1996).

And yet, suppose that George had been christened as "enlightened" by the Maharishi or the Hare Krishnas, or Elvis taken as an avatar by Daya Mata. (Presley actually "had messianic concepts of himself as the savior of mankind in the early 1970s" [Cloud,

2000].) One can then only imagine the profound *"darshan* energies" which their fans would have sworn, from their own experience, to be able to feel flowing from them. One can likewise easily picture the miraculous "coronas" and the like which The King might have manifested. (Even as it stands, Elvis believed that he could move clouds with the power of his thoughts, but that is another story. As one of his handlers noted, if you take enough drugs, you can see anything you want.)

Conversely, no small percentage of the disciples vouching for the divinity of their own guru-figures are the same group-thinking ones who can see coronas which aren't actually there, etc. Understood in that context, their testimonies as to the greatness of any guru-figure cannot be taken seriously. Yet, history and hagiography are filled to the bursting point with exactly such individuals.

The late Swami Radha, for one, again looked askance at the reverence displayed for the "mere mortals" constituting the Beatles. One suspects, however, that had the relevant ground been trodden upon by her own guru, the "miraculous god-man" Swami Sivananda Himself, she would have been among the first to devotedly scrape it up. Indeed, were she to have given that a miss, that irreverence would certainly have placed her in the minority among devoted spiritual seekers, and would in all likelihood have called her own loyalty to the guru into question.

> I watched as eager devotees grabbed at [Sai Baba's] footprints in the sand, joyfully throwing the holy sand on their hair, heads and children; and some, even eating it (Jack Scher, in [Warner, 1990]).

> When I attended my *Leaving Darshan,* I was given a small wooden box with something of Bhagwan [Rajneesh] in it—a hair, or nail clipping, I don't know what because you are supposed to never open it (in Palmer and Sharma, 1993).

> My mind was filled with joy to be able to eat some of Gurudev's [i.e., Nityananda's] leftover food. I would rub on my body particles of dust from where he had sat (Muktananda, 1978).

> [C]ommon forms of homage to one's guru include drinking the water with which his feet have been washed (Kripal, 1995).

> [A] discarded toilet seat from Jetsunma's house had been rescued and saved by her students as a relic (Sherrill, 2000).

Likewise, among the sacred objects offered in a recent auction of items which had been blessed by being touched by Adi Da was a used Q-tip "stained with Adi Da's precious earwax." Minimum bid: $108 (Elias, 2000). In a previous auction, a half-smoked cigarette butt reportedly sold for $800 (Elias, 2000a).

As Tarlo (1997) then finally noted:

> It was embarrassing to see these supposedly serious seekers behaving [around Andrew Cohen] like a bunch of rock-star fans.

Or conversely, as a woman once said to me at a David Bowie concert, with regard to the headliner: "This man is God." (Cf. "[Adi Da] is utterly God" [in Da, 1974; self-published].)

The psychology of the "believer," then, is obviously the same, whether the object touched by the "holy sage" is sand, a bowling ball or a toilet seat, and regardless of whether the sacred butt (on toilet or cigarette) in question belongs to Jetsunma, Adi Da or Ringo Starr.

For my own part, I would have more faith and trust in Sri Ringo.

* * *

Frances Vaughan (in Anthony, et al., 1987) gives the following set of questions, which potential new members of alternative religious movements are advised to consider before joining:

> Does the group keep secrets about its organization and the leader? How do members of the group respond to embarrassing questions?.... Do members display stereotypic behavior that emulates the leader?.... Are members free to leave?.... Does the group's public image misrepresent its true nature?

Reasonable questions, all. *But where to get an honest answer to them?* From the guru-figure? From his inner circle of disciples? From other loyal members of the group, anxious to have you join them? Surely it is obvious that any spiritual teacher or organization with things to hide would never tell the truth in response to those questions, instead giving the potential devotee the "right" answers which he/she wanted to hear in the first place. And is it not obvious that *all* organizations and leaders keep secrets from the public?

> Does the Vatican have secrets? Yes, as every government, corporation, NGO [i.e., non-governmental organization], and other institution does (Allen, 2004).

Is it not equally obvious that all groups (even secular ones) have "pod people" members who mimic their leaders? (Even physicist J. Robert Oppenheimer's graduate students used to unconsciously imitate his manner of smoking cigarettes. Oppenheimer, for his own group-thinking part, dismissed David Bohm's work as "juvenile deviationism," going so far as to suggest that "if we cannot disprove Bohm, then we must agree to ignore him" [Peat, 1997].) And obvious, too, that you're always "free to leave," even if being "pursued by disasters" to "drown in the dark sea of ignorance" afterwards ... and that the public image *never* properly represents the true nature of the spiritual teacher or community?

Were common sense to play a greater role, one might instead do the obvious, in evaluating any particular guru-figure: simply talk to former disciples who have split from the "master," and ask them why they left! That latter approach, indeed, is the *only* way (short of published exposés) to accurately gauge the character of the guru-figure and community.

> The best way to learn about a specific group is to locate a former member, or at least a former member's written account (Hassan, 1990).

Minimal thought applied to that subject would further disclose that the amount of perceived validity and "divine love" in the sage being evaluated at the beginning of the disciple's involvement or "testing period" has little relation to his or her real character. Indeed, such differential would be far greater than the difference in the degree of "perfection" seen in a potential romantic mate on a first date, say, versus after a decade of marriage.

You would not, unless you are a complete cad, hire a private investigator to quietly uncover dirt on a prospective mate, when falling in love with her or him. Neither could you objectively ask (or even covertly research) the intrusive questions suggested above by Vaughan of any "holy sage" and his or her organization, when you are already "falling in love" with them.

And then, where those two ideas cross:

> [Paulette Cooper] had in front of her pages of detailed reports from another [alleged] cult operative.... He had, for a short while, been very close to her, and pretended to be in love with her....
>
> The secret agent told his superiors that on the outside he was sympathetic [to her troubles] but inside he was laughing: "Wouldn't [Cooper's depressed talk of suicide] be a great thing for Scientology?" (Marshall, 1980).

As to Vaughan's suggested questions above, then: Even if you did ask them, you would truly have to be born yesterday to think that you would ever get an open and honest answer.

* * *

Jack Kornfield, years ago, penned a landmark exposé for *Yoga Journal*. There, he presented the results of his own research, disclosing that thirty-four of the fifty-three American yoga teachers whom he surveyed (64%) had had sex with their students. Those indulgences encompassed preferences ranging from heterosexual, bisexual, homosexual, fetishist, exhibitionist and monogamist, to polygamist.

How to react to that? As both the people at Kripalu and the Dalai Lama figured out for themselves through simple common sense, the proper response to father-figure gurus and teachers who reportedly cannot keep their hands off their disciples in spiritual incest is quite simple. That is, one must criticize them openly and, if they will not change, pack one's bags and leave.

Or, even better, wisely send the *teacher* packing.

Yet, just when we may be thinking that we have finally found a guru-figure, in the Dalai Lama, who can actually see things even halfway clearly ... well, we find the same man musing aloud that it may indeed be possible for great yogis such as Drukpa Kunley to sleep with other men's wives only *for their (wives') benefit*.

> Smiling slightly, His Holiness explained that Drukpa Kunley could understand the long-term effects of his actions because he had attained the nondual insight known as "One Taste." All experiences were the same to him: He could enjoy [eat-

> ing] excrement and urine just like the finest food and wine (Wheeler, 1994).

Ken Wilber himself, however, has again attained to the One Taste state of which the Dalai Lama speaks so highly, thus allegedly being able to "understand the long-term effects of his actions," e.g., in endorsing Adi Da and Andrew Cohen. (No word on Wilber's preferences of fine wine versus urine, etc.) Those endorsements, however, plus his continuing, insult-filled misrepresentations of David Bohm's brilliant work, absolutely prove that "choiceless awareness" cannot be a valid basis for one's allegedly "always behaving appropriately in every situation." Note also that even the Dalai Lama is thus guilty of romanticizing the spiritual accomplishments of persons whom he regards as being greater than himself. Indeed, he is probably doing that to a comparable degree as his own spiritual state is undoubtedly overestimated by his most loyal followers.

Further regarding Kunley himself:

> There is little doubt that Drukpa Kunley would have broken the incest taboo if he had thought that this might serve his mother's spiritual growth (Feuerstein, 1992).

> Drukpa Kunley ... when asked by a follower, Apa Gaypo, for a prayer to strengthen his religious resolve, answered:
>
> > Drukpa Kunley's penis head may stick,
> > Stick in a small vagina,
> > But tightness depends upon the size of the penis.
> > Apa Gaypo's urge to gain Buddhahood is strong,
> > So strong,
> > But the scale of his achievement depends upon the
> > strength of his devotion (French, 2003).

As prayers go, it's certainly one of the more interesting....

Kunley's exploits included claims of his having slept with five thousand women—but evidently no men—"for their spiritual benefit." So here we have someone who ostensibly drew no distinctions between excrement and urine, versus "the finest food and wine." That is, he potentially enjoyed both sets equally, for experiencing everything—including his own thoughts, sensations and emotions—as having the same "One Taste." In other words, he "experienced" them with no division between subject and object, and no recoiling from psychological engagement in those various psychic relationships. And yet, like the strictly heterosexual Wilber, he obviously still distinguished between men and women as sexual partners, only indulging in the female of the species in that regard.

Very fishy, that—to allegedly not distinguish between one's culinary enjoyment of filth versus appropriate foods, but to still be bound by largely learned/cultural sexual preferences.

Feuerstein gives many additional "fairy tales" of the violent "crazy wisdom" exploits of Kunley and others. None of those mythic stories could possibly be literally true. Yet, all of them have undoubtedly been used, at one time or another, to excuse the behaviors of foolish individuals masquerading as sages, both past and present.

Consider:

> [Adi Da] likes to compare his work to the crazy-wise teachings of some of the great adepts of the East. In particular, he once remarked, "I am Drukpa Kunley.... This is exactly what I am in your time and place" (Feuerstein, 1996).

* * *

> Traditionally, in Asia, vows and moral precepts have protected teachers and students from sexual and other forms of misconduct. In Japan, Tibet, India and Thailand, the precepts against harm by stealing, lying, sexual misconduct, or abuse of intoxicants are understood and followed by all members of the religious community....
>
> In modern America these rules are often dispensed with, and neither TV preachers nor Eastern spiritual teachers have clear rules of behavior regarding money, power and sex (Kornfield, 1993).

Yet as we have seen, contrary to the romantic belief that things are different in Asia: In Japan, local girls throw rocks over the monastery walls, receiving ready responses to those "calling cards." (Such enticement, though, is hardly needed, given the documented propensity of monks there to sneak out over the walls even without solicitation.) In Tibet, while masturbation and oral sex are taboo, whores are okay as long as you pay for their services yourself. In Thailand, with a population that is 95% Buddhist, monks get their names in the papers for having been caught with pornography, sexual paraphernalia, and more than one woman at a time. And that publicity is even independent of their Rajneesh-like collections of vintage cars, some of which were obtained via the misuse of temple funds. (Ironically, Kornfield himself practiced meditation "in the remote jungles of Thailand" under the guru Ajahn Chah in the early '70s [Schwartz, 1996]. Perhaps the jungles there are simply not "where the action is," but in any case, the idea that precepts are in general followed there or elsewhere in the East "by all members of the religious community" in no way matches the facts, as we have repeatedly seen. For more of the same purely wishful thinking regarding "Eastern gurus," see Andrew Harvey's [2000] conversation with Ken Wilber.)

And things could be different in contemporary India, building upon the constraints "obeyed" by Ramakrishna and the like? Sadly, no:

> That little seven year old is a real Lolita. She's the best lay in the ashram (in Mehta, 1979).

Or, as one five-year-old boy in Rajneesh's Poona center complained: "Fuck, fuck, fuck, all we ever do is fuck!"

At least one "older and wiser" six-year-old girl in the same community, however, saw things from a more adult perspective; for she

> delighted in grabbing men's genitals through their robes. Another offered to suck the penis of every man she saw in the public showers (Franklin, 1992).

Of course, that situation did not improve upon Rajneesh's messianic move to America, where one could easily find three-year-old girls sobbing their hearts out to their mothers:

> None of the boys will fuck me!.... It's not fair! Just because I wear diapers they won't fuck me. They said I'm a baby! (in Franklin, 1992).

To that, the mother's patient response was simply an encouragement to her child to stop wetting herself at night, at which point she would not have to wear diapers anymore.

With the additional penchant of early-teenage girls in Rajneesh's America for sleeping with men twice their age, Franklin went on to note:

> Scores of ranch swamis would have been considered child molesters out in the world.

Consider also the relevant problem of Tibetan lamas taking private female consorts in spite of their public vows of celibacy—reported by June Campbell on the basis of her own experience as such a consort to a universally revered lama. That rule-breaking was never lessened by tradition, hierarchy or lineage:

> [W]hile a lama would, to all intents and purposes, be viewed publicly as a celibate monk, in reality he was *frequently* sexually active, but his activities were highly secret (Campbell, 1996; italics added).

Further, note again that Chögyam Trungpa's teachings and behaviors, for one, were verified as authentic not merely by the (disillusioned, late) student Butterfield but *by the head of his own Nyingma School.* Indeed, by that verification, his behaviors were exactly in accord with that 1800-year-old tradition, dating back to Milarepa. Given that endorsement, it was obviously for *working within* the alleged "checks and balances" of his tradition, not for being freed of them when emigrating to the West, that Trungpa had people publicly stripped and humiliated. From the same "obedient following" of selected traditional rules—i.e., of only the ones which they felt like obeying, without meaningful censure for violating others—his successor again infected his disciples with AIDS, criminally believing that God would protect them.

Likewise, consider the reported non-effect on Trungpa when the Sixteenth Karmapa came to America in 1974:

> It had been six years since His Holiness and Chögyam Trungpa Rinpoche had last seen each other, and the Karmapa had doubtless heard lots of stories, some true, some exaggerated, about how this former monk had immersed himself in the Western world. But now as they met His Holiness smiled broadly, and it was clear that everything was all right (Fields, 1992).

Additional research, though, discloses that the same Karmapa actually later "non-recognized" Trungpa. Further, the Dalai Lama, too, pointedly canceled a scheduled visit to Trungpa's community from his itinerary during his first, historic tour of America in the 1970s (Clark, 1980). Part of the motivation for that cancellation no doubt arose from the suggestion, by an officer in Trungpa's paranoid, submachine-gun toting organization, that (in all seriousness) the Dalai Lama was conspiring to assassinate the Karmapa.

Neither of those quiet lamaic signs of disapproval, of course, did anything to keep Trungpa in check from making additional "mistakes." But it is still a little bit comforting to know that those two lamas at least had some sense left in them. For, one can easily contrast even that ridiculously mild censure with others who have touted Trungpa's teachings and *sangha* as being the first foray of "authentic Tibetan Buddhism" into America (Bharati, 1974).

Acharya Reginald Ray is another of Chögyam Trungpa's contemporary followers. He is thus undoubtedly familiar with the details of his "principal teacher's" life. He therefore had this to say regarding the effect of traditional "checks and balances" on the behaviors of gurus and their ilk:

> In Tibet, even the *tulkus*—these very well-trained people—were surrounded by people who were watching them all the time. Even the ordinary village people knew what was appropriate behavior and what wasn't. If a guy went off, he'd be nailed (in Caplan, 2001).

Yet, in spite of such claimed watchfulness and the supposed punishment for "going off" vouched for by Ray, Trungpa managed to sleep with women "since he was thirteen," actually getting one pregnant before having left Tibet, while still under a vow of celibacy. He further obviously suffered no discipline in response to that, from "ordinary village people" or otherwise, sufficient to get him to stop that blatantly "inappropriate behavior." In short, in no way did he get "nailed" for that.

One wishes, truly, that there was a visible correlation between the documented realities of situations like that, and the distortions which are presented to the Western public as factual by respected, life-long "experts."

> While I do not know what people mean when they claim that everyone is entitled to his own opinion, I do know that no one has a right to be wrong in his facts (Askenasy, 1978).

It was, further, not merely Trungpa himself who was transplanted into the West. More importantly, the closed communities, feudal/hierarchical power structures and "infallibility of the guru" teachings of his ancient Tibetan tradition formed the basis for his own little spiritual "kingdom" in Boulder (Marin, 1995). And it is *those* structures, not any excessive partying *per se,* which create the "superintendent/guard/prisoner" environment which ruins people's lives just as much in *non*-"crazy wisdom" surroundings as it does in "uncontrolled" contexts such as Chögyam's.

It is true that Trungpa (1981), for one, gave at least lip service to encouraging "an attitude of constant questioning, rather than ignoring our intelligence." Butterfield's descriptions of the interview process undergone during his own admission as a student, however, show that one could not become a member of Trungpa's community without buying into the full set of ridiculous superstitions. Consider also Merwin's fate, when he attempted to question rather than going blindly along with the dictates of the guru and his group-thinking community. It is issues like these, not half-baked, pulled-out-of-thin-air theory, which matter in evaluating the potential for harm present in any "true *sangha.*"

Note further that, by Feuerstein's own testimony, Drukpa Kunley's sexual exploits "did fly in the face of custom and propriety." That is, his "crazy wisdom" behaviors *were not constrained* by the agrarian society in which he lived.

Obviously, then, after all that, neither social nor cultural nor psychological-development variations can account for the "difference" between guru-disciple relationships as practiced in the East versus the West. Rather, when it comes to the demand for blind obedience, and to the reported abuse of sex and power, the problems and alleged abuses exist, *and have always existed,* just as surely "on the other side of the pond" as they do in North America. (Cf. Ramakrishna, and the history of Zen and of lama-sexing, child-torturing Tibetan Buddhism.)

Persons looking to account for a non-existent difference between East and West in all this further generally ignore the natural effect of the passage of time on the involved individuals. Someone like Trungpa was going to become increasingly self-destructive as the years went by regardless, for his childhood pains and otherwise. It was his own psychology, not "the West," which gave him license to drink himself into an early grave.

Further, being worshiped by one's disciples as a "god" for years on end would go to one's head in the East just as much as in the West. It would also predictably result in an increasing feeling that one could get away with anything, regardless of whether or not the surrounding society and culture had become more liberal at the same time.

If one goes from the East to the West, then, being worshiped equally in both as time goes by, one's increasing disregard for moral rules in that *later* West can in no way be reduced to a simple surrounding cultural or social matrix phenomenon. Rather, the bulk of that can be accounted for simply on the basis of the aforementioned grandiose inflation, fuelled by the willing obedience and obeisance of one's close, devoted followers.

Put more bluntly: Although power corrupts, it also takes *time* to thus corrupt. If other things are changing simultaneously with that passage of time, it may be easy to mistake them for the cause of the corruption. For nearly every guru-figure one could name, however, there was a time early in his (or her) life when he could have been regarded as exhibiting "impeccable integrity"; a later time when he allegedly began breaking rules which hurt others; and a yet later time when he had hurt so many people that his alleged sins began to find him out. Some such figures lived their entire lives in the West, some came to the West from the East, and some spent their entire lives in the agrarian East. For the latter, nothing of the "unconstrained" West can be regarded as the cause of their reported misdeeds; and yet the alleged corruption in the claimed misuse of power and sexuality happened all the same.

Likewise, regarding "tradition": Aside from Rajneesh, Sai Baba, the Caddys, Aurobindo, Ramana Maharshi, Ananda Moyi Ma and Ammachi (whom we shall soon meet)—plus L. Ron Hubbard and Werner Erhard—every other spiritual leader we have considered herein came from within a recognized teaching lineage. (Aurobindo might even claim Vivekananda as a teacher.) Yet, that has clearly done nothing to keep them in check, or even to ensure/test that they were anywhere near as enlightened as they claimed to be.

> Sex between clergymen and boys is by no means a uniquely Catholic phenomenon ... it's been going on in Buddhist monasteries in Asia for centuries.
>
> "Of course, this is against the Buddhist canon," [Dr.] Leonard Zwilling [said] "but it has been common in Tibet, China, Japan and elsewhere.
>
> "In fact, when the Jesuits arrived in China and Japan in the 16th century, they were horrified by the formalized relationships between Buddhist monks and novices who were still children" (Siemon-Netto, 2002).

* * *

After all that, it is almost a relief to find an actual instance of Eastern rules being "followed by all members of the religious community," as Kornfield and others claim:

> The real temptation many men face when they come here [to a Thai Buddhist forest monastery] is masturbation. You are not supposed to do it. Once you have been ordained, if you break this precept you must come and confess it to the senior monk. It's worse if you are a *bhikkhu* [monk]. Then a meeting of the *sangha* is required and penance must be handed down. The guilty monk has to sit at the end of the food line. For seven days no one can do anything for him. It's really embarrassing. I remember one fairly senior monk had a serious problem with this. Whenever the villagers came in to bring us food in the morning, they would see him sitting at the bottom of the line and laugh (Ward, 1998).

It is one thing for monasteries to focus on humiliating their residents for such a trivial activity—which surely affects, for harm or good, no one but the individual practitioners in the privacy of their own bedrooms, and should hardly merit *a meeting of the entire community to discuss it.* It is quite another, however, for them (or their "big city" counterparts) to overlook or attempt to cover up embezzlement, the use of prostitutes, and the indulgence in necrophilia and karaoke, etc., on the part of their other residents. Indeed, the situation is no different, in that regard, than one finds with the horrendous betrayals of trust reported within the Catholic Church, worldwide. Such major alleged abuses are then left to be brought out by muck-raking journalists whose conscience has evidently not yet been completely dulled by blind adherence to a set of archaic precepts.

One further cannot help but note that Buddhism has surpassed even the Catholic Church, here, in terms of the need for confession (to one's superiors) and humiliating *public* penance, for even ridiculously minor "sins." And that Church is by no means an easy one to surpass, in terms of guilt and ignorance:

> Even today, the official teaching of the Roman Catholic Church holds masturbation to be a mortal sin [i.e., one "punishable by eternal damnation, unless one repented in confession"], though few serious theologians consider it a cause for the loss of heaven (Berry and Renner, 2004).

* * *

Interestingly, had Rajneesh and his inner circle of followers not gone over a line with their public bioterrorism activities, etc., his ashrams would still be viewed today as fine models of how spiritual communities should be run—as J. Donald Walters' Ananda was, for example, prior to his own disgrace. That is in spite of the fact that, as early as 1979, the National Institute of Mental Health had been warned that Rajneesh's Poona ashram might become "another Jonestown" (Gordon, 1987). (Likewise, the San Francisco Zen Center had "long [been] thought of as the very model of a modern Zen center," prior to the "Apocalypse" following from the public airing of Richard Baker's hitherto-private reported activities there [Fields, 1992].)

> Until Rajneesh spoke publicly, the only charges pending against him or anyone else on the ranch were related to immigration fraud. If he hadn't exposed Sheela's wrongdoings, the authorities would probably never have found informants to testify, let alone obtained convictions on wiretapping, poisoning, and arson. And if Rajneesh hadn't tried to flee the country, both he and his commune would in all likelihood still have been in Oregon (Gordon, 1987).

The composition of that same ex-ashram is of significant interest:

> According to the Oregon University survey, 11% of the [Rajneeshpuram] commune members had postgraduate degrees

> in psychology or psychiatry and another 11% had B.A.'s in the field (Fitzgerald, 1986).

Thus, nearly one-quarter of the residents at Rajneeshpuram were trained psychologists. That documented fact does nothing to increase one's confidence in the ability of the profession to spot openly pathological behavior in contexts where its members have a vested interest. For, while most members of the Rajneesh community were not aware of the more grossly illegal activities going on there until after the fact, Sheela's own "duchy" included suppression of any "negativity." In her world, further, even constructive criticism qualified as that, and was punished accordingly. Of course, all that one gets out of that, other than an enforced obedience, is a superficially "happy" community of people—as in the Maharishi's ideal society—reminding one too much of the Python sketch involving an unhappy man sentenced to hang by the neck (or meditate) "until he cheers up."

The sociological studies of safely distant, academic "Rajneesh watchers," etc., would fall into the same category of deep concern. Indeed, for such scholars, publishers of exposés, by Milne for example, have been deemed worthy of denigration as "schlockmeisters" (cf. Palmer and Sharma, 1993).

Nor were Bhagwan's *sannyasin* psychologists merely at the bottom of the barrel in their professional abilities or standing:

> The "Hollywood crew" [included] the best-known therapists in town—all of them had taken *sannyas* (Strelley, 1987).

Rajneesh, interestingly, was actually regarded as "the intellectual's guru": "[T]he educational level of the followers of Rajneesh was far greater than most of the rest of the population" (Oakes, 1997).

> An astounding number of therapists and leaders of the human potential movement are current or former disciples of Bhagwan's, although few, if any of them, publicly acknowledge it (Franklin, 1992).

> Many of these therapists had the sense, before they came to Poona, that Rajneesh was at least a master therapist, that his work might represent the next step in the evolution of psychotherapy (Gordon, 1987).

Those, of course, are the same people who decide, through the peer review process and as a "community of competent, intersubjective interpreters," what constitutes truth within humanistic psychology. The same peer-adjudication of truth naturally occurs within consciousness studies in general, influenced by Wilber and his colleagues, for example.

Interestingly, from the early '70s until the collapse of his empire and IRS-inspired flight into Mexico in 1991, Werner Erhard reigned as the "guru of the human potential movement." Indeed, even in Anthony, Ecker and Wilber's near-worthless (1987) *Spiritual Choices,* the interview questions (led by John Welwood) put to Erhard centered only on whether est training granted an "enlightenment" comparable to that purportedly realized through traditional spiritual disciplines. That is, there was not even the slightest whisper of any concern expressed regarding its safety, in spite of those authors' own later characterization of the interview as being "spirited." (The interview itself was conducted in 1981—half a dozen years after Brewer's [1975] exposé of the alleged negative effects reportedly experienced by various est participants.)

Wilber has, in the past, sat on the Board of Editors of *The Journal of Transpersonal Psychology,* as have Ram Dass, Dr. Herbert V. Guenther, Ph.D., and "the best stripper in town," Chögyam Trungpa. Current members of that board include Michael Murphy, who again *genuinely believes* (1992) that Ramakrishna's spine lengthened during his Hanuman *sadhana.*

Murphy is "the leading integral theorist of his generation," according to Wilber's Integral Naked (2005) website.

Also on the JTP board is one Mr. Paul Clemens, whose Blue Dolphin publishing company catalog contains books by authors who can (they believe) literally hear God and Jesus speaking to them, and literally converse with leprechauns—the latter existing, fractal-like, in the "third-and-a-half dimension." None of those are financially lucrative best-sellers, which could then perhaps have been excused as being published only for their dollar value.

Note further: The above book on leprechauns, by the imaginative Tanis Helliwell, was actually endorsed by Jean Houston, the former *president* of the Association of Humanistic Psychology. Indeed, she there credited Helliwell with being a "deep seer."

Houston (1997) has, at other times, functioned as a non-guru to the White House:

> For almost a year and a half, I had served as a kind of intellectual sparring partner for First Lady Hillary Rodham Clinton, helping her focus ideas for the book she was writing.
>
> A report that the First Lady and I had engaged in an imaginative exercise in which we reflected on what Eleanor Roosevelt might have said about building a better society for our children sent the media scurrying for colorful copy. "Séance!" the front pages of the newspapers shouted. "Witchcraft!" And even that most dreaded of all epithets, "Guru!"
>
> Needless to say, the distortions both embarrassed Mrs. Clinton and played havoc with my life and career. Virtually every newspaper and news magazine in the world carried the stories, the facts hugely distorted, and liberally dosed with snickering asides by reporters who never bothered to find out anything about me or my work.
>
> As a result of this public ridicule, I found my reputation for thirty years of good work in the service of human betterment strained so badly that lectures were canceled by nervous sponsors and research grants were withdrawn. I felt that I had gone overnight from being regarded as a respected pioneer on the frontier of human capacities research to a laughable representative of the flaky fringe....
>
> What was it that turned the evening news into an Inquisition?
>
> I suspect that the answer lies in two great phobias—fear of the rising power of women and fear of the power of imagination and inner realities.

A "laughable representative of the flaky fringe" ... as opposed to being a "respected pioneer" in the field of humanistic psychology. There is, of course, no meaningful difference between the two categories.

Autobiographical claims on the part of Houston include supposed childhood friendships with both Albert Einstein and Teilhard de Chardin, and a status as Margaret Mead's adopted daughter. (Mead also served as the President of the Board of Directors of the Foundation for Mind Research [Houston, 1982].)

> As Advisor to UNICEF in human and cultural development, [Jean] has worked to implement some of their extensive educational and health programs, primarily in Myanmar [Burma] and Bangladesh (Houston, 2006).

Houston's own (1982) teachings have included the following wisdom:

> I have been known to begin seminars by asking people to tell each other three outrageous lies! The resistance that some people experience to such a suggestion may be indicative of the extremely literal mind-set that results from an acculturation that worships "the fact" and logical proof.

Houston's husband, Robert Masters, by his own "About the Author" testimony, is a "leading pioneer of modern consciousness research," "one of the founders of the Human Potentials Movement" ... and former director of the Library of Sex Research. Much of his "Work" (always capitalized) in the non-library regard has centered around Sekhmet, an Egyptian goddess possessing the head of a lioness and the body of a woman—ostensible a "Gateway to alien realms" of consciousness via the raising of the kundalini energy. The worldview within which Masters' (1991) Egyptian metaphysics functions includes the following ideas:

> The "Gods" of Chaos ordinarily "ascend" only to the realm of the KHU [the "fourth most subtle of the Five Bodies," cf. auras], when a "black magic" is practiced. However, some of the most potent sometimes invade the SÂHU [the "highest" of the Five Bodies] so that even the holiest of men or women is not secure from them. Also, the most powerful of black magicians can work with Metaeidolons representing the Ur-Gods of Chaos at this level, thus effecting the most potent evil.

Later in the same book, Masters expounds further on his view of reality:

> You can learn to extract from another body a [cf. astral] Double of that body and interact with it. In fact, this is what, at the lowest level of psychic development, a psychic does, whether for healing, for defense against psychic attack, or in an unscrupulous way to attack by psychic means.

In 1972, John Lennon blurbed for Masters and Houston's *Mind Games,* saying:

> I have read three important and revolutionary books in the last three years: Yoko Ono's *Grapefruit*, Arthur Janov's *Pri-*

mal Scream, and now *Mind Games.* I suggest you read and experience them.

The book itself is simply a series of exercises, done in groups, for entering altered states of consciousness. It does, however, aim for the creation of a "Group Spirit" by "a version of a method known and practiced for thousands of years in Tibet, where such entities are known as thought-forms, or *tulpas.*"

What caliber of thought, then, would you expect from a group of people among whom Houston is one of the level-headed, understated, thoughtful ones? What would you expect the lesser lights of the "profession" to look like? Would it surprise you to find that they seem to genuinely believe that the voices they hear, and the elfish beings they see, are real?

You may start out taking transpersonal/integral/parapsychological claims seriously, as David Lane, John Horgan, Susan Blackmore and I once did. And there is nothing so very wrong with that, up to a point. For, each one of us, at one stage or another in our lives, has committed to mistaken ideals and perspectives simply for not knowing any better, and for believing far too much of what we were told by people whom we trusted to have done at least minimally satisfactory research and vetting of their own beliefs and purported abilities. With regard to transpersonal, integral and parapsychological claims, however, if you simply keep reading and thinking widely, beyond the field itself, the transition from believer to skeptic is *unavoidable.*

Conversely, to exist for decades in those fields as a member in good standing is a sure sign that one is relying more on the part of one's brain that is responsible for mere wishful thinking, than on the section which is to credit for coherent, rational analysis.

Speaking of which: Dr. Roger Walsh is another respected member of the JTP board. He is also on the Board of Editors of the *Journal of Consciousness Studies.* Plus, he is another founding member of the Integral Institute, who has compared Wilber's (1995) *Sex, Ecology, Spirituality* to Hegel's work in its scope. Walsh has recently stated, with an absurd degree of exaggeration:

> Ken Wilber is one of the greatest philosophers of this century and arguably the greatest theoretical psychologist of all time (IntegralNaked, 2004).

Walsh actually teaches philosophy (among sundry other subjects) at the University of California at Irvine, and might therefore claim some measure of informed expertise in voicing the above opinion. Still, such puffery surely reminds one far too much of Wilber's own pontifications as to whom he imagines the top shabd yogis, Realizers, or "strongest dinosaurs" to be.

Frances Vaughan, incidentally, is Roger Walsh's wife. Both are close friends of Ken Wilber—and founding members of the Integral Institute—to the point of having introduced him to his second wife. Together, Walsh and Vaughan (1988) edited a book of selections from Helen Schucman's *A Course in Miracles* (ACIM)—attempted pithy sermons which were purportedly channeled from Lord Jesus Christ in 1965.

Wilber, interestingly, had this to say (in Klimo, 1998) about the *Course:*

> I'm not saying that there was not some transcendental insight involved and that Helen probably felt that it was certainly beyond her day-to-day self. *I think that's true* [italics added]. But there's much more of Helen in the *Course* than I first thought.... It's not all pure information, there's a lot of noise that gets in. I also found that if you look at Helen's own poetry, you're initially very hard pressed to find any difference between that and the *Course*.

Yes indeed. And, *why might that "non-difference" be?* The answer is obvious to anyone who isn't desperately trying to find spirituality and paranormality in what can much more reasonably be viewed as simply one woman's overactive imagination and inability to distinguish reality from her own fantasies.

Or do *you* believe that Jesus Christ spoke directly to Helen Schuchman in the mid-'60s, dictating over a thousand pages of garden-variety New Age musings to her?

Regardless, anyone who was actually impressed with ACIM to the point of compiling a "best of" from it that makes Andrew Cohen's books look wise and insightful by comparison, should think more than twice before considering himself to be in a position to rank the world's great philosophers. That applies, I think, even if the person in question is a *peer reviewer* amongst a field of comparably fine "scholars."

The same compiled book was endorsed as "marvelous ... inspired and profound" by Willis Harman, former president of the

Institute of Noetic Sciences. In a similar vein, Walsh and Vaughan's (1993) anthology, *Paths Beyond Ego,* has a foreword written by John E. Mack, M.D.—Harvard's now-late, laughably credulous alien abduction expert (Carroll, 2004). As if to close the circle, the foreword for Walsh's (1999) *Essential Spirituality* was written by the Dalai Lama, and is dedicated to Judith Skutch Whitson—president of the Foundation for Inner Peace, publisher of *A Course in Miracles.*

Of that same uninspiring book, Ken Wilber blurbed: "The field of spiritual books has been looking for its own Lewis Thomas or Carl Sagan, and I believe Roger Walsh may be that one." Sagan, however, was not merely a cogent popularizer of serious science, but also one of the world's more prominent skeptics, who would not for a moment have taken ACIM seriously. Any "Carl Sagan of spirituality" would be one who would keep asking pointed questions and demanding properly conducted research ... at which point even the most hitherto-certain claims of the transpersonal/integral field crumble rapidly into a pile of fairy dust.

As to the psychological profession in general, Storr (1996) has demonstrated that both Freud and Jung created personality cults —initially populated by many other respected psychological professionals—around themselves:

> Freud's dogmatism and intolerance of disagreement led to the departure of many colleagues, including Adler, Stekel, Jung, and eventually Rank and Ferenczi, from the psychoanalytic movement. When his associates remained faithful disciples, Freud gave them his approval; but when they disagreed, he abused them, or accused them of being mentally ill. Adler was described by Freud as paranoiac, Stekel as unbearable and a louse; Jung as brutal and sanctimonious.
>
> What is remarkable about Freud's leadership of the psychoanalytic movement is that although he quite clearly did not believe in any kind of supernatural creator, he adopted almost without exception the strategies of those who did. In effect he treated his own theories as if they were a personal revelation granted to him by God and demanded that others should accord to them the reverence which the sacred word usually commands (R. Webster, 1990).

And as we have seen, leading professionals in humanistic psychology thought that Rajneesh was "at least a master therapist." (Likewise, "Fritz Perls, founder of Gestalt therapy, defended [L. Ron] Hubbard's early work ... and briefly received Dianetic counseling" [Atack, 1990].) Comparably, transpersonal and integral psychologists today regard Ken Wilber as a rare genius and a compassionate bodhisattva.

Think about all of that before you feel obliged to take any of their other ideas or analyses seriously.

Interestingly, Richard Price had actually visited and subsequently repudiated Rajneesh's India ashram in the '70s. (Price was one of the co-founders of the humanistic potential Esalen community, that "hotbed of sexual experimentation" located three hours south of San Francisco.) That distancing, however, was strictly for the violence he observed in their encounter groups, not for any stated comprehension of the potential for pathological problems which exists inside every closed society.

Price actually noted a style of "manipulating group pressure to force conformity" (Fitzgerald, 1986) in those encounter groups, in his formal letter of protest sent to the ashram staff and to Rajneesh himself. One will, however, find that manipulation in *every* ashram setting, with or without encounter groups. In any case, Price's objections were not directed at the ashram in general, which environment he fully enjoyed. Yet that "enjoyable" community is exactly where the real pathologies later manifested.

Price and Murphy's Esalen, like Findhorn, is itself a relatively safe community. Or "safe," at least, when not being haunted by future mass murderers:

> Esalen was, at this time [i.e., August of 1969], just coming into vogue as a "growth center".... Obviously [Charles] Manson felt Esalen a prime place to espouse his philosophies. It is unknown whether he had been there on prior occasions, those involved in the Institute refusing to even acknowledge his visits there....
>
> Manson would tell Paul Watkins ... that while at Big Sur he had gone "to Esalen and played his guitar for a bunch of people who were supposed to be the top people there [Murphy? Price?], and they rejected his music" ... just three days before the Tate murders (Bugliosi and Gentry, 1974).

Prior to that, the Beach Boys had recorded (in September of 1968) one of Manson's songs, "Never Learn Not To Love," for their *20/20* album. Manson and his Family had actually lived in (drummer) Dennis Wilson's house in 1968-9. It was Dennis himself who had once taken Manson to Roman Polanski's house, at which the murder of the latter's wife (i.e., centerfold Sharon Tate) and others later occurred.

Between that and Mike Love's interest in the Maharishi, that the Boys managed to sustain any "good vibrations" at all is nothing short of amazing. (The Maharishi actually toured with the Beach Boys in 1968, to the complete disinterest of their fans, causing the tour to be cancelled halfway through, already half a million dollars in debt [Kent, 2001].)

* * *

> The inner circle [in Jetsunma's ashram] was always careful to protect newcomers from the darker side of the center—and the things they would not be able to comprehend *correctly* (Sherrill, 2000; italics added).

The present book is, of course, exactly an attempt to provide a relatively comprehensive disclosure about what reportedly goes on behind the ashram gates. That is, it is a cataloging of the alleged actions which one would not "comprehend correctly" if one were to find out about them too soon in one's involvement with any group. Informed decisions may then be made regarding one's participation in our world's nontraditional and traditional spiritual organizations.

Of course, each new approach which comes along may be the "one clean spiritual path" whose guru-figure is everything he or she claims to be, with an inner circle of disciples who care nothing for their own power or respect, and simply want to make the world a better place by first changing themselves.

And if you buy that, I've got an ashram in Florida I'd like to sell you ... because that's *exactly* what I once thought SRF was. And yet, even the holy Tara Mata's attitude toward other, lower members of that compassionate and "God-guided" society embraced the totalitarian ideal:

> In an organization, no one has a right even to *think* except the members of the Board of Directors (in Walters, 2002).

Comparably, as Thomas Doyle (2002) observed, with regard to the Catholic Church:

> There is a solid principle in political science that says the governing elite of an organization will eventually think *it is* the organization.

No surprise, then, that exactly the same principle would apply to our world's nontraditional religious organizations, in their ashrams and otherwise. How could it not? 'Tis simply human nature.

Interestingly, devotees who tire of SRF and Yogananda frequently end up following Sai Baba, Chinmoy, or the "hugging avatar" Mata Amritanandamayi (Ammachi).

> Many people have called Amma[chi] a saint or sage and believe that she is a great master, a reincarnation of Divine Mother, Krishna, Christ, Buddha, or Ramakrishna.... When asked if she believes this about herself, she responded that she basically did not want to claim anything or that she was any particular incarnation of a god or goddess (Cornell, 2001).

And yet—

> "The Mother of Immortal Bliss" [i.e., Amritanandamayi] claims to be the living manifestation of all the divine goddesses of the Hindu pantheon combined (Macdonald, 2003).

In presenting Amma with the Gandhi-King Award for Non-Violence in 2002, *the* Jane Goodall further reportedly characterized her as being "God's love in a human body" (in Ammachi, 2004).

Understandably—or not—then,

> Amritananda[mayi] went underground in 1983 when the police confronted about twenty-six women who claimed to be possessed by gods and goddesses (Premanand, 1994).

Sarah Macdonald's (2003) clear-eyed experiences with Ammachi in *darshan* leave one further wondering:

> Amid the push, shove, knee-crunch and head-yank I concentrate on my question.
>
> "What is my purpose, what does God want from me?"

> Again, the flash of the nose ring, the gentle hold of the neck and the whisper in the ear. The answer, my purpose in life is: "rootoongarootoongarootoongarootoongarootoongarootoonga."
>
> My shoulder nearly dislocated by the yank out of the Mother's midst, I wait for a vision. Is the purpose of my life to root?

* * *

One can again always find apologists for whom allegedly abusive gurus/teachers are only "a fraction of a percentage" (i.e., less than 1%) of the whole. To the same "compassionate experts," students attract to themselves the teachers and guru-figures they deserve:

> In almost all cases, the sincere student is with a corrupt teacher because he or she has areas of blindness that are either getting fed or reflected by the teacher....
>
> When I encounter someone who argues vehemently against the student-teacher relationship, almost inevitably they are unconsciously trying to heal something still unsettled either in their present life or in some former circumstance....
>
> It has been suggested that false prophets are decoys to deter the masses of less determined seekers so that only those who are serious enough to pay the price for true mastery will discover it (Caplan, 2002).

But did the "true prophet" Ramakrishna's (or Sai Baba's) young male disciples, faced with the alleged sexual interests of those gurus, and going along with them because they believed that their "God in the flesh" wanted them to, "bring that upon themselves"? Was David Bohm's brutal mistreatment at the hands of the "authentic sage" Krishnamurti a necessary price to pay for his own "true mastery"? (In Bohm's case, that cruelty was the primary component inducing his suicide-considering nervous breakdown. It ultimately led to electroshock therapy, not to any greater enlightenment at the hands of the "World Teacher.")

The Wilber-admiring Caplan does not "name names" in her evaluations of "decoys" and her spirited defense of the hierarchical guru-disciple relationship in general—though she does consider 95% (her figure) of gurus to not be worth following. However, it is quite obvious from the content of her writings and of the interviews within them that she and her interviewees specifically regard Krishnamurti, Aurobindo, Meher Baba, Trungpa, Muktananda, Ma Jaya Sati Bhagavati and Andrew Cohen as being "authentic sages."

Interestingly, Ram Dass' experiences with Bhagavati (in her "Joya" days, with "no escape clause") did not prevent Caplan from interviewing both of them in the same (2002) book. She further did that without giving any indication that "Ma" is anything less than (in Caplan's own words) "an internationally respected spiritual teacher, as well as a forerunner in the global fight for human rights and religious freedom." Bhagavati has received equally positive coverage, independent of Dass' well-known claims regarding her past, in Cohen's (2001) *What Is Enlightenment?* magazine. Conversely, in Caplan's view, it could apparently only be other, unspecified "bad apples" who are guilty of messing up their naïve followers' lives, not any of these "compassionate sages."

Perspectives such as that are again sadly what passes for wisdom in today's spiritual marketplace. One then follows such advice only at one's own peril. After all, if these "experts" are wrong, it is *your* life that will be at risk of being shattered, not theirs.

Interestingly, Caplan's largely misled (2002) book has been hyperbolically endorsed by the Trungpa-following Welwood as being "the most comprehensive, lucid, well-argued, utterly straightforward and honest work on the whole guru question that there is." Caplan herself is a devoted disciple of Lee Lozowick, the latter of whom has a "special relationship" with Adi Da, and is a friend of Andrew Cohen (Rawlinson, 1997). Lozowick himself, however, has been critiqued by at least one former disciple, as follows:

> I think he is deluding himself when he claims to be fully enlightened.... During public gatherings he would constantly use four-letter words, ramble on about sex and anal fixations, and generally behave and speak in a totally asinine way (in Feuerstein, 1992).

Of his prolific, if unknown, rock band ("Liars, Gods, and Beggars"), Lozowick has predicted: "LGB will be bigger than the Beatles" (Rawlinson, 1997).

And thus, "more popular than Jesus Christ," too.

The wise Lozowick is further of the opinion that Sai Baba is a "master [of] the physics of form," i.e., that the latter's purported materializations of *vibhuti* and the like are genuine (Caplan, 2001). It is more than ironic, then, that both of Caplan's relevant books are concerned in significant part with how to distinguish "authentic" guru-figures from "decoys."

* * *

After all that, are "delusions of enlightenment" alright? Some would ridiculously say so:

> Better these people should think they're enlightened, which is a wonderful aspiration, than be robbing stores or taking heroin or beating their wives or kicking their dogs. I think that one of the most wonderful things is the delusion of enlightenment, even if it is a delusion. At least it represents an aspiration that is better than an aspiration to be a murderer (Joan Halifax, in [Caplan, 2001]).

But, are the "best" of history's "sages" really better than our world's bank robbers, drug addicts, wife abusers or animal mistreaters? Are they not arguably worse? For, note that more than one of them has allegedly misused (i.e., effectively stolen) temple funds, or feasted while his most devoted followers starved, thus exhibiting less moral sense than the average bank robber. (Stealing from a church or from one's friends and admirers, after all, has got to be morally worse than stealing from a faceless corporation or a bank.)

In the same vein, more than one has been accused of physically beating or otherwise brutally oppressing his or her spouse. As the *Mill Valley Record* (Colin, et al., 1985) reported:

> On one occasion during a raucous party at the church sanctuary in Clear Lake, eyewitnesses say they saw [Adi Da] push his wife Nina down a flight of stairs. They also claim that during that party Jones pulled a sizable hunk of hair from her head.

> [Rajneesh] wasn't the Master [Deeksha had] fallen in love with. She'd witnessed him beating Vivek once, she swore (Franklin, 1992).

Recall also Swami Rama reportedly kicking women in the buttocks. And further:

> Chögyam Trungpa wrote that Marpa, the tenth-century Tibetan guru, "lost his temper and beat people." Marpa is also considered an incarnate Buddha, the spiritual father of Tibet's greatest yogi Milarepa. Maybe his beatings were compassion in disguise, but it is hard to understand why the same argument could not be made for the *drunk who abuses his wife and children* (Butterfield, 1994; italics added).

In terms of the aforementioned (and above-denigrated, by Halifax) use of illicit and abused prescription substances: Included among the usage attributed to various "genuine sages" have been LSD, mescaline, psilocybin, nitrous oxide, and the opium derivatives Percodan and Demerol. Also amyl nitrite, a blood vessel-dilator used to cause a "high" or to improve sex; and, it goes without saying, marijuana. Not to mention Quaaludes reportedly given as a medical treatment in Rajneeshpuram. (That only Percodan, Demerol, Quaaludes and nitrous oxide among all those are recognized as being—like the opiate heroin—physically addictive, seems somewhat beside the point.) And God only knows what the police were expecting to find when they raided Trungpa's Scottish center. (People with nothing to conceal generally do not feel the need to desperately hide themselves, as Trungpa did, in such circumstances.)

Even metaphorically, the analysis fares no better:

> Fred [Stanton]'s final comment on Andrew [Cohen] was, "Andrew creates addicts. It's like giving people heroin" (Tarlo, 1997).

On top of that, we again have "genuine masters" allegedly building secret passageways leading to the dormitories of young girls in their care. (Caplan quotes frequently and respectfully from Muktananda in her books, thus inadvertently providing a bad, *bad* example from him of how *not* to do the guru-disciple relationship properly. Both of her relevant books were written well after the 1994 *New Yorker* exposé of him by Lis Harris.) Plus, we have the reported pedophilia/ephebophilia of universally revered figures such as Ramakrishna, as an early precursor to the allegations against Sai Baba. Also, holy Zen masters "beating the crap out of" their disciples, even to the point of death, and being *celebrated* for their macho, "ego-killing" abuse by foolish persons who themselves have obviously never been thus "beneficially" beaten. And all of that is ever done, of course, "in the name of God, for the compassionate benefit of all sentient beings," by great bodhisattvas and otherwise. And woe unto any "disloyal" disciple who should even think otherwise, and thereby risk his "one chance at enlightenment" in this life.

I myself am again in no way anti-drug, anti-dildo, anti-secret-passageway-to-the-dormitory, anti-whorehouse, anti-orgy or anti-leprechaun. It is simply obvious, by now, that any of those, when put into the hands of "god-men" who have carved islands of absolute power for themselves in the world, only make an already dangerous situation much worse.

We can surely agree with Ms. Halifax in her three decades of experience, though, that the delusion of enlightenment generally "represents an aspiration that is better than an aspiration to be a murderer." Unless, of course, you're Charles Manson. For, he borrowed heavily from Eastern philosophy in creating his own pre-rational view of the world, hinted at "deity status" for himself, and believed that "since all is one, nothing is wrong."

> Manson ... called himself "a.k.a. Lord Krishna, Jesus Christ, Muhammad, the Buddha" during a 1986 parole hearing (Agence, 1999).

After all that, it should be painfully clear that the delusion of enlightenment is the most *dangerous,* not the most wonderful, delusion. (Again, Jim Jones and David Koresh had similar messianic regards for their own enlightenment as does the still-incarcerated Manson. In all three of those "worst" cases, the delusion of enlightenment/divinity undeniably helped create the violent tragedies for which they are each known.) That most-dangerous regard is so if for no other reason than the effect that it has on the ensuing naïve followers. For, those end up throwing their lives and sanity away on persons who, even while laying claim to the highest levels of enlightenment (whether validly or psychotically), grandiosely deceive themselves, and then mislead others, all with the apparent goal of being given the proper obeisance due to themselves as "enlightened masters."

And as far as the treatment of animals goes, the spellbinding writer Deborah Boliver Boehm (1996) relates her experiences in a Japanese Zen monastery in Kyoto, upon being presented with two stray kittens:

"Will you keep them?" Saku-san asked.

"What if I didn't?" I asked.

"Then they would be left to die, or to be found by someone else if they were lucky."

"But why doesn't the *sodo* adopt them?"

"Because then we would become a dumping ground for every unwanted cat in town, and they would tear up the tatami [straw meditation mats]. Besides, some monks have allergies."

"But what about the vow you take every day, to save all sentient beings?"

"It's a nice idea, but not very practical," said Saku-san with a wide-shouldered shrug.

[B]eneath the smiles Tibetans obviously are not perfect. It's not all loving-kindness here; *I see a monk beat a dog,* another one smokes and while Buddhist texts forbid meat, the fleshy bodies of sheep hang in roadside butcher boxes attracting swarms of flies and shoppers galore....

I know the Dalai Lama has *tried* to turn vegetarian but so long as he and other Tibetan Buddhists continue to eat meat, the tinge of hypocrisy will remain (Macdonald, 2003; italics added).

* * *

Having said all of that, one can still sadly strike a much more negative note, when it comes to the effects of messianic delusions of enlightenment/divinity on both leaders and their followers:

Adolf Hitler had a mystical awakening at Pasewalk Hospital in 1918, following the defeat of Germany; it led to his decision to enter politics (Oakes, 1997).

Hitler by now was possessed by delusions of grandeur.... Convinced that he was Germany's political messiah, his supporters unashamedly referred to Hitler as a prophet.... After reading *Mein Kampf,* Joseph Goebbels, later the Party's propaganda chief, wrote "Who is this man? half plebian, half God! Truly Christ, or only St. John?" For the growing number of "disciples" gathering around Hitler at this time—referred to as the "charismatic community"—Hitler was more than just a politician offering political and economic solutions, he was a messianic leader embodying the salvation of Germany (D. Welch, 2001).

As if to further close the circle, then, we find this, in Goodrick-Clarke's (1994) *Occult Roots of Nazism:*

> The Ariosophists, initially active in Vienna before the First World War, borrowed from the theosophy of Helena Petrovna Blavatsky, in order to prophesy and vindicate a coming era of German world rule....
>
> At least two Ariosophists were closely involved with Reichsführer-SS Heinrich Himmler in the 1930s, contributing to his ... visionary plans for the Greater Germanic Reich in the third millennium....
>
> Ravenscroft adapted the materials of Rudolf Steiner ... to the mythology of occult Nazism.

Nor was that the only relevance of Eastern metaphysics to the Nazi cause:

> Savitri Devi, the French-born Nazi-Hindu prophetess, described Hitler as an avatar of Vishnu and likened Nazism to the cult of Shiva with its emphasis on destruction and new creation....
>
> [She] was sure that Hitler had realized he was an avatar while still a youth (Goodrick-Clarke, 2003).

Overall, truly believing that you are "enlightened and can do no wrong"—as every "messiah" and nearly every "meditation master" has role-played himself into believing—gives you unlimited license to mistreat others "for their own good." Indeed, it actually places your conscience farther out of reach than if you were *knowingly* manipulating them purely for your own selfish benefit, as a simple con man (or woman).

As Professor J. H. von Dullinger insightfully observed over a century and a quarter ago:

> All absolute power demoralizes its possessor. To that all history bears witness. And if it be a spiritual power which rules men's consciences, the danger is only so much greater, for the possession of such a power exercises a specially treacherous fascination, while it is peculiarly conducive to self-deceit, because the lust of dominion, when it has become a passion,

> is only too easily in this case excused under the plea of zeal for the salvation of others.

For that primary reason, among many secondary others, the "guru game," even when enacted by "genuine masters" (such as the swooning Ramakrishna, the Force-ful Aurobindo, the caste-conscious Ramana Maharshi, the non-healer Meher Baba, and the firewalking Yogananda) is more dangerous than is any secular power-play or con game.

Even when performed with integrity and sincerity? Yes. In fact, doubly so:

> Nothing in the world is more dangerous than sincere ignorance and conscientious stupidity.
>
> —Martin Luther King, Jr.

And Lord, have we seen enough of that.

* * *

Most of the "great sages" whose behavior we have touched upon within these pages have been men. Notable exceptions, however, have included Ramakrishna's wife, Aurobindo's "Mother," Muktananda's Gurumayi, and Yogananda's Daya Mata and Tara Mata. Also, Ma Jaya Sati Bhagavati, Ammachi, Jetsunma, and Andrew Harvey's Mother Meera. The latter's original hope, at age fourteen in the 1970s, had actually been to replace Aurobindo's Mother in the Auroville ashram in Pondicherry, following that Mother's passing (Minor, 1999):

> She had ... received visions of both Sri Aurobindo and the Mother in which they told her that she was entrusted with the work of completing the transformation of the world they had begun. The language of Aurobindo and the Mother are regularly a part of her descriptions of these visions, but often, she said, Aurobindo and the Mother actually appeared to her and in their conversations commissioned her to continue the work.

The entirely non-mystical, twentieth-century, late Russian-American philosopher Ayn Rand (d. 1982), too, apparently managed to create a personality cult around herself. Loyalty there was evidenced to the point where one of her sincere followers reportedly floated (in the late '60s) the idea of murder as a means of dealing with an unfaithful (and otherwise married) former lover of the homely, yet eminently rational, Ms. Rand (Shermer, 1997).

The endangered ex-lover in question was the dashing Nathaniel Branden—Rand's "intellectual heir," to whom *Atlas Shrugged* was dedicated. (The book itself was the "greatest human achievement in the history of the world," according to Rand and Branden.) Together, they encouraged followers of Rand to consider them as being "the two greatest intellects on the planet."

Branden himself was later to host a delightful dinner, in the mid-'80s, for his good friend, Ken Wilber (1991). Branden is, further, another one of the founding members of Wilber's Integral Institute.

From the former's own website (www.nathanielbranden.net):

> The name Nathaniel Branden has become synonymous with "the psychology of self-esteem," a field he began pioneering over thirty years ago. He has done more, perhaps, than any other theorist to awaken America's consciousness to the importance of self-esteem to human well-being.

One would expect no less, though, from one of the two "greatest intellects on the planet."

So, it is a small, small spiritual world, after all. And even smaller when one considers what happens when other scholars "go bad":

> [Frithjof] Schuon, blessed by God and the Virgin Mary, [believes that he] radiates grace from his body—at all times but most potently when he is naked; and that this is itself a salvific act....
>
> [His given initiations] consist of Schuon in a state of semi-nakedness at the center of a circle of semi-naked female disciples (Rawlinson, 1997).

Even when fully clothed, Schuon was evidently no ordinary man:

> He himself says that "I was from the beginning a person different from the others, I was made from different material." An unpublished paper, *The Veneration of the Shaykh* [written by his Da-like fourth "wife"], says that Schuon is "an

> eminent manifestation of the eternal *sadguru* ... an 'avataric' phenomenon ... a 'prophetic' figure ... and a great bodhisattva"; that he demonstrates the qualities of Shiva and Krishna; and has affinities with Abraham, David, Christ, and Muhammad....
>
> One disciple who questioned Schuon's authority was branded as mad; another was called "a natural swine"; and many others (including these two) were excommunicated (Rawlinson, 1997).

Dr. Schuon, as a recognized expert in the perennial philosophy or transcendent unity of religions, was of course referred to respectfully, in far less interesting ways, in Wilber's early (e.g., 1982, 1983) writings.

Should the aforementioned male/female numerical discrepancy in guru-dom still irk, however, consider the revered Bengali mystic Ananda Moyi Ma, who herself claimed to be an avatar, or direct incarnation of the Divine Mother. Indeed, after meeting her in 1936, Yogananda (1946) expressed his evaluation of her degree of spiritual advancement thusly:

> I had found many men of God-realization in India, but never before had I met such an exalted woman saint.

Arthur Koestler (1960), however, added the following information regarding Ananda's character:

> [F]rom the age of twenty-eight onward, for an undefined number of years, she was unable to feed herself. "Whenever she tried to carry food to Her mouth, Her grasp slackened and a large part of the food slipped through Her fingers"....
>
> There were ... occasions when, at the sight of an Untouchable eating rice, or a dog devouring garbage, she would begin to cry plaintively, "I want to eat, I want to eat." On yet other occasions, she had fits of ravenous overeating....
>
> She was prone to weeping, and to laughing fits which often lasted over an hour. She liked to tease her devotees and to display a kittenish behavior, though sometimes her playfulness could more appropriately be called cruelty. When [one of her closest followers] was ill, she did not visit him for several months, and on certain occasions during his convalescence she expressly forbade that food be sent to him.

Ma herself was nevertheless credited with having profound healing abilities, as Yogananda's (1946) niece relates:

> At the entreaty of a disciple, Ananda Moyi Ma went to the home of a dying man. She stood by his bedside; as her hand touched his forehead, his death-rattle ceased. The disease vanished at once; to the man's glad astonishment, he was well.

All such claimed abilities and exalted realization aside, however, the following incident stands out and rankles:

> An old woman came forward, prostrated herself, and begged Ananda to intercede for her son, a soldier reported missing after a clash in the border area. Ananda kept chewing *pan,* ignoring her. The woman began to shout and sob in near-hysterics. Ananda said harshly, "Go away," brushing her aside with a single gesture, and the old woman, still crying, was led from the room (Koestler, 1960).

If there is compassion in such behavior, only one not yet suitably shaken from the pleasant fantasy that such actions might be a manifestation of God "working in mysterious ways" could find it.

Consider further that it has been reported that the vast majority of the individuals currently sitting on the SRF Board of Directors are nuns. And those have given no indication whatsoever of any wish on their part to give up the rigidly hierarchical structure of that organization, or their choice positions in it.

> To Daya Mata, we and everyone who disagrees with her are —to quote a favorite expression of hers—"pipsqueaks"....
>
> Daya Mata actually said once to Brother Anandamoy and me, "Let's face it, women are more spiritual than men" (Walters, 2002).

The revered Mata herself has been prominently featured in various magazines, in celebration of her role as one of the world's first female spiritual leaders, and thus as "part of the solution" to the world's problems.

Of course, the women in Rajneesh's ashrams were part of the same "solution":

> True to Rajneesh's vision of women as "the pillars of my temple," women dominated the leadership of the movement (except for Bhagwan "Himself"). Braun notes that women controlled over 80% of executive positions in Rajneeshpuram (Palmer and Sharma, 1993).

And Rajneeshpuram, as we know, was the Oregon ashram infamous for its salmonella, electronic bugging and alleged murder plots.

Undeterred, Ma Bhagavati has informed us:

> If people don't accept women teachers, that's the end of everything, because the men have made a real mess of things (in Caplan, 2002).

Bhagavati, recall, was the reportedly self-professed "incarnation of the Divine Mother" whom Ram Dass, on the basis of his own experiences, totally repudiated in the mid-'70s, in his "Das and Dasser" period, and her days as the gold-bangled "Joya."

"The end of everything," indeed.

Mother Teresa, sadly, fares no better in the harsh light of day, as Aroup Chatterjee's (2003) *Mother Teresa: The Final Verdict* has demonstrated:

> [Mother Teresa] has been quoted as saying that suffering is a means of attaining Christ; to suffer along with the suffering helps one come closer to God. In other words the poor and dying are to her only a means of attaining salvation for herself. Their suffering, which is a replay of the suffering of Christ, gives her spiritual succor. Hence the tremendous funds at her disposal have never been used to set up a state of the art hospital where much of the suffering could be alleviated or pre-empted; to establish schools which would rescue generations from poverty; to renew the slums of Calcutta and eliminate disease and crime. For, she has a vested interest in the perpetuation of poverty and sickness and death.

Nor were those religious issues by any means the only problems with Teresa's work and character:

> She inflated her operations and activities manifold in her speeches to journalists and supporters. Often her statements would have no connection with reality whatsoever. Many

> times she had been captured on television while telling very tall tales about her work. She prevaricated even in her Nobel Prize acceptance speech....
>
> [W]hen it comes to social issues, even the present pope is much more liberal than Mother Teresa....
>
> Mother was confronted on the issue of pedophile priests by the Irish journalist Kathy Ward. She replied, "Pray, pray and make sacrifices for those who are going through such terrible temptations." It is not that she was against custodial sentencing *per se:* a few times she said that she wanted to open a special jail for doctors who performed abortions.

Christopher Hitchens (1995) had earlier written his own less-detailed exposé of Teresa:

> [S]he once told an interviewer that, if faced with a choice between Galileo and the authority of the Inquisition, she would have sided with the Church authorities....
>
> "She also touched on AIDS, saying she did not want to label it a scourge of God but that it did seem like a just retribution for improper [e.g., homosexual or promiscuous] sexual conduct."

And how did Ken Wilber (2000a) jump the gun, in voicing his positive attitude toward Mother Teresa upon receiving (media) news of her death, nearly half a decade after Hitchens' exposé?

> Mother Teresa was much closer to that divine ray [than was Princess Diana, who died in the same week], and practiced it more diligently, and without the glamour. She was less a person than an opening of Kosmic compassion—unrelenting, fiercely devoted, frighteningly dedicated.
>
> I, anyway, appreciated them both very much, for quite different reasons.

Such opinions, sadly, are again exactly par for the course with Wilber, in his consistent vouching for other people's high degrees of enlightenment. For here too he obviously, if utterly wrongly, considers himself to be in a position to intuitively and intelligently separate the reality from the PR, even without having minimally familiarized himself with the long-extant, relevant research materials.

Likewise for his friend, Dr. Roger Walsh (1999):

> The few hours I spent with Mother Teresa and the Dalai Lama continue to inspire me years later, while films of them have inspired people around the world. Such is the power of those who devote their lives to awakening and service.

Or, rather, "such is the power" of those with good public relations machines and the ability to bury their indiscretions and prejudices. For, they shall be taken as saints and gods, even in the midst of cruel homophobia, bizarre sexual hang-ups, association with known criminals and the receiving of stolen goods. (Mother Teresa accepted over a million dollars in donations from Savings-and-Loan fraudster Charles Keating, and wrote a naïve letter in his defense during his trial. Following his conviction and imprisonment, the deputy district attorney of Los Angeles County contacted Teresa, encouraging her to return those "stolen" funds. He received no reply from the "great saint" [Chatterjee, 2003].)

Anyway, one might even begin to sympathize with such perspectives as Bhagavati's, above, in the face of nonsense such as Brooke's (1999) position. For there, he repeatedly expressed the desire to "out" (his word) the "wrangling bitch" and "vain effete peacock" (his phrases) Sai Baba. He also evinced a predictably "Christian" attitude toward female gurus in general:

> I had never met [Hilda Charlton] ... and had my own personal barriers and suspicions about women gurus. It just wasn't my style.

Gender-based "suspicions," however, cannot be reduced to mere matters of "style," even in the case of complete flakes such as Charlton. Nor can such dismal attitudes—whether coming from male born-again Christians or in reverse from celebrated contemporary female yogis—be viewed as a valid antidote to the problems which pervade the spiritual marketplace, or even the saner world in general.

We should not, therefore, attempt to split the power/sexual/psychological issues underlying these poor reported behaviors along male/female or patriarchal/matriarchal lines, as is often done. Indeed, should one even be tempted to do so, one should instead consider Janja Lalich's experiences in a "soul-crushing" political "cult" founded by thirteen feminist Marxist-Leninists. Eleven of those founders "self-identified as radical lesbians." And yet, even under their "nurturing, tolerant, egalitarian" rule:

> A well-respected doctor and party theoretician in his fifties said he was so tired he prayed daily for a heart attack to give him some release. A number of others said they secretly wished they would get killed in a car accident because they couldn't think of any other way of getting out (in Langone, 1995).

You're thinking of dabbling in something like paganism to slake your spiritual thirst, on the wishful supposition that it might be any less founded on lies, sexism, and unapologetic misrepresentations than is any other religion or form of spirituality? Please first read Charlotte Allen's delightful (2001) article, "The Scholars and the Goddess":

> In all probability, not a single element of the Wiccan story [of its own origins] is true. The evidence is overwhelming that Wicca is a distinctly new religion, a 1950s concoction influenced by such things as Masonic ritual and a late-nineteenth-century fascination with the esoteric and the occult, and that various assumptions informing the Wiccan view of history are deeply flawed.

Indeed, as Allen further notes, the idea—central to Wiccan belief—that any ancient civilization, anywhere, ever worshiped a single, archetypal goddess, is wholly rejected by contemporary scholars, on the basis of both written records and archeology. (Cf. Cynthia Eller's [2003] refreshingly insightful and devastating *The Myth of Matriarchal Prehistory.*)

Likewise for the purported superiorities of past Native American societies, or the like, to "fragmented, patriarchal, European" ones:

> The Mayas, whose cities were completely unfortified, were long thought to be "an unusually gentle, peaceful people living in a relatively benign theocracy." But as the Mayan writing system began to be deciphered and as new excavations were undertaken, a different picture emerged. Archaeologists found depictions of severed heads and bound captives under public buildings. As archaeologist Arthur Demarest concludes on the basis of this new evidence, "the Maya were one of the most violent state-level societies in the New World" (Eller, 2003).

All of which only goes to reinforce the wise observation that "a saint [or a fanciful mythology, or a 'Golden Age' culture] is what remains after a person's sins have been forgotten." Or, if not duly forgotten, at least prematurely buried by close disciples, as by the sage himself/herself—all of them having no small interest in presenting the best possible public face, for their own welfare in power and glory.

* * *

We have earlier touched on the idea of spiritual incest, in terms of sexual relations *usually* (but not always) initiated by the guru-figure with his (or her) trusting disciples. The respected theoreticians in the higher branches of psychology and consciousness studies may still be grappling with how to explain away such life-destroying "mistakes" on the part of their "enlightened" heroes. By contrast, others with far less commitment to the field, but far more insight, had already discerned the relevant dynamics and appropriate restrictions over a decade and a half ago:

> The power of the pastor over the congregant is tremendously enhanced by his authority, if he wishes to exercise it, to describe to a woman her status with God. A sexually abusive clergyman can easily exploit this authority by telling a woman that her sexual involvement is part of a divinely ordained plan. Even sophisticated women can have difficulty resisting this argument if they are devoted to the religious vision that the clergyman represents.
>
> [So-called religious] cults in which the guru or spiritual leader has sexual relationships with many of his female congregants are more blatant examples of this phenomenon (Rutter, 1989).

Rutter continues:

> The [related] issue of sexual relationships between professors and students draws attention because of their frequency, which [high frequency] can be *partially* [italics added] attributed to a traditional absence of a clearly demarcated forbidden zone [where sexual activities are not allowed] on the college campus. People who argue against such prohibitions usually claim that the women involved are consenting adults and that there is no duty to protect them....

> All of these arguments ignore important social and psychological realities. The social dynamic still places the power in the hands of the teacher or professor. The psychological dynamic is based on the underlying reality of continuing dependency issues, which must be taken into account in assessing the ethics of sexual relationships between female college and graduate students and their professors. Recently, some universities have begun articulating clear policies against faculty-student intimacies that do take the unequal power dynamics into consideration.

Chapter 7 of Singer and Lalich's (1996) *Crazy Therapies* covers similar topics to the above:

> Sex with a therapist or counselor [or guru] is not okay and is not going to benefit the client [or disciple]. If anything ... it will cause new problems and exacerbate previous ones.

> Gurus, like fathers, are in a context that gives them enormous power because of their disciples' needs, trust, and dependency. One reason incest is a betrayal of trust is what a daughter needs from her father is a sense of self-worth not specifically linked to her sexuality. Sex with the guru is similarly incestuous because a guru ostensibly functions as a spiritual father to whom one's growth is entrusted. Having sex with a parental figure reinforces using sex for power. This is not what young women (or men) need for their development. When the guru drops them, which eventually he does, feelings of shame and betrayal usually result that leave deep scars (Kramer and Alstad, 1993).

Note that none of the above ideas are puritanical, shadow-projecting or prudish. (In the words of the One Taste-realized Drukpa Kunley, hero to the Dalai Lama: "You like religion and I like cunt. May both of us be happy!") They are, rather, simply a minimal application of real compassion for the well-being of others, being directed in the spiritual world against individuals who make themselves out to be gods.

> When people do not have a clear idea of harm—and it is very hard to talk about sex and get it right—they accuse others of being Puritans. This is going on all over Buddhism today (Lew Richmond, in [Downing, 2001]).

As if to prove Richmond's point, the tantric initiate John Blofeld (1970) gave a fallacious defense which could have been applied to the vast majority of our world's guru-figures:

> [A]dvanced adepts are permitted to do what seems good to them, regardless of the normal [e.g., social] rules of conduct. To consider abiding by the rules as necessarily good or transgressing them as necessarily evil would be to tie themselves down with the dualism they have set out to transcend....
>
> Sordid people judge others by their own standards, reading crude motives into every sort of action. Hypocrites will be likely to see their own vice in every unconventional act of a man sincerely seeking spiritual advancement. It is hard to convince them that others may act from lofty motives. A true adept, however, will not be put out by misguided criticism.

But, to what extent, if any, have our world's guru-figures ever really acted from "lofty motives"? And might not any associated hypocrisy perhaps apply more to the teachers themselves than to their "puritanical" critics?

Further consider the twenty-five virgin girls who surely had their lives messed up by one deluded old man, Upasani Baba, regardless of what component of their marriage may have been only symbolic or spiritual. (For the young girls sleeping with Mahatma Gandhi, too, it was merely a "spiritual" arrangement. Yet, had his lust ever risen to the fore, the likely outcome would have been rape. How well would *you* sleep, with that lurking over your shoulder?)

That same Baba was again convinced that he could distinguish the "Avatar for this age" from the mass of spiritual seekers, which avatar just happened, against all odds, to be one of his own disciples. That is indeed "sordid," but not in any way which the apologetic Blofeld would ever have imagined. If one wishes to see the effects of "traditional agrarian" society on allegedly constraining what guru-figures are allowed to get away with, one need look no further than celebrated "spiritual discipline" like that.

To state the obvious, again: Any set of "rigid constraints" which grants a greater degree of latitude in allowable behavior to its god-figures than does Western society's own healthy permissiveness (among consenting adults, here) would, in practice, create an even more unconstrained society for those so fortunate as to be the "kings" of it. Indeed, in the same West where a "lack of social constraint" is regularly blamed for the excesses of its "crazy wisdom" practitioners:

> [Few] crazy-wisdom masters today are afforded the privilege of making use of their full bag of tricks. They are well aware that a single lawsuit brought against them ... could result in their losing the opportunity to continue their teaching function (Caplan, 2002).

Since those lawsuits arise predominantly from alleged sexual abuses (cf. Swami Rama), one cannot have it both ways. That is, one is welcome to state, with Ram Dass (in Caplan, 2002), that previously "impeccable" gurus fall from their lofty ideals because of the greater freedoms and promiscuity (in alcohol, drugs and sex) in the West. One would be hopelessly wrong—cf. Dass' own "seventeen-year-old jock," Neem Karoli Baba—but one is free to close one's eyes and propose that. Having stated it, however, one cannot then turn around and assert that "crazy wisdom" is practiced with *more* freedom in the East, where "the guru-principle is understood," and lawsuits need not be so feared should "Da Shit hit Da Fan"!

Note further that while even educational institutions have acknowledged the existence of relevant psychological dynamics between teachers and students, from which the students need to be protected, things are much worse for guru-figures and disciples. For, a student receiving unwanted attention from a professor or graduate supervisor might, at least in theory (i.e., notwithstanding "old boys' networks" and the like), transfer to another class/supervisor, or go over the prof's head to the dean, etc. There are no such courts of appeal, however, for wronged disciples. Rather, there is merely the fear that in saying "No" to anything that the guru-figure asks of you, you are being disobedient and egoic, and thus retarding your own spiritual growth. Further, to break with the guru at any stage of that may, one believes, cast one into "Vajra hell," or result in one "wandering the Earth for incarnations" before being given another chance at enlightenment, should you "waste" this one.

More obviously, no mere professor, graduate supervisor or employer could believably suggest that sleeping with him (or her) is part of a "divinely ordained plan." Guru-figures, on the other hand, can and do routinely advance exactly that idea. Thus, whatever constraints may be placed on secular classes should apply *even more* to guru-figures. For, in between the "voice of God" speaking through them, the constraints to obey, and the lack of any court of appeal, the power imbalance is *far* greater in the spiritual world than in the academic.

Sex between the father-figure guru and his (or her) disciples is again widely recognized as being of a comparable psychological status to incest or child abuse. One need not be stuck in any "puritanical" worldview, then, in order to feel the need to object to such activities, whether they are occurring in spiritual or in secular contexts. Nor can proponents of "idiot tolerance" for the same (alleged, spiritual) abuse safely hide behind the idea that such objections arise merely from followers wanting their sages to be "dead from the neck down."

Encouragingly, the California Yoga Teachers Association Code of Conduct (Lasater, 1995) admirably spelled out the minimal relevant constraints on the behavior of its members a decade ago, even though concerning itself only with imperfect teachers and their students, not "divine, infallible" gurus and their disciples. There, they recognized that "all forms of sexual behavior or harassment with students are unethical, even when a student invites or consents to such behavior or involvement." They further instructed:

> We do not make public ... statement[s] implying unusual, unique or one-of-a-kind abilities, including misrepresentation through sensationalism, exaggeration or superficiality.

One wishes that the frequently "one-of-a-kind" and "best," "enlightened avatars" in the world could see things as clearly—i.e., with such elementary, common-sense psychology and integrity—as its "unenlightened, mere mortal" teachers have. There would be far less garbage ("and the goddess") littering the long and winding spiritual road.

* * *

> Leaving a [so-called] cult is like experiencing a death of a loved one. There is a grieving process which will take time. Time to process the feelings of confusion, loss, guilt, disillusionment, anger, and lack of trust engendered (Bailey and Bailey, 2003).

For first-hand accounts as to the difficulties involved in disentangling oneself from spiritual and emotional commitments to enlightenment at the feet of any "great sage," plus personal descriptions of the power games and manipulation which are alleged to occur within the ashram environment, I have found the following books to be excellent:

- Michael Downing (2001), *Shoes Outside the Door*—San Francisco Zen Center, Richard Baker (this book is worth reading for the keen wit alone)
- Stephen Butterfield (1994), *The Double Mirror*—Chögyam Trungpa
- Peter Marin (1995), "Spiritual Obedience," in *Freedom & Its Discontents*—Chögyam Trungpa
- Satya Bharti Franklin (1992), *The Promise of Paradise*—Rajneesh
- Hugh Milne (1986), *Bhagwan: The God That Failed*—Rajneesh
- Kate Strelley (1987), *The Ultimate Game*—Rajneesh
- Andre van der Braak (2003), *Enlightenment Blues*—Andrew Cohen
- Luna Tarlo (1997), *The Mother of God*—Andrew Cohen
- Martha Sherrill (2000), *The Buddha from Brooklyn*—Jetsunma
- Barbara and Betty Underwood (1979), *Hostage to Heaven*—the Moonies
- Deborah Layton (1998), *Seductive Poison*—Jim Jones
- John Hubner and Lindsey Gruson (1990), *Monkey on a Stick*—the Hare Krishnas, exposed as the reportedly murderous, drug-running, wife-beating, child-molesting apocalyptic "cult" we were always reflexively warned to avoid. Yet, we chose instead to liberally tolerate and defend them as an "alternative religion," which should not be discriminated against simply for being "different."

  "Live and let live," right?

  Compare:

> When I first started to speak out about [alleged] cults approximately ten years ago [i.e., around 1982], I was one of an extremely small group of lawyers who

> were willing to address [so-called] cultic groups' broad range of challenges to individual freedom and personal liberty. The podium had in fact been largely forfeited to a strident, well-organized clique of "civil libertarian" experts who discoursed at length upon the inviolability of the First Amendment and the rights, vulnerabilities, and vitality of so-called new religious movements (Herbert Rosedale, in [Langone, 1995])

- Amy Wallace (2003), *Sorcerer's Apprentice*—Carlos Castaneda, another "world's savior," who was every bit the tragically equal fool in cruelly disciplining his followers as any of the other "Rude Boys" we have seen herein have been. The details Wallace gives of an insane community founded on a "skillful means" of reported lies and unspoken, rigid rules are nearly enough to cause one to lose one's faith in our sad species. Nor did Castaneda's own famous writings featuring the purported Yaqui sorcerer Don Juan fare any better in the light of truth:

  > As sociologist Marcello Truzzi was the first to say, Castaneda's books were the greatest hoax since the Piltdown Man (Gardner, 1999)

Anyone who has ever lived in an ashram/monastery environment, and recovered enough from that to see how much *less* "evil" the real world is, will find numerous significant points of contact in all of the above first-hand accounts—including Underwood's days with the Moonies, and Layton's gripping story of her narrow escape from Jonestown. For, as we have seen, the techniques used to keep residents in line and loyally "living in fear" of what will happen to their bodies or souls should they leave are constant across all paths. That is so, regardless of the specific beliefs involved in each case.

The total insanity underlying the use of "skillful means" of teaching, and the easy descent of followers into a chilling mob mentality, further come across frighteningly in Sherrill's book. Selected chapters from that text are available online, at Sherrill (2000a). The "Great Blessing" chapter there is an especially enlightening/sickening documentation of the madness too often allegedly perpetrated in the name of "purifying compassion." (For the difference between reality and hagiography, compare that exposé against the chapter on Jetsunma in Mackenzie's [1995] *Reborn in the West.* And then apply the same demythologizing proportionately to each of the other *tulkus* covered by Mackenzie.) That "purifying compassion" came, again, from a *tulku* whose spiritual greatness was formally recognized in the mid-'80s by Wilber's own Penor Rinpoche.

Also coming across clearly there are the jaw-dropping rationalizations created by disciples, in absurdly viewing such alleged violent abuses as being for their own benefit. That occurred within the context of ridiculously skewed ideas about merit and karma — including *tulkus* reincarnating as houses, wooden bridges, and equally wooden actors. Also, one cannot help but note the laughably superstitious interpretations of natural phenomena, and an equally hideous, Catholic-like insistence on the confession of any broken vows to one's superiors. For, the consequence of not confessing is that such breaks remain allegedly forever unmendable. That is, they supposedly create obstacles and produce more suffering "for countless sentient beings" by one's having failed to come forth quickly and voluntarily to admit them.

In any case, a primary idea to glean from all of the above-listed book-length testimonials is that, if you've once decided to leave a spiritual community, *follow through on it, and don't ever go back,* even if the community begs you to stay or to return. (Corollary: leaving in the middle of the night, without saying "goodbye," gives them less chance to talk you out of that.) Things won't get better by staying longer, and the nonsense which caused you to decide to leave in the first place will only get worse. None of those problems, further, are ever simply "tests sent by your guru" to see how loyal you are, regardless of what the guru himself or his committed disciples may try to tell you.

Leaving such a community after any meaningful length of stay of course means being ostracized by the remaining members, and being regarded as having left for not being able to take the discipline in that relationship. Or, being the subject of far worse allegations and/or reported violence. That, however, is a small price to pay for one's freedom and (literally) one's sanity.

Indeed, as to the treatment which one may expect upon leaving the average "divine guru": Andrew Harvey (2000) and his partner broke with and publicly repudiated Mother Meera shortly after having declared her to be "the avatar who would save the world"

(Blacker, 1996). They then claim to have encountered the following set of horrors:

> A vicious, callous, and sophisticated system was set up by a group of ex-"close friends," that included anonymous letters, death threats for nearly a year, horrible telephone harassment, visits to New York publishers to discredit Eryk's and my work, attempts to have me thrown out of my job in San Francisco, relentless public and private calumny—the complete cocktail, in fact, of [so-called] cult violence, demonization, and attempted destruction....
>
> I know of many cases of terrible abuse where ex-disciples of this or that "master" are too terrified to speak out.

Former members of Rajneesh's (Milne [1986]; Franklin [1992]) and Muktananda's (Harris, 1994) ashrams, to name but two more, have claimed to fear for their safety in comparable situations.

Interestingly, Ma Jaya Sati Bhagavati (Joya) apparently regards Andrew Harvey's claims of harassment and homophobia against mother Meera as being "baloney." She also, however, has reportedly recently defended Trungpa and Rajneesh, and spoken highly of Muktananda (Bostock, 1998). Simultaneously, she has evidently "forgiven" Ram Dass—the "fighting puppy" at her regal, parading "elephant feet"—for speaking out against her in the '70s. Again, the www.kashiashram.com website offers a valuable corrective to her public face and to any claims that she is doing "selfless, compassionate" work.

Comparably disturbing details as to the alleged treatment of ex-members by Adi Da's community are available online at Jewel (1999). A good summary of his reported behaviors in general can be found online at ThisTruth (2001).

See also the preface to Wakefield (1991) for her claimed frightening experiences, including alleged death threats, after having left Scientology. Plus, Chapter 9 of Wakefield (1996), and the epilogue of Malko (1970), for comparable allegations.

And yet, even after all that, the Muktananda-quoting Caplan, as recently as 2001, could still write:

> There is the occasional Jim Jones, Charles Manson, or Marshall Applewhite (Heaven's Gate) who comes into the spiritual scene and presents a physical danger to the very lives of the students whom they claim to be saving. But these in-

stances are negligible in comparison to the majority of spiritual schools and teachers, who present no danger of physical harm to their students.

The hard data, however, available for over twenty years by now, argues exactly the opposite. For, as Conway and Siegelman reported in 1982, based on a survey of over four hundred former "cult" members from forty-eight different groups:

> Incidences of physical punishment, reported by approximately one in five respondents, included beatings, starvation, physical bondage, cold showers and dousings and long hours of humiliating and degrading labor.

Nor were those the only alleged negative effects to be disclosed by Conway and Siegelman's study. Rather, nearly 20% of their respondents battled long-term health problems, while two in every three faced lasting emotional difficulties. Further, 14% claimed to have suffered from psychiatric delusions (e.g., hallucinations) for up to eight years after breaking away from their respective organizations. Also, more than one out of every five former members in the survey had suicidal or other self-destructive feelings during the rehabilitation period after leaving—a time which averaged more than sixteen months.

Interestingly, beyond the first three to six months, the impact of "cult ritual" and indoctrination did not correlate with the difficulties faced by the member after leaving the group. That is, "most of the damage appears to be done in the first few months" of (esp. residential) membership.

* * *

The "fury of a savior scorned" is generally not limited to former members of his world-saving group, but extends even to those third parties who dare to speak in too much unpleasant detail about our world's spiritual organizations. The aforementioned late "cult psychology" expert Margaret Singer (2003) apparently found that out for herself the hard way:

> Since the first edition of [*Cults in Our Midst*] came out, various [so-called] cults have sent people to ring the doorbell of my home at all hours of the night, often leaving menacing

> notes in my mailbox, then scampering away in the dark like mischievous kids on a Halloween night....
>
> In addition to this childish level of harassment, a lawsuit was brought against me and the book ... which I am sure was designed only to intimidate and to attempt to silence me and my work. The litigation was also, I believe, an attempt to dissuade my academic and clinical colleagues from publishing similar research and analysis of [alleged] cults in the United States and from testifying against [so-called] cults, as I do, in the many current criminal and civil court cases under way between [alleged] cults and their former victims.

Steven Hassan (2000) reported his own comparable experiences:

> When *Combatting Cult Mind Control* was first published in 1988, I became one of the most visible targets of [so-called] cult disinformation campaigns. There are [alleged] cult leaders who lecture their members on the evils of speaking with me and even reading the book. Scientology has a "Dead Agent Pack" about me. This folder contains material designed to assassinate my character—to "neutralize" me in members' minds as a respected person. Countless times, I've been threatened with lawsuits and have even received death threats from [alleged] cult members. Several groups, such as the Moonies, tell their members that I am Satan's agent.

> For the past twenty years, [David] Lane's books and articles exposing the [alleged] plagiarisms, lies, inconsistencies and scandals of a number of new religious movements have raised a fury among true believers. Members of various [alleged] cults have [reportedly] made death threats, written him letters with skeletons on them, broken into his apartment, threatened lawsuits, and generally harassed him....
>
> "They sent letters about me claiming I was the negative force, that I was predicted from the beginning of mankind" [says Lane] (Bellamy, 1995).

> It was easy for Theosophists to conclude that anyone who disagreed with them, however well intentioned, was working in the service of the Dark Forces (Washington, 1995).

As has been noted previously, it would be inconsistent for SRF to not view the present author as being, like the above "Dark

Forces," quite literally a deluded tool of *Maya*—the satanic cosmic delusive force, or devil.

Singer herself unfortunately downplayed the real and legitimate search for Truth in her list of reasons why people join and remain in spiritual communities. Instead, she focused on those joiners simply being vulnerable to proselytizing in "looking for meaning" after a personal loss, depression, loneliness or insecurity, etc. For my own part, however, I have *lived* that "seeker myth," with no proselytizing whatsoever on the part of any of Yogananda's followers. I therefore cannot take Singer's broad debunking of that principle seriously. Nor does one encounter anything in the first-person accounts of Butterfield, van der Braak, Milne, Franklin or Strelley which would match Singer's assertion of "active, sophisticated and unrelenting proselytizing" on the part of the relevant organizations (re: Trungpa, Cohen and Rajneesh). The Gurdjieff Society and his eponymous Institute likewise "never advertise and never recruit" (Washington, 1995).

The same is true even of Adi Da's group, at least with regard to non-celebrities: "[S]o far as I know, the community has never gone in for active recruiting, preferring to let people be drawn by Da Free John's writings" (Lowe, 1996). Layton's experiences in being pulled into the People's Temple, however, did include flattering attention/pressure from Jones himself. Underwood's (1979) and Hassan's (1990) reported experiences in becoming involved with the Moonies likewise fit much more closely with Singer's assertions.

In any case, for those nontraditional organizations which do actively recruit, university campuses remain the primary area of focus:

> University students are often vulnerable recruitment targets for potentially harmful groups (Smith, 2004).
>
> College campuses are the chief recruiting centers of most [alleged] destructive cults, and virtually every college campus in the country has been and continues to be visited by these organizations....
>
> At the University of California—Berkeley, for example, it is estimated that at least two hundred different religious sects on and off-campus are recruiting from the 30,000-student campus (in Rudin, 1996).

> In a survey done in 1980 by Zimbardo of more than one thousand high school students in the San Francisco Bay area 54% reported a [so-called] cult had attempted to recruit them and 40% said they had experienced multiple attempts (Ross, 2002b).

Indeed, in one survey (Singer, 2003) it was found that 43% of former "cult" members were students (in high school or college) at the time when they became involved with their respective organizations. Further, of those students, 38% dropped out of school after joining their groups.

> Some ... observers echo Richard Delgado's call for an intensive public education campaign about the [so-called] cults.... Dr. Lester Rosenthal ... believes ninth, tenth, and eleventh graders should be required to take courses in school on how the [so-called] cults recruit and operate (Rudin and Rudin, 1980).

Beyond the sorely needed education of young people in particular, the following reasonable suggestions have also been made:

> Federal funds should be appropriated for research and treatment of [so-called] mind control victims (Hassan, 1990).

> [T]he government might launch a campaign to raise awareness about the dangers of [so-called] cults, just as it has done for smoking, seat belts, and drunk driving (Hassan, 2000).

> Professor Richard Delgado asserts that the legal status of [alleged] religious cults should be analyzed within the context of the Thirteenth Amendment of the United States Constitution—which forbids slavery—rather than within the First Amendment alone. He believes the conditions of some [so-called] cult members do in fact constitute a state of slavery (Rudin and Rudin, 1980).

> U.S. courts have repeatedly ruled that the First Amendment provides only unqualified freedom of religious *belief,* not unlimited freedom to practice those beliefs in ways that may violate existing laws or pose a threat to the health and safety of individuals or society (Conway and Siegelman, 1982).

The means of getting into the organization may differ between non-proselytizing "true *sanghas*" and recruiting-based nontraditional organizations. Still, once one is inside, working long hours for minimal wages, in a "state of slavery" to a master whose orders you cannot disobey, leaving is just as difficult. That is true whether departing from the oppressive environment means "falling into Satan's power," being "pursued by disasters," or simply risking showing oneself to be a "bad disciple"—a weakling who "can't take the heat."

* * *

In my own case, after leaving Hidden Valley, I happened to get in touch with the monk (from a different order) who had taken over the position and workspace which I had vacated there. I then attempted to inform him as to the problems with that organization, as reported in Russell (1999), for example.

His response?

"If anything were going really wrong, Yogananda would step in and intervene. Until then, the Master was probably just looking down and laughing at the foibles of his disciples. In the meantime, we should just focus on changing *ourselves,* and not worry about things like that." Or words to that effect.

Oy vey. With "wisdom" like that, one does not need ignorance. With "compassion" like that, one does not need callousness. For, at what point in the slow descent into insanity of *any* of our world's guru-figures and organizations did God or the relevant line of "ascended, omniscient" Masters *ever* "step in" to stop alleged pedophilia, spiritual incest, intense psychological and physical abuse, or worse? When, even, did Jesus ever step in to stop the sodomizing of altar boys in the Catholic Church? And other guru-figures will then have more interest in, or ability to stop, abuses done in their name? And if they do not step in, "everything is going as it should, for your own benefit," so "bend over, here it comes"?

> That I was apparently poisoned and/or deliberately overdrugged [in Rajneesh's ashram] was the furthest thing from my mind....
>
> I took everything that happened at face value. The only ulterior motives I looked for were spiritual.... Everything was happening the way it should. It always did (Franklin, 1992).

> [T]o be a disciple [of Rajneesh] you had to believe that everything that happened was literally or mystically the guru's doing. If something appeared to be wrong or unjust or foolish, that was your myopia; it was otherwise in the guru's encompassing vision (Fitzgerald, 1986).

That attitude, of course, was nothing peculiar or pathological to Rajneesh, but is rather the essence of the guru-disciple relationship, in agrarian India and Tibet as in the postmodern West.

You think that your "divinely loving, omniscient" guru-figure is watching over you, and everything is always working out as it should, for your own greatest good? Tell that to Lisa McPherson.

Oh, you can't: She's dead.

* * *

We cannot take refuge in the idea that any of the individuals exposed herein are simply "false teachers," and that genuinely enlightened individuals would not behave so poorly. Nor is the problem simply with "naïve Westerners" following guru-figures who would not be taken seriously in the "spiritual East," as is sometimes wrongly suggested. For, if there is such a thing as a "genuine guru," who would ever have doubted that Vivekananda, Trungpa, Muktananda or Yogananda would qualify as such? These are not the *worst* of gurus, they are rather among the widely recognized *best!* Ramakrishna, likewise, was ostensibly one of

> the few indubitable Indian saints and sages amidst the veritable plague of so-called swamis, gurus, "enlightened masters," maharishis, "bhagvans" [*sic*] and the like of recent times (Oldmeadow, 2004).

After all that we have seen, then, it is easy to sympathize with the perspective of the insightful and democratic *1984* author, George Orwell (1980):

> Saints should always be judged guilty until they are proved innocent.

The bottom line with each of these figures is thus not whether one or another of their visions may have been real or imagined. Nor is it whether their actual degree of enlightenment is even one-tenth of what they and their loyal disciples claim it to be. (It is not.) Nor can our concerns be allayed by the suggestion that any reticence in approaching one or another of these figures is based merely in "fear of ego-annihilation" or in a "misunderstanding of the nature of obedience" to the guru. Nor is the problem with "projection/transference onto the perfect father/mother figure," or "intolerance for human imperfections" in evaluating the teacher's character and behavior. (Again, none of those issues were present in Zimbardo's prison study. Yet, he still could not avoid creating a toxic environment which exactly parallels ashramic society.)

Nor need we even worry about which of these organizations should be designated as a (prepersonal or transpersonal) "cult," or whether the alarming/alarmist term "brainwashing" should be used to describe any of their means of control. (Anyone who wishes to intelligently compare the tactics reportedly utilized by our world's ostensibly "safe" guru-figures and spiritual communities, against those in recognized "problematic" environments, however, will find *many significant* points of correspondence. For that, Denise Winn's [2000] *The Manipulated Mind* and Len Oakes' [1997] *Prophetic Charisma* are excellent.)

Rather, the root question to ask with regard to even these "best" figures is simply:

Would you trust your mental and physical health to any of them?

* * *

"Your spiritual teacher's an Enlightened Master? Join the club, buddy."

Maharshi. Trungpa. Muktananda. Swami Rama. Gurumayi. Chinmoy. Jetsunma. Andrew Cohen. Werner Erhard.

"Your spiritual teacher's an avatar? Impressive."

Vivekananda. Sivananda. Aurobindo. The Dalai Lama. Babaji. Lahiri Mahasaya. Sri Yukteswar. Yogananda. Ramakrishna's wife. Aurobindo's Mother. Ananda Moyi Ma. Mother Meera. Ma Jaya Sati Bhagavati. L. Ron Hubbard.

"Your spiritual teacher's *the* Avatar (Messiah, Teacher, etc.)? Hey, so's mine!"

Ramakrishna. Jiddu Krishnamurti. Meher Baba. Yogi Bhajan. Satya Sai Baba. Da Avatar. Rajneesh. Carlos Castaneda. Sun Myung Moon. David Koresh. Jim Jones. Charles Manson.

Jesus Christ.

"Guru, schmuru."

CHAPTER XXX

MAKE IT BETTER

> Nothing was true of all that she had believed, but the falsest thing of all was what she had mistaken for revealed truth.
>
> —François Mauriac, *Maltaverne*

WHERE THEN DOES ALL OF THIS leave spirituality and enlightenment?

First, one of Yogi Bhajan's former followers has rightly noted, of that guru's restrictive community environment:

> Certainly all those brainwashing hours of chanting and meditation hadn't been a worse way to spend my time than watching TV (K. Khalsa, 1994).

Likewise, the fact that most ashrams provide only vegetarian food need not be brought up with any raised eyebrows. The present author, for one, has been vegetarian since age twenty. (See www.newveg.av.org, www.vegdining.com, www.foodrevolution.org, www.veg.ca, Lane [1993] and John Robbins' [1987] *Diet for a New*

America.) That has included several years of adhering to a strict vegan (no eggs or dairy) diet.

Famous vegetarian rockers, interestingly, include many of the most creative and virile stars in the music world: Mick Jagger, David Bowie, Peter Gabriel and his former lover Sinead "the Anti-pope" O'Connor, Kate "Wuthering Heights" Bush, Elvis Costello, Bob Dylan, Bob Marley, Don "American Pie" McLean, Natalie Merchant, Stevie Nicks and Sarah McLachlan. Also, Tom Scholz—the 4.8 GPA M.I.T. Engineering graduate, mastermind guitarist/songwriter behind the group Boston—"guitar god" Jeff Beck, Tom Petty, Ozzy Osbourne, Paul McCartney, George Harrison ... Ringo ... and, ironically, Meat Loaf.

One may choose to focus on things like "hard-working disciples subsisting on [allegedly inadequate] vegetarian diets" or the absence of television as if they were part of the destructive "weirdness" of any "cult-like" situation. That, however, only dilutes the rest of one's objections to the *real* problems with the world's spiritual paths. (Full disclosure: By choice, I have no TV, either.)

The supposed differences between traditional and nontraditional religions are, further, again far less marked than one might like to believe:

> [T]he community that is spontaneously forming around Andrew [Cohen] in the midst of this modern, materialistic society so closely resembles the followings of the great Masters of ancient times (said complimentarily in [Cohen, 1992]).

No doubt that assertion was true, in celebrating Cohen's re-enacting of the countless, more notable guru-roles played before his own easily forgettable part in world history. But it is also valid in terms of reading backwards from the reported *problems* within and around Cohen to ascribe similar dysfunctionalities to earlier, archaic communities:

> [M]uch of the literature on Christianity in its first century of existence depicts the early Christians in totalistic and authoritarian terms (Robbins and Anthony, 1982).

Amazingly, Anthony and Robbins use that as an argument *in favor of* allowing our world's authoritarian "god-men" to operate unchecked. The Catholic Church has turned out so well, after all....

* * *

Given a dozen or more disciples and a guru-figure, the psychological dynamics inherent in the situation render it largely irrelevant whether the "one true/best guru" they are devotedly following is Jesus, Rajneesh or Da Savior, etc. Nor would the organizations created around those various gurus be particularly distinguishable after several centuries or millennia of cultural assimilation. Further, like it or not, what Adi Da's disciples believe of him, or what Cohen's followers accept of his claimed "perfection" and salvific potential, or what I once believed of Yogananda, is nowhere even one whit more ridiculous than what Christians believe of Jesus.

Or, compare L. Ron Hubbard's stories of Xenu and Teegeeack against the biblical Garden of Eden and Fall of Man. Taking each side equally literally, there is truly nothing to choose between them, in terms of (im)plausibility. Likewise, consider the idea that God would tell a prophet or a group of people how they should prepare food in order for it to be acceptable to Him. Were that notion not presented in an "acceptable," traditional context, it would be seen as a height of cultist absurdity. Indeed, it is far beyond any "weirdness" one could possibly ascribe to vegetarianism, for example. Yet, kosher foods get produced today all the same, with a special version of Coke® even being sold for Passover (Alter, 2004).

It is equally obvious that no such thing as "brainwashing" is inherently necessary in order to get people to ardently believe in ideas which, in the cold light of day, make no sense at all. Indeed, it should be clear to anyone not already committed to one side or the other that the taking of Jesus Christ as the sole Son of God is no more, *and no less* peculiar, than is the regard for a spiritual teacher and his wife as being the "parents" of humanity. Yet, beliefs like the latter have been claimed to be induced gradually and deceptively, via withheld information, love-bombing, sleep deprivation and other "mind control" techniques. The former "reasonable" delusion, on the other hand, occurs completely naturally and unforced, with its conversions even being actively welcomed by large segments of our everyday society.

The idea that "I used to be 'brainwashed' into thinking that some Guru was the Savior of humanity, but now I've recovered enough to be able to think clearly, and I realize that Jesus is the Savior," may or may not strike the reader as being completely hilarious. It is also, however, an eye-opening window into how even the most ridiculous ideas can be taken as being completely "normal" and "safe," if enough people believe in them.

Conversely, you may be safely and traditionally Jewish, for example, and believe, on the basis of holy scriptures written by the relevant ancient sages, that the Messiah is yet to come (cf. Rich, 2001). But then how do you know he won't come from Korea, for example? How do you distinguish "false" messiahs from the "true" one that you're expecting to come any day now? (And remember: Generally, if you fail to believe the "real" Messiah when he makes the same claims as the "false" ones do, your salvation is toast. Good reason to believe, then, to be on the safe side.) Is it by his manifesting of miraculous "signs and wonders" ... a la Sai Baba? By his claimed physical healing of others ... a la Yogananda? By his downplaying of the claims made on his behalf, i.e., "Only the true Messiah denies his divinity"? By his "divine love," as vouched for by his earliest followers on down, all of whom would probably have felt (i.e., imagined/projected) the same love and peace flowing from Jim Jones or the messianic Elvis Presley? By the characteristics explicated in your holy scriptures—the authors of which were surely no more wise or reliable than are the contemporary likes of Cohen, Da and Wilber?

Would the "real" Messiah reportedly own a machine-gun factory? Presumably not; but yet, as every devotee of the sun and moon knows, "God works in mysterious ways"—who are we to question the Divine, even in His human forms? If the Messiah doesn't conform to what the prophets of old said to expect, perhaps those ancient prophets got it wrong, right? Plus, Jesus himself overturned the tables of the money-lenders, even if not utilizing submachine guns in that, as a *real* "Rambo-dhisattva"—some things just require force.

If God spoke to Adam and to Abraham, why shouldn't He speak equally clearly to Ramakrishna and Sai Baba? Conversely, though, if none of the top forty "sages" of today are what they claim to be, what makes you think that things were any different for the equally "authentic" prophets millennia ago? Realistically, given the absence of the scientific method and the corresponding greater degree of superstition, those aged figures could only have been even *less* reliable.

Whether one is devoutly believing that a messianic Santa Claus lived two thousand years ago, or that Santa Claus is incarnate today, or that the real Santa Claus is yet to come on some long-anticipated Christmas Eve in the future, all are equally childish beliefs in something which blatantly *doesn't exist.* To regard one of those fairy tales as being believable, and the others as ridiculous or "obviously cultish," is more than I would personally be prepared to do.

If and when it turns out that the fat guy in the red suit at your local mall/ashram isn't the "real" Santa Claus, then, you might wisely take the hint, rather than sincerely searching throughout other malls across the world, convinced that one of them may harbor the genuine article.

Further, if someone keeps sneaking down your chimney in the middle of the night and molesting your wife or daughters while claiming to be a "Perfect Santa Claus Master," you'd want to know about it, right?

The *real* Santa Claus, though, would at least know where all the naughty girls live. Now there's a list worth checking twice!

* * *

The degree to which one is impressed by any purported sage's realization of a permanently enlightened, witnessing consciousness, will depend on what one takes the origin of self-awareness to be. That is, it will hinge on whether one believes that such witnessing self-awareness is an essential characteristic of Spirit and of one's realization of That, or rather takes it as deriving from mere biochemical reactions in the brain. For, in the latter case, such "realization" would indeed not be anything to get excited about. Either way, though, such "I am" awareness exists with our without the presence of thoughts in one's mental milieu.

Interestingly, then, Wilber himself claims (2000a) to be able to voluntarily enter a "brain-dead" state with no alpha, beta, or theta, yet "maximum delta" brainwaves, in *nirvikalpa samadhi.* Indeed, he has video of that EEG posted on the Integral Naked (2004) website. Presumably, none of that declaration has been exaggerated, i.e., one assumes that he has managed to hook the machine up correctly, and is not otherwise tampering with the results. If so, though, simply demonstrating the parapsychological component (if any) of that claim under properly controlled conditions could net him a cool million dollars at James Randi's JREF, in his Parapsychological Challenge. (My own impression is that such abilities might well be comparable to past incidents of yogis being able to put their hearts into a fast flutter, and then claiming that they had "stopped" the heartbeat [cf. Koestler, 1960]. That is, even valid claims are likely to be simple, untapped capabilities of the physical body—akin to the suspended animation sometimes accompanying hypothermia in humans, and now induced in mice via low doses of hydrogen sulfide. I, at least, would by now be surprised if there were anything "mystical" or paranormal about that.)

The same million-dollar qualifying nature would of course apply to the purported healing abilities of Barbara Ann Brennan, for example. Those are indeed claimed to be demonstrated regularly at her healing school (www.barbarabrennan.com) in Boca Raton, Florida.

Brennan has been regarded by the Da-admiring Elizabeth Kübler-Ross as being "one of the best spiritual ... healers in the Western hemisphere." Back in my "believer" days, I paid through the figurative nose for healing sessions with two of her graduates. One of them, grossly guilty of "playing psychologist" in his appointed hour, has since acted as a dean at her school. The beneficial effect of their healings on me? None at all, of course.

The dozen most frequently given excuses for claimed paranormalists not "putting their money where their mouths are" have already been compiled by Randi (2002). No sense reinventing that wheel, then.

For my own part, I am well past the point of accepting any parapsychological claims without them having been proved under appropriately controlled conditions.

* * *

No skeptic needs to "look through the microscope," or attempt to develop paranormal abilities himself, in order to validly have an opinion about whether the claims of purported mystics and healers are valid. Rather, it is more than sufficient for skeptics to insist that such abilities be demonstrated in experiments designed to directly or indirectly test for their existence, e.g., to distinguish one set of microscope slides from another at a better than "guessing" level.

You say you can see different auras around different people? Fine: Take two people, hidden behind baffles, with only their supposed energy fields extending beyond, for those to be visible to you. Ensure that there is no possibility of "cheating" or cueing. If you can really see their auras, you will be able to tell who is behind which baffle, in a series of trials, at a better than chance level.

You believe you can do astral remote viewing? Great: There's a five-digit number written down on a piece of paper, tacked to a wall in a specified location. It will be visible to you if, and only if, you can actually travel to that location in your astral body on an appointed day. If you can really do that viewing, then, you will have no difficulty at all in discerning the specific number in each of a series of trials.

Those are inexpensive, definitive, "yes-or-no" experiments—as opposed to, say, Marilyn Schlitz's recent "remote viewings" of "tourist sites in Rome from her home in Detroit" (Gorski, 2001), or Ingo Swann's purported subtle jaunts to Jupiter (the planet) in the late 1970s (Randi, 1982). Such elementary, not-subject-to-interpretation tests do not depend on any new theory, or on what the laws of physics may or may not allow. Rather, they simply ask that paranormalists demonstrate their claimed abilities to "use their microscopes" under properly controlled (e.g., double-blind) conditions, where they can't be fooling themselves or mistaking imagination for reality.

Both of the above definitive experiments, and many others like them, have been performed numerous times. (See Lane [1997] and Blackmore [1983]; plus the simple and correspondingly devastating [though unfortunately not double-blind] tests of Therapeutic Touch done by elementary schoolgirl Emily Rosa, related in Seidman [2001] and Randi [2003a].) That, though, has only been to the unfortunate acute embarrassment, and subsequent denial and excuse-making, of the tested individuals. For, their claimed paranormal abilities have invariably turned out to be merely imagined.

Worse, with regard to even "genuine enlightenment": As Richard Feynman could easily have noted, the mere *feeling* of being "one with all reality"—i.e., of having "no boundary" in consciousness—for example, does not mean that you really *are* thus undivided. After all, each one of us has all manner of internally produced feelings which have no objective correspondent. Until you can produce some verifiable artifact of knowledge through such purported superconscious states (whether astral, causal, witnessing, nondual, or whatever) which you could not have gotten any other way, it remains an utterly unsubstantiated claim, which *anyone* can make. *Nor can you yourself know whether your own experiences in those states are ontologically real, or merely imagined.*

Witnessing consciousness (i.e., self-awareness) can coexist with any physical, mental or parapsychological conditions, including indulgence in sex, alcohol, and drugs. Conversely, the latter may quite validly be used toward one's own "spiritual awakening," depending on one's preferences and constitution. If transcendent, witnessing awareness is anything short of "Spirit looking through you," however, that same awakening, whether temporary or long-term, will most likely have no more ontological reality than a *tulku's* rainbow. If you're having fun getting the rational mind out of the way via meditation, drugs, or trance, great; but as a life's goal or center, beyond pure selfishness....

Our world's "sages" in general, even when they are being honest, again consistently misinterpret utterly normal phenomena as being paranormal, and have mistaken innumerable hallucinations for meaningful visions. They have, that is, regularly proven themselves to be unable to distinguish between "real" mystical experiences, and merely imagined ones. Consequently, no one need feel obliged to take seriously their equally confident claims, filtered through the same addled mindset, as to even something so basic as the existence and nature of Spirit. Conversely, if one chooses to believe in the existence of That, it is *in spite of* the veracity of our world's "meditation masters," not *because of* their "personal authority."

* * *

Half of the practical problem with the very idea of witnessing and/or nondual enlightenment is that such a realization, even if it is ontologically real rather than just a subjective shift, regards everything equally. It thus, even in the standard and wholly noncontroversial accepted understandings, inherently does nothing whatsoever to make one a better person (via undoing one's psychological kinks or otherwise), or to make the world a better place. One could, in all seriousness, be the greatest living Realizer, and still be a pedophile, rapist or murderer.

Conversely, no crime or misbehavior, no matter how heinous, perpetrated by such a great "sage," could do anything to disprove his or her claimed realization. Thus, Ramakrishna's pedophilia, for example, "only shows how difficult it is for people afflicted with that orientation to grow past it," and says nothing about his realization: He was still "indubitably" a "great sage." Indeed, his behaviors may even be used to validate one's own comparable *sadhana*. (As to why Sai Baba's alleged pedophilia would not be equally tolerable, given his fully comparable claims to divinity: it basically depends on whom you started out naïvely believing to be "authentic" in the sagely arena.) The likes of Da, too, even given all of his alleged abuses, could still be Self-realized, just "patterned by partying behaviors."

Hell, you could be Jack the Ripper, attain to nondual awareness, and go right on ripping. You could be Adolf Hitler himself, not merely "mystically awakened" but nondually enlightened, and it wouldn't affect your actions one damned bit.

That exalted nondual realization—so beloved of Ken Wilber and Drukpa Kunley—even if ontologically real, is then worth pursuing ... why, exactly?

Of course, when one has "pledged enlightenment" for so long, it must be worth *something*. Even if auras and subtle energies don't exist, even if parapsychology was bogus from the beginning, even if every hoped-for superphysical phenomenon falls by the wayside, nondual enlightenment must be worth *something*.

Mustn't it?

* * *

There is no question that the "mind control" techniques cited earlier exist, that they are used, and that they do a lot to make things get worse, faster—as the deindividuation, force-feeding, humiliation and sleep deprivation did in Zimbardo's study. But even without them, in a "safe, traditional" religion, as soon as you have accepted the "divine guidance" and/or infallibility of those above you, you cannot disobey. And as soon as you have bought fully into the purported existence of hellfire and damnation or the like, you cannot leave that thought-environment without risking your eternal soul. That is, once deeply accepted, such "reasonable" and socially accepted beliefs again leave one no more able to freely choose to walk away from the traditional religion to face the possibility of eternal damnation, than one is free to walk away from a "destructive cult" and face a similar future.

Yet, that does not lessen the reality that people of sound mind and body, fully functional in the real world, will convert *completely voluntarily,* under no duress at all, to exactly such restrictive sets of tenets. In the face of such facts, the idea that "cult" members believe wacky things only because they were fed the belief system in incremental "bits and pieces," in the midst of love-bombing or the like, rather than having the entire theology dispassionately explained to them up front, is not supportable. The worst negatives may well not be presented until one has publicly committed to the best of the salvific positives. But those negatives are still just the flip side of the positives; one readily accepts them, if it means being part of the "saved" group.

And we all want to be part of the "in" group, or to be "chosen" by God, right? And to have the social support of others who are equally "special"? Why else would we find people barely escaping from nontraditional salvific "cults" to then join "safe," nontraditional religions? For the latter, in their early years of devotion and obedience to "the one true Savior" or to the relevant apocalyptic "prophets" preceding or following him, *were indistinguishable from the former.*

One should therefore not underestimate the human need to believe in Something—Anything—particularly if believing in that Big Something can be both a means of salvation and a route to social approval. Our species has never needed to be coerced into believing "six impossible things before breakfast." Rather, we have always done that quite willingly, even in the most ordinary circumstances. Indeed, the acceptance of the most hellish, fear-inducing of those beliefs occurs, with full social sanction, as part of every one of our world's "safe, traditional" religions.

(With equal willingness, newly freed people will vote for communist candidates if they think, from their own past and present experience, that their lives will improve in the short term for having that oppressive but comforting system reinstated [Hoo, 2005]. No "brainwashing" is required in any of that; it's just the sad nature of the species.)

Nor is the degree of "mature obedience" given by devoted Christians to Jesus any different from that given by any other loyal followers to their guru-figure: If (the Son of) God asks you to do something, you do it, right? The only "difference" is that Christians have found the "one true/best, living Savior," of whom every bizarre positive claim is necessarily "true"—as it was for Rajneesh, Jim Jones and David Koresh, etc., in the eyes of their devoted disciples in their own times.

Contrary to the frequently invoked comparison, the existence of fool's gold (i.e., "false gurus") does *not* mean that real gold (i.e., enlightenment and "true gurus") exists. Rather, it simply means that there are a lot of fools out there, who naïvely believe their eyes when they should rather be applying every possible rational test to the claims being placed before them.

I should know: I used to be one of those very same fools.

As David Lane has often noted, we would not think of buying a used car—whether sold by Bhagavan Das, Werner Erhard or otherwise—without first "kicking the tires." Yet, we do not think to equally properly question the assertions made by our world's "god-men" before giving up our independence and willingly/blindly following them. Further, *we again do that too often on the "good advice" of the "geniuses" and elders in transpersonal and integral psychology.* For, we quite reasonably assume that they have done at least minimal research, and thus that they would be in a position to offer more intelligent and informed opinions than our own.

Big mistake.

* * *

Of course, one is still free, even after all that, to believe that Jesus raised others (e.g., Lazarus) from the dead—as, it is claimed, did Yogananda and Meher Baba. (And as has Scientology: "Hubbard claims they brought a dead child back to life by ordering the thetan back and telling him to take over the body again" [Cooper, 1971].) And, that Christ fed the multitudes with manifested foodstuffs—as has Sai Baba. And, that J. C. rose from the grave himself—as, it is claimed, did Yogananda's guru, Sri Yukteswar.

As Lalich (2004) noted, however—apparently with unintentional yet heavy irony—in the context of our world's potentially harmful *nontraditional* groups:

> Countless examples—from making preposterous claims of raising the dead to taking multiple wives to committing ... murder ... clearly illustrate that some [so-called] cult members make seemingly irrational, harmful, and sometimes fatal decisions. Yet these acts are committed in a context that makes perfect sense at the time to those who enact them and are, in fact, consistent with an ideology or belief system that they trust represents their highest aspirations....
>
> Some [alleged] cults are totalistic when they are exclusive in their ideology (i.e., it is sacred, *the* only way).

Raising the dead: traditional Christianity.

Multiple wives: the Mormons, in their early days.

Committing murder in an ideological context where it makes "perfect sense" at the time: the witch hunts, the Crusades, etc.

"The only way": insert your preferred traditional religion here, whether petrified of condoms and masturbation, swigging Kosher-Cola, or fixated on modesty-enforcing burkas.

Further, when considering the purported "divinity" of the founders of any of our world's traditional religions, keep in mind that had any of the more recent "Christ-like" figures lived two thousand years ago, we would today know none of the reported "dirt" on them. That is, their "divinity" would remain intact, as Ramakrishna's *almost* did. Conversely, were Jesus alive today, all of his "Last Temptation"-like human indiscretions would have been put into print by journalists and disgruntled former followers. So, it is really just an accident of history that "Christ-like" gurus such as Sai Baba or Ramakrishna have been exposed enough for one to reasonably question their divinity and recognize the reportedly dangerous nature of their closed communities of disciples, while others such as Jesus have not.

> I had been trying to figure out the difference between a [so-called] cult and a religion—and had decided it was only two things: a matter of time and conformity (Sherrill, 2000).

> All religions, except perhaps the very earliest and most primitive, begin as new religious movements. That is, they begin as movements based on spiritual innovation usually in a state of high oppositional tension with prevailing religious practices. Often, they are begun by charismatic religious entrepreneurs (Zablocki, 1998).

> Conversely:

> In its first thousand years, the [Catholic] Church grew from a tiny, underground [so-called] cult into a vast, multinational power (Aarons and Loftus, 1998).

> Similarly:

> Like many groups that were formerly *enfantes terribles,* Scientology, if it continues in its current clean-up campaign, may one day become one of the world's most respected groups or Churches (Cooper, 1971).

Indeed, as Scientology's John Travolta once put it (in Gould, 1998): "I'm sure Christianity had some problems too in its first fifty years." (Tell that to Lisa McPherson. Oh, you can't....)

Saturday Night Fever ... or Saturday Night Mass. You decide.

> [O]ne asks oneself how much is really known about the founders and originators of the great classical religions of the past? How did they really begin? What were the true motives of their founders?.... Supposing that the world rolls on for a thousand years ... what then will the mythology of Scientology look like? And what stories will people be telling of Mr. Lafayette Ronald Hubbard, his teachings and his first disciples? (Evans, 1973).

In any case, if enough people believe that Jesus Christ (or Da Savior) is the sole Son of God, given to this world via Virgin/Dildo Birth and ascended into Glory, it ceases to be "weird," and the belief begins to be "inherited" by the children of each parent follower of that "one true/best guru." Comparably, as Strelley (1987) noted, even pathological events and beliefs within Rajneesh's ashram "all seemed familiar and 'normal' because that was the world we had built and were living in every minute of our lives." Indeed, as a general principle:

> A community is a community. Just as it is bizarre to those not in it, so it is natural ... to those who live it from within (Goffman, 1961).

If enough people believed that Adi Da was "the greatest Realizer," etc., the same homogenization and inheritance of belief would occur, and it would become weird to *not* believe that he was "the greatest."

Thankfully, that is not likely to happen.

Conversely, broadcasting the original meaning of Jesus' teachings in the Bible Belt today would produce every bit as much unrest as could be found in Rome two thousand years ago. It is not only contemporary so-called cults, after all, who encourage their members to "go and sell that thou hast, and give to the poor" (Matthew 19:21). Nor is that the only point of comparison:

> Many [alleged] cults put great pressure on new members to leave their families, friends, and jobs to become immersed in the group's major purpose. This isolation tactic is one of the

> ... most common mechanisms of control and enforced dependency (Singer, 2003).

Likewise:

> He that loveth father or mother more than me is not worthy of me: and he that loveth son or daughter more than me is not worthy of me.
>
> And he that taketh not his cross, and followeth after me, is not worthy of me (Matthew 10:37-8).

With all that, accepting a guru-disciple relationship in any context clearly calls for an attitude of "meditator beware":

> Of one hundred persons who take up the spiritual life, eighty turn out to be charlatans, fifteen insane, and only five, maybe, get a glimpse of the real truth. Therefore beware (Vivekananda, in [Nikhilananda, 1996]).

> [I]t is my belief that 90% of the so-called masters in the modern world are not enlightened at all (Harvey, 2000).

Of course, the "best" of the guru-figures we have covered herein—e.g., Ramakrishna, whom Harvey still quotes approvingly—would account for a good amount of the remaining 10%. (The fact that Harvey—"probably the preeminent mystic of our day" [Knight, 2003]—ridiculously considers the same 90% of "unenlightened masters" to be "occult magicians," holding their disciples in sway via real, supernatural powers, need not concern us here. Comparably, for the born-again Tal Brooke, Sai Baba was viewed as being closer to a literal "Antichrist" than a simple opportunistic conjuror. Yet projection and transference, which factor overwhelmingly into the guru-disciple relationship, are neither "occult" nor "from the devil." Or was the Beatles' earth-scooping, bladder-control-losing effect on their fans, too, based in "occult magic"?)

Nor was the situation any better in the days before our modern world:

> Buddha said that the chances of encountering a genuine teacher and getting enlightened were about on a par with the likelihood that a turtle coming to the surface in the middle of the ocean would put his head through a single ring tossed on the waves (Butterfield, 1994).

Even having ostensibly found that "ring," Stan Trout, a former decade-long swami follower of Muktananda, rightly observed:

> Those who willingly put aside their own autonomy, their own moral judgment, to obey even a Christ, a Buddha, or a Krishna, do so *at risk of losing a great deal more than they can hope to gain* [italics added].

One might take comfort, then, in the fact that Ramana Maharshi himself not only accepted no disciples, but had no human guru: "Guru is God or the Self." (At other times, however, Maharshi actually regarded Mount Arunachala—and presumably "all of the *siddhas* in it"—as his guru.) Aurobindo too (1953) "never took any formal initiation from anyone." The same is true of the Buddha.

Whatever spiritual evolution (real or imagined) might be realized under a guru, then, can obviously also be gotten without one. And given all of the problems we have noted with guru-figures, disciples, and their relationships, there is a lot to be said for erring on the side of caution in that regard.

Nor will simply asking for an honest opinion from the current followers of any purported sage keep one safe in all that. For, in the vast majority of cases, the loyal disciples who defend the "noble cause" are simply those who have not yet been sufficiently harmed by the guru. Or, they have not yet gotten close enough to him/her and the inner circle for long enough to comprehend what is really going on. Or, they are so close to the guru, and in need of preserving that position, as to lose all perspective, having wholly set aside their ability to impartially evaluate his actions, as they must if they are to be "good disciples."

As the head of Adi Da's Hermitage Service Order expressed his view of Da and his "Teachings" (in Colin, et al., 1985):

> He operates with the highest of integrity.... It is the most genuine thing I have ever encountered in my entire life.

Likewise, for another seclusive "avatar":

> Jim [Jones] is a man of absolutely unimpeachable character (in Layton, 1998).

> Eugene Chaikin, a Californian attorney who became a member of the [People's] Temple, [described Jim Jones] as the most loving, Christ-like human being he had ever met. An-

> other law graduate [actually, the assistant district attorney in San Francisco], Tim Stoen, called Jones "the most compassionate, honest and courageous human being the world contains" (Storr, 1996).

Similarly for Heaven's Gate:

> One early follower [of Applewhite and Nettles] recalled, "I just felt drawn to them. You could feel the goodness" (Lalich, 2004).

One takes such positive evaluations seriously—with the above being indistinguishable from the gushing which any loyal disciple would do over his or her "genuine/best/greatest" guru-figure—only at one's own grave risk.

So rather send a "deep, devotional bow" to Jim Jones than to the likes of Adi Da or Andrew Cohen, if you must at all. For at least Jones, like Applewhite, being long deceased, can do no further harm to persons so foolish as to trust him.

* * *

Rick Ross (2005c) gives ten characteristics to look for in a safe group and/or leader. Those range from the encouraging of critical thinking and individual autonomy in the followers, to the acceptance by the leader of constructive criticism, to a democratic environment, to willing financial disclosure on the part of the organization.

Good luck with finding any number of those characteristics in any "authentic, spiritually transformative" environment, though (or even in the typical business corporation, for that matter). For such a group begins, by definition, with a leader who is more "spiritually evolved"—i.e., who ostensibly sees truth more clearly—than the people around him. That is, he merits his position as leader not merely for having a greater, studied understanding of one or another set of holy scriptures, but rather for possessing a higher degree of enlightenment.

"Fortunately," though, the eager aspirants around him can attain to that same height if they simply follow his teachings and instructions. Thence follows role-playing, respect-hungering, and the understandable desire to distance oneself from anything that might interfere with one's most-valued spiritual progress (e.g., attachments, family, sex, etc.). And with the need to obediently endure anything which might accelerate the realization of one's becoming "as great as" the leader himself is, as quickly as possible, it's all downhill from there.

So it is, by now, in no way surprising that even the best of our world's spiritual communities have been found to quickly degenerate into "problematic" nests, leaving their idealistic followers wondering, "Where did it all go wrong?"

The point, again, is not that brainwashing, mind control, deceptive recruiting and enforced isolation do not exist, for they surely do. But even without them, things are *much worse* than would be imagined by theorists who point to such issues as being distinguishing characteristics of so-called cults.

If you cannot bring yourself to accept that, you are free to continue believing that the Roman Catholic Church, the U.S. Marines, and the average prison, for example, are "safe" places to be. And good luck to you in that—you're going to need it, should people you care about ever become trapped in those "non-cultic" environments.

* * *

The collection of "enlightened" individuals we have considered here are again in no way the *worst* of our world's spiritual teachers, but are rather among the universally recognized *best*. The disregard for the guru-disciple relationship evinced herein thus has nothing to do with simply rejecting it, whether wisely or blindly, in favor of an alternative emphasis on individuality and independence, without regard for the benefits of learning from a teacher wiser than oneself. Rather, such disdain is the simple and unavoidable outcome of recognizing the high probability that, in any given case, the guru-disciple relationship is very likely to do much more harm than good.

Conversely, the relevant question is not why anyone should be "anti-guru," but rather: How could anyone, in the face of all of the long-extant reported issues quoted herein, still be "*pro*-guru"? If the assertion is that the good mixed in with the bad (for any given spiritual teacher) offsets the latter, the appropriate response is that a mixture of nectar and poison is more dangerous than is one of poison alone. After all, animals die from drinking anti-freeze because it *tastes good*. Were it not for the good, they would not simultaneously swallow the bad.

As Dick Anthony (et al., 1987) quite unsuspectingly put it:

> [A] number of group leaders who evolved into dangerous, authoritarian tyrants seemed truly to have ... loving kindness, generosity, selflessness. These leaders were extremely dangerous precisely because they did combine such an unlikely mix of extreme beneficence and extreme abusiveness within them. The beneficence was prominent first, attracted a large, devoted following, and then gradually gave way to a "dark side" that came increasingly into expression over ten or twenty years, imperceptibly turning heaven into hell for the followers.

The point which Anthony has completely missed, of course, is that the hitherto "peacenik" student guards in Zimbardo's prison study likewise combined "extreme beneficence and extreme abusiveness" within themselves. Indeed, each one of those eventual "Nazis" again began the study congenially, only having his tyrannical authoritarianism brought out later by the closed, hierarchical environment.

* * *

If all of this seems too cynical, simply compare the reported behaviors we have seen herein with how any sensible and self-honest person would behave. Couldn't *you* (outside of the eventual, perspective-losing effects of imperial role-playing) do better than *every one* of the respected spiritual figures evaluated here, in guiding other people's evolution, regardless of whether the enlightenment claimed by each of these so-called sages is real or imagined? Even if your every hidden indiscretion was made public, wouldn't you still come off looking like a better human being than any of these bozos?

Then, factor in the orders-of-magnitude difference between the disinfected, hagiographic versions of the lives of undisputed "sages" such as Ramakrishna and Krishnamurti, versus their real natures. And in doing that, never be so naïve as to imagine that the distortions, cover-ups, group-think, wishful thinking and outright fabrications applied to any claimed saint's daily behavior by his vested-interest disciples would not be effected just as much with regard to his or her visionary experiences, other "miracles," and overall "compassionate" nature.

I would personally still *like* for most of the fairy tales told in the name of spirituality to be true. The problem which I have by now in accepting any of them is not that I would *a priori* or "scientifically" find it difficult to believe that human volition can affect the behavior of matter. Indeed, I would still actively prefer for auras, chakras, subtle energies, astral travel, manifested "loaves and fishes" and their ilk to exist. The issue I have by now is simply that the sources of information in all of those "miraculous" and mystical regards are so unreliable as to be less than worthless. Further, the claimed phenomena fail uniformly, on every point on which they have been properly tested, to stand up to simple rational questioning and reproducibility.

* * *

> If people were really well-informed, they would be immune to bad gurus (Robert Thurman, in [Watanabe, 1998]).

Well, you are now "really well-informed." And being thus wise, knowing of the Dalai Lama's admiration for Drukpa Kunley, and being cognizant of Richard Baker's reported behaviors at the SF Zen Center ... you would not be surprised to learn that Thurman is still a loyal admirer of the homophobic Lama, after having been a friend of SFZC during Baker's apocalyptic tenure there. Nor would you be taken aback to find that Thurman, in spite of his own "immunity to bad gurus" and foolish pandits after a lifetime of spiritual study and practice ... is a founding member of Wilber's Integral Institute. Nor would you nearly fall off your chair in learning that he has released a recording of dialogs on Buddhism and politics between himself ... and alternative medicine's Deepak Chopra.

Interestingly, both Thurman and the Dalai Lama endorsed Chopra's (2000) book, *How to Know God* ... as did Ken Wilber and Uri Geller. Thurman called it the "most important book about God for our times." Not to be outdone, *the* Mikhail Gorbachev elevated Chopra to the position of being "undoubtedly one of the most lucid and inspired philosophers of our times."

And all of that, while Thurman was simultaneously being named as one of *Time* magazine's twenty-five most influential people in 1997, and viewed as "America's number one Buddhist" by the *New York Times*. The point being that, with no particular disrespect intended toward Dr. Thurman, even the best and most-esteemed figures in Buddhism and elsewhere demonstrably cannot be relied upon to do other than lead us *directly to* spiritual teachers whom we would do much better to avoid, should we make the mistake of following their "really well-informed" advice.

Even someone like the Buddhist teacher Jack Kornfield has again failed to do even minimally adequate research regarding the alleged unpunished breaking of rules in the East, before offering a confident, watertight opinion. That is, he has presented a superficially convincing, but ultimately utterly false theory, as if it were inarguable, researched fact. Further, he was still maintaining that indefensible opinion nearly *two decades* after his own days teaching at Trungpa's Naropa during its most "wild and crazy" period. Those, too, were its most overtly "cult-like" times, as is painfully obvious for anyone with eyes even halfway open to see such things.

Few "experts" in Eastern spirituality are better informed, or more trustworthy or level-headed, than are Thurman and Kornfield. Yet, it is merely one small step from them and their "informed" opinions to find yourself following the likes of Trungpa, Richard Baker, or the "Tibetan Catholic" Dalai Lama.

Or, consider the work of Rabbi Michael Lerner—briefly dubbed the "guru of the White House" during the Clinton administration. (During a period of unpopularity, the Clintons also sought advice from the Muktananda-admiring, firewalking Tony Robbins. That self-help icon has guested on Wilber's Integral Naked forum, and has also been an interviewee of Andrew Cohen [1999a].) Lerner is a close friend of Ken Wilber, and another founding member of the Integral Institute. And, while his political Tikkun organization, groups and magazine may well be "safe and nourishing" ones, he also considers Wilber to be a "great mind," whose "brilliance pours out on every page" of his journals.

And then this from the same man—Lerner—blurbing for kw's (2001b) *A Theory of Everything:*

> Ken Wilber is one of the most creative spiritual thinkers alive today, and *A Theory of Everything* is an accessible taste of his brilliance. Like a masterful conductor, he brings everyone in, finds room for science and spirit, and creates music for the soul.

Suppose, then, that you, as a young but dedicated spiritual seeker and/or political activist, and an admirer of Lerner, were to attend one or another of the Tikkun functions. And suppose that you discovered the work of Ken Wilber through that, devouring his "brilliant" books in the following months. Not knowing any better, you would undoubtedly be impressed by the great man's "genius" and "compassion" on such a wide range of subjects—as I myself was for two months, many naïve years ago—particularly given Lerner's endorsement of that "brilliance."

How long would it be, then, before you followed kw's "good advice" in those writings? How long before you (perhaps not unlike Mr. Kowalczyk) found yourself "surrendered completely" as a non-celebrity to a "great Realizer," whose every alleged "Rude Boy" abuse was being indulged in only for your own benefit, as a wise "Teaching"?

Lerner himself has not only endorsed Andrew Cohen's *Living Enlightenment* (2002), but also been interviewed by Cohen (2001a) in *What Is Enlightenment?* magazine. Dr. Lerner has a Ph.D. in clinical psychology; Cohen, perhaps unique among human beings, has no psychological shadow (or so he claims). He would thus surely have made a fascinating case study for Lerner, had the latter's eyes been open to that rare, breakthrough opportunity.

Interestingly, other enthusiastic endorsers of Cohen's *Living Enlightenment* have included Jack Crittenden, Deepak Chopra, Lee Lozowick, Mariana Caplan, and the late Swami Satchidananda himself.

Yet, "with great power comes great responsibility." And if one is using one's good name in any field to give credibility to others, one has a grave responsibility to ensure that the latter are actually some semblance of what they claim to be. Yet, one struggles to find any comprehension of that fact among Wilber and the rest of these "experts." For, if they had understood that principle at all, they would be very humbled to realize the irreparable damage they have done in indefensibly encouraging others to throw their lives away in "surrendering completely" to the likes of Da and Cohen.

* * *

For my own part, the actions alleged of our world's "fire-breathing" gurus (e.g., at the WHAT enlightenment??! website) and their henchmen remind me of nothing so much as having transferred rural schools in grade seven.

The previous year, the "alpha male" in that new environment had, I was told, been forcing the boys in the grade below him to crawl through mud and endure other forms of mistreatment. Why? Just because he could exercise that power—no better reason or provocation, outside of his own insecure psychology.

Appropriately, the power-abusing boy got his comeuppance the following year, being beaten up by his peers in grade seven.

His brave response? To go crying to his pastoral parents about that, tearfully begging that they move to a different community, etc., but of course making no mention of how he had merited that retribution.

If only our world's guru-figures and spiritual seekers in general had as much sense as a bunch of thirteen-year-olds. They might, in that case, consider holding their peers and heroes responsible for their reported abuses of power, i.e., "As ye beat the crap out of others, so shall the crap be beaten out of you." With even that minimal application of intelligence and real compassion, there would be far fewer simpering "Rude Boys" in the world. Much less would those socially dysfunctional fools be *celebrated* for allegedly coercing others into enduring demeaning acts "for their own good."

* * *

The recurring phenomenon of "bad gurus," from which no one is immune so long as he holds on to the hope that one or another of them can lead him closer to enlightenment, is actually completely predictable. For, absolute power corrupts, not merely *some* of the time, but *all* (or at least 99.99%) of the time. (It was actually in response to the 1870 papal declaration of infallibility that Lord Acton coined the relevant phrase [Allen, 2004].) Against that psychological reality, whatever public face any "sage" may show in apparent tolerance for questioning by his celebrity followers or the like, is typically no more real than one's temporary mask shown at a news conference might be.

And beyond even any sagely "best behavior," human transference and projection can create a "god" even out of a pile of shit—as Nityananda knew well. One cannot afford to go into any such "spiritual" environment with a naïvely positive attitude, hoping for the best, seeing only the good in others while ignoring the red flags for the bad, and trusting the guru-figure and his guards/henchmen to guide you right. For, such Pollyanna-ish behavior is exactly, without exaggeration, how Jonestowns (and Rajneeshpurams, and "true *sanghas*" such as Trungpa's and Muktananda's and Yogananda's) get started.

No small part of what is supposed to separate mystics from the truly insane is exactly the ability to distinguish reality from their own fantasies or externalized voices/visions. Yet, that ability to distinguish is exactly what is apparently lacking in "astral moon cannibal slaves," subtle Allied Forces, irreconcilable reincarnations of Leonardo da Vinci, sprightly leprechauns and Paulsen's bad-science-fiction UFOs. And in that case, the relevant "sages" could potentially have simply imagined/hallucinated/self-hypnotized *every* step of their own "enlightening" spiritual experiences.

The preceding point makes the fact that a person can be simultaneously at a very high level of spiritual development, and at a very low level of conscious evolution along moral lines, essentially irrelevant. For, if one cannot tell the difference between "real" spiritual experiences and imagined ones, it is not simply one's lack of moral development or the like which invalidates the supposed wisdom in the teachings and behaviors which are based on those same experiences.

By comparison, a clinical schizophrenic with a high level of moral or empathic development would still make a very dangerous leader or guru-figure. That is true however clearly the imagined "voice of God" might be speaking to him or her and then enforced on the world "with integrity." It is further true even if that voice is experienced as a nondual (e.g., One Taste) phenomenon by the mentally unstable individual. Conversely, if one is going to surrender one's will to any guru-figure, one would hope to do better than an evaluation concluding, "Sure he's psychotic, but he's got a lot of integrity"!

One is then left with very little indeed to cling to in all of this. For, if even the widely recognized "best" Realizers apparently cannot distinguish between hallucination and their own ostensibly valid realizations, are lesser Realizers to be regarded as being *more* reliable?

Seen from that perspective, the most that any spiritual teacher can be is a decent, honest, unpretentious, even-tempered and caring human being, never "divinity in the flesh." Yet, if even one-tenth of the allegations made against those figures are valid, the overwhelming majority of them would fail miserably at even that minimal, level-headed decency. Thus, the bulk of what they would wish to teach us by their own behaviors, no sensible person would want to learn.

So even let each of them be every bit as enlightened as they have claimed to be, then. (Again, if these top forty spiritual leaders are not so divine, *who is?)* It makes no difference; for, with the endemic reported character flaws which they bring to the table, who of them could ever do more good than harm in the world? What use, then, is their vaunted "enlightenment"? And, if anything like karma and reincarnation exist, who could suffer more for their alleged actions, in future lives, than such respected holy fools, from the "Christ-like" Ramakrishna on down?

The good news, though, is that none of these grandiose god-figures, playing unconvincingly at being holy, compassionate and wise, have any power whatsoever over anyone else other than what you, or I, would give to them. Without our obedient submission and credulous swallowing of their untenable claims and widespread exaggerations, they will dry up and blow away as if they had never existed.

Put another way: They need us *much more* than we need them.

In the words of the formerly born-again *Hustler* magazine publisher, Larry Flynt (in Krassner, 1993):

> I believe that Jesus was not a more important teacher than Buddha, and that neither Jesus nor Buddha is more important than any individual.

Please explicitly note one more thing: The apparently unstable and/or radically unreliable "best" sagely individuals considered herein are in large part exactly the same ones upon whose claims and authority the very existence of the realization called "enlightenment" is widely accepted. If they cannot be trusted in the testable details and paranormal claims, however, can they really be relied upon to accurately represent the higher realizations from which they have derived their greatest fame? If so very, *very* much of what even the most revered spiritual Realizers in the history of our globe have said or written was a probable hallucination, provable misrepresentation, or demonstrable exaggeration, can you really afford to take *any* of their claims "on faith"?

And if not, what are we to make of the ageless, high regard for the institution of gurus, and the belief that they can lead you to an enlightenment which they themselves most likely do not possess beyond mere self-delusion, via your unconditional obedience to them? Is such belief and surrender any more of a mature, rational approach to life than is the belief in receiving comparable secular gifts from Santa Claus, through following his instruction to be "nice" (i.e., obedient) rather than "naughty"?

I, personally, do not believe that it is.

Of course, for over a decade of my own life, I bought as fully as anyone into the "myth of the totally enlightened guru." But in my own defense, I didn't have access to the wide swath of information, as gathered herein, which would have convinced any rational, thinking person that the practitioners of the "guru game" are not in any way what they present themselves as being. Indeed, without the Internet and over five thousand hours of research, I still wouldn't have it.

You, however, having gotten this far, *do* have easy access to that information. And you can save yourself, and those you care for, from undergoing a great deal of suffering, simply by using it wisely.

For, if we have learned one thing from Blaise Pascal, it is that "those who play at being angels, end up as animals."

There may still be more to religion and spirituality than mere hallucination, dissociation, psychoses, transference, conformity, massive co-dependence, belongingness needs, and hierarchical outlets for power-tripping authoritarianism and "Rude Boy" sadism. But the sad fact is that the above principles would fully suffice to create exactly the situation which we see in the imprisoning guru/savior-influenced "spiritual world" around us. Indeed, *they could not help but do so.*

* * *

Christopher Reeve (2002) then summed up his noteworthy, common-sense conclusions regarding spirituality. (Reeve's own genuine spiritual interests had previously led him to investigate both Muktananda and TM, in addition to Scientology.)

> Gradually I have come to believe that spirituality is found in the way we live our daily lives. It means spending time thinking about others.

It should not take "Superman" to point out what the revered avatars and theoreticians within the spiritual marketplace have so clearly failed to put into practice for so long, messing up others' lives in the process while congratulating themselves about their own supposedly shadow-less, "perfect" and nondual enlightenments. Of course, we all know that consideration for others is supposed to be a *prerequisite* for the spiritual path. That preliminary, however, is typically forgotten somewhere along the way to enlightenment:

> [A]s I began to spend time with people who'd devoted many years to meditation, people who had built their lives around spiritual practices aimed at transcending the ego, I saw that they had many of the same difficulties I did. Few of them behaved more compassionately, sensitively, or selflessly than the majority of people I knew who didn't meditate at all (Schwartz, 1996).

Robert Thurman (2004) told of his own related experiences with an acquaintance of his, widely known for being calm and holy, who had been excluding him from participating in the dialog at a conference she was leading. When questioned by another friend as to why he was not taking a more active role in the conversation, Thurman replied:

> "I'd love to, but So-and-so won't allow me to talk. It seems she has a bug in her ear about me!" I inflected my delivery in a nasty way, knowing full well that the friend in question, standing nearby, was overhearing what I was saying.
>
> It was a petty and rude way to speak, it showed how poor my own self-control was, and I am ashamed to tell the story. However, the reaction of the leader was an even greater shock. She rushed up to me, stuck her furious face inches from mine, and shrieked at the top of her lungs, "F—— you, Bob. F—— you! How dare you say such a thing about me!"

Further, any enlightenment which can be negated not only by the consumption of alcohol (cf. Wilber, 2000a) but even by a bad cold (or staph infection) is an interesting type of awakening: "I used to be enlightened, but I caught the flu." Indeed, that "fall" fully disproves the idea that "Great Masters, having attained their own enlightenment, meditate only for the good of others." That is, if the "permanent" realization of that highest evolution can be lost by something as seemingly irrelevant as temporary bodily illness, meditative practice is obviously being continued in order to maintain that state, regardless of any sage's protests that it is being done only "for others."

Even without those concerns, however, the quantity of woefully ignorant advice and self-serving misrepresentation dispensed by our world's "enlightened" individuals makes it impossible to ascribe any actual inherent wisdom or intelligence-guided compassion to that state. The dismal lack of commitment to reality in situations where it does not flatter the "enlightened" figure should be another blatant red flag in that regard. It should further underline the danger of subverting/surrendering one's own judgment to the alleged "greater insight" of such individuals. Indeed, that warning exists wholly independent of arguments as to whether one is "childishly/blindly/submissively following" or "maturely/consciously surrendering and obeying" the same figures. For, bad advice from others is best resisted regardless of what one's own flaws or present stage of psychological development may be.

On top of all that, if there are a mere *dozen* "deeply enlightened" Zen masters on the Earth right now, for example, that figure surely pales in comparison to the thousands if not millions of people who have had their lives devastated by the same paths—or even by the very same stick-wielding "wise masters." The fact that such followers may too often lack the independence and initiative to realize how much they have given up in thus being willingly mistreated does not in any way excuse the actions of the "superior beings" who sit in authority over them.

Following in the footsteps of such "sagely" individuals, then, could hardly be a confident step toward alleviating even one's own suffering. Much less could it be a sensible means of enacting a bodhisattva vow to liberate all others, for that same vow would surely imply *easing* others' suffering on the average, not *increasing* it.

> Of what use is any future or enlightenment that does not restore a just and fully human world? (Marin, 1995).

By contrast, in cultivating our own independence, learning from *our own* errors rather than "making other people's mistakes," and attempting to understand how our own actions affect others, we may at least know that we're heading in the right direction as human beings. That is so even if such a direction is, in practice, too often the exact opposite of where the "spiritually enlightened" guru-figures of this world, and their apologists, would have us obediently go.

Further, real life provides more than enough "learning experiences" for each one of us, should we choose to take advantage of those toward introspection and personal change. No one needs a guru-figure or a constricting, independence-robbing ashram to fabricate crises for that.

> I described to my friends my own disillusionment with spiritual practice, and my discovery that craving and greed infect the spiritual life just as they do every other aspect of life. "What I thought I was leaving behind," I said, "I found right here [at Kripalu]—the *kleshas* [afflictions], the erroneous beliefs, creating new spiritual knots" (Cope, 2000).

As Butterfield (1994) then reasonably concluded, after years of devotedly following Trungpa and his successor, Osel Tendzin:

> I gave up trying to base personal relationships on dharma consciousness, or the bodhisattva ideal, neither of which led to my establishing an enduring bond with another human being. Instead I looked for what I could do at any given moment to respect and care about myself and others, communicate honestly, and live my needs and experiences as they actually arose, with no thought that I was on a spiritual journey or had to bring everything to an all-consuming path.

Or, as Carlos Castaneda's potential successor—who later wisely repudiated that role—came to realize:

> [M]y incursion in the world of Carlos Castaneda gave me many things. It showed me the reality of relying on yourself and not projecting your fantasies upon others. It showed me that the only true magic is "ordinary magic" and that the most important thing in life is the way we treat each other (Tony Karam, in [Wallace, 2003]).

Deborah Boehm (1996; italics added), following her own experiences with Zen Buddhism in Japan, likewise noted:

> I realized now that any enlightenment I might ever attain would come from living, from making mistakes, from thinking things through, just as the most valuable lessons I had learned in Kyoto about how to be a less-flawed mortal mammal took place *outside* the meditation hall.

No new guru, no new religion, no new church or ostensibly channeled readings are needed for that, nor is their presence even beneficial toward real spiritual growth (whatever that might be).

Rather, it is simply up to each one of us to use our own independence and intelligence to make the world a better place, and to make ourselves better people, with or without taking up meditation on top of that.

Monica Pignotti (1989) then opined, after spending half a decade in Scientology:

> I know that no one is going to give me the answers to life. I now realize that I have a mind that is fully capable of guiding me through the decisions I make in life and I will never put anyone or anything above what I know and feel. I now know the techniques that are [allegedly] used to control people's minds and that people exist in this world that have no compunction about using these techniques to manipulate people.... My life and my mind are now my own and I will never give them up again.

Those are very hard lessons to learn for any man or woman who, too trustingly, wants to believe in the "myth of the totally enlightened guru." But anyone who simply keeps questioning what he or she has been told by the authorities on any spiritual path will eventually come to exactly the same conclusions and resolve. It is inevitable, for the long-extant reported information can lead to no other end.

So let each of us then go our own way, following our hearts, utilizing unbiased, multi-perspectival reason to the best of our abilities, and courageously speaking truth as best we can, regardless of whether or not that fits into "the world according to" any "enlightened" sage's authoritarian view of reality.

That may not be a flawless way of proceeding but, after all that we have seen herein, it couldn't get much worse.

So let's do what we can to make it better.

ESSENTIAL ONLINE RESOURCES

OVERALL

If you value your mental and physical health, please don't even consider joining any nontraditional religion, with or without a guru-figure at its helm, without having first researched it through these websites:

Freedom of Mind Center (Steven Hassan, author of *Combatting Cult Mind Control* and *Releasing the Bonds*) — www.freedomofmind.com

The Ross Institute — www.rickross.com

Cult News — www.cultnews.com

GuruRatings Yahoo! Group — http://groups.yahoo.com/group/GuruRatings

Sarlo's Guru Rating Service — www.globalserve.net/~sarlo/Map.htm (some of Sarlo's higher ratings should absolutely be downgraded on the basis of the information presented throughout this book)

reFOCUS — www.refocus.org

International Cultic Studies Association (ICSA), *Cultic Studies Review* — www.csj.org

Ex-Cult Resource Center — www.ex-cult.org

Cult Information Centre (UK) — www.cultinformation.org.uk

Yahoo! Groups — www.groups.yahoo.com

MSN Groups — http://groups.msn.com

Flameout — www.flameout.org/flameout/gurus/index.html

BEWARE the Cult Awareness Network — www.cultawarenessnetwork.org (this is now a "Scientology-related" entity)

INFORMATION ON SPECIFIC SPIRITUAL LEADERS AND ORGANIZATIONS

Adi Da — http://lightmind.com/library/daismfiles,
www.adidaarchives.org

Andrew Cohen — http://whatenlightenment.blogspot.com
http://what-enlightenment-uncensored.blogspot.com
http://jekyllhyde.homepage.dk/home.html

Buddhism — http://www.american-buddha.com/CULTS.htm

Chinmoy — www.chinmoycult.com

Kriyananda, Ananda Church of Self-Realization —
www.anandainfo.com
www.anandauncovered.com

Ma Jaya Sati Bhagavati — www.kashiashram.com

Maharaji, Divine Light Mission — http://ex-premie.org
http://www.prem-rawat-maharaji.info

Maharishi Mahesh Yogi — http://onwww.net/trancenet.org
www.suggestibility.org
www.angelfire.com/cantina/donandmarcy/TM.html

Muktananda, SYDA — www.leavingsiddhayoga.net

Paramahansa Yogananda, Self-Realization Fellowship —
www.yogananda-dif.org
Cult Busters—SRF Division:
http://p208.ezboard.com/bcultbusterssrfdivision
SRF Walrus: www.angelfire.com/blues/srfwalrus
Kriya Yoga Discussion Board:
www.boards2go.com/boards/board.cgi?&user=Kriya

Satchidananda — http://meltingpot.fortunecity.com/albania/148

Sai Baba — www.exbaba.com
www.snowcrest.net/sunrise
http://www.npi-news.dk/page152.htm
http://home.no.net/anir/Sai/enigma/index.htm
http://bdsteel.tripod.com/More/index.html

Scientology — www.xenu.net
www.factnet.org
http://home.snafu.de/tilman
www.lisamcpherson.org
http://lisatrust.bogie.nl/home.htm

Zen — www.darkzen.com

For archives of sites which move or disappear: The Internet Archive Wayback Machine (http://web.archive.org/collections/web.html).

BIBLIOGRAPHY

With many of these books being out of print, I have found the used book emporium at www.abebooks.com to be invaluable for my own research.

Aarons, Mark and John Loftus (1998 [1991]), *Unholy Trinity: The Vatican, The Nazis, and the Swiss Banks* (New York: St. Martin's Griffin).

Actualism (2006), "Selected Correspondence Peter: Jane Goodall" (http://www.actualfreedom.com.au/actualism/peter/selected-correspondence/corr-goodall.htm).

Adriel, Jean (1947), *Avatar: The Life Story of Avatar Meher Baba* (Berkeley, CA: John F. Kennedy University Press).

Agence France-Presse (1999), "Australian Teenager Sent Threat via Charles Manson," March 22 (http://www.rickross.com/reference/manson/manson13.html).

Alexander, Meredith (2001), "Thirty Years Later, Stanford Prison Experiment Lives On," in *Stanford Report,* August 22 (http://news-service.stanford.edu/news/august22/prison2-822.html).

Allegro, John M. (1970), *The Sacred Mushroom and the Cross: Fertility Cults and the Origins of Judaism and Christianity* (New York: Doubleday & Co.).

Allen, Charlotte (2001), "The Scholars and the Goddess," in *Atlantic Monthly,* January (http://www.rickross.com/reference/wicca/wicca31.html).

Allen, John L., Jr. (2004), *All the Pope's Men: The Inside Story of How the Vatican Really Thinks* (New York: Doubleday).

Alter, Rabbi (2004), "Ask Rabbi Alter" (http://web.archive.org/web/20040216042603/http://www.jewmich.com/askthe.htm).

Ammachi (2004), "Amma" (http://www.ammachi.org/amma/index.html).

Amritanandamayi, Mata (1994), *For My Children* (San Ramon, CA: Mata Amritanandamayi Center).

Anandamoy, Brother (1995), *Spiritual Marriage* (Los Angeles: Self-Realization Fellowship).

Anandamoy, Brother (1982), *Is Peace Possible in Today's World?* (Los Angeles: Self-Realization Fellowship).

Anandamoy, Brother (1979), *Closing the Generation Gap* (Los Angeles: Self-Realization Fellowship).

Ananthanarayanan, N. (1970), *The Inspiring Life-Story of Swami Sivananda* (New Delhi: Indraprastha Press).

Anthony, Dick, Bruce Ecker and Ken Wilber (1987), *Spiritual Choices: The Problem of Recognizing Authentic Paths to Inner Transformation* (New York: Paragon House).

Areddy, James T. (1989), "Sri Chinmoy Seeks to Claim a Title: Stunt Man Supreme," in *The Wall Street Journal,* January 13 (http://www.rickross.com/reference/srichinmoy/srichinmoy9.html).

Arendt, Hannah (1992 [1963]), *Eichmann in Jerusalem: A Report on the Banality of Evil* (New York: Penguin Books).

Arya, Rohit (2004), "Paramahansa Yogananda—Reports from the Inside of Indian Spirituality" (http://www.indiayogi.com/content/indsaints/yogananda.asp).

Askenasy, Hans (1978), *Are We All Nazis?* (Secaucus, NJ: Lyle Stuart Inc.).

Associated Press (2003), "Celebrities Push for Transcendental Meditation Center in L.A." (http://www.rickross.com/reference/tm/tm59.html).

Associated Press (1991), "Swami's Former Followers Say He Demanded Sexual Favors," August 2 (http://www.rickross.com/reference/yogaville/yogaville9.html).

Atack, Jon (1992), "The Total Freedom Trap: Scientology, Dianetics and L. Ron Hubbard" (http://www.factnet.org/Books/TotalFreedomTrap/TFTrap.html?FACTNet).

Atack, Jon (1990), *A Piece of Blue Sky: Scientology, Dianetics and L. Ron Hubbard Exposed* (New York: Carol Publishing Group; text available online at http://www.clambake.org/archive/books/apobs/).

Aurobindo, Sri (1953), *Sri Aurobindo on Himself and on the Mother* (Pondicherry, India: Sri Aurobindo Ashram).

Austin, Bill (1999), "Rev. Thomas Alhburn, Writer of Endorsements, Finally Meets Da" (http://lightmind.com/thevoid/daism/alhburn-leela.html).

Baba, Meher (1967), *Discourses* (San Francisco, CA: Sufism Reoriented).

Baba, Upasani (1978), *The Talks of Sadguru Upasani-Baba Maharaja,* Volume 2, Part B (Sakori, India: Upasani Kanyakumari Sthan).

Bailey, David and Faye Bailey (2003), "The Findings" (http://web.archive.org/web/20031214164954/http://www.npi-news.dk/page152.htm).

Barry, Dave (1992), *Dave Barry Does Japan* (New York: Random House).

Bart, Peter (1998), "Defenders of the Faith Should Stand at Ease," in *Daily Variety,* June 27 (http://www.rickross.com/reference/scientology/celebrities/celebrities1.html).

BBC (2003), "The Conquest" (http://www.bbc.co.uk/radio4/history/sceptred_isle/page/8.shtml?question=8).

Behar, Richard (1991), "The Thriving Cult of Greed and Power," in *Time,* May 6 (http://www.rickross.com/reference/scientology/scien413.html).

Belfrage, Sally (1981), *Flowers of Emptiness: Reflections on an Ashram* (New York: The Dial Press).

Bellamy, Dodie (1995), "Eckankar: A Former Member Revisits the Movement," in *San Diego Reader,* June 22 (http://www.geocities.com/eckcult/dodie.html).

Berry, Jason (1992), *Lead Us Not into Temptation: Catholic Priests and the Sexual Abuse of Children* (New York: Doubleday).

Berry, Jason and Gerald Renner (2004), *Vows of Silence: The Abuse of Power in the Papacy of John Paul II* (New York: Simon & Schuster).

Berzin, Alex, tr. and ed. (1978), *The Mahamudra* (Library of Tibetan Works and Archives).

Beyerstein, Dale (1994), *Sai Baba's Miracles: An Overview* (http://www.exbaba.de/files/A_Critical_Study.html).

Bhajan, Yogi (1977), *The Teachings of Yogi Bhajan: The Power of the Spoken Word* (Pomona, CA: Arcline Publications).

Bharati, Agehananda (1980), *The Ochre Robe: An Autobiography* (Santa Barbara, CA: Ross-Erikson).

Bharati, Agehananda (1976), *The Light at the Center* (Santa Barbara, CA: Ross-Erikson).

Bharati, Agehananda (1974), "Fictitious Tibet: The Origin and Persistence of Rampaism," in *Tibet Society Bulletin,* Volume 7 (http://www.serendipity.li/baba/rampa.html).

Blacker, Hal (2001), "Enlightenment's Divine Jester Mr. Lee Lozowick," in *What Is Enlightenment?* Issue 20 (http://www.wie.org/j20/lee.asp).

Blacker, Hal (1996), "The Kramer Papers: A Look Behind the Mask of Antiauthoritarianism," in *What Is Enlightenment?* Issue 9 (http://www.wie.org/j9/kramer.asp).

Blackmore, Susan (1986), *The Adventures of a Parapsychologist* (Buffalo, NY: Prometheus Books).

Blackmore, Susan (1983), "Are Out-of-Body Experiences Evidence for Survival?" in *Anabiosis—The Journal for Near-Death Studies,* Volume 3 (http://www.susanblackmore.co.uk/Articles/Anabiosis%201983.htm).

Blanco, Jodee (2000), *The Complete Guide to Book Publicity* (New York: Allworth Press).

Blass, Thomas (2004), *The Man Who Shocked the World: The Life and Legacy of Stanley Milgram* (New York: Basic Books).

Blavatsky, Helena P., edited by Elizabeth Preston and Christmas Humphreys (1967), *An Abridgement of The Secret Doctrine* (Wheaton, IL: The Theosophical Publishing House).

Blofeld, John (1970), *The Tantric Mysticism of Tibet: A Practical Guide* (New York: E. P. Dutton).

Bob, Sri (2000), *The Knee of Daism: Deconstructing Adi Da* (http://lightmind.com/Impermanence/Library/knee/).

Boehm, Deborah Boliver (1996), *A Zen Romance: One Woman's Adventures in a Monastery* (New York: Kodansha International).

Bohm, David and Basil J. Hiley (1993), *The Undivided Universe* (New York: Routledge).

Bonder, Saniel (2003), "Waking Down in Mutuality" (http://www.wakingdown.org).

Bonder, Saniel (1990), *The Divine Emergence of the World-Teacher* (Clearlake, CA: The Dawn Horse Press).

Bose, Nirmal Kumar (1974), *My Days with Gandhi* (New Delhi: Orient Longman Limited).

Bostock, Cliff (1998), "Guru with a Schtick: An Interview with Ma Jaya," in *Creative Loafing,* April 18 (http://web.archive.org/web/20040309150200/http://www.soulworks.net/writings/paradigms/site_027.html).

Boston Globe, Investigative Staff of the (2003), *Betrayal: The Crisis in the Catholic Church* (New York: Little, Brown & Company).

Braun, Kirk (1984), *Rajneeshpuram: The Unwelcome Society—"Cultures Collide in a Quest for Utopia"* (Medford, OR: Scout Creek Press).

Brennan, Barbara Ann (1993), *Light Emerging: The Journey of Personal Healing* (Toronto: Bantam Books).

Brennan, Barbara Ann (1987), *Hands of Light: A Guide to Healing Through the Human Energy Field* (Toronto: Bantam Books).

Brent, Peter (1972), *Godmen of India* (London: Allen Lane).

Brewer, Mark (1975), "'We're Gonna Tear You Down and Put You Back Together,'" in *Psychology Today,* August (http://www.rickross.com/reference/est/estpt8.html).

Brooke, Tal (1999 [1990]), *Avatar of Night: Special Millennial Edition* (Berkeley, CA: End Run Publishing).

Brown, Mick (2000), "Divine Downfall," in *The Daily Telegraph Saturday Magazine,* October 27 (http://www.rickross.com/reference/saibaba/saibaba3.html).

Browning, Christopher R. (1998 [1992]), *Ordinary Men: Reserve Police Battalion 101 and the Final Solution in Poland* (New York: HarperPerennial).

Bruni, Frank and Elinor Burkett (2002 [1993]), *A Gospel of Shame: Children, Sexual Abuse and the Catholic Church* (New York: Perennial).

Brunton, Paul (1935), *A Search in Secret India* (New York: E. P. Dutton & Co., Inc.).

Bugliosi, Vincent and Curt Gentry (1975), *Helter Skelter: The True Story of the Manson Murders* (New York: Bantam Books).

Burke, Abbot George (1994), *An Eagle's Flight: Autobiography of a Gnostic Orthodox Christian* (Geneva, NE: Saint George Press).

Burroughs, William S. (1995 [1972]), *Ali's Smile/Naked Scientology* (Bonn, Germany: Expanded Media Editions).

Burroughs, William S. (1974), *The Job: Interviews with William S. Burroughs by Daniel Odier* (New York: Penguin Books).

Buswell, Robert E. (1992), *The Zen Monastic Experience: Buddhist Practice in Contemporary Korea* (Princeton, NJ: Princeton University Press).

Butler, Katy (1990), "The Shadow of Buddhist America," in *Common Boundary,* May-June.

Butler, Katy (1985a), "Sex Practices Did Not Cease, Marin Cult Officials Admit," in *San Francisco Chronicle,* April 9 (http://www.rickross.com/reference/adida/adida9.html).

Butler, Katy (1985), "Guru's Fiji Haven Called 'Paradise,'" in *San Francisco Chronicle,* April 5 (http://www.rickross.com/reference/adida/adida11.html).

Butterfield, Stephen T. (1994), *The Double Mirror: A Skeptical Journey into Buddhist Tantra* (Berkeley, CA: North Atlantic Books).

Caddy, Eileen (1976), *Foundations of Findhorn* (Forres, Scotland: Findhorn Publications).

Campbell, June (1996), *Traveller in Space: In Search of Female Identity in Tibetan Buddhism* (New York: George Braziller).

CANDER (2001), "Latest News" (http://web.archive.org/web/20031201170313/http://www.savemtwashington.org/).

Caplan, Mariana (2002), *Do You Need a Guru?* (London: Thorsons).

Caplan, Mariana (2001), *Halfway Up the Mountain: The Error of Premature Claims to Enlightenment* (Prescott, AZ: Hohm Press).

Carlson, Peter (2002a), "Chakra Full of Scandal: Baring the Yogis," in *Washington Post,* August 27 (http://www.washingtonpost.com/ac2/wp-dyn?pagename=article &node=&contentId=A64895-2002Aug26¬Found=true).

Carlson, Peter (2002), "'Taking a Yogic Flier on 'Peace Bonds,'" in *Washington Post,* August 29 (http://www.rickross.com/reference/tm/tm37.html).

Carnahan, Sumner (1995), *In the Presence of My Enemies* (Santa Fe, NM: Heartsfire Books).

Carroll, Robert T. (2004e), "Jean Houston and The Mystery School," in *The Skeptic's Dictionary* (http://www.skepdic.com/houston.html).

Carroll, Robert T. (2004d), "Anthroposophy, Rudolf Steiner (1861 – 1925), and Waldorf Schools," in *The Skeptic's Dictionary* (http://www.skepdic.com/steiner.html).

Carroll, Robert T. (2004c), "Firewalking," in *The Skeptic's Dictionary* (http://www.skepdic.com/firewalk.html).

Carroll, Robert T. (2004b), "Incorruptible Bodies," in *The Skeptic's Dictionary* (http://www.skepdic.com/incorrupt.html).

Carroll, Robert T. (2004a), "Cold Reading," in *The Skeptic's Dictionary* (http://www.skepdic.com/coldread.html).

Carroll, Robert T. (2004), "Alien Abduction," in *The Skeptic's Dictionary* (http://www.skepdic.com/aliens.html).

Carroll, Robert T. (2003), "The Skeptic's Dictionary Newsletter 38" (http://www.skepdic.com/news/newsletter38.html).

Castro, Stephen J. (1996), *Hypocrisy and Dissent Within the Findhorn Foundation: Towards a Sociology of a New Age Community* (Forres, Scotland: New Media Books).

Chadwick, David (1999), *Crooked Cucumber: The Life and Zen Teachings of Shunryu Suzuki* (New York: Broadway Books).

Chadwick, David (1994), *Thank You and OK! An American Zen Failure in Japan* (New York: Penguin/Arkana).

Charlton, Hilda (1990), *Hell-Bent for Heaven: The Autobiography of Hilda Charlton* (Woodstock, NY: Golden Quest).

Chatterjee, Aroup (2003), *Mother Teresa: The Final Verdict* (Kolkata: Meteor Books; text available online at http://www.meteorbooks.com).

Chelishev, E. (1987), "Swami Vivekananda—The Great Indian Humanist, Democrat and Patriot," in Harish C. Gupta, ed. (1987), *Swami Vivekananda Studies in Soviet Union* (Calcutta: Ramakrishna Mission Institute of Culture).

Chew, Sally (1998), "Paradise Lost," in *Out Magazine,* December/ January (http://leavingsiddhayoga.net/homophobia_in_sy.htm).

Chinmoy, Sri (1985), *The Master and the Disciple* (Jamaica, NY: Agni Press).

Chinmoy, Sri (1978), *Meditation: Man-Perfection in God-Satisfaction* (Jamaica, NY: Aum Publications).

Chopra, Deepak (2000), *How to Know God: The Soul's Journey into the Mystery of Mysteries* (New York: Harmony Books).

Chopra, Sonia (1999), "Satchidananda's Yoga Ashram Caught Up in a New Controversy, Past Sexual Charges Begin Resurfacing," in *Rediff on the Net,* June (http://www.rickross.com/reference/yogaville/yogaville21.html).

Christopher, Milbourne (1975), *Mediums, Mystics, & the Occult* (New York: Thomas Y. Crowell Co.).

Christopher, Milbourne (1970), *ESP, Seers & Psychics* (New York: Thomas Y. Crowell Co.).

Churchill, Pola (1996), *Shiva Mahavatar Babaji* (Beverly Hills, CA: Churchill Publishing Co.).

Cialdini, Robert B. (2001), *Influence: Science and Practice* (Toronto: Allyn and Bacon).

Clark, Tom (1980), *The Great Naropa Poetry Wars* (Santa Barbara, CA: Cadmus Editions).

Clayson, Alan (1996 [1990]), *The Quiet One: A Life of George Harrison* (London: Sanctuary Publishing Limited).

Cloud, David W. (2000), "Elvis Presley: The King of Rock & Roll" (http://www.wayoflife.org/fbns/elvispresley.htm).

Cohen, Andrew (2005), "Endorsements for *What Is Enlightenment?* Magazine" (http://www.andrewcohen.org/pressroom/WhatIsEnlightenmentquotes.asp).

Cohen, Andrew (2002), *Living Enlightenment* (Lenox, MA: Moksha Foundation).

Cohen, Andrew (2001a), "From What Is to What Ought to Be," in *What Is Enlightenment?* Issue 19 (http://www.wie.org/j19/lerner.asp).

Cohen, Andrew (2001), "Don't Ask Why—Just Do Something," in *What Is Enlightenment?* Issue 19 (http://www.wie.org/j19/majaya.asp).

Cohen, Andrew (2000a), "Yoga, Ego and Purification," in *What Is Enlightenment?* Issue 17 (http://www.wie.org/j17/desai.asp?page=1).

Cohen, Andrew (2000), *Embracing Heaven & Earth* (Lenox, MA: Moksha Foundation).

Cohen, Andrew (1999a), "'I CAN' vs. 'I AM': What is the Relationship Between Self-Mastery and Enlightenment?" in *What Is Enlightenment?* Issue 15 (http://www.wie.org/j15/andrew.asp).

Cohen, Andrew (1999), *In Defense of the Guru Principle* (Lenox, MA: Moksha Foundation).

Cohen, Andrew (1992), *Autobiography of an Awakening* (Corte Madera, CA: Moksha Foundation).

Cohen, Andrew (1989), *My Master is My Self* (Larkspur, CA: Moksha Foundation).

Cohen, Susan (2002a), "Swami Satchidananda, Integral Yoga Institute, Yogaville—A Survivor's Story," August 31 (http://www.rickross.com/reference/yogaville/yogaville61.html).

Colin, Molly, Peter Seidman and Tony Lewis (1985), "Defectors Voice Several Charges," in *Mill Valley Record,* April 3 (http://www.rickross.com/reference/adida/adida19.html).

Colman, E. A. M. (1974), *The Dramatic Use of Bawdy in Shakespeare* (London: Longman Group Limited).

Conway, Flo and Jim Siegelman (1982), "Information Disease: Have Cults Created a New Mental Illness?" in *Science Digest,* January (excerpt at http://www.amazing.com/scientology/cos-mind-control.html?FACTNet).

Cooper, Paulette (1997), "Harassment Diary" (http://www.lermanet.com/cos/cooperdiary.htm?FACTNet).

Cooper, Paulette (1971), *The Scandal of Scientology* (New York: Tower Publications, Inc.; full text available online at http://www.clambake.org/archive/books/tsos/sos.html).

Cooperman, Alan (2005), "Harassment Claims Roil Habitat for Humanity" (http://www.newsobserver.com/nation_world/story/2194735p-8576011c.html).

Cope, Stephen (2000), *Yoga and the Quest for the True Self* (New York: Bantam Books).

Cornell, Judith (2001), *Amma: Healing the Heart of the World* (New York: HarperCollins Publishers Inc.).

Cornwell, John (1999), *Hitler's Pope: The Secret History of Pius XII* (New York: Viking).

Corydon, Bent and L. Ron Hubbard, Jr. (1998 [1987]), *L. Ron Hubbard: Messiah or Madman?* (Secaucus, NJ: Lyle Stuart Inc.; full text online at http://www.clambake.org/archive/books/mom/Messiah_or_Madman.txt).

Da, Adi (1995), *The Knee of Listening: The Early-Life Ordeal and the Radical Spiritual Realization of the Divine World-Teacher* (Middletown, CA: The Dawn Horse Press).

Dakota (1998), "Paramahansa Yogananda: A Different Light" (http://www.yogananda-dif.org).

Dalal, A. S., ed. (2000), *A Greater Psychology: An Introduction to the Psychological Thought of Sri Aurobindo* (Los Angeles: Jeremy P. Tarcher).

Daniélou, Alain (1987), *The Way to the Labyrinth: Memories of East and West* (New York: New Directions).

Das, Bhagavan (1997), *It's Here Now (Are You?)* (New York: Broadway Books).

Das, Sushi (2003), "Hardly Krishna," in *The Age* (Australia), June 2 (http://www.theage.com.au/articles/2003/06/02/1054406108753.html).

Dass, Ram (2000), *Still Here: Embracing Aging, Changing, and Dying* (New York: Riverhead Books).

Dass, Ram (1990), *Journey of Awakening: A Meditator's Guidebook* (New York: Bantam).

Dass, Ram (1979), *Miracle of Love: Stories About Neem Karoli Baba* (New York: E. P. Dutton).

Dass, Ram (1971), *Be Here Now* (San Cristobal, NM: Lama Foundation).

Dass, Ram and Stephen Levine (1977), *Grist for the Mill* (Santa Cruz, CA: Unity Press).

Davis, Roy Eugene (2000), *Seven Lessons in Conscious Living* (Lakemont, GA: CSA Press).

DeRopp, Robert S. (1968), *The Master Game: Pathways to Higher Consciousness Beyond the Drug Experience* (New York: Dell Publishing Co., Inc.).

Desai, Yogi Amrit (1985), *Working Miracles of Love* (Lenox, MA: Kripalu Publications).

Desai, Yogi Amrit (1981), *Kripalu Yoga: Meditation-in-Motion* (Lenox, MA: Kripalu Publications).

Dhargyey, Geshe Ngawang (1974), *Tibetan Tradition of Mental Development* (Library of Tibetan Works and Archives).

Disciples, Eastern & Western (1979), *The Life of Swami Vivekananda* (Mayavati: Advaita Ashrama).

Dittmann, Melissa (2003), "Lessons from Jonestown," in *APA Monitor,* Volume 34, No. 10, November (http://www.apa.org/monitor/nov03/jonestown.html).

Downing, Michael (2001), *Shoes Outside the Door: Desire, Devotion, and Excess at San Francisco Zen Center* (Washington, DC: Counterpoint).

Doyle, Thomas P. (2003), "Roman Catholic Clericalism, Religious Duress, and Clergy Sexual Abuse," in *Pastoral Psychology,* Volume 51, No. 3, January.

Doyle, Thomas P. (2002), "They Still Don't Get It and Probably Never Will," in *Irish Times,* March 22.

Dreyer, Peter (1975), *A Gardener Touched with Genius* (New York: Coward, McCann & Geoghegan, Inc.).

Dutt, Anuradha (1988), "The Troubled Guru," in *The Illustrated Weekly of India,* July 17 (http://www.trancenet.org/news/weekly/).

Dykema, Ravi (2003), "An Interview with Sakyong Mipham Rinpoche," in *Nexus* (http://www.nexuspub.com/articles/2003/may2003/interview.htm).

Dynes, Michael and Dominic Kennedy (2001), "I Sought Peace and Couldn't Find It," in *The Times British News,* August 27 (http://www.rickross.com/reference/saibaba/saibaba9.html).

Ebon, Martin (1968), *Maharishi, the Guru: An International Symposium* (Toronto: The New American Library of Canada Limited).

Economist (2000), "Monkey Business: Thailand's Monkish Scandals," in *The Economist,* November 30 (http://www.economist.com/displayStory.cfm?Story_ID= S%26(X%20%2BQQ%3F*%0A).

Edwards, Harry (1995), "Incorruptibility: Miracle or Myth?" in *Investigator*, 45, November (http://www.adam.com.au/bstett/PaIncorruptibility.htm).

Edwards, Harry (1994), "Firewalking," in *Skeptoon, An Illustrated Look at Some New Age Beliefs* (New South Wales, Australia: Harry Edwards Publications; http://www.indian-skeptic.org/html/ byhedwa3.htm).

Ehrlich, Richard S. (2000), "Buddhist Crimes" (http://www.scoop.co.nz/mason/stories/HL0011/S00003.htm).

Eisenstadt, Merry M. (1993), "Former Cult Members Recall Group They Left," in *Washington Jewish Week,* March 25.

Elias (2002), "Yogic Masturbation in Adidam" (http://lightmind.com/blogs/blogarchive-007.html).

Elias (2000a), "The New Pattern" (http://lightmind.com/thevoid/daismreport-04.html).

Elias (2000), "Adidam Fundraising" (http://lightmind.com/thevoid/daismreport-03.html).

Elias (1999a), "Is Daism Vulnerable to a Class Action Suit?" (http://lightmind.com/blogs/blogarchive-036.html).

Elias (1999), "For a Man Who Had a Vision of Frank" (http://lightmind.com/blogs/blogarchive-016.html).

Eller, Cynthia (2003), *The Myth of Matriarchal Prehistory: Why an Invented Past Won't Give Women a Future* (Boston, MA: Beacon Press).

Ellis, Mark (2003), "Dalai Lama: I've Missed Sex," in *The Mirror,* July 29 (http://www.mirror.co.uk/news/allnews/content_objectid=13231174_method=full_siteid=50143_headline=-DALAI-LAMA--I-VE-MISSED-SEX-name_page.html).

EmpireNet (2003), "Lawsuits Against TWI and Allegations of Sexual Misconduct" (http://www.empirenet.com/~messiah7/tw_suits-sex.htm).

England, Mark and Darlene McCormick (1993), "The Sinful Messiah," in The Waco Tribune-Herald Series, *Fort Worth Star-Telegram,* March 3 (http://www.rickross.com/reference/waco/waco9.html).

Epstein, Edward (1995), "Politics and Transcendental Meditation," in *San Francisco Chronicle,* December 29 (http://www.rickross.com/reference/tm/tm3.html).

Evans, Christopher (1973), *Cults of Unreason* (London: Harrap).

Extra (1999), "Extra: Family at War," September 27 (http://www.rickross.com/reference/yogaville/yogaville27.html).

Falk, Geoffrey (2008 [2006]), *"Norman Einstein": The Dis-Integration of Ken Wilber* (Toronto: Million Monkeys Press).

Falsani, Cathleen (2002), "All He's Saying Is...," in *Chicago Sun-Times,* July 11 (http://www.rickross.com/reference/tm/tm34.html).

Farrow, Mia (1997), *What Falls Away: A Memoir* (New York: Nan A. Talese).

Feuerstein, Georg (1998), *The Mystery of Light: The Life and Teaching of Omraam Mikhael Aivanhov* (Lower Lake, CA: Integral Publishing).

Feuerstein, Georg (1996), "Holy Madness: The Dangerous and Disillusioning Example of Da Free John," in *What Is Enlightenment?* Issue 9 (http://www.wie.org/j9/feuerstein_madness.asp?page=2).

Feuerstein, Georg (1992), *Holy Madness* (New York: Arkana).

Fields, Rick (1992), *How the Swans Came to the Lake: A Narrative History of Buddhism in America* (Boston, MA: Shambhala).

Findhorn Community (1980), *Faces of Findhorn* (New York: Harper & Row, Publishers).

Fitzgerald, Frances (1986), *Cities on a Hill: A Journey Through Contemporary American Cultures* (New York: Simon & Schuster).

Flaccus, Gillian (2001), "Ore. Town Never Recovered from Scare," in The Associated Press, October 19 (http://www.rickross.com/reference/rajneesh/rajneesh8.html).

Forem, Jack (1973), *Transcendental Meditation; Maharishi Mahesh Yogi and the Science of Creative Intelligence* (Toronto: Clarke, Irwin & Company Limited).

France, David (2004), *Our Fathers: The Secret Life of the Catholic Church in an Age of Scandal* (New York: Broadway Books).

Frank, Arno (2000), "Intimidation of the Waldorf Kind," in *TAZ,* August 4 (http://www.rickross.com/reference/waldorf/waldorf2.html).

Franken, Al (1996), *Rush Limbaugh is a Big Fat Idiot* (New York: Delacorte Press).

Franklin, Satya Bharti (1992), *The Promise of Paradise: A Woman's Intimate Story of the Perils of Life with Rajneesh* (Barrytown, NY: Station Hill Press).

French, Patrick (2003), *Tibet, Tibet: A Personal History of a Lost Land* (New York: Alfred A. Knopf).

Friedman, Roger (2003), "Will Scientology Celebs Sign 'Spiritual' Contract?" on *Fox News,* September 3 (http://www.rickross.com/reference/scientology/celebrities/celebrities32.html).

Furlong, Monica (1987), *Thérèse of Lisieux* (London: Virago Press).

Futrelle, David (1997), "How Strange Were They? The San Diego Cultists Have More in Common with Other Religious Enthusiasts Than You Might Think," in *Salon,* March 28 (http://www.rickross.com/reference/heavensgate/gate30.html).

Galloway, Paul (1991), "Gonzo Guru," in *Chicago Tribune,* September 20 (http://www.rickross.com/reference/srichinmoy/srichinmoy1.html).

Garden, Mary (1988), *The Serpent Rising: A Journey of Spiritual Seduction* (Fortitude Valley, Australia: Brolga Publishing).

Gardner, Martin (2000), *Did Adam and Eve Have Navels? Discourses on Reflexology, Numerology, Urine Therapy, and Other Dubious Subjects* (New York: W. W. Norton & Company).

Gardner, Martin (1999), "Carlos Castaneda and New Age Anthropology," in *Skeptical Inquirer,* Volume 23, No. 5, September/ October.

Gardner, Martin (1996), *Weird Water and Fuzzy Logic* (Buffalo, NY: Prometheus Books).

Gardner, Martin (1978), "White and Brown Music, Fractal Curves and One-Over-f Fluctuations," in *Scientific American,* April.

Gardner, Martin (1957 [1952]), *Fads and Fallacies in the Name of Science* (New York: Dover Publications).

Geisler, Norman (1991), "The Rise of the Cults," lecture at The New England Institute for Religious Research, November 2.

Ghosh, Sananda Lal (1980), *Mejda: The Family and the Early Life of Paramahansa Yogananda* (Los Angeles: Self-Realization Fellowship).

Ginsberg, Alex (2004), "Ex-Followers Rip 'Sleazy' Sri," in *New York Post,* May 23 (http://www.rickross.com/reference/srichinmoy/srichinmoy28.html).

Giri, Swami Satyeswarananda (1992), *Babaji, Volume III: Masters of Original Kriya* (San Diego: The Sanskrit Classics).

Giri, Swami Satyeswarananda (1991b), *Kriya: Finding the True Path* (San Diego: The Sanskrit Classics).

Giri, Swami Satyeswarananda (1991), *Babaji, Volume II: Lahiri Mahasay, The Polestar of Kriya* (San Diego: The Sanskrit Classics).

Giuliano, Geoffrey (1989), *Dark Horse: The Secret Life of George Harrison* (Toronto: Stoddart Publishing Co. Limited).

Giuliano, Geoffrey (1986), *The Beatles: A Celebration* (Agincourt, Ontario: Methuen Publications).

Goa, Helen (1999), "Sex and the Singular Swami," in *The San Francisco Weekly,* March 10 (http://www.rickross.com/reference/ananda/ananda1.html).

Goffman, Erving (1961), *Asylums: Essays on the Social Situation of Mental Patients and Other Inmates* (Garden City, NY: Anchor Books).

Goldberg, Michelle (2001), "Untouchable?" in *Salon,* July 25 (http://dir.salon.com/people/feature/2001/07/25/baba/index.html).

Goldhammer, John D. (1996), *Under the Influence: The Destructive Effects of Group Dynamics* (Buffalo, NY: Prometheus Books).

Goldman, Albert (1991), *Elvis: The Last 24 Hours* (New York: St. Martin's Paperbacks).

Goldman, Albert (1981), *Elvis* (New York: Avon).

Goodrick-Clarke, Nicholas (2004 [1994]), *The Occult Roots of Nazism: Secret Aryan Cults and Their Influences on Nazi Ideology* (New York: New York University Press).

Goodrick-Clarke, Nicholas (2003 [2001]), *Black Sun: Aryan Cults, Esoteric Nazism and the Politics of Identity* (New York: New York University Press).

Goodstein, Laurie (1998), "Hare Krishna Faith Details Past Abuse at Boarding Schools," in the *New York Times,* October 9 (http://www.rickross.com/reference/krishna/krishna5.html).

Gordon, James (1987), *The Golden Guru: The Strange Journey of Bhagwan Shree Rajneesh* (Lexington, MA: The Stephen Greene Press).

Gorski, Timothy N. (2001), "Hearing on Swindlers, Hucksters and Snake Oil Salesmen: The Hype and Hope of Marketing Anti-Aging Products to Seniors," in *United States Senate Special Committee on Aging,* September 10 (http://www.quackwatch.org/01QuackeryRelatedTopics/Hearing/gorski2.html).

Gould, Martin (1998), "Travolta Dragged into Bizarre Gay Lawsuit," in the *Star,* August 18 (http://www.rickross.com/reference/scientology/Scien58.html).

Gourley, Scott R. and Rosemary Edmiston (1997), "Adidam Comes to the Northcoast," in *Northcoast Journal Weekly* (http://www.rickross.com/reference/adida/adida4.html).

Govindan, Marshall (1997), *How I Became a Disciple of Babaji* (Eastman, Quebec: Babaji's Kriya Yoga and Publications, Inc.).

Gracious, God Is (2000), "Barbara Marx-Hubbard Meets Adi Da" (http://lightmind.com/thevoid/daism/hubbard-leela.html).

Grout, James (2003), "The Death of William the Conqueror" (http://itsa.ucsf.edu/~snlrc/britannia/hastings/williamdeath.html).

GuruNet (2003), "Sri Aurobindo: Overview of His Life" (http://gurusoftware.com/Gurunet/AurobindoMother/Aurobindo.htm).

Gyan, Satish Chandra (1980), *Sivananda and His Ashram* (Madras, India: The Christian Literature Society).

Gyanamata, S. (1984), *God Alone: The Life and Letters of a Saint* (Los Angeles: Self-Realization Fellowship).

Hajdu, David (2003), "Hustling Elvis," in *The New York Review of Books* (http://www.nybooks.com/articles/16598).

Hall, Elizabeth (1975), "The Sufi Tradition: 'Some Gurus are Frankly Phonies, and They Don't Try to Hide It from Me, They Think I am One Too,'" in *Psychology Today,* July.

Hamilton, Craig (1999), "Excellence is Not Enough: An Interview with Anthony Robbins," in *What Is Enlightenment?* Issue 15 (http://www.wie.org/j15/robbins.asp).

Hamilton, Rosemary (1998), *Hellbent for Enlightenment: Unmasking Sex, Power, and Death with a Notorious Master* (Ashland, OR: White Cloud Press).

Haney, Craig and Philip G. Zimbardo (1998), "The Past and Future of U.S. Prison Policy: Twenty-Five Years After the Stanford Prison Experiment," in *American Psychologist,* 53 (text available online at http://www.prisonexp.org/pdf/ap1998.pdf).

Haney, Craig and Philip G. Zimbardo (1975), "The Blackboard Penitentiary: It's Tough to Tell a High School from a Prison," in *Psychology Today,* June.

Haney, Craig, William Curtis Banks and Philip G. Zimbardo (1973), "Interpersonal Dynamics in a Simulated Prison," in *International Journal of Criminology and Penology,* 1 (text available online at http://www.prisonexp.org/pdf/ijcp1973.pdf).

Harper, Marvin Henry (1972), *Gurus, Swamis, & Avatars* (Philadelphia, PA: The Westminster Press).

Harpur, Tom (2001), "Guru Shrugs Off Sex Allegations," in *The Star,* January 14 (http://www.rickross.com/reference/saibaba/saibaba5.html).

Harris, Lis (1994), "O Guru, Guru, Guru," in the *New Yorker,* November 14 (http://www.ex-cult.org/Groups/SYDA-Yoga/leave.txt).

Harris, Michael (1991 [1990]), *Unholy Orders: Tragedy at Mount Cashel* (New York: Penguin Books).

Harvey, Andrew (2000), *The Return of the Mother* (Berkeley, CA: Frog, Ltd.).

Harvey, Bob (2000a), "The Man Believers Think is God," in *The Ottawa Citizen,* December 19 (http://www.rickross.com/reference/saibaba/saibaba4.html).

Harvey, Peter (2000), *An Introduction to Buddhist Ethics: Foundations, Values and Issues* (Cambridge, England: Cambridge University Press).

Hassan, Steven (2000), *Releasing the Bonds: Empowering People to Think for Themselves* (Somerville, MA: Freedom of Mind Press).

Hassan, Steven (1990 [1988]), *Combatting Cult Mind Control* (Rochester, VT: Park Street Press).

Hatengdi, M. U. (1984), *Nityananda: The Divine Presence* (Cambridge, MA: Rudra Press).

Hausherr, Tilman (2002), "Cult Apologist FAQ" (http://home.snafu.de/tilman/faq-you/cult.apologists.txt).

Hawken, Paul (1976), *The Magic of Findhorn* (New York: Bantam Books).

Hayward, Jeremy and Francisco Varela (1992), *Gentle Bridges: Conversations with the Dalai Lama on the Sciences of Mind* (Boston, MA: Shambhala).

Heath, Chris (2000), "The Epic Life of Carlos Santana," in *Rolling Stone,* March 16 (New York: Straight Arrow; http://www.rickross.com/reference/srichinmoy/srichinmoy18.html).

Hislop, John (1978), *Conversations with Sathya Sai Baba* (San Diego, CA: Birth Day Publishing Company).

Hitchens, Christopher (2001), *Letters to a Young Contrarian* (Cambridge, MA: Basic Books).

Hitchens, Christopher (1998), "His Material Highness," in *Salon,* July 13 (http://www.salon.com/news/1998/07/13news.html).

Hitchens, Christopher (1995), *The Missionary Position: Mother Teresa in Theory and Practice* (New York: Verso).

Hoffer, Eric (1951), *The True Believer* (San Francisco, CA: Harper & Row, Publishers).

Holmes, David S. (1988), "The Influence of Meditation Versus Rest on Physiological Arousal: A Second Evaluation," in Michael A. West, ed., *The Psychology of Meditation* (Oxford: Clarendon Press) (http://www.american-buddha.com/meditation.arousal.htm).

Holmes, David S. (1984), "Meditation and Somatic Arousal Reduction. A Review of the Experimental Evidence," in *American Psychologist,* 39(1).

Hoo, Stephanie (2005), "Many in Mongolia Nostalgic for Communism" (http://www.boston.com/news/world/asia/articles/2005/05/21/many_in_mongolia_nostalgic_for_communism?mode=PF).

Horgan, John (2003a), *Rational Mysticism: Dispatches from the Border Between Science and Spirituality* (New York: Houghton Mifflin Company).

Horgan, John (2003), "The Myth of the Totally Enlightened Guru" (http://www.johnhorgan.org/work8.htm).

Horgan, John (1999), "The Anti-Gurus" (http://www.johnhorgan.org/work5.htm).

Houston, Jean (2006), "Bio" (www.jeanhouston.org/bio.html).

Houston, Jean (1982), *The Possible Human: A Course in Extending Your Physical, Mental, and Creative Abilities* (Los Angeles: J. P. Tarcher, Inc.).

Hubner, John and Lindsey Gruson (1990 [1988]), *Monkey on a Stick: Murder, Madness, and the Hare Krishnas* (New York: Penguin Books).

Huchzermeyer, Wilfried (1998), *Mother: A Short Biography* (Silver Lake, WI: Lotus Press).

Inner Culture (1935), "Inner Culture News," in *Inner Culture,* December (http://www.ananda.it/en/yogananda/india1935/india9.html).

Integral (2004), "History" (http://web.archive.org/web/20031205084501/www.integralinstitute.org/history.htm).

Integral (2003), "Integral Institute" (http://www.integralinstitute.org).

IntegralNaked (2005), "Michael Murphy" (http://www.integralnaked.org/talk.aspx?id=35).

IntegralNaked (2004), "Who is Ken Wilber?" (http://www.integralnaked.org/contributor.aspx?id=1).

Jackson, Devon (1996), "Bless You, Sir, May I Jog Another?" in *Outside* magazine, October (http://outside.away.com/outside/magazine/1096/9610febl.html).

Jacobsen, Jeff (2004), "Lisa McPherson" (http://www.lisamcpherson.org).

James, William (1990), *The Varieties of Religious Experience* (New York: Vintage Books/Library of America).

Jenkins, Philip (2001), *Mystics and Messiahs: Cults and New Religions in American History* (Oxford: Oxford University Press).

Jewel (1999), "How Devotees Became 'Dissidents' in 1985" (http://lightmind.com/archives/daism-05/daism-05.mv?module=view&viewid=3252&row=270).

John, Bubba Free (1974), *Garbage and the Goddess: The Last Miracles and Final Spiritual Instructions of Bubba Free John* (Lower Lake, CA: The Dawn Horse Press).

John, Da Free (1985), *The Dawn Horse Testament* (Middletown, CA: The Dawn Horse Press). Foreword at http://www.beezone.com/Wilber/ken_wilbur_praise.html.

John, Da Free (1980), *Scientific Proof of the Existence of God Will Soon Be Announced by the White House!* (Middletown, CA: The Dawn Horse Press). Foreword at http://www.beezone.com/Wilber/onherocults.html.

Johnson, K. Paul (1994), *The Masters Revealed: Madame Blavatsky and the Myth of the Great White Lodge* (New York: State University of New York Press).

Joy, W. Brugh (1990), *Avalanche: Heretical Reflections on the Dark and the Light* (New York: Ballantine Books).

Kamala (1964), *The Flawless Mirror* (Nevada City, CA: Crystal Clarity Publishers).

Kashi (2004), "Kashi Center for Advanced Spiritual Studies Presents Bhagavan Das Chanting Concert and Workshop" (http://www.kashi.org/Flyers/BhagDas.pdf).

Kashi (2003), "Ma Jaya Sati Bhagavati" (http://www.kashi.org/bio.htm).

Kasturi, N. (1971), *The Life of Bhagavan Sri Sathya Sai Baba* (Santa Ana, CA: Sai Baba Society).

Katz, Donald (1992), *Home Fires* (New York: Harper Collins).

Kaufman, Robert (1995 [1972]), *Inside Scientology/Dianetics: How I Joined Dianetics/Scientology and Became Superhuman* (http://www.factnet.org/Books/InsideScientology/?FACTNet).

Kaur, Now Aware (1998), "3HO—Is It a Toxic Faith System?" (http://www.rickross.com/reference/3ho/3ho44.html).

Kazlev, Alan (2003), "Ken Wilber and Adi Da" (http://www.kheper.net/topics/Wilber/Da.html).

Keegan, Paul (2002), "Yogis Behaving Badly," in *Business 2.0,* September (http://www.rickross.com/reference/general/general478.html).

Keene, M. Lamar (1977), *The Psychic Mafia* (New York: Dell Publishing Co., Inc.).

Kennedy, Dominic (2001), "Suicide, Sex and the Guru," in *The Times British News,* August 27 (http://www.rickross.com/reference/saibaba/saibaba11.html).

Kent, Stephen A. (2001), *From Slogans to Mantras: Social Protest and Religious Conversion in the Late Vietnam Era* (Syracuse, NY: Syracuse University Press).

Khalsa, Kamlapadi Kaur (1994), "In the Magical Soup: Meditations on Twenty Years of Cult Living (Within Yogi Bhajan's 3HO)" (http://www.rickross.com/reference/3ho/3ho19.html).

Khalsa, Kamlapati Kaur (1990), "The Dysfunctional 3HO Family," in *Visions* (http://www.rickross.com/reference/3ho/3ho72.html).

Khalsa, Shakti Parwha Kaur (1996), *Kundalini Yoga: The Flow of Eternal Power* (New York: Perigee).

Kjernsmo, Kjetil (1997), "A Preliminary Empirical Study of Firewalking" (http://www.skepsis.no/english/subject/firewalk/kpreemp1).

Klein, Aaron E. and Cynthia L. Klein (1979), *Mind Trips: The Story of Consciousness-Raising Movements* (Garden City, NY: Doubleday & Company).

Klimo, Jon (1998), *Channeling: Investigations on Receiving Information from Paranormal Sources* (Berkeley, CA: North Atlantic Books).

Knight, Steve (2004), "Uri Geller: Chronological Bibliography" (http://www.zem.demon.co.uk/index.htm).

Koestler, Arthur (1960), *The Lotus and the Robot* (New York: Harper & Row Publishers, Inc.).

Kornfield, Jack (2000), *After the Ecstasy, the Laundry: How the Heart Grows Wise on the Spiritual Path* (New York: Bantam).

Kornfield, Jack (1993), *A Path with Heart: A Guide Through the Perils and Promises of a Spiritual Life* (New York: Bantam).

Kramer, Joel and Diane Alstad (1993), *The Guru Papers: Masks of Authoritarian Power* (Berkeley, CA: Frog, Ltd.).

Krassner, Paul (1993), *Confessions of a Raving, Unconfined Nut: Misadventures in the Counter-Culture* (New York: Simon & Schuster).

Kraus, Daniel (2000), "Roo the Day," in *Salon*, August 25 (http://dir.salon.com/people/feature/2000/08/25/roos/index.html).

Kripal, Jeffrey (1995), *Kali's Child: The Mystical and the Erotic in the Life and Teachings of Ramakrishna* (Chicago: The University of Chicago Press). For a critique of Kripal's work, from a monk of the Ramakrishna Order, see Tyagananda (2000). For Kripal's response to his critics, see http://www.atman.net/kalischild/index.html.

Kripalu (2003), "Kripalu Center for Yoga and Health" (http://www.kripalu.org).

Krishnamurti, Jiddu (1969), *Early Writings,* Volume 1 (Bombay: Chetana).

Kriya Yoga Discussion Board (2001), "Kriya Yoga Discussion Board" (http://www.boards2go.com/boards/board.cgi?&user=Kriya).

Kriyananda, Swami (1979), *The Path: Autobiography of a Western Yogi* (Nevada City, CA: Ananda Publications).

Kriyananda, Swami (1974 [1973]), *The Road Ahead: World Prophecies by the Great Master, Paramahansa Yogananda, Edited with Commentary by his Disciple Swami Kriyananda* (Nevada City, CA: Ananda Publications).

Kuncl, Tom (2001), "George W. Bush and the Moonies," in *The National Examiner,* January 9 (http://www.rickross.com/reference/unif/unif106.html).

Lake County (1985), "Believers 'Surrender' to Spiritual Master," in *Lake County Record-Bee,* April 4 (http://www.rickross.com/reference/adida/adida13.html).

Lalich, Janja (2004), *Bounded Choice: True Believers and Charismatic Cults* (Berkeley, CA: University of California Press).

Lalich, Janja (1997), "CNN Interview with Yanya [*sic*] Lalich" (http://www.rickross.com/reference/heavensgate/gate25.html).

Lama, Dalai (1999), *Ethics for the New Millennium* (New York: Riverhead Books).

Lama, Dalai (1996), *Beyond Dogma: Dialogues & Discourses* (Berkeley, CA: North Atlantic Books).

Lane, David Christopher (1997), "Occam's Razor: Critical Essays" (http://elearn.mtsac.edu/dlane/paranormal.htm).

Lane, David Christopher (1996a), "The Paradox of Da Free John" (http://vm.mtsac.edu/~dlane/datext.html).

Lane, David Christopher (1996), "Critique of Ken Wilber" (http://elearn.mtsac.edu/dlane/kendebates.htm, also posted with greater usability at http://www.geoffreyfalk.com/books/LaneMenu.asp).

Lane, David Christopher (1995), *The Enchanted Land* (http://elearn.mtsac.edu/philosophy/quest.htm).

Lane, David Christopher (1994), *Exposing Cults: When the Skeptical Mind Confronts the Mystical* (New York: Garland Publishing; text online at http://www.geocities.com/eckcult/cults.html).

Lane, David Christopher (1993), "Why I Don't Eat Faces: A Neuroethical Argument for Vegetarianism" (http://articles.animalconcerns.org/ar-voices/archive/faces.html).

Lane, David Christopher (1992), *The Radhasoami Tradition: A Critical History of Guru Successorship* (http://vm.mtsac.edu/~dlane/radhabook.html).

Lane, David Christopher (1983), *The Making of a Spiritual Movement: The Untold Story of Paul Twitchell and Eckankar* (Del Mar, CA: Del Mar Press; text online at http://www.geocities.com/eckcult/index.html).

Lane, David Christopher and Scott Lowe (1996), *Da: The Strange Case of Franklin Jones* (http://vm.mtsac.edu/~dlane/dabook.html).

Langone, Michael D., ed. (1995 [1993]), *Recovery from Cults: Help for Victims of Psychological and Spiritual Abuse* (New York: W. W. Norton & Company).

Larabee, Mark (2000), "Two Rajneeshee Members Plead Guilty," in *The Oregonian,* December 16 (http://www.rickross.com/reference/rajneesh/rajneesh6.html).

Lasater, Judith (1995), "California Yoga Teachers Association Code of Conduct," in *Yoga Journal,* November/December (http://www.rickross.com/reference/3ho/3ho52.html).

Lattin, Don (1994), "Best-Selling Buddhist Author Accused of Sexual Abuse," November 10 (http://www.american-buddha.com/sogyal.htm).

Lattin, Don (1985a), "Hypnotic Da Free John—Svengali of the Truth-Seeking Set," in *San Francisco Examiner,* April 5 (http://www.rickross.com/reference/adida/adida12.html).

Lattin, Don (1985), "Guru Hit by Sex-Slave Suit: Stories of Drugs, Orgies on Free John's Fiji Isle," in *San Francisco Examiner,* April 3 (http://www.rickross.com/reference/adida/adida16.html).

Layton, Deborah (1998), *Seductive Poison: A Jonestown Survivor's Story of Life and Death in the Peoples Temple* (New York: Anchor Books).

Lehnert, Tomek (1998), *Rogues in Robes: An Inside Chronicle of a Recent Chinese-Tibetan Intrigue in the Karma Kagyu Lineage of Diamond Way Buddhism* (Nevada City, CA: Blue Dolphin Publishing).

Lewy, Guenter (2000 [1964]), *The Catholic Church and Nazi Germany* (Cambridge, MA: Da Capo Press).

Leydecker, Mary (1985), "Suit Shatters Calm for Sect Members," in *Marin Independent-Journal,* April 5 (http://www.rickross.com/reference/adida/adida10.html).

Lifton, Robert (1989), *Thought Reform and the Psychology of Totalism: A Study of Brainwashing in China* (Chapel Hill, NC: University of North Carolina Press).

Light, Search For (2003), "Short Life-Sketch" (http://www.searchforlight.org/TheMother_lifeSketch.htm).

Lightmind (2004), *Daism Research Index* (http://lightmind.com/library/daismfiles/).

LNI (2003), "History of Nityananda Institute and Swami Chetanananda" (http://www.leaving-nityananda-institute.org).

Lowe, Scott (1996), "The Strange Case of Franklin Jones" (http://www.american-buddha.com/franklin.jones.htm).

Lutyens, Elisabeth (1972), *A Goldfish Bowl* (London: Cassell & Co.).

Lutyens, Mary (1988), *Krishnamurti: The Open Door* (London: John Murray).

Lutyens, Mary (1983), *Krishnamurti: The Years of Fulfillment* (London: John Murray).

Lutyens, Mary (1975), *Krishnamurti: The Years of Awakening* (New York: Avon Books).

Macdonald, Sarah (2003 [2002]), *Holy Cow: An Indian Adventure* (New York: Broadway Books).

Mackenzie, Vicki (1999), *Cave in the Snow* (London: Bloomsbury Publishing Plc.).

Mackenzie, Vicki (1995), *Reborn in the West* (New York: Marlow & Company).

Maharishi Mahesh Yogi (1995), *Science of Being and Art of Living: Transcendental Meditation* (New York: Penguin).

Maharshi, Ramana with Robert Powell, ed. (2000), *Talks with Ramana Maharshi: On Realizing Abiding Peace and Happiness* (Carlsbad, CA: Inner Directions).

Malko, George (1970), *Scientology: The Now Religion* (New York: Delacorte Press; full text online at http://www-2.cs.cmu.edu/~dst/Library/Shelf/malko/malko.htm).

Mallia, Joseph (1998), "Church Wields Celebrity Clout," in *Boston Herald,* March 5 (http://www.rickross.com/reference/scientology/Scien39.html).

Mandelkorn, Philip, ed. (1978), *To Know Your Self: The Essential Teachings of Swami Satchidananda* (Garden City, NY: Anchor Books).

Mangalwadi, Vishal (1992), *The World of Gurus* (Chicago, IL: Cornerstone Press).

Manseau, Peter and Jeff Sharlet (2004), *Killing the Buddha: A Heretic's Bible* (New York: Free Press).

Marin, Peter (1995), *Freedom & Its Discontents* (South Royalton, VT: Steerforth Press).

Marshall, Anne (1963), *Hunting the Guru in India* (London: Victor Gollancz, Ltd.).

Marshall, John (1980), "Files Show Spy Reported Woman's Intimate Words," in *Globe and Mail,* January 25 (http://www.rickross.com/reference/scientology/canada/canada6.html).

Mason, Bobbie Ann (2003), *Elvis Presley* (New York: Viking Penguin).

Masters, Robert (1991 [1988]), *The Goddess Sekhmet: Psychospiritual Exercises of the Fifth Way* (St. Paul, MN: Llewellyn Publications).

Masters, Robert and Jean Houston (1972), *Mind Games: The Guide to Inner Space* (New York: Dell Publishing Co.).

Mata, Daya (1971), *Only Love* (Los Angeles: Self-Realization Fellowship).

Mata, Durga (1992), *A Paramhansa Yogananda Trilogy of Divine Love* (Beverly Hills, CA: Joan Wight Publications).

Matsakis, Aphrodite (1996), *I Can't Get Over It: A Handbook for Trauma Survivors* (Oakland, CA: New Harbinger Publications, Inc.).

McCafferty, Dennis (1999), "Old Bhagwan, New Bottles," in *Salon,* October 20 (http://www.salon.com/books/feature/1999/10/20/osho/).

McDermott, Robert A., ed. (1984), *The Essential Steiner: Basic Writings of Rudolf Steiner* (San Francisco, CA: Harper & Row, Publishers).

McGehee, Overton (1991), "Ex-Followers Say Swami Demanded Sexual Favors," in *Richmond Times-Dispatch,* August 2 (http://www.rickross.com/reference/yogaville/yogaville8.html).

Mehta, Gita (1979), *Karma Cola* (New York: Simon & Schuster).

Meier, Barbara (1992), "Interview: Jerry Garcia," in *Tricycle: The Buddhist Review,* Spring 1992.

Michel, Peter (1992), *Krishnamurti, Love and Freedom* (Woodside, CA: Bluestar Communication Corporation).

Midal, Fabrice (2004), *Chögyam Trungpa: His Life and Vision* (Boston, MA: Shambhala).

Miles, Barry (1989), *Ginsberg: A Biography* (New York: Simon & Schuster).

Milgram, Stanley (1974), *Obedience to Authority* (New York: Harper & Row).

Miller, Russell (1987), *Bare-Faced Messiah: The True Story of L. Ron Hubbard* (Toronto: Key Porter Books Limited; full text online at http://www.discord.org/~lippard/bfm).

Milne, Hugh (1986), *Bhagwan: The God That Failed* (New York: St. Martin's Press).

Minor, Robert N. (1999), *The Religious, the Spiritual, and the Secular: Auroville and Secular India* (Albany, NY: State University of New York Press).

Motoyama, Hiroshi (2000 [1992]), *Karma and Reincarnation: A Key to Spiritual Evolution and Enlightenment* (London: Piatkus).

MSS (2003), *Karmayogi* (Pondicherry, India: The Mother's Service Society; text online at http://www.motherservice.org/Life & Teachings/Life and Teachings.htm).

Mukerjee, Dada (1996), *The Near and the Dear: Stories of Neem Karoli Baba and His Devotees* (Santa Fe, NM: Hanuman Foundation).

Muktananda, Swami (1999), *The Perfect Relationship: The Guru and the Disciple* (South Fallsburg, NY: SYDA Foundation).

Muktananda, Swami (1996), *Bhagawan Nityananda of Ganeshpuri* (South Fallsburg, NY: SYDA Foundation).

Muktananda, Swami (1981), *Where Are You Going? A Guide to the Spiritual Journey* (South Fallsburg, NY: SYDA Foundation).

Muktananda, Swami (1978), *Play of Consciousness: A Spiritual Autobiography* (South Fallsburg, NY: SYDA Foundation).

Murphy, Michael (1992), *The Future of the Body: Explorations into the Further Evolution of Human Nature* (Los Angeles: Jeremy P. Tarcher, Inc.).

Murphy, Padraic (2000), "Scandal Engulfs Guru's Empire," in *The Age* (Australia), November 12 (http://www.rickross.com/reference/saibaba/saibaba2.html).

Mussolini, Benito (1927), "Science and Religion," in *East-West* magazine, May/June, Volume 2, No. 4 (http://www.mysticalportal.net/2-4.html).

Muster, Nori J. (1997), *Betrayal of the Spirit: My Life Behind the Headlines of the Hare Krishna Movement* (Chicago: University of Illinois Press).

Nahar, Sujata (1989), *Mirra the Occultist* (Paris: Institut de Recherches Évolutives).

Naman, Mard (1980), "The Pure Ones," in *New West,* December (http://www.rickross.com/reference/3ho/3ho1.html).

National Post (2000), "'Have Rabbit, Will Travel': Yogic Flyer's Natural Law Party Failed to Capture the Imagination," in *National Post* (UK), February 9 (http://www.rickross.com/reference/tm/tm7.html).

Neary, Walt (1985a), "Crazy Wisdom Bent Minds, Say Ex-Cultists," in *Lake County Record-Bee,* April 11. (http://web.archive.org/web/20031227113341/lightgate.net/archives/daism-02/daism-02.mv?module=view&viewid=715&row=228).

Neary, Walt (1985), "Inner Circle Privy to Parties," in *Lake County Record-Bee,* April 12 (http://www.rickross.com/reference/adida/adida7.html).

Nickell, Joe (2002), "Psychic Pets and Pet Psychics," in *Skeptical Inquirer,* Volume 26, No. 6, November/December (http://www.csicop.org/si/2002-11/pet-psychic.html).

Nickell, Joe (2001), *Real-Life X-Files: Investigating the Paranormal* (Lexington, KY: University Press of Kentucky).

Nickell, Joe (1998), *Looking for a Miracle: Weeping Icons, Relics, Stigmata, Visions & Healing Cures* (Amherst, NY: Prometheus Books).

Nikhilananda, Swami (1996), *Vivekananda: A Biography* (Calcutta: Advaita Ashrama).

Nikhilananda, Swami, tr. (1984 [1942]), *The Gospel of Sri Ramakrishna* (New York: Ramakrishna Vivekananda Center).

Nirodbaran (1990), *Sri Aurobindo for All Ages: A Biography* (Pondicherry: Sri Aurobindo Ashram).

Nisbet, Matt (2000), "The Physics Instructor Who Walks on Fire," in *Generation sXeptic,* October 25 (http://www.csicop.org/genx/firewalk/index.html).

Nityatmananda, Swami (1967), *SriM Darsan* (Calcutta: General Printers & Publishers Pvt. Ltd.).

Nixon, Bob (2004), "Fire Walking Explained," in *"the Skeptic" Journal* (http://www.skeptics.com.au/journal/firexplain.htm).

Nordquist, Ted (1978), *Ananda Cooperative Village: A Study in the Beliefs, Values, and Attitudes of a New Age Religious Community* (Uppsala, Sweden: Borgströms Tryckeri AB).

Oakes, Len (1997), *Prophetic Charisma: The Psychology of Revolutionary Religious Personalities* (Syracuse, NY: Syracuse University Press).

Oates, Robert M. (1976), *Celebrating the Dawn* (New York: Putnam).

Occhiogrosso, Peter (1996), *The Joy of Sects: A Spirited Guide to the World's Religious Traditions* (New York: Image Books).

Odajnyk, V. Walter (1993), *Gathering the Light: A Psychology of Meditation* (Boston, MA: Shambhala Publications, Inc.).

Oldmeadow, Harry (2004), *Journeys East: 20th Century Western Encounters with Eastern Religious Traditions* (Bloomington, IN: World Wisdom).

Olson, Helena (1979), *Maharishi at "433": The Story of Maharishi Mahesh Yogi's First Visit to the United States* (Los Angeles).

Orwell, George (1980 [1949]), "Reflections on Gandhi," in *The Collected Essays, Journalism and Letters of George Orwell, Volume 4: In Front of Your Nose, 1945-1950,* Sonia Orwell and Ian Angus, ed. (Harmondsworth: Penguin).

Paine, Jeffery (1998), *Father India: How Encounters with an Ancient Culture Transformed the Modern West* (New York: HarperCollins Publishers, Inc.).

Palmer, Susan J. and Arvind Sharma (1993), *The Rajneesh Papers: Studies in a New Religious Movement* (Delhi: Motilal Banarsidass Publishers).

Panchen, Ngari and Pema Wangyi (1996), *Perfect Conduct: Ascertaining the Three Vows* (Boston, MA: Wisdom Publications).

Partridge, Eric (1947), *Shakespeare's Bawdy* (New York: Routledge).

Paulsen, Norman (1984), *Christ Consciousness* (Salt Lake City, UT: The Builders Publishing Company).

Peat, F. David (1997), *Infinite Potential: The Life and Times of David Bohm* (Reading, MA: Addison-Wesley).

Penny, Bob (1993), *Social Control in Scientology: A Look at the Methods of Entrapment* (http://www-2.cs.cmu.edu/~dst/Library/Shelf/xenu/scs.html).

Perez-Rivas, Manuel (2000), "A Search for Serenity," in *Washington Post,* July 6 (http://www.rickross.com/reference/tm/tm10.html).

Phelps, Richard (1997), "Woman Wins $1.8M for Lecherous Swami," in *The Philadelphia Daily News,* national edition (via Associated Press), September 5 (http://www.rickross.com/reference/swami_rama/swami_rama1.html).

Pignotti, Monica (1989), *My Nine Lives in Scientology* (http://www.factnet.org/Books/9LivesScientology/nine_lives.html?FACTNet).

PlanetSave (2001), "Sex Scandal Monk Steps Down," October 18 (http://web.archive.org/web/20041128090733/http://www.planetsave.com/ViewStory.asp?ID=1515).

PLANS (2004), "Our Concerns About Waldorf Schools" (http://www.waldorfcritics.org/active/concerns.html).

Premanand, Basava (2005), "An Indian Skeptic's Explanation of Miracles" (http://www.mukto-mona.com/Articles/yuktibaadi.htm).

Premanand, Basava (1994), *Science Versus Miracles,* Volume 1 (http://www.indian-skeptic.org/html/svm_cont.htm).

Pressman, Steven (1993), *Outrageous Betrayal: The Dark Journey of Werner Erhard from est to Exile* (New York: St. Martin's Press).

Radha, Swami Sivananda (1992), *From the Mating Dance to the Cosmic Dance: Sex, Love, and Marriage from a Yogic Viewpoint* (Kootenay Bay, BC: Timeless Books).

Radha, Swami Sivananda (1978), *Kundalini Yoga for the West* (Kootenay Bay, BC: Timeless Books).

Radzik, Jody (2005), "The Perils of Pedestalization" (http://www.globalserve.net/~sarlo/Yworship.htm).

Rae, Stephen (1991), "The Guru Scene: Yes, They're Still at It! (Celebrity Cult Followers)," in *Cosmopolitan,* August (http://www.rickross.com/reference/ramtha/ramtha1.html).

Raftery, Mary and Eoin O'Sullivan (2001), *Suffer the Little Children: The Inside Story of Ireland's Industrial Schools* (New York: Continuum International Publishing Group).

Rajendra (1976), *Journey to the New Age* (Sumneytown, PA: Kripalu Yoga Ashram).

Ramakrishna (2003), "Sri Ramakrishna: Biography" (http://www.ramakrishna.org/Rmk.htm).

Rampa, T. Lobsang (1956), *The Third Eye* (New York: Ballantine Books).

Randi, James (2003a), "Swift: Online Newsletter of the JREF," March 14 (http://www.randi.org/jr/031403.html).

Randi, James (2003), "Swift: Online Newsletter of the JREF," October 17 (http://www.randi.org/jr/101703.html).

Randi, James (2002), "Swift: Online Newsletter of the JREF," June 28 (http://www.randi.org/jr/062802.html).

Randi, James (2000), "Commentary," December 8 (http://www.randi.org/jr/12-08-2000.html).

Randi, James (1995), *An Encyclopedia of Claims, Frauds, and Hoaxes of the Occult and Supernatural* (New York: St. Martin's Press).

Randi, James (1993), *The Mask of Nostradamus: The Prophecies of the World's Most Famous Seer* (Buffalo, NY: Prometheus Books).

Randi, James (1982), *Flim-Flam! Psychics, ESP, Unicorns and Other Delusions* (Buffalo, NY: Prometheus Books).

Rawlinson, Andrew (1997), *The Book of Enlightened Masters: Western Teachers in Eastern Traditions* (Chicago, IL: Open Court).

Read, Richard (2001), "In the Grip of the Guru," in *The Oregonian,* July 15 (http://www.oregonlive.com/special/guru/index.ssf?/news/oregonian/lc_11gside15.frame).

Reeve, Christopher (2002), *Nothing is Impossible* (New York: Random House).

Reeves, Jay (2005), "FBI Probes Alabama Boy Scouts Membership" (http://abcnews.go.com/US/wireStory?id=442654).

Rich, Tracey R. (2001), "Judaism 101" (http://www.jewfaq.org/moshiach.htm).

Richardson, John H. (1993), "Catch a Rising Star," in *Premiere,* September (http://www.rickross.com/reference/scientology/Scien12.html).

Riddell, Carol (1990), *The Findhorn Community: Creating a Human Identity for the 21st Century* (Findhorn, Scotland: Findhorn Press).

Rinpoche, Patrul (1998), *The Words of My Perfect Teacher* (Boston, MA: Shambhala).

Robbins, John (1987), *Diet for a New America* (Walpole, NH: Stillpoint Publishing).

Robbins, Thomas and Dick Anthony, ed. (1982), *In Gods We Trust: New Patterns of Religious Pluralism in America* (New Brunswick, NJ: Transaction Books).

Rodarmor, William (1983), "The Secret Life of Swami Muktananda," in *CoEvolution Quarterly* (http://www.ex-cult.org/Groups/SYDA-Yoga/leave.txt).

Ross, Rick (2005c), "Warning Signs" (http://www.rickross.com/warningsigns.html).

Ross, Rick (2005b), "Deepak Chopra" (http://www.rickross.com/groups/deepakchopra.html).

Ross, Rick (2005), "Frederick Lenz" (http://www.rickross.com/groups/lenz.html).

Ross, Rick (2004d), "Narconon" (http://www.rickross.com/groups/scientology.html#Narconon).

Ross, Rick (2004c), "Church Universal and Triumphant and Elizabeth Clare Prophet" (http://www.rickross.com/groups/cut.html).

Ross, Rick (2004b), "Lisa McPherson—Death of a Scientologist" (http://www.rickross.com/groups/scientology.html#mcpherson).

Ross, Rick (2004a), "Clergy Abuse" (http://www.rickross.com/groups/clergy.html).

Ross, Rick (2004), "Welcome to the Rick A. Ross Institute of New Jersey" (www.rickross.com).

Ross, Rick (2003e), "AP Picks Up NY Times Story About Scientology-Related Program and NYC Firemen," in *Cult News,* October 5 (http://www.cultnews.com/archives/week_2003_10_05.html).

Ross, Rick (2003d), "Sri Chinmoy Discusses Sex, Celibacy and How To Be a Good Guru" (http://www.rickross.com/reference/srichinmoy/srichinmoy21.html).

Ross, Rick (2003c), "Is a Yoga Website Promoting 'Cult' Groups?" in *Cult News,* March 24 (http://www.cultnews.com/2003_03_23_archive.html).

Ross, Rick (2003b), "Goldie Hawn to Appear at 'Cult' Leader's Birthday Bash," in *Cult News,* August 18 (http://www.cultnews.com/archives/week_2003_08_17.html).

Ross, Rick (2003a), "Time Magazine Plugs a 'Cult' Guru's Plan," in *Cult News,* July 31 (http://www.cultnews.com/archives/week_2003_07_27.html).

Ross, Rick (2003), "Is Dick Anthony a Full-Time Professional 'Cult Apologist'?" in *Cult News,* March 27 (http://www.rickross.com/reference/apologist/apologist44.html).

Ross, Rick (2002b), "Cult Influence Growing?" in *Cult News,* November 13 (http://www.rickross.com/reference/apologist/apologist45.html).

Ross, Rick (2002a), "Still Crazy After All These Years?" in *Cult News,* August 1 (http://www.cultnews.com/archives/week_2002_07_28.html).

Ross, Rick (2002), "Another Hollywood 'Cult' Craze," in *Cult News,* August 20 (http://www.cultnews.com/archives/week_2002_08_18.html).

Ross, Rick (1998), "Feats of Prowess Show Spirit's Inner Strength," November 3 (http://www.rickross.com/reference/srichinmoy/srichinmoy17.html).

Royalty (2003), "William the Conqueror: The Conqueror's Childhood" (http://www.royalty.nu/Europe/England/Norman/WilliamI.html).

Rudin, James and Marcia Rudin (1980), *Prison or Paradise? The New Religious Cults* (Philadelphia, PA: Fortress Press).

Rudin, Marcia (1996), *Cults on Campus: Continuing Challenge* (Bonita Springs, FL: American Family Foundation).

Russell, Peter (1977), *The TM Technique: An Introduction to Transcendental Meditation and the Teachings of Maharishi Mahesh Yogi* (Boston, MA: Routledge & Kegan Paul).

Russell, Ron (2001a), "Exhuming the Truth: Ben Erskine Says He's the Swami's Love Child and He Wants a Chance to Prove It," in *New Times Los Angeles,* November 29 (http://www.rickross.com/reference/selfreal/selfreal4.html).

Russell, Ron (2001), "The Devotee's Son," in *New Times Los Angeles,* July 5 (http://www.rickross.com/reference/selfreal/selfreal3.html).

Russell, Ron (1999), "Return of the Swami," in *New Times Los Angeles,* July 1-7 (http://www.rickross.com/reference/selfreal/selfreal2.html).

Rutter, Peter (1989), *Sex in the Forbidden Zone: When Men in Power—Therapists, Doctors, Clergy, Teachers, and Others—Betray Women's Trust* (Los Angeles: Jeremy P. Tarcher, Inc.).

Salkin, Allen (2002), "Emperor of Air," in *Yoga Journal,* September/October (http://www.yjevents.com/views/738_1.cfm).

Sanat, Aryel (1999), *The Inner Life of Krishnamurti* (Wheaton, IL: The Theosophical Publishing House).

Sannella, Lee (2001), *The Visionary Life* (http://www.skaggs-island.org/humanistic/sannella/visionarylife.html).

Satchidananda, Swami (1977), *Guru and Disciple* (Pomfret Center, CT: Integral Yoga Publications).

Savage, Dan (2005), "Savage Love" (http://www.thestranger.com/current/savage.html).

Schell, Orville (2001), *Virtual Tibet: Searching for Shangri-La from the Himalayas to Hollywood* (New York: Henry Holt & Company, Inc.).

Schumacher, Michael (1992), *Dharma Lion: A Biography of Allen Ginsberg* (New York: St. Martin's Press).

Schwartz, John (2004), "Simulated Prison in '71 Showed a Fine Line Between 'Normal' and 'Monster,'" in the *New York Times,* May 6 (http://query.nytimes.com/gst/abstract.html?res=F40D11FB34590C758CDDAC0894DC404482&incamp=archive:search).

Schwartz, Tony (1996), *What Really Matters: Searching for Wisdom in America* (New York: Bantam Books).

Scott, R. D. (1978), *Transcendental Misconceptions* (San Diego, CA: Beta Books).

Seidman, Barry F. (2001), "Medicine Wars: Will Alternative and Mainstream Medicine Ever Be Friends?" in *Skeptical Inquirer,* Volume 25, No. 1, January/February (http://www.csicop.org/si/2001-01/medicine-wars.html).

Seidman, Peter (1985), "Sexual Experiments Continued After '76, JDC Officials Admit," in *Mill Valley Record,* April 10 (http://www.rickross.com/reference/adida/adida8.html).

Self, Jane (1992), *60 Minutes and the Assassination of Werner Erhard: How America's Top Rated Television Show was Used in an Attempt to Destroy a Man Who was Making a Difference* (Houston, TX: Breakthru Publishing).

Sennott, Charles M. (1992), *Broken Covenant: The Story of Father Bruce Ritter's Fall from Grace* (New York: Simon & Schuster).

Siemon-Netto, Uwe (2002), "Buddhism's Pedophile Monks," in UPI (http://www.american-buddha.com/pedophile.monks.htm).

Shambhala (2003), "Vidyadhara Chögyam Trungpa" (http://www.shambhala.org/teachers/vctr/ctrbio.html).

Shapiro, Marc (2002), *Behind Sad Eyes: The Life of George Harrison* (New York: St. Martin's Press).

Shermer, Michael (1997), *Why People Believe Weird Things: Pseudoscience, Superstition, and Other Confusions of Our Time* (New York: W. H. Freeman and Company).

Sherrill, Martha (2000a), *The Buddha from Brooklyn* (http://www.american-buddha.com/buddha.brook.htm).

Sherrill, Martha (2000), *The Buddha from Brooklyn* (New York: Random House).

Shy, David (2004), "Abstracts of Articles in Psychological Journals concerning est and The Forum" (http://www.rickross.com/reference/landmark/landmark22.html).

Sil, Narasingha P. (2004), personal email communication.

Sil, Narasingha P. (1998), *Ramakrishna Revisited: A New Biography* (Lanham, MD: University Press of America, Inc.).

Sil, Narasingha P. (1997), *Swami Vivekananda: A Reassessment* (Mississauga, ON: Associated University Presses).

Silverman, Steve (2003), "William the Conqueror" (http://home.nycap.rr.com/useless/william_the_conqueror).

Simon, Stephanie (2004), "Cattle Video Stirs Kosher Meat Debate" (http://failedmessiah.typepad.com/failed_messiahcom/kosher_meat_scandal/).

Singer, Margaret T. (2003 [1995]), *Cults in Our Midst: The Continuing Fight Against Their Hidden Menace* (San Francisco, CA: John Wiley & Sons, Inc.).

Singer, Margaret T. and Janja Lalich (1996), *Crazy Therapies: What Are They? Do They Work?* (San Francisco, CA: Jossey-Bass Publishers).

Singh, Siri Scandal (2000), "More Predictions and Observations from 'The Master'" (http://www.rickross.com/reference/3ho/3ho18.html).

Singh, Siri Scandal (1998a), "3HO Foundation Teachers Training Courses" (http://www.rickross.com/reference/3ho/3ho9.html).

Singh, Siri Scandal (1998), "Predictions from 'The Master'" (http://www.rickross.com/reference/3ho/3ho13.html).

Singh, Siri Scientific (1999), "More from the Master's Mouth" (http://www.rickross.com/reference/3ho/3ho55.html).

Sivananda, Swami (1958), *An Autobiography of Sivananda* (Sivanandanagar, India: Yoga-Vedanta Forest Academy Press).

Skolnick, Andrew (1991), "Maharishi Ayur-Veda: Guru's Marketing Scheme Promises the World Eternal 'Perfect Health,'" in *JAMA, The Journal of the American Medical Association,* October 2 (http://web.archive.org/web/20040419100603/http://www.aaskolnick.com/mav.html).

Sloss, Radha R. (2000), *Lives in the Shadow with J. Krishnamurti* (Lincoln, NE: iUniverse.com, Inc.).

Smith, Ryan (2004), "Cults Targeted at Campus Security Conference" (http://www.uofaweb.ualberta.ca/arts/nav02.cfm?nav02=27097&nav01=18478).

SRF (1976), *Paramahansa Yogananda, In Memoriam: The Master's Life, Work, and Mahasamadhi* (Los Angeles: Self-Realization Fellowship).

Steiner, Rudolf (1963 [1923]), *Atlantis and Lemuria* (Mokelumne, CA: Health Research).

Steiner, Rudolf (1959), *Cosmic Memory: Prehistory of Earth and Man* (West Nyack, NY: Rudolf Steiner Publications, Inc.).

Steiner, Rudolf (1947), *Knowledge of the Higher Worlds and its Attainment* (Hudson, NY: Anthroposophic Press).

Storr, Anthony (1996), *Feet of Clay: Saints, Sinners, and Madmen: A Study of Gurus* (New York: The Free Press).

Strelley, Kate with Robert D. San Souci (1987), *The Ultimate Game: The Rise and Fall of Bhagwan Shree Rajneesh* (San Francisco, CA: Harper & Row, Publishers).

Sturlson, Snorri (1997), *Heimskringla—Norwegian Kings* (Seattle, WA: The World Wide School; http://www.worldwideschool.org/library/books/hst/european/heimskringla/HeimskringlaVolume6/chap97.html).

Sullivan, Kelly (2003), "Religious Sect's Leader Visits Local Church Site," in *Chariho Times,* July 10 (http://www.rickross.com/reference/ananda/ananda7.html).

Tarlo, Luna (1997), *The Mother of God* (Brooklyn, NY: Plover Press).

ThisTruth (2001), "Twisted Examples of 'Crazy Wisdom' from Adi Da's Fantasy World" (http://www.luckymojo.com/esoteric/religion/tt200112adidabubbafreejohnscandal.txt).

Thompson, Geoff (2000), "Scandals Follow Thailand's Monks," in *ABC Online News,* Friday, November 24 (http://www.abc.net.au/pm/stories/s216493.htm).

Thurman, Robert A. (2004), *Infinite Life: Seven Virtues for Living Well* (New York: Riverhead Books).

Time (1977), "Yogi Bhajan's Synthetic Sikhism," in *Time,* September 5 (http://www.rickross.com/reference/3ho/3ho94.html).

Tobias, Madeleine Landau and Janja Lalich (1994), *Captive Hearts, Captive Minds: Freedom and Recovery from Cults and Other Abusive Relationships* (Alameda, CA: Hunter House; Joya-related excerpt online at http://www.kashiashram.com/blinded.htm).

Todd, Douglas (2001), "Holy Man? Sex Abuser? Both?" in *Vancouver Sun,* February 27 (http://www.rickross.com/reference/saibaba/saibaba6.html).

Toscani, Oliviero, et al. (2000), *Cacas: The Encyclopedia of Poo* (Los Angeles: TASCHEN America, Llc.).

TranceNet (2004), "Shameless Mind" (http://www.trancenet.org/chopra/index.shtml).

TranceNet (2003), "TranceNet: Independent TM Research Archive" (http://onwww.net/trancenet.org/research/index.shtml).

Trimondi, Victor and Victoria Trimondi (2003), *The Shadow of the Dalai Lama: Sexuality, Magic and Politics in Tibetan Buddhism,* tr. Mark Penny (http://www.trimondi.de/SDLE/Index.htm).

Trungpa, Chögyam (1981), *Journey Without Goal: The Tantric Wisdom of the Buddha* (Boulder, CO: Prajna Press).

Trungpa, Chögyam (1977), *Born in Tibet* (Boston, MA: Shambhala Publications, Inc.).

Trungpa, Chögyam (1973), *Cutting Through Spiritual Materialism* (Boulder, CO: Shambhala Publications, Inc.).

Turner, Joseph (2001), "Who is Joseph Turner?" in Tommy Ryden, ed., "Arya Kriya Information" (http://www.tommyryden.com/kriya/turners_life.htm).

Tworkov, Helen (1994 [1989]), *Zen in America: Five Teachers and the Search for an American Buddhism* (New York: Kodansha America, Inc.).

Tyagananda, Swami (2000), *Kali's Child Revisited: Or, Didn't Anyone Check the Documentation?* (http://home.earthlink.net/~tyag/Home.htm).

Underwood, Mick (2005), "Social Influence—Conformity" (http://www.cultsock.ndirect.co.uk/MUHome/cshtml/socinf/conform.html).

Underwood, Barbara and Betty Underwood (1979), *Hostage to Heaven: Four Years in the Unification Church by an Ex Moonie and the Mother Who Fought to Free Her* (New York: Clarkson N. Potter, Inc.).

Van de Wetering, Janwillem (2001 [1999]), *Afterzen: Experiences of a Zen Student Out on His Ear* (New York: St. Martin's Press).

Van de Wetering, Janwillem (1999 [1973]), *The Empty Mirror: Experiences in a Japanese Zen Monastery* (New York: St. Martin's Press).

Van der Braak, Andre (2003), *Enlightenment Blues: My Years with an American Guru* (Rhinebeck, NY: Monkfish Book Publishing Company).

Van Wolferen, Karel (1990), *The Enigma of Japanese Power: People and Politics in a Stateless Nation* (New York: Vintage Books).

Vaughan, Frances (1982), "A Question of Balance: Health and Pathology in New Religious Movements," in *Journal of Humanistic Psychology*.

Vernon, Roland (2001), *Star in the East: Krishnamurti, The Invention of a Messiah* (New York: Palgrave).

Victoria, Brian Daizen (2003), *Zen War Stories* (New York: RoutledgeCurzon).

Victoria, Brian (Daizen) A. (1997), *Zen at War* (New York: Weatherhill, Inc.).

Vivekananda, Swami (1947), *The Complete Works of Swami Vivekananda* (Hollywood, CA: Vedanta Press & Bookshop).

Vosper, Cyril (1997 [1971]), *The Mind-Benders: Scientology* (London: Neville Spearman; full text online at http://members.chello.nl/mgormez/books/vosper/).

Wakefield, Margery (1996), *Testimony: The Autobiography of Margery Wakefield* (http://www-2.cs.cmu.edu/afs/cs/Web/People/dst/Library/Shelf/wakefield/testimony.html).

Wakefield, Margery (1993), *The Road to Xenu: A Narrative Account of Life in Scientology* (http://www-2.cs.cmu.edu/~dst/Library/Shelf/xenu/).

Wakefield, Margery (1991), *Understanding Scientology* (Tampa, FL: Coalition of Concerned Citizens; full text online at http://www-2.cs.cmu.edu/~dst/Library/Shelf/wakefield/us.html).

Waldman, Amy (2002), "Old Rajneesh Commune Lightens Up in Afterlife," in the *New York Times,* December 11 (http://www.rickross.com/reference/rajneesh/rajneesh10.html).

Walker, David (1968), *William the Conqueror* (London: Oxford University Press).

Wallace, Amy (2003), *Sorcerer's Apprentice: My Life with Carlos Castaneda* (Berkeley, CA: Frog, Ltd.).

Wallis, Roy (1976), *The Road to Total Freedom: A Sociological Analysis of Scientology* (London: Heinemann Educational Books Ltd.).

Walls, Jeanette (2003), "Is Madonna Converting Britney Spears to Kabbalah?" on MSNBC, September 11 (http://www.rickross.com/reference/kabbalah/kabbalah42.html).

Walls, Jeanette (2002), "Could Scientology Have Saved Elvis?" on MSNBC, October 1 (http://www.rickross.com/reference/scientology/celebrities/celebrities11.html).

Walrus, SRF (2004), "SRF Walrus Discussion Forum" (http://www.angelfire.com/blues/srfwalrus).

Walsh, Roger (1999), *Essential Spirituality: Exercises from the World's Religions to Cultivate Kindness, Love, Joy, Peace, Vision, Wisdom, and Generosity* (New York: John Wiley & Sons, Inc.).

Walsh, Roger and Frances Vaughan, ed. (1993), *Paths Beyond Ego: The Transpersonal Vision* (Los Angeles: Jeremy P. Tarcher, Inc.).

Walsh, Roger and Frances Vaughan, ed. (1988), *A Gift of Healing: Selections from A Course in Miracles* (Los Angeles: Jeremy P. Tarcher, Inc.).

Walters, J. Donald (2002), *A Place Called Ananda: The Trial by Fire That Forged One of the Most Successful Cooperative Communities in the World Today* (http://www.ananda.org/inspiration/books/place/index.html).

Walters, J. Donald (1995), "Deposition of Mr. J. Donald Walters: September 6 – November 30, 1995" (http://www.anandaawareness.com/walters_testifies.html).

Ward, Tim (1998), *What the Buddha Never Taught* (Toronto: Somerville House Publishing).

Warner, Brad (2004), "Enlightenment Blues" (http://www2.gol.com/users/doubtboy/enlightenmentblues.html).

Warner, Brad (2003), *Hardcore Zen* (Boston, MA: Wisdom Publications).

Warner, Judy (1990), *Transformation of the Heart* (York Beach, ME: Samuel Weiser).

Washington, Peter (1995 [1993]), *Madame Blavatsky's Baboon: A History of the Mystics, Mediums, and Misfits Who Brought Spiritualism to America* (New York: Schocken Books).

Watanabe, Teresa (1998), "Teachers or Tyrants?" in *L.A. Times,* August 15 (http://www.themotherofgod.com/latimes.htm).

Webb, James (1976), *The Occult Establishment* (La Salle, IL: Open Court).

Webster, Katharine (1990), "The Case Against Swami Rama of the Himalayas," in *Yoga Journal,* December (http://www.rickross.com/reference/swami_rama/swami_rama2.html).

Webster, Richard (1990), *A Brief History of Blasphemy: Liberalism, Censorship and "The Satanic Verses"* (Oxford: The Orwell Press).

Welch, Chris (1995), *Teenage Wasteland: The Early Years* (Surrey, England: Castle Communications).

Welch, David (2001), *Hitler: Profile of a Dictator* (New York: Routledge).

Wettig, Hannah (2002), "'King of the World' Preaches Peace Through 'Yogic Flying,'" in *The Daily Star,* November 11 (http://www.rickross.com/reference/tm/tm41.html).

WHAT Enlightenment??! (2005), "WHAT enlightenment??! An Uncensored Look at Self-Styled 'Guru' Andrew Cohen" (http://whatenlightenment.blogspot.com).

Wheeler, Kate (1994), "Toward a New Spiritual Ethic," in *Yoga Journal,* March/April (http://www.anandainfo.com/new_ethic.html).

White, John (1997), "The Experience of God-Realization," in *Noumenon: A Newsletter for the Nondual Perspective* (http://www.noumenon.co.za/html/summer_1997.html).

Wiener, Sita (1972), *Swami Satchidananda* (New York: Bantam Books).

Wikipedia (2003), "Dalai Lama" (http://en.wikipedia.org/wiki/Dalai_Lama).

Wilber, Ken (2002), "Sidebar A: Who Ate Captain Cook? Integral Historiography in a Postmodern Age" (http://wilber.shambhala.com/html/books/boomeritis/cook/part3.cfm).

Wilber, Ken (2001a), *A Theory of Everything: An Integral Vision for Business, Politics, Science and Spirituality* (Boston, MA: Shambhala).

Wilber, Ken (2001), "Response to McDermott" (http://www.integralworld.net/mcdermott2.html).

Wilber, Ken (2000a), *One Taste: The Journals of Ken Wilber* (Boston, MA: Shambhala).

Wilber, Ken (2000), *Integral Psychology: Consciousness, Spirit, Psychology, Therapy* (Boston, MA: Shambhala).

Wilber, Ken (1998b), "An Update on the Case of Adi Da" (http://wilber.shambhala.com/html/misc/adida_update.cfm).

Wilber, Ken (1998a), "Letter to the Adi Da Community" (http://www.beezone.com/Wilber/ken_wilbers_letter.html).

Wilber, Ken (1998), *The Eye of Spirit: An Integral Vision for a World Gone Slightly Mad* (Boston, MA: Shambhala).

Wilber, Ken (1996a), "The Case of Adi Da" (http://wilber.shambhala.com/html/misc/adida.cfm).

Wilber, Ken (1996), *A Brief History of Everything* (Boston, MA: Shambhala).

Wilber, Ken (1995), *Sex, Ecology, and Spirituality* (Boston, MA: Shambhala).

Wilber, Ken (1991), *Grace and Grit: Spirituality & Healing in the Life & Death of Treya Killam Wilber* (Boulder, CO: Shambhala).

Wilber, Ken (1983b), *A Sociable God: Toward a New Understanding of Religion* (Boulder, CO: Shambhala).

Wilber, Ken (1983a), *Up from Eden* (Boulder, CO: Shambhala).

Wilber, Ken (1983), *Eye to Eye* (Boulder, CO: Shambhala).

Wilber, Ken (1982), *The Holographic Paradigm and Other Paradoxes* (Boulder, CO: Shambhala).

Wilber, Ken (1977), *The Spectrum of Consciousness* (Wheaton, IL: The Theosophical Publishing House).

Willey, David (2002), "Firewalking Myth vs. Physics" (http://web.archive.org/web/20031203013713/http://www.pitt.edu/~dwilley/fire.html).

Wills, Garry (2000), *Papal Sin: Structures of Deceit* (New York: Doubleday).

Wills, Garry (1972), *Bare Ruined Choirs: Doubt, Prophecy, and Radical Religion* (Garden City, NY: Doubleday & Company, Inc.).

Wilson, Ian (1988), *The Bleeding Mind* (London: Weidenfeld and Nicolson).

Winn, Denise (2000 [1983]), *The Manipulated Mind: Brainwashing, Conditioning and Indoctrination* (Cambridge, MA: Malor Books).

Woman #2 (1995), "Declaration of XXX in Support of Cross-Defendants' Special Motion to Strike Cross-Complaint" (http://www.anandaawareness.com/woman_2.html).

Yogananda, Paramahansa (1998), *Autobiography of a Yogi* (Los Angeles: Self-Realization Fellowship).

Yogananda, Paramahansa (1987 [1953]), *The Science of Religion* (Los Angeles: Self-Realization Fellowship).

Yogananda, Paramahansa (1986), *The Divine Romance* (Los Angeles: Self-Realization Fellowship).

Yogananda, Paramahansa (1985), *Beholding the One in All* (Los Angeles: Self-Realization Fellowship).

Yogananda, Paramahansa (1984 [1956]), *SRF Lessons* (Los Angeles: Self-Realization Fellowship).

Yogananda, Paramahansa (1982), *Man's Eternal Quest* (Los Angeles: Self-Realization Fellowship).

Yogananda, Paramhansa (1946), *Autobiography of a Yogi* (Nevada City, CA: Crystal Clarity; http://www.ananda.org/inspiration/books/ay/index.html).

Yukteswar, Swami Sri (1977), *The Holy Science* (Los Angeles: Self-Realization Fellowship).

Zablocki, Benjamin (2001), "Methodological Fallacies in Anthony's Critique of Exit Cost Analysis" (http://www.rci.rutgers.edu/~zablocki/Anthony.htm).

Zablocki, Benjamin (1998), "The Birth and Death of New Religious Movements" (http://www.rci.rutgers.edu/~zablocki/birth%20and %20death%20of%20new%20religious%20movements.htm).

Zimbardo, Philip G. (2004b), "A Situationist Perspective on the Psychology of Evil: Understanding How Good People are Transformed into Perpetrators," in A. G. Miller, ed., *The Social Psychology of Good and Evil* (New York: Guilford Press; chapter text available online at http://www.prisonexp.org/pdf/evil.pdf).

Zimbardo, Philip G. (2004a), "Power Turns Good Soldiers into 'Bad Apples,'" in *The Boston Globe,* May 9 (http://www.boston.com/news/globe/editorial_opinion/oped/ articles/2004/05/09/power_turns_good_soldiers_into_bad_apples/).

Zimbardo, Philip G. (2004), "Stanford Prison Experiment Slide Show" (http://www.prisonexp.org).

Zimbardo, Philip G. (2002), "Mind Control: Psychological Reality or Mindless Rhetoric?" in *APA Monitor,* Volume 33, No. 10, November (http://www.apa.org/monitor/nov02/pc.html).

Zimbardo, Philip G. (1971), "The Power and Pathology of Imprisonment," in the Congressional Record (Serial No. 15, October 25). Hearings before Subcommittee No. 3, of the Committee on the Judiciary, House of Representatives, Ninety-Second Congress, *First Session on Corrections, Part II, Prisons, Prison Reform and Prisoner's Rights: California* (Washington, DC: U.S. Government Printing Office; text online at http://www.prisonexp.org/pdf/congress.pdf).

Zimbardo, Philip G., Christina Maslach and Craig Haney (2000), "Reflections on the Stanford Prison Experiment: Genesis, Transformations, Consequences," in Thomas Blass, ed., *Obedience to Authority: Current Perspectives on the Milgram Paradigm*

(Mahwah, NJ: Erlbaum; chapter text online at http://www.prisonexp.org/pdf/blass.pdf).

Zimbardo, Philip G., Craig Haney, William Curtis Banks and David Jaffe (1973), "The Mind is a Formidable Jailer: A Pirandellian Prison," in *The New York Times Magazine*, April 8 (text online at http://www.prisonexp.org/pdf/pirandellian.pdf).

Zoll, Rachel (2005), "Bishops: New Sex Abuse Claims Top 1,000" (http://www.usatoday.com/news/religion/2005-02-18-bishops-abuse_x.htm?POE=NEWISVA).

Zupp, Adrian (2003), "What Would Buddha Do? Why Won't the Dalai Lama Pick a Fight?" in *Counterpunch,* October 11/13 (http://www.counterpunch.org/zupp10112003.html).

PERMISSIONS

Every effort has been made to trace copyright holders of material in this book. The author and editors apologize if any work has been used without permission and would be glad to be told of anyone who has not been consulted. Grateful acknowledgment is made for permission to quote from the following publications:

Quotations from Dodie Bellamy's (1995) article, "Eckankar: A Former Member Revisits the Movement," reprinted with permission of the *San Diego Reader.*

Quotations from Mick Brown's (2000) article, "Divine Downfall," reprinted with permission of *The Daily Telegraph Saturday Magazine.*

Quotations from Stephen Butterfield's (1994) book, *The Double Mirror: A Skeptical Journey into Buddhist Tantra,* published by North Atlantic Books, copyright © 1994 by Stephen T. Butterfield. Reprinted by permission of the publisher.

Quotation from Susan Cohen's (2002a) article, "Swami Satchidananda, Integral Yoga Institute, Yogaville—A Survivor's Story," reprinted with permission of Rick Ross and the Ross Institute (www.rickross.com).

Quotations from Lake County's (1985) article, "Believers 'Surrender' to Spiritual Master," reprinted by courtesy of the *Lake County Record-Bee.*

Quotation from John Marshall's (1980) article, "Files Show Spy Reported Woman's Intimate Words," reprinted with permission of *The Globe and Mail.*

Quotations from Walt Neary's (1985) article, "Inner Circle Privy to Parties," reprinted by courtesy of the *Lake County Record-Bee.*

Quotations from Narasingha P. Sil's (1998) book, *Ramakrishna Revisited: A New Biography,* reprinted with permission of University Press of America, Inc.

Quotations from Andre van der Braak's (2003) book, *Enlightenment Blues: My Years with an American Guru,* reprinted with permission of Monkfish Book Publishing Company.

INDEX

ABOUT THE AUTHOR

Geoffrey D. Falk (www.geoffreyfalk.com) is author of *The Science of the Soul: On Consciousness and the Structure of Reality*, *"Norman Einstein": The Dis-Integration of Ken Wilber*, and *Hip Like Me: Years in the Life of a "Person of Hair."* He studied electrical engineering and physics at the University of Manitoba. Following that, he kicked ass as a best-in-class computer programmer. He currently divides his time between writing, software development, and music composition.

www.ingramcontent.com/pod-product-compliance
Lightning Source LLC
Chambersburg PA
CBHW060424100426
42812CB00030B/3293/J
* 9 7 8 0 9 7 3 6 2 0 3 1 3 *